Worldview Theory, Whiteness, and the Future of Evangelical Faith

Worldview Theory, Whiteness, and the Future of Evangelical Faith

Jacob Alan Cook

LEXINGTON BOOKS/FORTRESS ACADEMIC
Lanham • Boulder • New York • London

Published by Lexington Books/Fortress Academic
Lexington Books is an imprint of The Rowman & Littlefield Publishing Group, Inc.
4501 Forbes Boulevard, Suite 200, Lanham, Maryland 20706
www.rowman.com

86-90 Paul Street, London EC2A 4NE, United Kingdom

Copyright © 2021 by The Rowman & Littlefield Publishing Group, Inc.

All rights reserved. No part of this book may be reproduced in any form or by any electronic or mechanical means, including information storage and retrieval systems, without written permission from the publisher, except by a reviewer who may quote passages in a review.

British Library Cataloguing in Publication Information Available

Library of Congress Cataloging-in-Publication Data

Names: Cook, Jacob Alan, 1986– author.
Title: Worldview theory, whiteness, and the future of evangelical faith / Jacob Alan Cook.
Description: Lanham, Maryland : Lexington Books/Fortress Academic, [2021] | Includes bibliographical references and index.
Summary: "Examining key white evangelical voices from the last century, Jacob Cook deconstructs the concept of 'worldviews' based on current conversations in psychology, sociology, critical race studies, and theology. He engages Dietrich Bonhoeffer's theology of relationality for a constructive alternative to imperial ways of knowing and ordering the world"—Provided by publisher.
Identifiers: LCCN 2021033589 (print) | LCCN 2021033590 (ebook) | ISBN 9781978708198 (cloth) | ISBN 9781978708204 (epub)
Subjects: LCSH: Christian philosophy. | Philosophy. | Evangelicalism—United States.
Classification: LCC BR100 .C767 2021 (print) | LCC BR100 (ebook) | DDC 230.01—dc23
LC record available at https://lccn.loc.gov/2021033589
LC ebook record available at https://lccn.loc.gov/2021033590

Contents

Foreword *by David P. Gushee*	vii
Acknowledgments	xi
Introduction	1
PART I: SELF-REVELATIONS	25
1 The Neo-Calvinist World-View of Abraham Kuyper	27
2 A Contemporary Psychological Discussion of Selfhood	69
PART II: SOCIAL REVELATIONS	111
3 The New Evangelical World-View of Harold Ockenga	113
4 A Sociohistorical Analysis of White, American Evangelicalism	155
PART III: DIVINE REVELATION	199
5 The Evangelical Calvinist World-View of Richard Mouw	201
6 A Theological Criticism of the Modern Preoccupation with Epistemology	245
Coda	289
Bibliography	299
Index	313
About the Author	329

Foreword
David P. Gushee

It is a time of profound deconstruction of white American evangelical Christianity. The illusions and delusions, the prejudices and harms of a religious group with whom many of us once identified are currently being unveiled, attacked, and abandoned. Where #exvangelicals have not given up entirely on faith, seedlings of postevangelical Christian discipleship are being planted.

When my protégé Jacob Cook first started his research at the flagship evangelical Fuller Seminary, probably he had no idea how powerfully his work would fit into the current project of evangelical deconstruction and postevangelical rebirth. But now, in finished book form, Jacob's project offers a stunningly important contribution to both aspects of that work.

Jacob's unique focus is on the evangelical "world-viewing" project. Those of us who have spent any considerable time teaching or leading in evangelical higher education since the 1970s will know exactly what he is talking about. We read books about "The Christian/Biblical Worldview." We held faculty workshops. We went to conferences.

Back at our home schools, we were asked to demonstrate how we would "integrate our academic discipline with the Christian worldview," in fields ranging from accounting to zoology. We were challenged not to allow the supposedly secular presuppositions of contemporary academia to pollute our presentation of our fields to our impressionable young charges. We were reminded that we were the holders of truth revealed through Scripture and that all fields of human inquiry must be run through biblical categories rather than be allowed to stand on their own.

The supposed payoff of this world-view project was protecting our young from ideological corruption, forming their souls, and winning the war of ideas in secular America.

Jacob Cook argues here that the "world-viewing" project needs to be deconstructed both as a way of thinking about knowledge and as a paradigm for forming Christian disciples. He presents considerable evidence that the very concept of *Weltanschauung* was tainted by European white supremacism from the beginning, that it was deployed as part of the European colonial project, and that it has always dripped with cultural chauvinism. He also aptly describes it as part and parcel of "whiteness," defined in one place here as the social imaginary that sees white people as "the norming group in any given room, [with] the privilege of not questioning whether one really can or ought to try ordering, grasping, or even viewing the whole world."

Those of us who read or heard Abraham Kuyper, Harold Ockenga, Richard Mouw (all of whom Cook examines closely here), or many other "world-viewish" figures, can easily recall the hubristic confidence with which these men strode the intellectual world, confidently classifying, categorizing, and organizing the realities they had encountered, including different types of human beings and human communities. He is right in concluding that the world-viewers "never really resolved the dilemma of epistemic certainty in a fallen world," mainly because they acted as if (their reading of) the Bible lifted them above that problem. But now we can see, and Cook gives us ample new evidence, that very, very often the white/straight/Protestant/evangelical world-viewers simply imported their social location and its blind spots into "The Christian Worldview," with effects sometimes just irritating and sometimes truly disastrous. Cook's analysis certainly helps to make sense of why so many non-white-etc. once-evangelicals dissented from "mainstream" white evangelicalism and often found themselves voluntarily or otherwise abandoning any association with it.

All these discoveries are crucial and would be enough of a contribution from this wonderful young scholar in his first book. But what I think is especially profound here is Cook's reminder, with a nice assist from Dietrich Bonhoeffer, that world-viewing is not the best way to live in a community, engage other human beings, or follow Jesus. World-view thinking takes us away from flesh-and-blood people into conceptual abstractions, which block communion. Here we meet this particular human being, made in the image of God, with a story to tell and a journey into which we are invited to enter. But we world-viewers are more interested in floating once again to our "God's-eye" vantage point to classify them according to our categories. Once we have done that, what is the point of looking them in the eye ever again?

Jacob Cook reminds us that this is not how Jesus knew people. It is not the spirit of the church that he founded. For those leaving evangelicalism behind, here is one more seed for the rebirth: on the other side of world-viewish evangelicalism, let us seek that "creaturely kind of knowing that flows from free relationship in communion with, for, and (in some ways) over-against other persons, including God."

We had wanted certainty based on epistemology, and instead we got the reinforcement of our own socially located prejudices, with all kinds of blockages to the communion of souls. Let us now choose interpersonal knowing, based on relationship with God and people. As Jesus did.

Acknowledgments

Though this book has been six years in the making, its completion has come as something of surprise to me. Laying out a research pathway in early 2015, I could never have foreseen how seismic shifts already underway below the surface would give way to a dramatic refiguring of the US social landscape, the conversation around race and equity, or the discourse around "evangelicalism" itself. As the months passed, I had to change my grip on this material multiple times to wrestle this project into a form that would make sense once it hit the printers. If ever there was a moment to deliberate on the liabilities of world-viewing and search out possibilities for a fundamentally more relational, interdependent, and human way of inhabiting faith in a world of difference, it is now.

My own story bears the formative influence of numerous others who have opened their lives to me, shown me my limit, and taught me to wrestle with complex ideas while walking in love. No blow fell harder than the death of my dear teacher, Glen Stassen. I am so very thankful for my years spent learning from him "ethics as if Jesus mattered"—within and beyond the classroom's walls. Glen's method and sensibility are thick in this project's pages, including an intense concern for honesty around moral formation and the psychological realities underneath it but also an unwavering focus on following after the living, biblical, historical Jesus.

I am immensely grateful for the many roles David Gushee has played in my story. We met in his first year teaching at Mercer University, when I was a young, green seminarian. His introductory Christian ethics course taught me to see and seek the kingdom of God where I had not looked before. As I was burning out and sought to retreat from the academy into a more familiar life in college-ministerial work, David offered to mentor me. From him I have learned a great deal, and some of the greatest lessons have been more human than academic—how to navigate challenges to one's convictions, weather storms while following one's conscience, and nurture a genuine relationship with God in which hope springs eternal.

When Glen, our common friend, died, I was left in a precarious situation with regard to this project, which Glen had been mentoring. David provided some continuity in the formative stage of this project, and he has guided me through the process of bringing it to print. For these and so many other kindnesses along the way and, most of all, an enduring friendship, I give thanks.

Tommy Givens provided masterful guidance to this project as well. While I have put in years of work to round out the research base and improve the writing, some of its best lines are almost certainly cribbed from Tommy's comments on earlier drafts. Abigail and I moved to be nearer my family about midway through the early writing process, and when I was languishing in the throes of bearing the last two chapters to completion, Tommy spent a week of his sabbatical coaching me through a writing retreat that saw the work to its end. All errors here are my own, but this project may never have seen the light of day without Tommy.

Within my generation of Christian scholars, Ryan Newson stands out among friends and colleagues as a most rewarding conversation partner. We cut our teeth together in many ways (as did our first children, born 10 days apart) so we share a grammar that helps us reach the heart of so many matters in short order. Some months back, Ryan read a review draft and, undaunted by the unique challenges of the pandemic season, used some vacation time to work through the project and provide helpful feedback—cheering me to keep my head in the game.

I have immensely enjoyed continued fellowship with Tim Scherer, Brian Robinson, Andrew Wright, and Michael Beardslee as well as members of my "Atlanta family" Eric Cain and Karla and Joel Sarmiento. And over the last several years, I have appreciated the support of my writing group, Jeremy Gallegos and Keas Keasler. Old friends like Jeff Elsbury, also my fair-weather running partner, have consistently proven themselves to be interested in what I am working on and ready to talk. And countless others in classrooms at the church, the university, and online have helped me better understand the connections between knowing, being, and doing.

One thing any reader needs to know about this book is that its underlying spirit has been forged in life together with people in my church community, where I must practice holding my beliefs with an open hand and consistently work to unhinge the world-viewing impulse in my own soul. I think especially of the late Paul Longhofer, whom I got to know through several years of small groups and classes together. He always thought my original title for this project was terrible (the work was called "Evangelicals and Identity Politics"), and I spent an inordinate amount of time working to improve just that feature. But more importantly, Paul actively worked to see and treat very diverse others as valuable children of God. My pastor, Jeff Gannon, as well as my friend Trevor Hinz have been not only supportive along the way but also key examples of wrestling toward faith in the living God.

My family has supported me in countless ways. Many pages of this book were researched and written on time borrowed from my parents, grandparents, and in-laws. Ongoing conversations in family circles have impressed upon me the hope of inhabiting faith in a way that can honestly probe the source and meaning of our convictions. My parents, Tamara and Corky, have been an endless and unwavering source of support over the years. Even while not fully understanding why this project would be worth so much of my time and energy, they have shown me what it means to see, love, and support someone as a unique other and not merely a reflection of the self.

Eleven years ago, Abigail and I graduated from seminary together, got married, and moved across the country to continue exploring life together in God's kingdom. We have discovered together many joys (and a few sorrows) of wrestling with faith and life's big questions. Abigail is brilliant, and she knows what it takes to do hard work well. So, she has been overly kind in helping me carve out the time and space to make this project happen amid the fullness of life. My closest friend and lovest of loves, Abigail, thank you for your steady care and grace for me. I am so grateful we are in this together.

Our first child, Judah, was born as I worked on the proposal for this project. We have since welcomed with joy Eleanor and Silas Glen into our lives. They have never known a dad who was not working on this book. And some of that is to the good, as the kids have taken to writing their own books regularly—often with enviable speed and clarity of vision. Now ages seven, five, and three, they together ensure that, however far my mind wanders into the ideal worlds of my own design, I ever remain one creature in the world of God's making.

Thanks be to God for these many wonderful creatures who embody for me such lovable limits.

Introduction

On social media pages and in news media shout fests, but also around dinner tables and in church fellowships, the polarization of worldviews is on full display across the United States. In nearly every sector of life, we can perceive the impulses toward cancellation and support, coercion and toleration, exclusion and embrace. We feel this problem. We worry about it. And we can also, in a way, quantify it. A quick scan of Pew Research Center reports on political polarization from the past several decades reveals numerous angles of concern.[1] Along one line of research, when American adults were recently asked about some 30 political values ranging from gun policy and racial attitudes to the social safety net and the role of government, the ideological gap between those who identified with the two major parties averaged around 39 percent.[2] Along another line, those who supported one ticket or the other in the 2020 election cycle largely agree that "those who supported the other candidate have little or no understanding of people like them."[3] And this problem is not merely about people in some other part of the country or even across town; it appears at fault lines within local churches, within families.[4]

While it is no wonder that we feel this way, naming the actual worldviews in conflict is not a particularly straightforward task. Much of the loudest rhetoric paints one side over against the other, dramatizing the competition of grand visions for how the world should work and casting other perspectives as threats to the very things that everyone should cherish. Adapting to meet the perceived threats du jour, the visionary battle can take up or leave off elements over time (e.g., partisan-politics, race and ethnicity, class, or religion) often without explicitly naming them, especially when doing so would create a political liability. Still, we must ask: Are we talking primarily about top-level religious differences? Political partisanship? The cultures and perceptions built around race in America? Why should creatures so complex as human beings rely upon such a simplistic, us-them framework? Instead of answering such questions, social critics and political leaders have too often seized the felt problem as grounds for defending their own angle amid the competition of worldviews, in which the solution is winning more people over to the right side—or at least getting a hand on the levers of power to keep others in check.

This competition certainly presents itself with religious energy. But according to the latest numbers from Gallup, Inc., Americans' membership in religious congregations has steadily declined since the early years of the George W. Bush administration.[5] It may be no mere coincidence that pollsters and pundits have increasingly foregrounded evangelical Christians as a powerful voting bloc in the same timeframe. And not a few younger Americans have been disaffected by the seemingly easy fit between Christian religion and this season's troubled politics—from war-making in the Middle East to stodginess around racial justice and LGBT+ rights. Taken together, the new Pew and Gallup data might suggest that attempts to wed the Christian and the American into a singular worldview in recent history have, in effect, diverted energy from religious congregations into political ideologies, including in reaction over against policies contentiously presented as commonsense and Christian. Watching the ease with which polarizing worldview energy can be passed back and forth between church and party (and race and gender, etc., even when unnamed), we might be hoping for a way out—pathways toward one another in reconciliation and communion.

In this book, I will argue that the spiritual disease of division is symptomatic of a deeper problem: the posture and practice of "world-viewing" in itself. This diagnosis will be confirmed by a good, hard look at how and why religious energy has been channeled into ideological battles framed by the worldview concept, which has proven itself vulnerable to all manner of unholy alliances among interest groups. Searching for paths forward, I will mark trailheads for a fundamentally different way of inhabiting the world, as an alternative to world-viewing. The security we are after cannot be found in merely holding to, and maybe advancing, the right world-view within the world itself, even if it is relatively easy to imagine why we would want to believe this were the case. Rather, I will argue that we may find ourselves to be truly secure only in genuine, ongoing communion with other persons who, in their complexity, stand with, for, and sometimes over-against us in the presence of the living God. Shifting the focus and energy away from epistemology and how we (think we) know what we know and toward a renewed relationality may free us to see the limits of our ideas and ideals—however much we love them—in and through life together with actual persons in the world we have.

STUDYING WHITE EVANGELICAL WORLD-VIEWING

Underneath the intuitive problems of our time, the political division and family table derision are problematic notions of identity and worldview. In the pages that follow, I will be deconstructing the very concept of worldview, both as a philosophical structure for knowledge and as a formational paradigm for faithful human lives together before God. Much of what follows in this book is historical in nature, but this book is not *about* history so much as attempting to learn its lessons about possibilities for, and obstacles to, following Jesus today. And while, this book is built around case studies of powerful "evangelical" expositors of the worldview concept, my aim is wider than this movement as I explore—and cut a path to escape—the worldview impulse that corrupts Christian faith and witness.[6] My reader need not have extensive knowledge of American evangelicals or the perpetual conversation about what it means to be evangelical to fruitfully engage this project. I will do my best throughout to set the stage for my argument with the necessary context. All the same, here I will very briefly survey some developments over the last century that highlight significant connections between evangelicalism, the worldview concept, and what I am calling "whiteness" in the loaded American racial context.

In early drafts for this project, I organized my research around the notion that evangelicalism had emerged in American public life as something like an "identity politics"—a term that requires some unpacking in the twenty-first century.[7] I was thinking of the way some highly visible folks had seized a useful identifier (namely, evangelical) for engaging in politics to promote a self-interested agenda. There is a kind of identity politics that works to build up a tribe, to inspire political action on behalf of one's most salient aggregate or social group(s). We might interpret such activism, at its most vulgar, as on par with the kind of social devolution that Plato saw in democracy—everyone voting their appetites and in danger of demagoguery. Yet even within more legitimately liberative identity politics, visible leaders often represent only a portion of the named identity group—and even then, only imperfectly. For example, the midcentury civil rights movement saw a public struggle between the visions of a possible future cast by Martin Luther King Jr., Stokely Carmichael, and others. For another example, womanists are wary of the racism of white feminist leadership as well as the patriarchy of Black male leadership. So, the goal of this or that identity politics is not necessarily liberation, full stop, but often liberation as conceived by those who happen to be visible and convincing group representatives. Thus, bad forms of power can be reinscribed within such groups, albeit along different lines. Like other identity-political movements, no public evangelical voice has actually represented the perspectives of the whole identifiable group, alienating some amid the totalizing rhetoric within evangelical spaces and in public. This was part of what I thought I would expose through this project, and I will return to question the evangelical fit with "identity politics" in chapter 3.

But after I started my research, the tone and trajectory of American politics leading up to and following the 2016 election cycle dramatically altered this conversation. Recently, the deliberations of many mainstream American evangelical leaders around what it means to be "evangelical" in the first place have been dedicated to understanding the complex set of motivations that led 81 percent of rank-and-file evangelicals to vote for Donald Trump in his first presidential campaign. Even how to read that number has been the subject of some controversy.[8] After all, are we talking about *self-identified* evangelicals in exit polls? Would the number break differently if centered on those who hold evangelical beliefs (e.g., measured against the Bebbington Quadrilateral)?[9] How did race factor into the evangelical bloc? Black Protestants tend not to claim the "evangelical" identity for themselves even when they share the beliefs that define the label for research organizations like LifeWay and the Barna Group. But they overwhelmingly supported Hillary Clinton in 2016 and Joe Biden in 2020 (around the 90 percent level, maybe 80 percent if prescreened for evangelical beliefs).[10] As historian Mark Noll summarized the whole situation, "The very high level of evangelical support for Donald Trump is like nothing seen in America's recent religious-political history—except for the even higher percentage that since the 1960s Democrats have received from Bible-believing, born-again African Americans."[11] When political pundits gestured toward evangelicals as a relatively homogenous voting bloc in the George W. Bush years (and pollsters counted them that way), fissures were already simmering. Now after two Trump presidential campaigns, cracks in any perceived unity are giving way to a crumble, especially along the color-line.

What it means to count evangelicals, to speak to and on behalf of evangelicals, to conceive of "evangelicalism" as a unified project is in flux. But much about this historical moment would not be particularly controversial if not for the parallel reality that, over the last century, key individuals and groups on the inside have attempted to marshal evangelicalism into, and represent it as, something of a self-conscious, unified moral movement among American churches and within the wider society. This activity does not account for everything that has happened around this label, of course, as this same timeframe has also seen the explosive growth and increasing visibility of evangelical expressions of faith around the globe, sometimes with little to no contact with American evangelicals. Looking at this overall picture, a focus on something like the Bebbington Quadrilateral (i.e., emphasis on Scripture's authority in thought and life, concerns for missionary activism, etc.) may help one identify a common spirit across vast geographic and ideological terrain.

But stateside, starting in the 1940s, an intentional and contentious deliberation has unfolded around certain players convinced that evangelical faith and piety, in a basic sense, ought to animate a common social and political cause within a capacious view of American society as a microcosm of God's will for all humankind.

In 2021, it seems increasingly clear in the prevailing conversation about American evangelicals that those who already had privilege and power (i.e., upwardly mobile, white, heterosexual males) have commandeered identity-political mechanisms, bending them to their service while decrying the identity politics of others.[12] And within these circles, social power ascribed on the basis of race, gender, class, sexual orientation, citizenship, and other categories is transfigured into *theopolitical* power, such that those who already enjoy social power also become de facto authorities on Jesus's identity, God's will, and so on. As overt rhetoric changes and policy planks are swapped out, what remains to be studied is how the worldview concept and its underlying impulse have facilitated the consolidation and concealment of these salient but unspecified interests in what has passed as "evangelical," both inside the movement and in public life. The histories of American evangelicalism and the worldview concept itself hold lessons about how we got here. And as I work to mine those lessons in the project ahead, I will regularly lead us up to the scene of a wrong turn, prospecting for truer pathways forward.

The worldview concept as developed within evangelicalism starting in the 1940s was part of a conscious attempt to end the cultural isolation and infighting that had characterized Christian fundamentalism for decades. In general, religious fundamentalisms are about strict adherence to basic convictions, especially as derived from particular readings of holy texts. And these specific fundamentalists were struggling to find a new way of speaking of faith in a society that was increasingly marked by "Modernism"—the traditional-religious-worldview-shattering complex of rationalism, materialism, and scientific naturalism. This struggle sometimes spilled into public view, as in the Scopes Trial that took place in Tennessee in 1925. Exacerbated by a sense of alienation from the wider culture, Christian fundamentalism during this period was marked by divisive infighting about theological and moral minutiae. The rhetoric ran hot, and friendly fire abounded. Some members of a new generation hoped to soften some of the sharp theological edges by promoting a common sense of public responsibility under the standard of a "new evangelical" or sometimes "biblical Christian" worldview. Early spokesman and pastor-theologian Harold John Ockenga (1905–1985) imagined "a progressive Fundamentalism with a social message."[13] Seeing threats like fascism and Communism abroad and interpreting them as the fruition of godless worldviews, these new evangelicals endeavored to stop their fundamentalist ilk from eating each other alive (a "progressive" notion for some) while the world burned down around them.

As they foregrounded their spiritual identity, the neo-evangelicals insisted that their resolve for social engagement did not displace but rather built upon the bundle of core convictions they inherited. While recognizing the need to continue working out the theological details, they seemed to believe the particulars of a worldview framing social life together (including, for them, Christian nationalism, free enterprise, and individual liberty) would be easier to agree upon, even commonsensical among the "unvoiced multitudes" of evangelicals. And movement leaders enjoyed lively, congenial conversations that buoyed their prediction that a fundamentally unified public witness and political activism would indeed attend their revival of "the evangelical worldview"—a notion they have often styled more simplistically and more presumptuously as "the biblical worldview." But statements of faith like the one used to galvanize the National Association of Evangelicals (NAE) in the 1940s were formulated and affirmed within a broader social imaginary already shared by, yet essentially invisible to, founding members. As we will see in chapter 4, historical realities like this have a lasting impact on institutional cultures. Those who did not already enjoy status in this powerful social network were left out of the conversations; institutions were founded and cultures were formed without much variety of input. And when diversity is excluded from the start, as sociologist Korie Edwards will help us see in chapter 4, practice norms and values are forged out of some unspoken commonalities (e.g., race, class, political partisanship). Once this has happened, even if membership is cast as free and voluntary and explicitly not limited by factors like race (i.e., colorblind), cultural pressures can conserve the homogeneity of *voices* while welcoming diverse *faces* to the table.

Sharpening the criticism, the genuine like-mindedness of many founding leaders and more than a few enthusiastic early supporters extended transparently (to them) beyond any official theological statements into a constellation of unspoken solidarities, especially race and political ideology in a still-segregated United States, but also gender and sexuality among others.[14] How else could Ockenga get away with maintaining that "the freedom or liberty which we prize as an ideal must be within certain limitations" starting with race (1948), panning efforts to force integration as "selfish" (1957), or later suggesting that "even the most mild blacks" were becoming Black Power revolutionaries (1972)?[15] One struggles to imagine how such rhetoric would invite or maintain a dialogue with real-life Black evangelicals. The power dynamics of unvoiced identities (to say nothing of the more overtly exclusive aspects of the movement) have been de facto causes for a number of rather diverse others who subscribed to the statements of faith or connected with the primitive lexis of the evangel to keep their distance from the evangelical establishment and its leaders.[16] Some Black Protestants founded other institutions, like the National Black Evangelical Association (1963), while others simply maintained other affiliations rather than identifying with the "evangelical" movement. To them, the reality was not so transparent: many mainstream white leaders within the growing number of neo-evangelical organelles maintained and articulated a "worldview" that was both more and less than "biblical."

To be sure, stopping the infighting about the fundamentals turned out to be a greater challenge than neo-evangelicals seemed to expect—especially on the nature of Scripture, which seems to serve as an epistemological lynchpin—but even the semblance of political unity was only possible at relatively homogenous convening tables. By the early 1970s, a progressive cohort of evangelicals—including folks like Richard Mouw (1949–), Bill Pannell (1929–), and Jim Wallis (1948–)—gained momentum and public visibility to challenge the neo-evangelical establishment.[17] These folks were more diverse along gender, racial, and denominational-traditional lines, yet they shared some common concerns (and criticism of the mainstream elites) around social issues like racial justice, economic inequality, and the war in Vietnam. They noticed the protraction of theological squabbling among mainstream leaders who were missing opportunities to reflect deeply on social issues like racism, economic inequality, and American militarism from within their theological frame. As we will find Mouw saying of Ockenga and company in chapter 5, "While evangelicalism's watchmen on the wall have scanned the horizons for bearers of a Bultmannian hermeneutic, a 'honky hermeneutic' has taken over the city."[18] Young evangelicals in the 1970s did not readily see the political fruits of the neo-evangelicals' labors; instead, they imagined themselves as the originals in bringing about true *social* concern among evangelicals who had not yet grasped that the work of evangelism (i.e., spreading the good news) meant also working for the common good in society. They even used some of their forebears' rhetorical lines against them, deploying the "evangelical" brand in their favor. But within a decade, the rise of the Moral Majority as an evangelical voice in American politics demonstrated that the right-wing vineyards planted in the 1940s were coming into their season. By this point, if not before, the weather-eyed observer could perceive competing worldviews under the evangelical umbrella.

Political activity at the heights of the evangelical movement, however, has tended to mask the politics internal to the identity itself all along. A consistent, if shifting, sense of overlap between those who *identify as* evangelical and those who *can be identified as* evangelical according to certain fundamental beliefs—along with the steady stream of rank-and-file evangelicals who generally support mainstream evangelical institutions—has served to maintain the public image of evangelicalism as a reliable bloc. But the evangelical demographic in America has always comprised more persons and dissenting ideas than highly visible leaders have been willing to acknowledge—except to the extent that dissenting others add to the bottom line of surveys that, in turn, confirm the heft of the constituency they claim to represent. This numbers game can serve to reinforce the authority of mainstream institutions' visible leaders, validating their possession and profession of the evangelical worldview's sanctioned, comprehensive details. But when there is disagreement about the social or moral implications of identifying as evangelical, the dissenting insider's voice typically goes unacknowledged by highly visible leaders—is not "owned," so to speak. And when evangelical leaders get together to develop new, thin consensuses, the (conscious and unconscious) preselection of players in those conversations ensures that the "right" consensus is reached. To put the matter more directly, the worldview concept is the means by which motivated evangelical leadership has constructed a stable identity to claim "true" evangelicals (or Christians!), to influence them, to box in their opponents, and to gain power in the public sphere. So, worldview is the stuff of the politics internal to an evangelical identity even as it spills into public engagement with polarizing, identity-political energy.

Notable about this time period is the ongoing use of the "evangelical" label and sweeping "biblical worldview" rhetoric even in the presence of genuine diversity among those who identify, or could be identified, as evangelicals by the illustrious standard held forth. More specifically, it would seem that those most likely to claim the evangelical brand and use biblical worldview rhetoric in public also, like Ockenga's social network, tend to share a number of unspoken social statuses, locations, and other realities in common. And more directly, we may rightly sense that racial fault lines exert a formative influence on the details of the worldview articulated as "evangelical" or "biblical." In view of the data above, the cynic might conclude that race and political fit—with all its complex demographic overtones—have been more significant in the "evangelical" worldview than the expressed biblical-theological fundaments. In any case, evangelical posturing within American politics in recent years has proven that the world-viewing approach to Christian faith and witness flatly does not improve the polarization within or beyond religious borders. Instead, it seems to expand the context to be polarized and, in some ways, raises the stakes. Every issue can become, can *feel* fundamental when framed as essential to the biblical worldview.

THE INTERTWINED HISTORIES OF WORLD-VIEWING AND WHITENESS

Deeper still than the history of American evangelicalism over the last century is the story of how the worldview concept codeveloped with the racial framework in the colonial period. To better establish how I am thinking about whiteness and world-viewing as conceptual frameworks throughout this project, I should now map some important points in the development of worldview language and conceptuality. The German term *Weltanschauung* tumbled into the English language in the mid-nineteenth century but, as evangelical philosopher David Naugle registers in his celebrated history and encomium of the worldview concept, its coinage can be traced to the 1790 publication of Immanuel Kant's (1724–1804) *Critique of Judgment*.[19] This mention turned out to be an *hapax legomenon* in Kant's body of work, a throwaway description of the almost-indescribable "power that is supersensible, whose idea of a noumenon cannot be intuited but can yet be regarded as the substrate underlying what is mere appearance, namely, our intuition of the world [*Weltanschauung*]."[20] By naming this specific *Anschauung* (intuition, a term that in itself represents a can of worms in Kant's phenomenology), Kant seemed to underscore an innate sensibility that the whole world is coherent in and of itself as part of his wider argument about synthetic a priori judgments. I will argue in part I that, whatever this power or substrate may be, the actual cognition of individual human minds (including intuitions) is structurally complex and socially formed. As a kind of example, it is also important to recognize, though Naugle makes no mention of such elements in any thinker he draws support from, that concluding the *Critique*, Kant confined the attainment of the natural, universal end of humankind (i.e., self-perfection in view of human freedom) to bourgeois European males.[21] Kant's own intuitions located human powers (e.g., intuition and reason) and even universality itself within a racial hierarchy fit for Europe's so-called Age of Discovery.

Bearing this in mind, we might follow Naugle to note, "Kant's Copernican revolution in philosophy, with its emphasis on the knowing and willing self as the cognitive and moral center of the universe, created the conceptual space in which the notion of worldview could flourish."[22] In the work of Romantic philosopher Friedrich Wilhelm Joseph von Schelling (1775–1854), the term *Weltanschauung* picked up new conceptual freight as "a self-realized, productive as well as conscious way of apprehending and interpreting the universe of beings."[23] In Schelling's view, white Europeans had altogether escaped the process by which "the other part" of humankind "degraded into races" and, in fact, belonged to no race themselves.[24] And other German Idealists like G. W. F. Hegel, who can often be found lurking in the background of this project, further developed the worldview concept throughout the nineteenth century even as the wider academy contested, criticized, and sometimes rejected such conceptual moves. Hegel theorized on the relative merits of various racial-ethnic worldviews within his epistemology, favoring the achievements of modern Europe toward reason and freedom over against the supposed lack of development among dark-skinned Africans. For example, he claimed, "In

Negro life the characteristic point is the fact that consciousness has not yet attained to the realization of any substantial objective existence."²⁵ Hegel maintained that dark-skinned Africans' souls remained in their natural state, in which the free, self-conscious Spirit lies unawakened, that is to say, about as far as humanly possible from the rational worldview to which white Europeans had ascended collectively.

More broadly, worldview conceptuality and "civilization" are bound up together in the history of European colonization of foreign lands, in which a special kind of "civility" was used to dispatch what was conceived as barbarity and general heathenism.²⁶ While we will explore this more fully with theologian Willie Jennings in chapter 4, here we might start to think of the worldview concept in terms of an *impulse*: it was nascent in the minds of early European globetrotters as they encountered and categorized very different "others" around the world relative to the norms of their own white Christian civilization.²⁷ The moment of classifying others in this way shared its effect with a move internal to the seafaring Europeans: in the experience of profound cultural difference, individual persons assumed something like a Western, Christian worldview was a part of themselves, bound to their bodies and not confined to their homelands, and projected over space and time as a skin-color spectrum. The scale of this thinking and the unquestioned normativity of the world-viewing subject is a function of a racial logic (namely, whiteness) pervading the power structures of the modern West. And what is more, Jennings tells us, white folk began to imagine their cross-racial contact, including the process of enslavement and their twisted form of inculturation, as initiating a Christian order of salvation.

The philosophical discourse above appears to be one source for the worldview concept when some influential Christian thinkers took it up around the turn of the twentieth century. Under the heading "Original Worldview Thinkers in Protestant Evangelicalism," Naugle names Scottish fundamentalist Presbyterian minister and scholar James Orr (1844–1913) and Dutch neo-Calvinist polymath Abraham Kuyper (1837–1920).²⁸ Orr and Kuyper were both familiar with German intellectual currents, and their respective philosophical methods for understanding and framing worldviews noticeably bear "idealist" marks.²⁹ While the germ of a worldview concept seems to have been already present in the imaginations of American fundamentalist Christians through other terms (e.g., "life-principle") available around the turn of the century, these two thinkers introduced the language and energy of a "worldview" into the streams of Calvinism and fundamentalism that would produce the neo-evangelical harvest in the 1940s.³⁰ Many neo-evangelical leaders—including Harold Ockenga and Carl F. H. Henry (1913–2003)— whet their intellects in the discourse of world- and life-views in the intellectual vortex formed by Wheaton College, Princeton Theological Seminary, and Westminster Theological Seminary. Several highly influential scholars in faculty posts at these schools in the early twentieth century were, like Orr and Kuyper, keen to instill in their students an epistemology fit to do battle with (or at least to persuasively debunk) what they called "Modernism."[31] And in many cases, these American fundamentalist professors had been in touch with Orr and Kuyper (or learned from those who had been). Significantly, both of these European thinkers delivered the prestigious Levi P. Stone Lectures at Princeton, and their writings (in Kuyper's case, introduced to an American readership by esteemed Princeton theologian and apologist B. B. Warfield) made the rounds among lettered evangelicals, especially their respective works on the Christian worldview.[32]

But just as the worldview concept helped Kant, Hegel, and company project their cultural chauvinism across more of the world and more of its people, it also failed to help Kuyper and others see more of the world more clearly. On full display in chapter 1 will be Kuyper's embrace of a Hegelian racial hierarchy for conceiving of peoples and their worldviews (and those who had not yet risen to the level of world-viewing), adding his own biblical rationale for that hierarchy and justifying a form of colonialism as indispensable to the divine mandate to "fill the earth and subdue it" (Gen. 1:28). He made such claims as his native Netherlands and England persisted in conflict over their stakes in South Africa, where a certain Christian worldview soon came to entail law and order within radically segregated spheres under white hegemonic rule. Kuyper's advocacy, as one who is upheld as an exemplar of Christian world-viewing, stings especially because we know he did not have to arrive at the conclusions he did about race and colony merely because of his cultural milieu. Even as he developed and defended his theological worldview, other Christians advocated a radically different racial sensibility—even in the prior century, as in the famous case of William Wilberforce (1759–1833). As a keynote speaker in this history, Abraham Kuyper will be my first case study (chapter 1).

In the United States, the history of the worldview concept shares a number of pages with neo-evangelicalism. In the decades before the "new evangelicals" organized their first institutions, "world- and life-view" and its cognates were markedly absent in the English-speaking world.[33] Worldview language found its footing in American discourse through early 1930's media coverage of ideologies on the march in Europe and, thus, was consciously connected with the German concept of *Weltanschauung* for reasons beyond the strictly philosophical.[34] As historian Molly Worthen puts it, "The rise of Nazism prodded some Westerners to realize that the conflict required not only manpower and matériel but a coherent intellectual front as well."[35] Here is a second sense in which we might understand world-viewing as a kind of *impulse*—a somewhat involuntary response to external ideological threats.

Speaking of the need to carry a full-orbed evangelical worldview into vigorous public engagement for the reclamation of American society, Ockenga preached, "Let us learn something from the Soviets and the Nazis. If the children of this world are wiser than the children of the light, then it is time for the children of the light to open their eyes and learn how to carry on God's work."[36] He was concerned with both the foreign threats posed by the potential spread of fascist and Communist worldviews and the domestic threat of a disintegrating, secularizing Modernism (capitalized here for effect vis-à-vis worldview theory); furthermore, Ockenga predicted fascism as the probable end of any decidedly secularizing worldview. This is noteworthy because, as chapter 6 will reveal, some Nazi-sympathizing Protestant theologians in Germany operationalized their "orders of creation" framework as grounds for supporting the needs of *das Volk* and for submitting to its will. Thus, contrary to Ockenga's analysis of the problem, these theologians imagined their ethnonationalism within what they took to be the biblical *Weltanschauung* or worldview. Suffice it to say, for now, the Ockenga quote above suggests that the worldview concept glittered in this historical moment as promising, an even more total response to threatening concretions of invasive alternative worldviews. "Now the way to understand one's enemy," Worthen explains, "was to see beyond his rhetoric, decipher his *Weltanschauung*—and defend one's own."[37] As one such worldview defender, Harold Ockenga will be my second case study (chapter 3).

Many current evangelical thinkers, following some of the original neo-evangelical ones, see the modern worldview contest as but an iteration of a universal and timeless problem, tracing "the struggle over first principles" (and all that supposedly follows from them) back through time as a mark of the human condition in a fallen world.[38] And these thinkers persist in identifying a battle between basic worldviews unfolding on a massive, global scale—whether the "war on terror" and the new cold war with the Communist bloc or the denouement of Modernism's godlessness in the *Post*modern "incredulity toward metanarratives."[39] Declinist narratives of the relationship between Westerners and their traditional sources of (moral) authority and of selfhood have been making the rounds for some time; even in the 1940s, one could cite philosophers who "say we have reached the eventide of the West; the end of an age; the crisis of an era; the conclusion of a civilization."[40] Once-prevalent worldviews have been dragged into perpetual deconstruction processes and power analyses, and as Naugle warns, all that "remains for the postmodern denizen is a plethora of socially and linguistically constructed meaning systems, each unprivileged, nonhegemonous [sic], and thoroughly tolerated."[41] Richard Mouw and the other editors of *Stained Glass*, a volume of papers on worldviews and social science presented at Calvin College in the 1980s, lamented the possibility that "we are now on the threshold of the end of the age of worldviews."[42] As a representative of evangelical world-viewing in this age and an heir to both Kuyper and Ockenga, Mouw will be my third case study (chapter 5).

Considered as a general, abstract concept bearing on reality with no history of its own, worldview has a certain ring to it. The concept of a worldview implies that one can meaningfully abstract from the real world a leaner structure of principles that make sense of the whole, including oneself and God. Particularly for those who come to understand their world-view (now hyphenated to emphasize the present point) as the very stuff of God's own self-revelation, the temptation is to use this principial structure as a mold for both "knowing" others—with questions of *how* someone represents the general human condition rather than *who* they are as a person—and reforming the world. Likening the biblical world-view to the fabled "Archimedean point," Naugle implies the regenerate individual is lifted out of their subjective vantage within the world and placed on a celestial point that offers an objective and total view of the whole world, *including themselves*.[43] I will consciously maintain the hyphenated form "world-view" throughout this project to keep before us the sense that this concept is, for its proponents, just such a vantage. When appropriate, I will sometimes amplify this aspect of world-viewing with adjectives like "comprehensive" and "total" that convey how the cases under study believe themselves to have received the God's-eye view that can and should be formulated as timeless principles and universally applicable laws—all of which carry divine force.

At this point, I can explain more clearly that the meaning of the world-view concept is found in the history of its use.[44] When I talk about "whiteness" throughout this project, it is not exactly about ethnicity or specifically about skin color. Among other things, whiteness can be understood through a culinary metaphor as a kind of blandness, a basicness that is home to the dopamine-releasing fats and sugars our bodies crave. Whiteness means involvement in the ubiquitous, transparent norms of reality. It means feeling right, feeling like a well-meaning person (i.e., good intentions even if a sinner), and so on. We call it whiteness because some of its most obvious features can be imagined as coevolving in the colonial moment and because we have the testimony of Black voices throughout this history naming the reality and their exclusion from it—like W. E. B. Du Bois's double consciousness or Frantz Fanon's inferiority complex or Ralph Waldo Ellison's invisible man. Whiteness is an ability to blend in, to be part of the norming group in any given room, the privilege of not questioning whether one really can or ought to try ordering, grasping, or even viewing the whole world. To qualify in another way, the advent of colonialism and the racial scale to support the myth of white European supremacy and its destiny of conquest did not coincide with the very first world-view-style thinking. Powerful Christians in the

West tended to assume they had a grasp on world order before the colonial moment, making civilizational progress on the confident natural theologies and moral teleologies of old. But whiteness is one prevailing head of an enduring, hydra-like problem generated atop humankind's deep insecurity following the first humans' alienation from the garden and its God. World-viewing is the capacious framework for humans' cognitive rebellion, which offers the vehicle for principalities and powers (racism, economic exploitation, militarism, and the like) to generate hegemony and strife across time and space. These powers include whiteness, but this phenomenon is neither delimited nor determined by skin color.

While I will be focusing on white evangelicalism a fair amount in this project, I am particularly concerned with how agenda-setting, world-view-style thinkers are positioning churches vis-à-vis the formation of their people. To what degree are we giving people the tools and the motivation to resist enlistment in the work of the principalities and powers that hold sway in our society? I know we do not want to believe ourselves party to the problem, and white folks like myself are especially challenged to be self-critical in ways that are psychologically taxing, but we need a reality check. American evangelicalism over the last century has participated in rather than unseating the divisive and polarizing dynamics of the modern world. The movement has not invited people to live in a new way, to see and inhabit the world differently because they walk with the living God. It has invited people to live the same way but to play for a new team. In this book, I will argue that church-community is to embody a clear and compelling alternative to this competitive and coercive way of seeing and inhabiting the world. Church-community is a God-initiated and God-maintained communion where all worldly identities and the security that attends them are questioned and shown their relative value in view of the coming fullness of God's kingdom. Christian faith is not a more certain (if presuppositional) way of knowing we are right so that we can work to transform the world. We must learn to hold our faith and our convictions differently, to embrace our status as creatures in a world only God can view in its totality. But the world-viewing impulse needs to be disarmed before we can openly and humbly hear the Spirit's call to change, to grow, to be courageous in the face of unrelenting pressure to conform.

THE TASK BEFORE US

Though I have already introduced much of what will follow, a sketch-map of key landmarks along the way may help the reader navigate this project. In part I, I will examine human beings' inner lives to discover the liabilities of imagining that something like a coherent, single-sourced world-view could take shape in such a cognitively complex creature. The first chapter centers on Abraham Kuyper and the details of his own particular world-view in light of his speculative philosophical theory about how world-views develop in human minds, especially among the born-again. He romanticized about an inner life reunified by the Holy Spirit and infused with biblical principles, conflating this idealized psychology with both a confident epistemology and the actual details of what he thought he knew about the world. Kuyper represents the colonial mentality that one can see and touch and think the whole world and all its people together at once, at least in all meaningful ways. Moreover, he theorized his comprehensive world-view concept as a divine vocation and inborn *impulse* (yes, this word is his), so he felt compelled to weave whatever convictions he had into a coherent web only to make *all these factors disappear* (again, his words) as he balanced the whole upon Scripture in the end. So, Kuyper also reveals how intelligent, powerful individuals in history can misconceive themselves through an abstract theory and, thus, feel pious and reasonable as they project some grizzly, subjective ideas (e.g., racism, colonialism, and patriarchy) into a space conceived as God's own mind and will. Among other problems, this posture opens the door to self-deception as well as self-defense in the form of mystification and resistance to adverse feedback. That Kuyper worked to leave a legacy based on the story he lived by may be seen as an indicator of psychological wellbeing. But morally, theologically, we must inquire about practices and norms for self-scrutiny, genuine deliberation on key ideas and frameworks—especially those that bring pain to other persons—and ongoing cognitive change.

Chapter 2 is the first of three intervening chapters that deconstruct world-view theory itself from a particular angle (here, current discussions across several branches of psychology) and then offer constructive prospects for a more honest, more viable, more faithful theology of identity. I open with the counter-testimony of W. E. B. Du Bois (1868–1963) who published his account of the jarring experience of double consciousness among African Americans before Kuyper visited America. This account begins to demonstrate the privilege of assuming your conscious awareness of yourself and your perspective overall are rational, virtuous, and universally normative. Over time, the perfidious supposition of virtue by white folk, beginning with those who commodified other human beings as chattel, has generated a color-line that excludes dark-skinned humans from this self-aggrandizing, norming power. Current cognitive psychological theory has taken what Du Bois registered as "double consciousness" in some new directions, conceptualizing the inner life of healthy individual persons as an adaptive network of numerous "selves" rather than a single, unified one. At the same time, developmental psychology confirms that people do tend to conceive of themselves as fundamentally consistent and come to emphasize coherence, growth, and other such values as they narrate their lives. This too is part of *the world-viewing impulse*: one's own world-view is subjectively assumed to be an adequate and honestly formulable description of the most basic and the most (or even the only) influential story one lives by.[45] But what we might describe as common or "healthy" does not necessarily fit the moral truth, particularly in that communion into which God is calling together so many very different people, by God's own will and action, beyond human control. Here, all our loyalties and convictions are to be cross-examined, shown their disharmony and relative value in light of the ultimate reality of God's coming kingdom. We narrate our lives relative to a new reality, yet God, the church as God's people, and the story of their relationship in time and space all remain bigger than us—drawing us, story and all, *into their orbit*.

In part II, I will explore the in-some-ways-hidden, or more nearly transparent-to-some, impacts of sociohistorical dynamics on what a person or group articulates as their world-view. The third chapter will take up the case of Harold Ockenga, who was less interested in a rich philosophical treatment of world-view conceptuality than seeding a broad, Spirit-infused movement with an impulse toward a commonsense Christian nationalism. His world-viewing rhetoric crystalized in a historical moment when the term "evangelical" served a more generic function and "evangelicals" were not widely held to be a distinct group or movement. With the support of other restless fundamentalists, Ockenga founded the NAE and Fuller Seminary and otherwise called American Christians to gather under a broad but distinct "new evangelical" standard. But the world-view he articulated found its roots and sprouted within a relatively homogenous social network, which allowed convictions and commitments from numerous overlapping social groups and aggregate interests (e.g., affluent, conservative, white, Republican) to pass through without being recognized or named as features. This historical reality allowed a partisan political and economic agenda along with the status quo of white authority—over against civil rights legislation and efforts to hasten desegregation—to hide within what he nominalized as the "evangelical" or "biblical Christian" world-view. Ockenga represents a kind of historical bridge character in that he (a) articulates a white identity politics more explicitly in keeping with past generations (b) within the seemingly more neutral form of omnicompetent world-viewing that renders the operations of whiteness more transparent in and to later generations. Here we will see how what is intended as evangelical witness picks up some silent letters as w(h)it(e)ness among those who cannot recognize when they are acting socially and not merely as individual, rational agents with common, biblical sense.

I will begin chapter 4 by engaging a different kind of evangelical arising in the late 1960s, namely, "the father of Black evangelicalism," William E. "Bill" Pannell. He openly identified the wedding of wealthy, partisan, white interests to the "evangelical" program, and he contested the claim that his own evangelical convictions must lead to the same detailed, "psycho-political" world-view. Describing his own formation within predominantly white evangelical institutions, Pannell concluded, "From a cultural and theological perspective we were white men."[46] And he narrated coming to grips with the reality that evangelicals were acting socially without even beginning to reflect *theologically* on the significance of humankind's social nature. What follows is a study of how evangelical churches in America persist as "white institutional spaces"—even those that intend to be multiracial. Current critical theory will help us understand how Ockenga and others, both then and since, could perform evangelicalism within racialized structures without necessarily meaning to do so—and why reforming these structures presents an uphill battle. Because the white American imagination comprises freewill individualism and the notion that our meaning-making and identity-defining commitments are voluntary associations, demonstrating the impacts of a whiteness that is transparent to its bearers is a genuine challenge. Pushing a layer deeper in history, I will highlight how the impulse to imagine the whole world and all of its people(s) at once through something like a "biblical world-view" has been bound up in the colonial framework of the modern West since its inception. While mainstream evangelical institutions have sloughed off a great deal of their overtly racist conceptuality, the enduring focus on broad, universal categories for world-viewing fails to adequately describe, let alone address, actual evangelicals, their relationships, or those persons and things nearest to them. Jesus's call to follow him finds us within a constellation of sociopolitical realities that structure our external world and our inner life. We must reckon with such spirited powers in our (hi)story—as they play out in our actual relationships, which make us responsible as agents. Our approach to identity security and the levers of power must be refigured to fit the new reality of God's kingdom and a new life through death-to-self by a thousand cuts (i.e., to the ways, certainties, and powers of old selves).

In part III, I will layer in a more robust theological critique of, and alternative to, what has amounted to a rather philosophical argument for world-viewing framed by epistemological assumptions. The fifth chapter will focus on Richard Mouw, who emerged as an American evangelical leader in a younger cohort that included Pannell in the 1970s. Much of this study will inquire about the epistemic confidence that Mouw gains from his Kuyperian tradition, which both motivates his work toward a broader, "generic" evangelical engagement in the wider society and provides the actual grounds for his public-theological claims. This chapter will expand our view of the whiteness at work in at least two ways. First, we will see how it becomes transparent in projects and institutions helmed by those who actually see the enduring color-line and know it represents structural sin, that is to say, how cultural pressures may conserve the homogeneity of *voices* even while learning to welcome diverse *faces* to the table. Second, by exploring Mouw's advocacy against same-sex marriage, I will pursue further questions about how a colonial-imperial framework for knowing and organizing the whole world turns out various forms of "essentialism" while participating in the sometimes coercive power dynamics of knowledge. He demonstrates how one can claim insider status, even representative power to chart the faithful course for whole traditions and movements, while both dissenting from positions maintained by other insiders (whether visible leaders like Ockenga or even a perceived majority of the rank and file), absolving the sins of problematic insiders (Mouw ascribes "warm evangelical faith" to Kuyper despite his glaring errors), and denying the social group identity to still others who dissent on different issues (e.g., same-sex marriage). All the while, Mouw leans on the supposed prestige of his thicker tradition's epistemology, which has never really resolved the dilemma of epistemic certainty in a fallen world. I will argue that it is no mystery why human beings feel confident in the details of their knowledge of good and evil, even to the point of using advocacy in the church, and too often in public, to put the squeeze on those who think differently. It is the substance of the fall in the garden, the original turn to epistemology for self-security, searching below and behind the relationship with God for a more haveable source of certainty.

Moving into the sixth chapter, I will argue that *epistemology itself* is central to the problems of polarized strife and alienation—is a diversion from the proper, creaturely kind of knowing that flows from free relationship in communion with, for, and (in some ways) over-against other persons, including God. This learning emerges from the writing and example of Dietrich Bonhoeffer, who met the living Jesus in a Black church-community in Harlem and returned to a depressed Germany with a new outlook on what it means to follow-after him in a broken world. Over against folks like Paul Althaus, who continued to make general, principled arguments about how Christians should live relative to the orders of creation that God had placed them in (including their specific German people) in full view of Nazis benefitting from such conceptuality, Bonhoeffer argued that we must turn toward Jesus, who speaks a word here and now. This word comes to us out of the future fullness of God's kingdom and makes us responsible without being able to retrieve a more graspable, more secure worldview from our lost beginning. Grasping after original-creational categories allows humans to project too much of themselves from their sociohistorical location into God's will while evading even the possibility that the living God might have something to say. This God we encounter in Jesus, who enters into the human situation with compassion and works to deliver all people into communion with God's presence at its center. The living, biblical, historical Jesus embodies and points toward the future consummation of God's kingdom, and in light of this, shows all present forms their relative, penultimate value. As such, we cannot rely on the principial forms we have derived from our lost beginning, for they may not—and as they reflect the texture of a fallen world, *will not*— reliably direct our lives toward the ultimate, interdependent existence of life together with God. A brief closing chapter will function like a coda, drawing the critical concerns and constructive themes from the book together in light of these theological moves.

For my part, I have envisioned and inhabited this project, painful as its message is at times, as a labor of love for the church. What I am after is a patient, thorough exploration of why world-viewing gets who we are—individually, together, and before the living God—wrong. I will examine why we slip into this kind of thinking, what structures and mechanisms in the world (social and epistemological and psychological) help prop up this way of thinking and make it feel like the right, the obvious, the only way of thinking about and living in the world. And also, I will sketch out some possibilities for a humbler path forward and a fundamentally different way of inhabiting faith in Jesus. I am guessing that many readers live and, thus, will understand the kind of faith that I will underscore throughout yet, when reaching for an intellectual form, feel compelled, drawn, under pains to articulate a world-view. But instead of merely participating in this way of thinking and living that the world itself has put before us, trying to use the form toward godly ends, Christian community can actually become the site for unhinging the impulse after self-secure knowledge of good and evil in the presence of God. We can pursue such community not by avoiding theological debate or withdrawing from scientific pursuits, but by changing our grip on what we think we know—holding it with an open hand such that, relative to all our beautiful thoughts, faith and trusting relationship change. Our side of this relationship must change if we are to become more open to the living God, more likely to grow in Christlikeness, and less anxious (and combative and polarizing) as we live truthfully with and for others.

NOTES

1. "Political polarization" can be applied as a topic filter on the Pew Research Center website at https://www.pewresearch.org/topics/political-polarization.
2. "In a Politically Polarized Era, Sharp Divides in Both Partisan Coalitions," Pew Research Center, December 17, 2019, accessed March 2, 2021, https://www.pew research.org/politics/2019/12/17/in-a-politically-polarized-era-sharp-divides-in-both -partisan-coalitions/.

3. Amina Dunn et al., "Voters Say Those on the Other Side 'Don't Get' Them. Here's What They Want Them to Know," Pew Research Center, December 17, 2020, accessed March 2, 2021, https://www.pewresearch.org/politics/2020/12/17/voters-say-those-on-the-other-side-dont-get-them-heres-what-they-want-them-to-know/.

4. A quick online search for "families divided by politics" will produce many examples and analyses.

5. Jeffrey M. Jones, "U.S. Church Membership Falls Below Majority for First Time," Gallup, Inc., March 29, 2021, accessed April 6, 2021, https://news.gallup.com/poll/341963/church-membership-falls-below-majority-first-time.aspx.

6. Many books do that kind of thing. For a helpful introduction to the conversation about evangelical history as it has unfolded over the last 35 years, see Mark A. Noll, David W. Bebbington, and George M. Marsden, eds. *Evangelicals: Who They Have Been, Are Now, and Could Be* (Grand Rapids: Eerdmans, 2019). In addition to the editors, several of the contributors have written books around this history (e.g., Kristin Kobes Du Mez, D. G. Hart, and Molly Worthen). And I have also appreciated the work of Matthew Avery Sutton, who provided helpful feedback on my project in an earlier form; see his *American Apocalypse: A History of Modern Evangelicalism* (Cambridge, MA: The Belknap Press, 2014).

7. In a helpful (and helpfully brief) exploration of "The Politics of Identity," Kwame Anthony Appiah illuminates seven possible meanings; see his essay by this title in *Daedalus* 135, no. 4 (Fall 2006): 15–22.

8. See, for example, Joe Carter, "No, the Majority of American Evangelicals Did Not Vote for Trump," November 15, 2016, accessed March 2, 2021, https://www.thegospelcoalition.org/article/no-the-majority-of-american-evangelicals-did-not-vote-for-trump/.

9. David Bebbington's classic definition of evangelicalism by way of four hallmarks (conversionism, activism, biblicism, and crucicentrism) appears in *Evangelicalism in Modern Britain: A History from the 1730s to the 1980s* (1989; repr., New York: Routledge, 1993), ch. 1; it is also reproduced in Noll, Bebbington, and Marsden, 31–55.

10. The data on these trends is ubiquitous and easy to find through a quick online search. Compare Frank Newport, "Religious Group Voting and the 2020 Election," Gallup, Inc., November 13, 2020, accessed March 2, 2021, https://news.gallup.com/opinion/polling-matters/324410/religious-group-voting-2020-election.aspx, and LifeWay Research, "Most Evangelicals Choose Trump Over Biden, But Clear Divides Exist," September 29, 2020, accessed March 2, 2021, https://lifewayresearch.com/2020/09/29/most-evangelicals-choose-trump-over-biden-but-clear-divides-exist/.

11. Mark A. Noll, "One Word but Three Crises," in Noll, Bebbington, and Marsden, 3.

12. See, for instance, Anthea Butler's very recent *White Evangelical Racism: The Politics of Morality in America* (Chapel Hill, NC: The University of North Carolina Press, 2021); Kristin Kobes Du Mez, *Jesus and John Wayne: How White Evangelicals Corrupted a Faith and Fractured a Nation* (New York: Liveright, 2020); and Robert P. Jones, *The End of White Christian America* (New York: Simon & Schuster, 2016).

13. Harold John Ockenga, introduction to *The Uneasy Conscience of Modern Fundamentalism*, by Carl. F. H. Henry (1947; repr., Grand Rapids: Eerdmans, 2003), xx.

14. George Marsden, *Reforming Fundamentalism: Fuller Seminary and the New Evangelicalism* (Grand Rapids: Eerdmans, 1987), 29.

15. See Harold John Ockenga, *Faithful in Christ Jesus* (New York: Fleming H. Revell, 1948), 232 (quotation); Owen Strachan, *Awakening the Evangelical Mind: An Intellectual History of the Neo-Evangelical Movement* (Grand Rapids: Zondervan, 2015), 62; and Harold John Ockenga, *Faith in a Troubled World* (Wenham, MA: Gordon College Press, 1972), 7–8.

16. Molly Worthen, *Apostles of Reason: The Crisis of Authority in American Evangelicalism* (New York: Oxford University Press, 2014), 37–38 and ch. 4.

17. See David Swartz's treatment of the young evangelicals in *Moral Minority: The Evangelical Left in an Age of Conservatism* (Philadelphia: University of Pennsylvania Press, 2012).

18. Richard J. Mouw, "Evangelicals in Search of Maturity," *Theology Today* 35, no. 1 (April 1978): 47–48.

19. David K. Naugle, *Worldview: The History of a Concept* (Grand Rapids: Wm. B. Eerdmans Publishing Co., 2002), 58–59. If we were to read this intellectual history from its underside, we might get a sense for the framing role of race in the history of worldview discourse, and, as a result, the figures who appear in the following paragraphs might impress us less. On this history, see Susanne Lettow, "Modes of Naturalization: Race, Sex and Biology in Kant, Schelling and Hegel," *Philosophy and Social Criticism* 39, no. 2 (2013): 117–31.

20. Immanuel Kant, *Critique of Judgment*, trans. Werner S. Pluhar (Indianapolis: Hackett Publishing Company, 1987), 111.

21. Lettow, 121.

22. Naugle, 59.

23. Martin Heidegger, *The Basic Problems of Phenomenology*, 1975, trans. Albert Hofstadter (Bloomington: Indiana University Press, 1982), 5. This quotation is found near the head of Heidegger's own brief history of the philosophical concept of *Weltanschauung*.

24. Lettow, 124.

25. G. W. F. Hegel, *The Philosophy of History*, 1892, trans. John Sibree (New York: Dover Publications, 1956), 93. See also Lettow, cited above, and Ronald Kuykendall, "Hegel and Africa: An Evaluation of the Treatment of Africa in The Philosophy of History," *Journal of Black Studies* 23, no. 4 (June 1993): 572–73.

26. Niall Ferguson, *Civilization: The West and the Rest* (New York: Penguin Books, 2011), ch. 1. Though the term "world-view" emerged in the English-speaking world around 1858, the rising popularity of "world-view" language in English is roughly concurrent with the emergence of an anthropological sense of "culture" (around the 1920s). Soon the two began to cover similar terrain, centering on the (a) religious core of whatever social group was studied and concerned with that group's "total way of life." Cf. Kathryn Tanner, *Theories of Culture: A New Agenda for Theology* (Minneapolis: Fortress Press, 1997), ch. 2.

27. Willie James Jennings, *The Christian Imagination: Theology and the Origins of Race* (New Haven: Yale University Press, 2010), ch. 1.
28. Naugle, 5; cf. Worthen, 27.
29. On the German Idealist influence on Kuyper, particularly his philosophical method, see James D. Bratt, *Abraham Kuyper: Modern Calvinist, Christian Democrat* (Grand Rapids: Wm. B. Eerdmans Publishing Co., 2013), 30–33. On the same in Orr, see James W. Sire, *Naming the Elephant: Worldview as a Concept*, 2nd ed. (Downers Grove, IL: InterVarsity Press, 2015), 45–46.
30. Worthen, 27; Peter S. Heslam, *Creating a Christian Worldview: Abraham Kuyper's Lectures on Calvinism* (Grand Rapids: Wm. B. Eerdmans Publishing Co., 1998), 92–96; and Bratt, 207. Despite the coinage of the English-language term "world-view" around 1858, when Kuyper asked his States-side colleagues how he should translate his Dutch concept *levens- en wereldbeschouwing*, they recommended the term "life-system" in circulation at Princeton around that time (*Calvinism: Six Stone Lectures* [Amsterdam: Höveker & Wormser, 1899], 3n1).
31. Worthen, 26–32.
32. Arguably the most-referenced works of each are Kuyper, *Lectures*; and James Orr, *The Christian View of God and the World as Centering in the Incarnation* (New York: Anson D. F. Randolph and Co., 1893).
33. Cf. Heslam, 89.
34. Worthen, 27–28. Despite his constructive theological ambitions for this work, Naugle's historical study is pegged to academic usage of the world-view concept. He does not really do the kind of historical work on evangelicalism necessary to see how neo-evangelical world-view offerings were framed at least partly as a response to Nazism, Communism, and so on.
35. Worthen, 28.
36. Harold John Ockenga, "The Unvoiced Multitudes," in *Evangelical Action!* (Boston, MA: United Action Press, 1942), 25.
37. Worthen, 28.
38. Naugle is clearly one of these thinkers. For another example, see James H. Olthuis, "On Worldviews," in *Stained Glass: Worldviews and Social Science*, ed. Paul A. Marshall, Sander Griffioen, and Richard J. Mouw (New York: University Press of America, 1989), 26–27. And for an early twentieth-century example, see J. Gresham Machen, *Christianity and Liberalism* (Grand Rapids: Wm. B. Eerdmans Publishing Co., 1923).
39. Jean-François Lyotard, *The Postmodern Condition: A Report on Knowledge*, trans. Geoff Bennington and Brian Massumi (Minneapolis: University of Minnesota Press, 1984), xxiv.
40. Harold John Ockenga, "The Challenge to the Christian Culture of the West" (presidential address, opening convocation of Fuller Theological Seminary, Pasadena, CA, October 1, 1947), accessed March 2, 2021, https://fullerstudio.fuller.edu/the-challenge-to-the-christian-culture-of-the-west-opening-convocation-october-1-1947/. Cf. Naugle, 262–63, 300ff.
41. Naugle, 174.
42. Marshall, Griffieon, and Mouw, 12.

43. Naugle, 28–29.

44. This phrasing is consciously connected with Ludwig Wittgenstein's claim, "For a *large* class of cases of the employment of the word 'meaning'—though not for all—this word can be explained in this way: the meaning of a word is its use in the language" (*Philosophical Investigations*, 4th ed., ed. P. M. S. Hacker and Joachim Schulte, trans. G. E. M. Anscombe, P. M. S. Hacker, and Joachim Schulte [Malden, MA: Blackwell Publishing, 2009], 25).

45. Naugle connects world-viewing to the individual's experiential sense of self-unity, explaining that biblical world-view conceptuality "provides a narrative context by which believers can establish their own identities, make sense of their lives, and discover their place in the world" (343).

46. William E. Pannell, "Evangelism and the Struggle for Power," *International Review of Mission* 63, no. 250 (April 1974): 201.

Part I

SELF-REVELATIONS

Chapter 1

The Neo-Calvinist World-View of Abraham Kuyper

The harsh realities of daily life for the many during the Western world's second industrial, or "technological," revolution grew increasingly clear as the nineteenth century drew to its close. When Christians began addressing the "social question"—from Christoph Blumhardt in Germany to Walter Rauschenbusch in the United States—their pronouncements regularly included litanies against material problems like the poverty and squalor of rapid urbanization, unsustainable working conditions, child labor, and the breakdown of family life. That such a crisis could develop in the first place was, to Abraham Kuyper, an unmistakable sign that runaway capitalist egoism and rank materialism (even Mammonism) were rending the social fabric itself asunder. Assessing these prime threats to God's original design for a beautiful, tapestried human community, he traced them all to a single source. And at the opening of his 1898 Levi P. Stone Lectures at Princeton Theological Seminary, Kuyper underscored this source in a disquieting juxtaposition. Though he was thrilled to be in the United States, where "so many divine potencies, which were hidden away in the bosom of mankind from our very creation, . . . are now beginning to disclose their inward splendor," he sensed the dismaying possible future of "Modernism," in which "the vast energy of an all-embracing *life-system*" depraves this hopeful new world and its fatherlands.[1] Facing the challenges of godless Modernism, Kuyper argued that one would do well to understand what delivered the West's Christian nations to this precipice—and the tectonic activity that produced those heights in the first place.

Throughout a long and distinguished career, Kuyper's lifework became the development and promulgation of a world-view meant to inspire Christians to submit all sectors of their lives to God's sovereign rule. But as activist energy—that is, the energy of an identity politics—Kuyper's Calvinism would not run its course until the particulars of God's will have been (super) intended over all persons and fashioned into political forms that preserve religious freedom and constrain evil in the wider society. He found many outlets for concretizing his world-view. In addition to church work, Kuyper started a newspaper (and served as its chief editor), founded a university (serving as its first Rector Magnificus and a faculty member), and helped establish a political party (serving as its head for some 40 years). He was elected to public office for the first time in 1874, and after a 20-year hiatus, returned to the House of Representatives. By 1901, his party made significant gains, and Kuyper became prime minister. All told, he served his country with almost 15 (nonconsecutive) years in the House, four years as prime minister, and seven years in the Senate. Kuyper entered politics as a young man because he sensed that convictions, and the world-view within which they come to be articulated, are of deepest consequence.[2] And given the slide into Modernism and the rampant materialism that comes with it, grasping the levers of power in culture-making institutions seemed perhaps the only way to make an impact.

Kuyper's name has become nearly synonymous with Christian worldviewing in some American evangelical circles. Speaking of his enduring appeal, historian and Kuyper biographer James Bratt cites distinguished colleagues Mark Noll and James Turner to say, "Neo-Calvinism [initiated by Kuyper] is the only resource available besides neo-Thomism to rescue American evangelicalism from cultural irrelevance, to unite the warm heart at which evangelicalism excels with the furnished mind that public engagement requires and the responsible pluralism that modern society demands."[3] And moving into his own commendation, Bratt argues,

> Above all he taught a critical method for measuring the socio-political agenda that one draws from the gospel, to see if it is of God. At this writing [2013] it is clearer than ever that evangelicals need more than ever to differentiate their professed Christian allegiance, and also their supposed social conservatism, from the gods of the market and of militaristic nationalism to which this group is so perpetually beholden.[4]

In the context of my overall project focused on white, American evangelicals, we study Kuyper from the outset partly because his Stone Lectures positioned him to bear a significant influence on the American faith leaders who would set the stage for the evangelicalism we see around us today. But also, the success of post–World War II neo-evangelicalism was boosted by the assimilation of European ethnic communities, not least the Dutch. As Noll explains, "Evangelicals offered the Dutch Reformed an important reference point as their immigrant community moved closer to American ways. For their part, the Dutch confessionalists gave their American counterparts a heritage of serious academic work and experienced philosophical reasoning."[5] And among my project's case studies, Kuyper develops the most explicit defense of the world-viewing impulse as an aspect of God-given human nature.

So, after reviewing his historical setting as motivation to get about the business of world-viewing, I will explore Kuyper's systematic theory of what a world-view is, how it develops in Christian minds, and what we should expect a Christian world-view to motivate—all the way up to sustained theological reflection and a conceptual articulation of the world-view itself. This major section will read as especially heavy on the situation of world-view conceptuality within human psychology, especially the cognitive structures for our convictions about the world and our related self-conceptions. We will find Kuyper to be quite confident in his own intellectual products' unity and coherence as a regenerate Christian who has ascended the heights of systematic theology and speculative philosophy. Yet some flagrant problems (e.g., Christian nationalism, cultural chauvinism, advocacy for colonialism, and white supremacy) in the details of his world-view will become evident in the penultimate section of this chapter. Many of his contemporary disciples are keen to dismiss Kuyper's grave errors as a side issue while attempting to rehabilitate what they take to be the gleaming principles of his universal, world-viewing framework. But I will argue that we need to attend honestly to how and why he could develop and disseminate all these thoughts together and ask searching theological questions about world-viewing as a conceptual form. The world-view concept presented itself as a boon in a broken historical setting, masking its emergence as an impulse among deeply troubled intuitions about the colonial subject, the world around them, and their place within it. As Kuyper's case will make clear, the conceptual form inaccurately represents and sinfully mishandles everyone it imagines while providing exhilarating psychological motivation for the powerful world-viewer to press on. I do not imagine the concept can be rehabilitated for use in a more humble, creaturely communion, nor do I underestimate the challenges of seeing or arriving at these conclusions from the broken conceptual moment in which we still live and move and have our being. These intellectual structures and the convictions that fill them out have become deeply intertwined with our sense of self—our identity.

PLACING KUYPER IN HISTORICAL CONTEXT: WORLD-VIEW AS THREAT AND PROMISE

However much Kuyper resisted Modernism, Bratt notes that the German Idealism (especially G. W. F. Hegel) he studied at Leiden University heavily influenced his view of human history and its most salient details.⁶ Simply put, he "literally [could] not think outside the Hegelian method by which Mind(s) developing down through time constituted the essence of history."⁷ When seen through the lens of his theological convictions, each life-system sprouts from a distinct principle about *the relationship between God and humankind*, which yields two more principles—concerning *social relations within humankind* and *the relationship between humans and the world*.⁸ Whether consciously or not, the first principle produces "logically and systematically the whole complex of ruling ideas and conceptions that go to make up our life- and world-view."⁹ In Kuyper's view, only a handful of such world-views had risen to prominence on the world stage in human history: paganism, Islam, Roman Catholicism, Calvinism, and now Modernism. Beginning with the midpoint, the Roman Catholic Church situated itself as the earthly mediator (this is its first principle) between God and all persons, between God and all sectors of society. And Kuyper traced many problems in his time back to the medieval period in which the Roman Catholic Church sought worldly splendor and cozied up to the rich and powerful, leaving the church vulnerable to a reversal in the flow of cultural transformation.¹⁰ With Hegelian terminology, he described Martin Luther as the "world-historic" individual in whom the Protestant movement began as an antithesis to Roman Catholicism.¹¹

In the magisterial reformers, Kuyper saw two paths diverge from the single, distinctive principle that animates all Protestantism, namely, that God enters into unmediated fellowship with the creature. While Luther took a "subjective, anthropological" path of justification by faith, John Calvin embarked on the "objective, cosmological" path of God's direct sovereignty over the whole cosmos and each of its constituent elements.¹² Considering the relation between humankind and the world, Kuyper called attention to the existential paradox in Luther (i.e., between church and world) that contrasts with how "Calvinism put its impress in and outside the Church upon every department of human life."¹³ In and after the Reformation, as Kuyper narrated this history, the Holy Spirit warmed hearts throughout Europe. And following the experience of being born again and restored to personal fellowship with God, many submitted all sectors of their lives—moral, social, and otherwise—to the direct, unmediated lordship of Christ, generating a certain instinctive (i.e., without extended reflection or personal, logical action) "form for life." And while many Protestants contributed to their societies from the overflow of God's work in their hearts, Kuyper credited only a small (if influential) number of faithful *Calvinists* with comprehending the full implications of their first principle.¹⁴

Notwithstanding this positive appraisal, Kuyper suspected that his theological tradition had been the object of widespread but undue criticism, so he took up for the Calvinist brand. He flatly denied that he would "claim honors for Calvinism which belong to Protestantism in general."[15] The Holy Spirit's total effect varies from person to person, and other Protestant traditions have diverged (or simply stalled) at some point from *the* logical development of their common first principle. "Only of Calvinism can it be said that it has consistently and logically followed out the lines of the Reformation, has established not only churches but also States, has set its stamp upon social and public life, and has thus, in the full sense of the word, created for the whole life of man a world of thought entirely its own."[16] In terms of political states, Kuyper had in mind his native Netherlands, its colonies in South Africa, (sometimes) England, and the United States as bearing the marks of "Calvinism." So, while we might best understand his three-element approach to world-views as a heuristic device for interpreting the social world(s) of humans in the West, he also used it as a rhetorical device for presenting Calvinism as "the completed evolution of Protestantism."[17] Ultimately, Kuyper identified the Calvinist brand with a diverse, somewhat diffuse spirit in a social-scientific, philosophical, or political sense.[18]

As a life-system, Calvinism had developed organically and made significant progress on many fronts, but the tradition had not, in Kuyper's estimation, disclosed an all-encompassing "form for thought" during the same period. He lamented this lack as perhaps *the* major contributing factor to Modernism's success as a world-view: it got a head start in bringing a comprehensive world-view to expression. Calvinism had entered the world through concrete lives changed rather than the pen of some folks who sat down to construct a logical and all-encompassing world-view. And, Kuyper speculated in a positive light, "The need of a theoretical and systematical study of so incisive and comprehensive a phenomenon of life only arises when its first vitality has been exhausted, and when, for the sake of maintaining itself in the future, it is compelled to greater accuracy in the drawing of its boundary lines."[19] But, Kuyper's tone on this point varied such that elsewhere he observed Calvinist thinkers had failed to strike while the spiritual iron was hot. The ebb tide of faith characterizing much of the nineteenth century created a vacuum in which Modernism could thrive and increasingly win the complicity (if not the witting collaboration) of many.

Under these circumstances, beginning in 1789 with French revolutionaries' cries for freedom and emancipation from divine authority, Kuyper found that Modernism had increasingly denied Calvinism its leading influence.[20] From within nations that already witnessed the Calvinist spirit's significant development, Modernists had successfully advanced the deceptive claim that human reason deserves all the glory for social progress. For example, Kuyper tied the Calvinist first principle to the conceptions of liberty, equality, and fraternity on which French revolutionaries capitalized.[21] And soon after, German thinkers took up the Modernist starting point (i.e., "no God, no master") and spelled out in more rigorous intellectual terms an expansive world- and life-view centering on human reason—sometimes shrouded in pantheistic conceptuality. Lacking any reliable first principles to guide or constrain their "logical" developments, Modernists' forms for thought could only be the product of fallen human intellects—from the sentimental world-spirit of some Romantics and the ethnonationalism of others to the natural evolution of things or the will to power. We must not imagine, however, the corrosive threat of Modernism as entirely external to the church; it also inspired missteps and profanations within Christian circles. Let us not forget that Hegel, the great light of German Idealism, had been a Lutheran seminarian and imagined his own philosophical project as ushering the Reformation to its logical conclusion. Also weighing on Kuyper's conscience in this vein was J. H. Scholten, one of his former Leiden professors who took up modern trends "toward the empirical and away from the ideal-historical and metaphysical construction" in a later commentary on the Gospel of John; reading this work brought home for Kuyper what a change in first principles can generate.[22]

Though its proponents seemed unaware, Kuyper argued, any good product of Modernism could only be but a dim reflection "of the brilliant ideal proclaimed by Calvinism" with no real substance of its own.[23] Moreover, Modernism depended on Calvinist moral capital and could not replenish the spiritual energy stores that had animated its actual progress—let alone inspire future developments.[24] So, even the most advanced Western societies were bound, over time, to degenerate into any number of excesses or deficiencies. Most notably, "in response to the breakdown of medieval Europe's church-centered society and the rise of nationalism, capitalism, and scientific and technological innovation, two secularizing perspectives came to dominate life and thought in the late nineteenth century: liberal individualism and socialist collectivism."[25] To be clear, individualism was not the *root* principle but one *derived* from the godless fundament of Modernism. Social democracy was the fullest fruit of this root principle, and "the liberal makes an arbitrary stop on a road that, in accord with his own system, has to be pursued."[26] Without the influence of steeled Calvinist theocrats, democracy tended to yield one of these positions—both of which upheld money as the valuation standard in place of the goodness of God's original design.

Nominal Christians who lacked personal awareness of the Calvinist worldview's essential elements were prone to follow suit (even if unintentionally). They might seat bald human reason in critical authority over God's self-revelation or, if less intellectually inclined, submit much of their lives to the individual ego, the collective spirit, or otherwise the vapid materialism of the broader culture.[27] Even if the many had a vague, pietistic sense that their faith *should* play a role in all aspects of their lives, the citizens of Protestant nations under the assault of Modernism were not deliberating *as Christians* on the common good or the role of individuals in pursuing it. To Kuyper, these folks could not be "integrated men; they lead an ambiguous life."[28] In this situation, Christians can err in many ways. For instance, he lamented, "That we in our age under a variety of Anabaptist and Methodist influences abandoned the field to the forces of unbelief is a fault of our fathers, the bitter consequences whereof we are now experiencing."[29] Kuyper associated Methodists and Pietists with the "evangelical" stream, which for him entailed both a tradition-minimizing individualism and a zeal for conversion that would not engender proper catechesis or good discipleship.[30] On down the line, this error would foster a tendency to lose one's grasp of the objective rights of the church community and the electing will of God over against the will and subjective rights of the individual.

This was no mere quibble for Kuyper, who placed heavy emphasis on the role of historical traditions in moving the theological conversation forward, particularly in providing a stable basis for bringing individual subjects to share in a world-view, to live it out, and maybe even to contribute to its logical development. Perhaps this complaint offers a window into why Kuyper opted to rehabilitate the Calvinist brand rather than adopting a seemingly more inclusive term like "evangelicalism."[31] But in the same way twenty-first-century Christians use the latter term, Kuyper applied "Calvinism" to both the minimal s/Spirit animating a historical type that lays claim to many instinctive or anonymous Calvinists (e.g., some Anglicans and Methodists)[32] and the maximal manifesto of neo-Calvinist emphases that he presented as the logical fruit of regenerate Christian faith.[33] As a matter of rhetoric, the former provided him with the historical test to demonstrate the influence of the Calvinist spirit in particular Western societies; the latter channeled that story's energy into his comprehensive theopolitical program, which promised further civilizational progress.

From the Stone Lectures platform, Kuyper warned all reflective Christians about the steady advance of godless Modernism. "Against this deadly danger, ye, Christians, cannot successfully defend your Sanctuary, but by placing, in opposition to all this, *a life- and world-view of your own, founded as firmly on the base of your own principle, wrought out with the same clearness and glittering in an equally logical consistency.*"[34] Protestantism needed to acknowledge it had spent its first-stage engine. To complete its climb to orbit for a full view of the world, it would need to prepare for stage two. Alert to the threat and promise of world-viewing, Kuyper and company could imaginably develop a thought-form for what had been primarily a lived reality. Addressing a highbrow crowd in his Stone Lectures, he framed his life-system as the finest fruit of *palingenesis* (a broad new beginning that includes rebirth in an evangelical sense),[35] called the audience to nourish the spiritual life that is so vital to good Christian theologizing, and lobbied others to magnify and disseminate a *new Calvinist* world-view (thus neo-Calvinism)—to hang it in full view like an Aeolian Harp.³⁶ Then, the Holy Spirit like a rushing wind could use the harp's song to awaken the unvoiced multitudes of (at least nominal) Christians from their spiritual slumber so that they might get about the work of restoring the Christian heritage of the West and carrying humankind to still greater heights.

THE WORLD-VIEW CONCEPT IN KUYPER'S THEOLOGY

In this section, I will explore how Kuyper presented the world-view concept and its underlying impulse by clarifying, elucidating, and sometimes juxtaposing key concepts in his Stone Lectures with salient passages from his larger body of work. He brought home the world-view concept with philosophical command and historical force in his Stone Lectures, and for many, then and now, these talks are their best taste of Kuyper's thinking. But to better understand his project, we must dig into both its philosophical-theological development in his wider systematic work—especially a lengthy portion of an "encyclopedic" text introduced to the US audience by Princeton theologian B. B. Warfield shortly after the lectures—and its fruit in the social and political life of the Dutch polymath himself.³⁷ Notably absent will be a discussion of "sphere sovereignty," which will appear in chapter 5. The section closes with a review of what Kuyper took to be the task of faithful theologians, which, given its self-involving nature, is a crucial jumping-off point for part I of my project. By taking a more in-depth look at what exactly he thought he was doing with his Calvinist world-view, we might see its unseemly features (as articulated in the next major section) exhibiting a problem endemic to the world-viewing impulse itself. To help the reader get into Kuyper's theological work, I will temporarily break with the conventions of historical studies to present his theory in the present tense.

The *Imago Dei*: World-Viewers by Design

Kuyper interprets the *imago dei* as the natural human capacity to produce an all-encompassing mental image of the cosmos and its inner workings, including God's place and our own within it all. Exhibiting a strong resemblance to Hegel's phenomenology of spirit, Kuyper argues the ultimate aim of God's self-revelation from creation on is that humankind would glorify their creator by becoming conscious of what God has revealed of God's character and will, searching out more and more such knowledge wherever it may be found, and consciously living that knowledge into more robust material reality, thereby reflecting an increasingly textured image back to God.[38] As such, he links divine revelation and its telos to the biblical language of *imago dei*:

> Man himself is the richest instrument in which and by which God reveals Himself . . . chiefly on account of that deepest and most hidden part of his being [viz. the rational soul], in which the creaturely reaches its finest and noblest formation. . . . We define it as being both the choicest jewel in the diadem of revelation and the instrument by which man transmutes all revelation into *knowledge of God*. Both are expressed in the creation of man after the *image of God*.[39]

So, the human soul is simultaneously the crowning achievement in the whole of creation and the part of the person in which "the *logos* operates," enabling one to appropriate God's manifold revelation as personal knowledge.[40] Leading into his working definition of science (and anticipating how he will frame theology as the queen science), Kuyper connects the *impulse* or thirst for knowledge to the *imago dei*:

> However much we may speculate and ponder, no explanation can ever suggest itself to our sense, of the all-sufficient ground for this admirable correspondence and affinity between object and subject, on which the possibility and development of science wholly rests, until at the hand of Holy Scripture we confess that the Author of the cosmos created man in the cosmos as microcosmos "after his image and likeness."
>
> Thus understood, *science* presents itself to us as *a necessary and ever-continued impulse in the human mind to reflect within itself the cosmos, plastically as to its elements, and to think it through logically as to its relations; always with the understanding that the human mind is capable of this by reason of its organic affinity to its object*.[41]

Made in God's image and set within the created cosmos, the human soul thirsts after a comprehensive world-view that takes in the universe of God's creative, self-revealing activity, including God's eternal will for human patterns of life. Those operating within a Modernist framework might see the promise of more voluminous and more accurate knowledge (i.e., the relentless quest for the truth) as an intrinsic motivator and guarantor of scientific investigations in diverse fields. But Kuyper wrests the very impulse to generate a world-view from the control of Modernist philosophers; like it or not, the call to comprehensive, systematic thought reverberating within the rational soul is an echo of God's voice.

As a matter of process, Kuyper explains that unfallen humans would have compiled a wide-ranging world-view primarily through their life with God and their experience of and in creation thanks to their inborn "capacity to draw knowledge of God from what had been revealed."[42] This aspect of their knowledge is an "innate or concrete theology," which has three elements: "(1) the inworking and manifestation of God Himself in Adam's inner being; (2) faith, by which the subject perceives and grasps this inworking and manifestation; and (3) the logical action, by which of himself and of necessity he reduces this content in his heart to *knowledge of God*, in the form of thought and word."[43] These three, down to the last and most self-involving one, are all original elements of God's intended mechanism for self-revelation; human minds are both part of and *participant in* the revelation of God by design, acting upon what has been revealed to become and assemble a richer picture of the cosmos. God did not impress a catechism of true knowledge onto the tablet of Adam's mind, but rather created Adam such that "in his awakening to self-consciousness, he arrived of necessity at this original theology from the data that were present in him."[44] Beyond the innate or concrete theology, Kuyper speaks of an additional "acquired theology"—a fullness or elaboration that would progressively unfold in the course of human life.[45] This reflects something of the dualism in Hegel's "philosophical history," which maintains that a higher spiritual reality is progressively realized in the material world through the increasingly self-conscious work of humankind. Human life in the world is to become the fullest expression of God's designs for the world, which are primarily ideas in the mind of God until they take material shape in creation.

Sin and Lies in Science and World-Viewing

In a world without sin, Kuyper thought Hegel's way of understanding history as progress toward the goal of a self-conscious, free society (with some creative cultural accouterments) would be essentially correct. But Kuyper would not have us dwell long on "the particulars of a supposed possibility cut off by sin. This would be to lose ourselves in fiction."[46] He offers an idealized account of the first humans' epistemology only because one "who has before his eyes the straight line understands the crooked line. . . . And the negative or privative character of sin makes this also necessary with the study of Theology."[47] Kuyper argues that while sin does not injure the person's *being* (i.e., stripping away one's cognitive faculties or thirst for knowledge), it does corrupt human *nature* by bending one's "attributes, workings, and influences" to defy God even unto death.[48] Faculties like faith, reason, and conscience remain as permanent elements in human cognition, but they cease to function normally.

Take faith as a leading example. Kuyper sees it as the function of every human soul that "obtains certainty directly and immediately, without the aid of discursive demonstration."[49] Faith, he argues, is always online underneath the investigating subject's logical activity, unconsciously operationalizing their convictions (e.g., about God, human nature, and the world) to shape their ways of seeing and reasoning. The individual subject can surely reflect on the stuff of their faith, but it comes online at the level of perception and intuition. So, rather than denying faith as a foundation for science (with Modernists) or arguing that one must move beyond faith to a unitive, rational philosophy (with Hegel), Kuyper contends the faith function and its attendant first principles play a major role in all human investigations.[50] That said, sin inverts faith,

> affects injuriously the consciousness of man, and not merely puts into his hands fantasy for reality, and fiction for history, but intentionally brings into our mind a representation of existing things which proscribes reality, with the avowed aim of estranging us from it.[51]

The fallen human consciousness is darkened by a loss of love for, or affinity with, the central "object" of the very reality that science investigates.[52] So, instead of feeling connected with God, with other humans as God's image-bearers, or with the cosmos as God's creation, humans become isolated, turned in upon ourselves, and lack the bond of love that would lead us to seek out knowledge in and of reality.

For our purposes, we might focus on those investigations that Kuyper categorizes under the "spiritual sciences" (e.g., theology, political science, and psychology). One's faith is of utmost importance in these sciences because they examine "objects" that are also living, thinking "subjects."[53] As such, one can more or less observe the forms and relations of these objects but not their true essence. Getting the spiritual sciences right is so difficult primarily "because [their] relations are so uncertain in their manifestation and are therefore almost always bound to the self-communication of the object."[54] In a fallen world, the necessity of self-revelation as the typical mode of knowing others introduces many troubles: people must have accurate self-knowledge, be willing and able to reveal it, tell the truth, and so on. Furthermore, the endless variations found in unique human souls make it basically impossible to draw reliable, wide-ranging conclusions about essential qualities.[55] Ignorance of reliable, eternal principles that genuinely connect with spiritual objects invalidates one's scientific and philosophical conclusions. "You may excel in all these studies," he says, "and not know the least thing about your own soul, which subjectively forms the center of all psychic investigation. And what is more serious still, in this way you run a great risk of, unknown to yourself, falsifying the object of your science, if not of denaturalizing it."[56] For example, theology has God as its object, and the investigating subject makes a methodological error when (a) focusing on the observable data of human religious expressions, in general, while (b) supplying a supposedly self-evident, but truly idiosyncratic, concept of religion as the basis of their study.[57] In this case, one has failed not only to describe oneself (i.e., one's own "religion") but also to say anything about the living God who is the object of true religion.

Notice Kuyper is not saying sin deadens the human impulse to put together a comprehensive world-view in the first place; rather, he disputes any assessment of sin as *merely* privative, partly by recognizing the hellish products of human intellective powers working in an abnormal direction.[58] Sin misdirects our natural capacities, introducing several practical problems into our scientific investigations and their results (i.e., what humans claim is knowledge), including unintentional mistakes in observation, memory, and logical action; self-delusion and self-deception; unconscious motivation by self-interest; and the influence of other sinful minds (i.e., socialization) over time. Addressing the risk of a wayward imagination in putting together a scientific and comprehensive world-view, Kuyper explains, "In strongly impassioned natures, [the boundary line] is sometimes absolutely undiscoverable, so that fantasy and reality frequently pass into one another. . . . This imaginary world will then assert its dominion over us and weaken the susceptibility in us for knowledge of ourselves and of the cosmos."[59] The problem here is not necessarily moving forward with a subjective approach to whatever study; in any science, the knowledge that animates a person in their innermost places need not, and indeed cannot, be proven. The real problem is one's ignorance of reliable, eternal principles that genuinely connect with spiritual "objects" and so could underpin and validate one's results. Thus, we might come to see why claims about certain truth (e.g., in metaphysics) vary so dramatically from person to person: many people live in false worlds of their own design.

Putting together the wide-ranging truth by way of science is only possible when the individual subject has a mystical awareness of God and a love that draws them toward God, but even among the unregenerate, the impulse after knowledge remains and produces some truth—when properly qualified, especially in the natural sciences. With godless Modernism ever on his mind, Kuyper speaks of a lie that, under the direction of "a hidden impelling power" (i.e., Satan), weaves a convincing web of false representations and offers it as the result of objective, or faith-less, science. As such, sin precipitates not only a break in our inner unity—including our motivations—but also our estrangement from reality, and thus our unity with the organic-cosmic whole.[60] The result is an antithesis so radical that the dialectical history of humankind, *in general*, will not reach synthesis in a point of rest. Kuyper says, "the fact that there are two kinds of *people* occasions of necessity the fact of two kinds of human *life* and *consciousness* of life, and of two kinds of *science*."⁶¹ Humankind's joint endeavor for knowledge—particularly those efforts higher up the hierarchy of sciences—inevitably will not come together. In place of the ubiquity of first principles (i.e., axioms) that many expect of the natural sciences, the spiritual sciences see hopes for unity and a common sensibility give way to contention and rivalrous schools of thought.

Better Knowing through Regeneration

If the Calvinist first principle is to mend our web of knowledge and "put its stamp upon our entire life," Kuyper tells us, "it must start from that point in our consciousness in which our life is still undivided and lies comprehended in its unity, ... where we disclose ourselves to the Eternal One."⁶² As we have seen, he argues that sin has essentially changed the *normal* (i.e., Godward) orientation of the human heart and, from this inner core, continuously works against the possibility of rightly knowing or relating to God (or to anything or anyone God has made). So, we must now try to understand how Kuyper believes this situation can be reversed. In the second of his Stone Lectures, Kuyper offers this summary: "Soteriological religion, next to the *necessitas* of inward *palingenesis*, demands also the *necessitas* of an assistant light, of revelation to be kindled in our twilight."⁶³ From this statement, we might seek further clarity about both the object and the subject of theology. Specifically, what, if anything, has changed about God's *revelation* itself in view of the fall? And how does this inward *palingenesis* recondition humans' faculties for knowing God, vouchsafe the fruits of their knowledge of God and God's creation, and thus restore their likeness to the *imago dei* as world-viewers?

As to the first question, neither God's self-revelation nor its telos has fundamentally changed since the fall. For concrete theology before the fall to have any hope of achieving its end in a full-orbed *imago dei*, God's revelation had to be complete already. The same is true today, and God's now-complete special revelation in Christ and Scripture materially extends what may be known of God "so as to include the knowledge of God's relation to the sinner."⁶⁴ As a matter of course, God's revelation still "flows from the archetypal knowledge of God and strives to become ectypal knowledge of God in man."⁶⁵ With the addition of special revelation in the inscripturated Word, Kuyper warns against misidentifying the ultimate object and telos of Christian theology. The Bible itself is not *the* object of theological science; rather, "Scripture here is taken as a plant, whose germ has sprouted and budded, and has unfolded those buds. It is not, therefore, the naked principium, but the principium together with what it has brought forth."⁶⁶ The final cause or goal of theology is to know and glorify the living God, and Kuyper strongly resists the possibility of reaching behind the Holy Spirit's witness for greater certainty in our knowledge of God—not even an objectively true, infallible Scripture.[67] Notwithstanding these caveats, theology advances over time not as a matter of *creatio continua* but as human consciousness actualizes its potential to reflect God's revelation, which is already complete in creation plus Scripture.

As to the second question, sin's damage to human nature extends to the two elements in theology by which humans make something of God's revelation—faith and logical action. The faith function can only be reset "by bending right again, from the root up, the direction of [one's spiritual] life."[68] And in regeneration, the Holy Spirit not only does this but also enlivens and harmonizes the indivisible soul, imparts assurance of a mended relationship with God, restores one's affinity with the object of the theological science, and seeds first principles that reflect biblical truth.[69] Lest we think the process of reversing sin's effects is thereby complete, Kuyper sets regeneration within the total life of the believer as the particular act of God by which "the wheel of life in the centrum of our being (the wheel of nature or of birth, James 3:6) is merely replaced upon its pivot; but this by itself has not changed the world of our *conscious* life."[70] This wider sense of regeneration, which entails the transformation of one's conscious life, relies on the Holy Spirit's progress into the soul's higher faculties, which Kuyper (after Calvin) numbers at two: understanding and will.[71] Consequent to the quickening that largely occurs below the level of consciousness, *enlightenment* is the transformation of a person's knowledge, understanding, and thought life while *sanctification* is the transformation of a person's will and behavior.[72]

We will focus on understanding and enlightenment, with this driving question: What changes has sin wrought in human "logical action" as an element in theology? Kuyper observes up front, "It is not so easy to lay a hand on the change, necessitated by sin in the entire scheme of revelation, with reference to the third factor."[73] Sin does not utterly destroy the inner locus of concreate theology in the fallen human, but it does shrink this element into a mere kernel of itself—what Calvin called the *sensus divinitatis* or *semen religionis*. As one might imagine, any growing knowledge is inextricably linked to a saving faith.[74] No human could get to the place of doing proper theology by the Cartesian route of finding an idea of the perfect God innate within their own fallen mind; rather, God must intervene to formally restore what sin corrupted, making the *semen religionis* burst forth into life. The Holy Spirit also implants a new potential nature to be actualized through the Spirit's ongoing work over time. Borrowing "old man, new man" language from the apostle Paul, Kuyper explains that, before regeneration, the person is "identified with the old man so completely that [it is] his very ego. He [has] no other life or existence."[75] But in *palingenesis*, God brings about "the union between our ego and this germinating life" in the "controlling center" of the self, and, "in that vital germ, God supports the formative power, which at His appointed time He will cause to come forth, by which our ego will manifest itself as a new man."[76] Regenerate human *nature* is set on a new course, such that one becomes increasingly willing to consciously use their God-given capacities in the service of a new first principle. Still, Kuyper argues that nothing about the regenerate person's *being* has changed; their formal cognitive capacities are the same as they ever were. Radical as the shift in identity with the "new man" is, regeneration is thinkable only if a singular ego endures.[77]

Kuyper offers a grafting metaphor to provide some texture to this account. We rightly confess that the regenerate person is truly and essentially changed—a tree is *entirely* transformed when grafted. But this change is effected "in such a way that, putting on the new nature in principle, [the person] still continues to *work* through the *old* nature.... The new nature must draw its saps through the *old* nature; apart from the graft, the trunk remains wild."[78] Describing how the biblical world increasingly takes hold and provides the true basis for integrating and expanding one's world- and life-view, Kuyper improves (he thinks) upon Calvin's well-known "spectacles" metaphor for relating specially revealed knowledge of God to what we may learn by natural means. "The special knowledge [of Scripture] is, indeed, a new and proper principium, but this principium joins itself to the vital powers of our nature with its natural principium; compels this principium to let its life-sap flow through another channel; and, in this way, cultivates ripe fruit of knowledge from what otherwise would have produced only wood fit for fire."[79] In sum, with their *being* intact and their *nature* redirected toward the proper object of theology, the regenerate can assemble an esemplastic, organic knowledge that draws from not only special principles and means but also natural capacities—all pursuing the original and ultimate telos of God's revelation. A normal, healthy soul comprises a unified mind contemplating the sovereign God and the universe of his creating and ordering work.

When discussing a more reliable basis for investigating the spiritual sciences, Kuyper describes the human need for a principled view from beyond ourselves and our limited place within the cosmos to really understand how everything really fits together. To this end, he quotes the ancient Greek philosopher Archimedes, saying, δός μοι πᾶ στῶ (give me a place to stand)—the first half of his famous claim, which concludes, καὶ τὰν γᾶν κινάσω (and I shall move the earth).[80] Once he gets down to explaining how we gain this place to stand, Kuyper argues that, since the unregenerate stand before Scripture as "a foreign object which [does] not suit his world of conceptions," the Holy Spirit must first create "in our sense and in our consciousness a modified view of ourselves, of the things of this world, and of the unseen world."[81] Put differently, God repopulates the regenerate Christian's inner world with better first principles regarding spiritual realities like those operationalized by the faith faculty when investigating psychology and other spiritual sciences. Regardless of whether the discord generated by this principial enlightening rises to the level of existential crisis or remains *essentially unconscious* (i.e., unnoticed by the individual subject),[82] its resolution comes when the Holy Spirit opens one's eyes to the Bible as "a world of energies, a world of full and beautiful life, which stands in direct opposition to his ordinary world, but which proves to agree in a wonderful way with the new life that has sprung up in his heart."[83] In this new, deeper consciousness, the regenerate receive what Archimedes could only seek in vain, namely, a standpoint for proper world-viewing.

Acquired theology takes center stage in postlapsarian life, and the subject of comprehensive knowledge shifts from the individual person to the church community.[84] Now, the object of theology must approach and confront us from the outside—in the incarnation and, following that, in the church gathered before the Bible—and this with great effect on the method of theology.[85] "By faith we perceive that an eternal Being manifests Himself in us, in order to place Himself over against our ego, in the same way in which we discover the presence of light by our eye; but *what* this eternal Being is and what it demands of us, is not told us by faith, but by the innate knowledge of God, presently enriched by the acquired."[86] This basic relationship between God and humans is the only proper context for any talk about knowledge of God; the person must first walk with God (i.e., in faith) and know they are doing so (i.e., the starts of concreate theology) before they can proceed with truly *theo*logical action. The individual person continues to be the bearer of the *imago dei*, which is the indelible essence of human nature, and God's self-revelation within creation fully arrives at its goal only when it comes to be reflected in humankind as a self-conscious, material image—what Kuyper calls an "ectype"—of God's original, ideal designs.

Some deeply Hegelian contours emerge as Kuyper argues that theological knowledge (and, really, advanced knowledge of all kinds) must first establish itself in *the collective consciousness* and can only be known by the individual from there. The way our knowledge of God is produced—as the very form that revelation can, and indeed *must*, take among humankind—necessarily involves some logical action upon the available data.[87] Yet while the possibility of logical action is *formally* restored to the individual person, Kuyper believes the collective consciousness of the church is the primary site of true, logical activity in a fallen world. He sees the first steps of growth *practically* as more about social formation and catechesis in a church and its tradition. Saving faith in God fosters a basic trust in the way one's own church works out the details of revelation, the implications for a life-system, such that a person will grasp its singular content as the stuff of their own world-view more and more. And through the churches in which the Holy Spirit has planted them, individual Christians participate in regenerate consciousness and logical action.[88] Primacy is given not to the personal assembly of knowledge from various data sources—as in the days of the garden (i.e., concreate theology)—but to acquired theology, which approaches the individual from outside the self, in Scripture and particularly in the community that teaches the individual how to read it for meaning.

More broadly, Kuyper argues that people—Christian or otherwise—balance their "instinctive life" and the personal impulse to reflect on and logically work out the implications of their faith in one of three ways: (1) "know nothing of 'learning,' live on the air of the instinctive life, and let themselves be guided by their practical good"; (2) "devote almost all their time and best energies to study"; and (3) live in between these two, typically feeding off the studies of others.[89] For the first and largest group, the *practical wisdom* necessary for making it through life functions at the level of instinct, with content appropriated by way of communal formation rather than conscious, logical action. The practical wisdom Kuyper has in mind here is what has guided arts and trades for all of human history; only later (if at all) have these received reflective study, and this is not such a bad thing—after all, reflection and logical action (at their best) concern real human lives. Kuyper connects this broad observation with the sentiment about Calvinism in history that we have seen expressed already: "Practical spiritual knowledge of God had been the rich possession of thousands upon thousands long before the idea of a scientific theology was suggested."[90] The Calvinist spirit has always entailed an inspired form for life; it is an all-encompassing form for thought that Kuyper seeks to develop. Between the other two ways of life, Kuyper clearly prefers the "amphibious" group that lives between the instinctive and reflective. He identifies clergypersons as most likely to bring "the instinctive and the reflective life into a higher synthesis"; however, he will also describe the ideal theologian as one who does firsthand reflection and logical action but retains their grounding in the instinctive life of faith.[91]

The Work of Theologians as Sanctified, Speculative Reasoning

Now, we can explore the source of Kuyper's confidence in the deliverances of his own world-view logic, which become the basis for his real-world cultural engagement and political activity *in the name of* Calvinism. For those who engage in reflective, *theo*logical action, the impulse to do so emerges within the instinctive life of faith. Kuyper sees the experience of being born anew and the consequent impression that this newness should affect "our entire sensibility" as the forces motivating any Christian "to give himself an intelligent account of all the consequences which flow from it and which are bound to affect his entire world- and life-view."[92] As a God-given function of the person's soul, faith serves as both the instinctive-directional stuff of a personal world-view and the cognitive basis for synthesizing and logically (and imaginatively) developing a comprehensive life-system. The potential totality or comprehensiveness of the Calvinist world-view corresponds with a belief in the restored unity of the individual Christian's inner self. So, the most important question of human identity centers on the world-view one possesses—or by which one is possessed.

According to Kuyper, one of the theologian's key tasks is to winsomely articulate their own cognitive landscape in a conceptual form that others may grasp and appropriate. Their most important work lies in the fields of Scripture, but, for Kuyper, once we realize the Holy Spirit was bound to logic in the illuminating work of generating Scripture, we may retain appropriate confidence in human intellectual development beyond what is explicitly revealed there.[93] By Kuyper's definition, all science involves personal logical action upon one's knowledge and experience that allows the thinker to loop their knowledge into the intellectual fabric that shares in the singularity and cohesiveness of God's creation. "It is by entering into *this order* and into this cosmical character of the object that science celebrates her triumphs."[94] This work is not for one thinker to do on alone—a descriptively true statement since theologians start their work amid a historical tradition, but also a conviction about the way variously gifted thinkers are spread across different scientific fields.[95] But in sum, a proper theological method entails reflecting on what one has discovered to be true and then depersonalizing that truth and bearing witness to it in order to help others discover and assimilate this knowledge into their own lives and thoughts.[96] If the impulse that sets the whole theological enterprise, as the queen of the sciences, into motion for the individual is to find "its point of rest," then it must reflect the fullness of God's self-revelation in the consciousness of regenerate humankind—starting with its thinking organs, the theologians.[97]

Something must change as the theologian depersonalizes their mental world, puts their thoughts into words, and subjects the resultant world-view to the crucible of their living church and its tradition. Kuyper makes plain the way a theological system takes shape in the course of concrete humans' thinking: "The beginning is made under the influence of all sorts of other factors; while the task is not ended until, at the end of the way, all these factors are made to disappear, so that finally our well-balanced conviction rests upon nothing but the Holy Scripture."[98] Perhaps the handiest example here is how all theologians, even revolutionary ones, begin their work within the traditions that have nourished them. "No theologian, following the direction of his own compass, would ever have found by himself what he now confesses and defends on the ground of the Holy Scripture."[99] The great reformer Calvin himself, Kuyper reminds his reader, constantly appealed to Augustine and Thomas Aquinas, and in general, theologians will stay close to the fields that have nourished them as their logical activity unfolds. Theologians are responsible, in part, for conceptually articulating what has been true in the community's "form for life"—making the "form for thought" clearer for and on behalf of *this* church, thus contributing to the objective spirit of their tradition and participating in the Holy Spirit as the true communal spirit of regenerate humankind.

We should not be under the impression that communicating one's theology—let alone their more comprehensive world-view—*scientifically* is either simple or easy. First of all, it "demands intense application of thought, because it is not enough that we take up in ourselves the loose elements of the revelation, but we must take those elements as constitutive parts of one organic whole, and thus in our thoughts, also, order them in one system."[100] More than that, though, the theologian shares in human nature such that, as they approach the Scripture they seek to comprehend, their subjective consciousness is no blank slate ready to receive a pure, biblical impress. Plenty of theologians reach their "point of rest"—that place of confidence in the system they have erected as framing the ectypal revelation of God in Scripture—under the *illusion* that they have merely been working with the material of Scripture without remainder. In the course of their intensive logical activity, theologians are duty-bound to "to expel from our [Kuyper clearly includes himself among this number] consciousness what is criticized by revelation as untrue, and to weave together what remains with the content of revelation, so that the unity of our world- and life-view shall not be lost."[101] But how?

We need Kuyper to address an elephant in the room—particularly the one he identifies like this: "By what infallible standard can it be determined how much of the old nature enters into the expressions of the new life? Is there no hypocrisy? Are there no conditions unexplained? Are there no obstacles to spiritual development?"[102] I might sharpen this line of questioning as follows: How does a theologian with such a detailed account of the many ways sin warps human thinking explain his confidence that the intellectual deliverances—the expressed world-views—of at least some theologians (not least himself) are a reliable, expansive image of God's self-revelation? Elsewhere, Kuyper explains that the wider sense of regeneration must embrace some mystery, partly due to the disparity between (a) the Christian's experience of the process and (b) the psychological realities beneath, and metaphysical realities beyond, their consciousness.[103] In light of our current questions, we might see this disparity manifest in the experiential (or at least confessional) sensibility that "I am a Christian, and that matters most (or solely) in my world-view" versus the psychological reality that one's convictions have been shaped by many sources—and some of them are bound to be out of step with reality.

These questions and tensions are adequately resolved in the life of the ideal theologian, Kuyper thinks, in the integration of instinct and reflection. Reflecting on many examples around him, he concludes that diving deeply into the reflective or intellectual life tends to dampen the practical good and vitality of the instinctive life.[104] For example, theology routinely diverges from genuine faith (Hegel himself serves as a case in point). But even if this is too often true, it is not the way things *must* go. "Theology has flourished," Kuyper explains, "only at the times when theologians have continued in prayer, and in prayer have sought the communion of the Holy Spirit, and . . . on the other hand, it loses its leaf and begins its winter sleep when ambition for learning silences prayer in the breast of theologians."[105] There is a mystical, spiritual reality beyond the self into which the theologian must be networked, such that theology is really just spelling out what has been experienced within this reality. For Kuyper, Christian theology is predicated on a fully integrated life marked by three factors: *palingenesis*, personal enlightenment, and the communion of saints (i.e., ongoing involvement in the life of a vibrant church).[106] Thus, theologians should be increasing in holiness by way of pious practice so as to grow personally in their faith-level affinity with reality (centering on God) even as they pursue a greater intellectual understanding of that reality.

Kuyper does not say what exactly this piety does for the individual thinker's progress in enlightenment, except that love for the reality they are trying to describe is inextricably linked to the quality of their cognitive access to that reality. "The world of our *conscious* life [is changed] only when the Holy Spirit, having taken up His abode in us, transfers His working from this centrum to our *facultates*, to the faculty of the understanding by enlightening and to the faculty of the will by sanctification."[107] Kuyper mystifies the process of personal enlightenment here apart from what may be attributed to the communion of saints—that collective consciousness in the background of this section.[108] The wider sense of the church as the body of Christ is also in view here, such that the true head of restored humanity is Christ, in whom the knowledge of God is complete, and the Holy Spirit functions as the true communal mind/spirit.[109] But given the situatedness of the individual theologian within a larger body, this too may amount to mystification, for even as the church forms the individual thinker, that thinker acts as one of the church's thinking organs: "The subject of theology presents itself to us in the renewed consciousness of restored humanity, and every individual theologian allows this subject to work its effect *pro parte virili* [to the best of one's ability]."[110] Kuyper idealizes those performing at the highest level of cognitive activity and with the greatest *awareness* that it is actually the Holy Spirit's indwelling work that enables them to interpret reality accurately. When a theologian is only dully conscious of the inner working of the Holy Spirit as they exegete

Scripture, the sense of connection they feel with the spiritual reality is bound to reflect only "the tenor of his inner life."[111] But a stark contrast is provided in the theologian who

> understands and feels that he is an organ of service, on the ground of which he may confidently expect lasting fruit of his labors so long as he puts himself in the service of the Holy Ghost. . . . Without this sense of service all study becomes subjectivistic, unhistorical, and arrogant, while, on the contrary, the placing of oneself at the service of the truth, i.e., in this instance of the Holy Ghost, banishes all pride, curbs the desire to be interesting by exhibiting new discoveries, feeds the desire of theological fellowship.[112]

On the one hand, this comparison reveals that Kuyper is concerned that God not be understood as an "object" in the wrong sense. Without continuous awareness of God working within—the living, indwelling, and self-revealing one—we only identify our own cognitive "stuff" as reality and, thus, live in our own little worlds and project them for others. On the other hand, we must genuinely wonder to what extent Kuyper is alert to, and on spiritually on guard against, the ways such sinful projection can occur among, and be unconsciously justified by, intellectually capable folks who claim to be highly "aware" of the Spirit's inner work.

POLITICS IN THE NAME OF "CALVINISM"

In this section, I turn to examine some of Kuyper's political commitments as they emerged in his public advocacy. While the theory above may already occasion questions about a theologian's self-awareness and whether Christian formation might be a bit more complicated than Kuyper imagines, here we will find reasons to probe the layers of motivation and formation in moral psychology. I have chosen to survey two key areas of his political thought for very different reasons in view of my wider project. The first subsection below explores Kuyper's approach to the social crises and injustices of the industrial revolution with a special focus on solutions that would read as problematic to many American evangelicals in the post–World War II period. So, this material will establish some tension in the more detailed elements of the purportedly singular "biblical world-view" that Kuyper and our case study in part II, Harold Ockenga, espouse. But the second subsection will move into Kuyper's cultural chauvinism and explicit defense of Dutch colonial activity, both of which reveal that racism runs deep in his intellectual principles. These problems also reveal the psychological conditioning of "whiteness"—a concept that will gain detail and come under greater scrutiny in chapters 2 and 4.

On the Social Question

Kuyper's sustained analysis of what was going on may bewilder an American evangelical audience expecting full-throated support for free-market economics along with a sense that personal sin is the real root of all social ills.[113] He saw the social crisis of his day as a black eye on those who claimed to follow Jesus. Before the 1891 Christian Social Congress, Kuyper argued,

> Only one thing is necessary if the social question is to exist for you: you must realize the untenability of the present state of affairs, and you must account for this untenability not by incidental causes but by a fault in the very foundation of our society's organization. If you do not acknowledge this and think social evil can be exorcised through an increase in piety, or through friendlier treatment or more generous charity, then you may believe that we face a religious question or possibly a philanthropic question, but you will not recognize the *social* question. This question does not exist for you until you exercise an architectonic critique of human society.[114]

Kuyper's proposed solution was social-ist in the sense that it gives primacy to "a God-willed *community*, a living, human organism" and not to the rights of the individual—their appetites and whims. To be clear, he also thought "social democracy" problematically centered on the base desires of sinful humans. But, given human beings' social nature, laissez-faire and liberal-individualist positions could not last; they simply would not satisfy the God-given impulse, and humans cannot function well without principles grounded in God's creational designs.[115]

Neither laissez-faire capitalism nor modern liberal individualism was compatible with the Christian principles Kuyper held dear. In his commentary on economics, he asserted God's preferential option for the poor and highlighted Jesus's criticism of the rich and powerful. As Bratt relays, "The merit of any economic system, both as to its theory and practice, had to be measured by the respect it exercised for human beings as bearers of the image of God and the basic security it provided for human existence."[116] Work is only a blessing under these circumstances. Criticizing US policy during his trip around the Stone Lectures, Kuyper "told Baltimore reporters that the United States' lack of an income tax constituted a clear and inequitable burden upon the poor. Even worse was the absence of laws protecting workers."[117] Observing the operations of money at the highest levels of influence and power, Kuyper was concerned that Mammonism and gross materialism might win the day—even in the church. "What the synodical boards were in the Dutch Reformed Church, 'the richer class' threatened to become in American Protestantism, demanding a gospel that endorsed the world in which they prospered."[118] This worry (as we will note with irony in chapter 3) did materialize to some degree in the postwar white American evangelism that sits somewhere behind the concern of twenty-first-century social critics who see hope in Kuyper's neo-Calvinism.

While he did find some ideas in the Social Democratic platform worthwhile, Kuyper was also wary of what today might be called "social democracy," even before the rise and fall of "centralized, communist, Marxist-Leninist governments."[119] Citing James 5, which begins, "Come now, you rich people, weep and wail for the miseries that are coming to you," Kuyper stated, "If words as strong as these were not found in the Bible, and if anyone should dare to pen them now on his own initiative, people would brand him as a crypto-socialist. For those who hope for money and who would build on the power of money, the Holy Scripture is a despairing book."[120] That said, absolute property is possible only for God; all others—including the modern individual *and* the collective "people"—can only be stewards.[121] The root issue in view of the radical antithesis is the rejection of God's sovereignty as the first principle. "If one sees in all the structures of our present society only the product of arbitrary human will; then, in consequence, one will feel justified in overthrowing everything that hinders the gigantic task of building anew on the vacant plot."[122] Given the overall character of Christian nations as under the influence of common grace, revolution would be unnecessary for the progress of Christian ideals.[123] All the same, Kuyper saw "solidarity" as a significant element in Christian ethics that curbs many Modernist impulses, ranging from the sense that the individual is supreme and has certain incontrovertible rights (e.g., to property) to any positive interpretation of the perpetual struggle of social classes with each other.

On Colonialism, Race, and Civilization

By contemporary standards of decency, Kuyper's Stone Lectures unraveled as he brought the first lecture to its ecstatic close and made evident his reliance upon then-standard but fundamentally flawed social theories. Here he worked to credit Calvinism decisively and exclusively "with the honor of having led humanity, as such, up to a higher stage in its development" to attain "the right to claim for itself the energy and devotion of our hearts."[124] As Bratt argues, Kuyper's reading of history and humankind's stewardship in Western civilization clearly owed "more to Hegel than to Scripture, and Kuyper did not hesitate to link it into the racial hierarchies of the day."[125] And so, as he worked to prove Calvinism's pride of place in human history, Kuyper's rhetorical strategies came to include (1) boasting in the commingling of once-tribal blood among white Europeans wherever Calvinism had flourished and (2) denigrating various regional and racial-ethnic life-systems around the globe.[126]

As to the first strategy, Kuyper pointed to *"the commingling of blood* as, thus far, the physical basis of all higher human development," and he named the American melting pot as the "highest conceivable realization" of this development.[127] Some twenty-first-century readers might wonder if Kuyper's comments on the commingling of blood in his Stone Lectures would have made them somewhat controversial in an 1898 US context. But he was speaking both from and into social contexts that would have assumed he was referring to the genetic coalescence of white Europeans only. Of his own context, elsewhere he propagandized the contrast between English and Boer colonial activity in South Africa, falsely claiming, "Liaisons with Negro women, which have always been the disgrace and scourge of colonizing nations, are among the Boers absolutely unknown."[128] Of the American context, antimiscegenation legislation had recently been bandied about in Congress and would pick up steam over the next several decades. So, explaining his "commingling" theory before his American audience, Kuyper operated within white supremacy, which he supported with an archaic racial-ethnic interpretation of Genesis 9.[129] "In entire conformity to the prophetic blessing of Noah the children of Shem and of Japheth have been the sole bearers of the development of the race. No impulse for any higher life has ever gone forth from the third group [i.e., the children of Ham's son Canaan]."[130] As Kuyper's perspective on race, civilization, and colony unfolds below, we must remember that he thought of these ideas as logical extensions of biblical principles and stories into a world-scale social theory, that is, as part of the "biblical world-view" itself.

To fill out our picture, we would do well to break for a moment from Kuyper's Stone Lectures rhetoric and consider more fully his take on "The South African Crisis." It is important to see exactly here how Kuyper's world-view was interlaced with a racial logic with which white evangelical world-viewers—not least those who knowingly sanitize Kuyper's "principles" of what they construe as merely faulty "practical applications"—have failed to grapple adequately. Building from his understanding of the mandate to "fill the earth and subdue it" in Genesis 1:28, Kuyper argued,

> We must never, as long as we value God's Word, oppose colonization.... Is it not simply human folly to remain so piled up in a few small places on this planet that men must crawl away into cellars and slums, while at the same time there are other places a hundred times larger than our native land, awaiting the plow and the sickle, or on which herds of the most valuable cattle wander without an owner?[131]

Describing the Boers as "men of practical genius," he praised the way "they understood that the Hottentots and the Bantus [both colonialist terms for

Africans that have become derisive] were an inferior race and that to put them on an equal footing with whites, in their families, in society, and in politics, would be simple folly."[132] With comments like these, the trail from Kuyper's expansive neo-Calvinist world-view to the white Dutch architects of South Africa's *apartheid* regime was made less strenuous.[133] Immediately after this particular comment, he returned to the theme of "mixed liaisons," which the Boers had polemicized as an incestuous "scourge." Finishing this thought, Kuyper described how, in contrast to other European missionaries, "the Boers have always faced squarely the difficulty of the color question which the English have persistently kept out of view. The blacks are increasing in South Africa to an extent that may well give cause for uneasiness. Of old, they had massacres among themselves every autumn."[134]

While the population numbers looked to become "ere long . . . menacing for whites" on all sides, he did not overlook that many whites were hopeful about the possibility of Christianity spreading among Black South Africans. In conference with some African Methodist Episcopal leaders in the United States, "a colored Methodist bishop ha[d] been appointed president of a kind of Negro council in Africa."[135] But not so fast, Kuyper counseled his reader: "Do not believe that Christianizing these blacks has obliterated their racial passion."[136] At this point, Kuyper crossed over to comment on race relations in the United States with impressions from his 1898 visit for the Stone Lectures. While in the States, he learned not that many Black Americans had a vibrant Christian faith, but that "conquest over the white man does and always will remain their chimerical ideal. They believe that Abel was black and that the sign of the curse which God put upon Cain was that he certainly became white. . . . Between blacks and whites there will never be lasting reconciliation."[137] Much could be said here, but it would seem that Kuyper's sanctified imagination could not generate a possible future in which dark-skinned humans were animated by his Calvinist spirit or possess its logically extended world-view. Painful as this conclusion may be, the Calvinist spirit at the center of his thought was decisively white and predicated on the supremacy of what he imagined as the commingled race of whites only.

As to his second rhetorical strategy while closing the first of his Stone Lectures, Kuyper lampooned China, Mexico, and Peru (referring to ancient civilizations like the Incas), and "the Slavic races," reserving his harshest criticism for the descendants of Ham. "The life of the colored races on the coast and in the interior of Africa," he illuminates, is "a far lower form of existence, reminding us not even of a lake but rather of pools and marshes."[138] To Kuyper, the perceived isolationism of each of these life-systems—lacking the drive to (super)intend the order of their world-view over all the world— betrayed the low energy in their inferior world-view(s) and descriptively ruled out their bearing the "promise of the future." He found this promise to have been carried alone upon that "one world-stream, broad and fresh" that "had its rise in Middle Asia and the Levant and has steadily continued its course from East to West."[139] Kuyper's derisive move here was but the flip side of his triumphalism. He proposed the comprehensive world-viewing concept (which, having studied his corpus, we have now seen worked out more systematically than most in his audience at Princeton) and the impulse to achieve it as the measure of all available life-systems, and here he operationalized that concept in his defense of Calvinism as the only viable option for the Christian West. Kuyper's theopolitical program was enmeshed in a revisionist history of the modern West that showcased a few narrowly defined "Christian nations"— where the social fabric bore the enduring imprint of common grace, refined to a peak through the energies of influential Calvinists.[140] More specifically, his grand history linked the United States, the Netherlands, the Dutch colonies of South Africa, and (sometimes) England together as sharing in the Calvinist (or sometimes "Reformed and Puritan") spirit or world-view.[141] And centering his account of humankind's civilizational achievement on these publics, framed in just this way, Kuyper claimed all perceived social progress as support for his Calvinist world-view.[142]

Working toward the end of his final lecture, Kuyper keyed on Calvinism's brilliance amid the great cultural diversity of humankind. He reminded his audience, "Half-measures cannot guarantee the desired result. Superficiality will not brace us for the conflict. Principle must again bear witness against principle, world-view against world-view, spirit against spirit."[143] In this place, Kuyper commended Calvinism as the firmest bulwark he knew when "*pagan* thought, *pagan* aspirations, *pagan* ideals [were] gaining ground even among us and penetrating to the very heart of the rising generation."[144] But the work of the Holy Spirit alone, according to God's foreordination of all things, would produce the kind of (re)awakening that Kuyper hoped for his Calvinist spirit and its logically produced, comprehensive world-view. Leading into this commendation, Kuyper recalled God's utter determination of history down to the details of "differentiation" and "inequality" of individuals' lives, the perception of which is itself "the very source of our human consciousness": "To put it concretely, if you were a plant you would rather be rose than mushroom; if insect, butterfly rather than spider; if bird, eagle rather than owl; if a higher vertebrate, lion rather than hyena; and again, being man, rich rather than poor, talented rather than dullminded, of the Aryan race rather than Hottentot or Kaffir [a third derisive, colonialist term for Africans derived from the Arabic word for 'infidel']."[145] At bottom, Kuyper's doctrine of election cast a strange light on his defense of Calvinism as the precipice of human world-viewing because, in so many cases, regeneration and especially its richest enlightenment also seemed to be distributed along other, more tangible lines of difference like race and nation.

PRELIMINARY CONCLUSIONS

Problems in the relationship of world-view theory to human psychology are particularly conspicuous in Kuyper's case because he theorizes so much in this arena even as he exhibits inconsistencies and errors. But I should also at least name how he presents the other two intertwined strands of critical concern that will occupy my attention as this project unfolds. I wager that the most obvious strand is the sociocultural as evidenced by his defense of Calvinism on the merits of white Western cultural supremacy from within a European colonial imagination. Like Hegel before him, Kuyper boiled world-viewing down to a self-conscious form for life, in general, and clearly also understood it as a racial capacity perfected among white Protestants in the West—lying dormant among dark-skinned Africans (including those in America). This conceptual framework set his standard for measuring other cultural forms of life in history. And given the seemingly clear location of the Netherlands, the United States, and maybe England at the pinnacle, his unquestioned judgments also boosted his confidence in the world-view concept itself as a meaningful tool for interpreting, valuing, and ordering the components of the world around him. I will return to consider the world-viewing significance of the racial scale and the colonial episteme of whiteness in chapter 4, but I will also engage in some related psychological discussions in chapter 2. A second, more directly theological strand arises in Kuyper's understanding of God's self-revelation (from the beginning, through the twilight of the fall, and into the *palingenetic* dawn). Specifically, his idealist epistemology originated in speculative philosophy but became deeply enmeshed with his understanding of the task of theology as well as his interpretation of the *imago dei* itself. To Kuyper, it made sense of the universe and our place within it as rationally structured and thus logically discernible, thus he assumed he should be speculatively theologizing (i.e., that it is a divine vocation). However, I find that Kuyper typifies theologians whose work exceeds a proper, creaturely mode for knowing and relating to God by turning God into a concept, a first principle in the vast, systematic universe to be reduplicated in human imaginations. And a similar judgment hangs over communion among humans who, in many ways, conceptualize one another as so many instances of the generic "human" type. This is a big claim suggesting the need for a seismic shift in theological studies and education, and my theological rationale will occupy much of chapter 6.

Understandably, Kuyper's contemporary followers desire to leave behind the offensive and otherwise embarrassing details of his world-view. As he deals with Kuyper's problematic legacy in the final pages of his biography, Bratt suggests, "The final test of a thinker might be whether her critical method can be used to expose and correct her substantive mistakes—whether, in Kuyper's language, his principles can work through unhappy iterations to reach a better application."¹⁴⁶ And, in the final paragraph or so of his biography, Bratt gestures toward some ways this may be true or at least some ideas that may be helpfully applied as an interpretive grid for progress in the world we know. Allan Boesak draws positively from Kuyper's sentiments about "the tenderness of conscience"¹⁴⁷ and predicts a major role for Calvinism in "the building of a modern, pluralistic democracy in today's globalizing world."¹⁴⁸ In a 2005 book, he glosses on Kuyper's Stone Lectures in a footnote:

> These lectures are at times unbearably triumphalistic, and Kuyper does not escape the religious chauvinism of his times, nor has he been able to overcome the benighted racial bigotry which characterized so much of European intellectual expression. Nonetheless one cannot but have appreciation for the universality and timelessness of the insights he espouses here on this particular issue.¹⁴⁹

Introducing one of his books on public theology in the line of Kuyper, Vincent Bacote casts this disclaimer over his embrace of Kuyper:

> Every theologian is a human being with flaws. I learned this early while reading Kuyper. Like many of his time, he made assumptions about civilization and race, namely, that Europeans were superior to other people, especially those with African heritage. My encounter with Kuyper's statements on race led me to become a critical thinker.... As I thought about it, it became clear that his views on race actually contradicted the best aspects of his theology. Kuyper could not transcend his own cultural biases and completely live up to the implications of his theology.¹⁵⁰

In his *Letters to a Young Calvinist*, James K. A. Smith commends Kuyper's Stone Lectures as "an essential part of your library" to aid the titular young, restless, and Reformed seeker-after-truth in the discovery of a "wide-angle Calvinism."¹⁵¹ Not wishing to get dragged into the weeds of Kuyper's racist colonialism at a sensitive moment in his argument for Calvinist world-viewing, Smith offers the uninitiated a vague proviso: "Now, I would disagree with him on some of the specifics, but...."¹⁵² So, for these thinkers, Kuyper evidently passes Bratt's test.

In the twenty-first century, many theologians acknowledge the impact of social location on their thinking to some degree, and among Kuyperians, the strategy is to name Kuyper's sociohistorical context as a problem while clearing debris to recover the supposedly orthodox skeleton of his principles. Even in Bratt's estimation, Kuyper's racial theory and its hierarchies belong in the same set as the National Socialists of early twentieth-century Germany.¹⁵³

And, we might add, his white supremacy (e.g., in his conviction that God makes people racially and also prefers some over others) shares much with his segregationist contemporaries in the United States who argued that racial differences and hierarchies "pleased the Divine will."[154] But Kuyper's devotees allege that his better principles can be read against himself to diagnose and correct his particular shortcomings—(implicitly) judged by historical standards as not principles but *applications*. In other words, Kuyper's racism and colonialism are problems, to be sure, but they represent historical aberrations in light of his supposedly deeper Christian principles. I find this assessment remarkable because Kuyper's sense that he could see and theorize the whole world in the first place is inextricably bound up with his historical moment. Of course, many intellectuals in his time trotted out the same tired ideas. But over against those who had no investment in Calvinism, Kuyper could add: God mandates cultural development that includes colonialism at this point, the color-line represents ancient biblical prophecy (i.e., the "Curse of Ham"), and God elects us to our sociohistorical locations. So, we ought to be grateful for our role, for our place in a history that is drawing so near to a complete image of God's original revelation. For Kuyper, the prevailing racial theory and colonial intercultural realities proved the merits of the world-view concept and, more than that, the supremacy of his white, neo-Calvinist worldview. This is, ironically, what it meant for Kuyper himself to acknowledge his social location. His world-viewing pride emerged from his partly accidental, partly biblical-prophetic, entirely divinely elected sociohistorical location as a blessed, powerful, white, European man. Allowing more diverse people into the group of confident world-viewers and world-orderers under the rubric of colorblindness—or of appreciating cultural accouterment—does not yet ask crucial theological questions about the historical tradition itself. Does the form for thought itself share in the problems of racist or colonial mentalities?

I maintain that Kuyper simply fails Bratt's test, for these historical problems have roots among his supposedly good theological principles themselves. To begin, Kuyper's race essentialism and its attendant white supremacy present *principial, theological problems* even if they reflect the historical attitudes and concrete structures of the world around him. Furthermore, they are indicative problems endemic to all essentialist thinking. History has shown that one can believe, generally, in the universal design and equal dignity of all human beings by way of their generalized "essence" and yet consistently deal with actual persons according to the accidental classes to which they belong (e.g., "all men are created equal" can be read to privilege white, land-owning males of a certain age). This problem dates at least to Aristotle, who upheld the superiority of wellborn, male Greeks on the basis of his observations and thus blurred the principial lines *he drew himself* between the "accidental" qualities of nature and essential qualities of being. Kuyper's racial categories were not only hierarchical in view of God's election of the total person in their historicity, but race for him took on an essential, even teleological quality, which, for some, amounted to an inescapable *privative* quality. Much of the same could be said for his approach to gender roles, which was arguably even more basic and essential in his way of thinking.[155]

At his Hegelian best, Kuyper may have guessed some of his own idiosyncrasies would be progressively synthesized out of his tradition. But as will become clear in our discussion of African American sociologist W. E. B. Du Bois (1868–1963) in chapter 2, at least some of Kuyper's contemporaries (not to mention other Christians before him) were more advanced in their thinking about race and the personhood of Black folk. Suffice it to say for now that, as an academic position, Kuyper did not have to maintain white supremacy or a colonial mandate. So, on what grounds could he possibly defend his understanding of not just the "formal" but the real-world potential of Black Africans and African Americans if he believed in the indelible, universal *being* of humankind? Pushing deeper than his belief in God's sovereignty, and circumscribing everything he would say on its basis, was Kuyper's white supremacy. Even as he employed Greek universalist thinking in his broader theory, he also deployed elements of the historical-particular Jewish and early Christian stories to justify the enduring significance of certain accidental qualities like race.[156] Both this severing of Christianity from its historical roots in Israel to become serviceable through generic "creational" categories and this faulty doctrine of election applied in support of essential, haveable qualities affecting particular humans' natures defy the biblically accountable identity of a people established and preserved by the word of the Creator, thus always contingent upon relationship with the living God.[157] Kuyper's racialized social theory was part and parcel of the world-view he presented as the logical outworking of Scripture, and he read history through this social theory to vindicate Calvinism as the once and future custodian of human consciousness.

Kuyper represents the colonial mentality that one can see and touch and think together at once the whole world and all its people, at least in all meaningful ways. And he justified this claim to an Archimedean point with his supposed grasp of God's revelation concerning how and by whom the world is to be ordered. White Europeans may have assumed the power and promise of Christian civilization to have a universalizing trajectory before the so-called Age of Discovery, but, in living contact with dark-skinned people from Africa, they intuited their sense of cultural superiority and the significance of human skin color as coterminous. This colonial mental framework, especially as it handles other persons out there in the world, will become more apparent as this project unfolds. For now, I want to call attention to the experience of the powerful subject who senses no need to, who encounters no situation or person to make them, question their social location or, more to the point, their cognitive unity, their rational lucidity, or their self-normativity. From within this space, Kuyper projected a world-view theory meant to explain the situation of the fallen world relative to God's creational intentions, from the location of the world's peoples down to his own psychology. What appeared to him as a rationally consistent, Bible-extending theory of everything actually held together in nineteenth-century colonial race logic, and his reading of Scripture undergirded his racism and cultural imperialism. Kuyper's contemporary disciples have not adequately analyzed his historical-particular problems as theological and principial in nature and, thus, have also failed to assess the dependence of neo-Calvinist public-theological concepts or world-view theory in general upon a racialized colonial framework. I cannot avoid the conclusion that neo-Calvinism in the line of Kuyper—and much of the broader "world-view" angle within American evangelicalism that developed following his Stone Lectures—instantiates the intuitive posture of whiteness.

What we have seen happen with Kuyper's social theory (i.e., historical particularity being drawn into the supposedly generalized world-view) is also manifest in his understanding of human nature, including its underlying psychological realities. The problem appears in a different register, however, since the fundaments of his psychological theory were read into the biblical world not just anywhere, but into God's original designs. In Kuyper's view, the world-viewing "impulse" is integral to the human's very *being* because it is instilled by God as an aspect of the *imago dei*, and making good on this impulse is part of glorifying God and constituent to creation's integrity as a logical whole. By his own account, however, he was awakened to this impulse not simply by the Calvinist spirit but also (largely) by the perceived threat already manifest in an expansive Modernist world-view that glittered in its logical consistency. Furthermore, Kuyper followed Hegel and others to appropriate the image of the human spirit as *microcosmos* from ancient Greek streams of philosophy (some place the concepts as far back as Democritus or Pythagoras) for explaining the *imago dei* in terms of a universal, rational soul situated within a logically ordered cosmos. His understanding of human minds is crucial—not least his views of the damage sin has wrought in human nature, God's total election of the person, and regeneration and the radical antithesis. Spelling out his psychological principles, Kuyper explained the restoration of unity in one's innermost place such that, as one increases in affinity with God through personal piety, that unity expands (often unconsciously) throughout one's thought-world. And he argued the regenerate should use their Holy Spirit-implanted, biblically communicated principles (e.g., about human psychology) in the spiritual-scientific investigation of real human persons/groups, who are otherwise rather unreliable self-revealers. Put differently, the world-viewing impulse pushed him to understand *himself* through his supposedly biblical principles within the abstract forms of his antithetical anthropological construct—and to doubt at least some disconfirming feedback.[158]

But Kuyper's psychological operating principles obscured the true origin and nature of his world-view's errors and also engendered his self-deceptive mystification of the longer process by which God enlightens and sanctifies the Christian. From the start, given the actual views he espoused, the concept of a singular, coherent, and comprehensive world-view simply does not accurately describe his own inner life or even his method for getting there. All wrapped up together are the problems of seeing the world through colonial-racist eyes, a theological commitment to world-viewing as a divine mandate, an overly simplistic spiritual sensibility that mystifies the ongoing process by which God enlightens and sanctifies the Christian, and the lack of practical resources for opening oneself to change. That he got so much patently wrong suggests the multiplicity of sources informing his world-view even as his theological convictions assured him otherwise—and his sentimental sense of personal piety reinforced the latter. From our place in the middle of history, we must deal with the problem that, if all that counts is the intent to glorify God as one engages in world-viewing and -transforming, then an avowedly Christian world-view may be found justifying any number of bad policies or alarming platforms in real time. The problem is not so much the attempt to theorize about a lot of different things or seek some kind of interdisciplinary conversation or even theoretical coherence; rather, it is the enduring assumption that these theories will connect with essential, universal truth corresponding to God's original creational intentions for all humankind. This pushes us to keep looking for ideal frameworks rather than approaching the data of the fallen world, with due humility about our own imperfect and self-interested psychology even as we confess and practice loyalty to Jesus. From within such world-views, any details deemed to be historical or accidental can be tossed (colonialism and later paternalism, patriarchy, etc.) as the thinker whittles down what must yet be essential about this or that identifiable group (e.g., race, nation, gender). Just where is the line between principle and application? I submit we must ask better *theological* questions about the whole thing.

Judging by Kuyper's own world-viewing attempt, we might start to see that efforts to "treat anthropological questions with presuppositions from epistemology" (to misplace a phrase from Clifford Green)[159] will not get us very far. Kuyper seemed blinded by both the subjective, somewhat Romantic experience or feeling of extending logical coherence across vaster terrain and the assumption that human beings and communities (himself and his own included) could be identified by their views of the whole world.[160] As an individual Christian person, he felt assured of his position on the regenerate side of the antithesis, was aware of many attributes God had gifted him in election (ranging from his whiteness to his intellectual prowess), actively cultivated pious affinity with the object of his study, and participated in the collective consciousness of the organic church by way of his Calvinist tradition and his local church. In his formal theological and philosophical activity, therefore, Kuyper thought himself fit to participate *pro parte virili* in the collective project of humankind: to glorify God by bearing the *imago dei qua microcosm*. But from our vantage, we can tell his abstract anthropological principles fail to accurately describe even Kuyper himself, though he seemed to be doing his level best to conceive of himself in terms of those principles. If we were looking for an element within Kuyper's Calvinist world-view that could account for how glaring errors like this get lodged in a world-view, we might look to his own explanation of how ignorance and sin coalesce in human ways of knowing. To do so, however, undercuts much of what he thought he was doing as a regenerate scholar piously seeking, in affinity with the help of God's irresistible power, to rid his mind of whatever conflicted with God's revelation. Kuyper acknowledged other factors in a limited sense (e.g., as matters of pride), but he could not imagine how other sources of knowledge—namely, the spirits that animate historically particular socialities—actually and actively *resist* the Holy Spirit's scrutiny even within a born-again, God-loving soul.[161] He could not anticipate or detect the incoherence of his own logical and self-narrating action as continuously impacted by principles and practices foreign to the evangel yet operating within his own innermost places.

World-viewing matters as a conceptual framework because it enables psychological tricks to avoid responsibility for the problems in one's view, not least when those problems are ubiquitous in one's social location. The ever-expanding scope of knowledge to be tied into one's world-picture—as an image that God wills humans to assemble of the world God created, ordered, and continues order—almost requires him to project some grizzly, subjective positions onto the mind of God. And Kuyper saw the pious theologian's final task as conceptually articulating their subjective world-view, depersonalizing it, and holding it before the church as an inspiration by making the whole thing *appear to hold together* as the deliverance of Scripture itself. Presupposing his own consciousness was essentially (re)unified in his innermost place and furnished with biblical first principles regarding God, human nature, and our sociality, Kuyper also presumed all the other thoughts he finds within himself cohere as a microcosm of the created order. But he deceived himself, lived in a world of his own making, just like everyone else, even as his convictions about God's self-revelation, the *imago dei*, the world-viewing impulse, and regeneration's cognitive effects drove him to present his intellectual deliverances as the comprehensive, "biblical," "Calvinist," and so on world-view. Kuyper's wider account of regeneration vis-à-vis enlightenment and sanctification offers some helpful balance conceptually. Yet, it is ultimately unable to correct his overblown and conveniently contradictory ways of conceptualizing and describing Christian identity. The way Kuyper linked a restored faith-instinct in one's innermost place together with the logical production of comprehensive knowledge in the highly developed intellectual space is exactly the problem with world-viewing: this *principial claim* fails to describe the cognitive life of concrete human beings and actually serves as an instrument of self-deception.

In the end, Kuyper veiled the historical process by which he arrived at these conclusions in a cloud of mystification. Folks come to see things straight somewhere in the nexus of the Holy Spirit's enlightening work and the individual's personal logical action. And he named the piety of the theologian and an awareness of God's activity within as the safeguards against their theology reflecting merely "the tenor of his inner life" along with any sinful errors lodged within. Kuyper tied the efficacy of the Holy Spirit's work in exegesis and theological understanding to the theologian's *awareness of the Holy Spirit's activity as such*—and to their (self-reported) conscious affinity with this work, as a matter of ongoing inspiration. Of course, it sounds good to say: the more in tune you are with reality by holy living in relationship with God, the more accurate your world-view will be in its details. But the grounds for justifying this or that logical development within this kind of view are ultimately subjective, such that you can do a whole lot of world-shaping in God's name without having any practical sites for correction and repentance. Furthermore, the mystification of God's activity can conceal dubious assumptions about the wider realities, one being the tendency to (probably unconsciously) identify the highest level of enlightenment (i.e., an imagination sanctified to uncover the details of God's will) *in oneself* and one's allies. To read him generously, we might construe his language about the unity of any given self and its total conversion as "confessional"—the proleptic claim of a promised future being worked out in real time. Such a reading would, however, require overlooking a great deal of Kuyper's more explicit developments to the contrary, particularly when understood as the work of a theologian who considers himself to be quite piously in tune with the (theo)logic of God's work in himself and the surrounding world. When he named the possibility that a pious, *regenerate* philosopher could successfully weave together the best of human knowledge into an organic whole, when he spoke of how the Holy Spirit guards against "subjectivistic, unhistorical, and arrogant" tendencies in thinkers who are aware of the Holy Spirit's inner work, and when he disclosed his belief that unity of consciousness can be found in regenerate humankind, Kuyper was commending the specific results of his own logical action to his audience.

No one, not even theologians at the top of their game, can be and do what Kuyper claimed. But world-viewing via abstractions and generalizations pushes us to cram ourselves into ill-fitting categories while providing the activist energy to engage in political action based on our world-viewing identity. In our quest for self-unity, we objectify even ourselves as instances of the universal ideas we hold dear and, thus, often cannot allow ourselves (whether consciously or not) to be honest about where we are on the journey. Moreover, when we mystify the processes by which the Holy Spirit works within to enlighten and sanctify, we may establish further prohibitive blocks to engaging honestly with our inner complexity. Then, as we engage in world-viewing, we risk turning God, self, and others into concepts, constructs, objects in our mental world that we fail to treat appropriately as persons. We would do better to work within and work to develop a concrete set of practices that keep us open to the Holy Spirit and honest to ourselves such that we might change over time. One place we might start is observing honestly (and in some ways without judgment, in freedom) the distance between our confessional ambition that "Christian" be the only identity that matters in our psyche and the lived reality of many influences, many loves working both within us and from the outside. The low-hanging fruit may be the practices that cut directly against the self-serving, self-deceptive piety Kuyper prescribes. However, the underlying sense that he is (or should be) unified, with a coherent web of beliefs already formed without consciously doing the hard work, may be more challenging to address. But the ideals of inner unity, identity singularity, and world-viewing omnicompetence persist, especially among those who represent or aspire to status as normative guardians. This fundamental error in psychological principles cannot be corrected without serious examination, putting the detailed, self-involving theology in conversation with the best theorizing in contemporary psychology. And this simply has not happened within this specific tradition or among America's evangelicals since. If we should not think of ourselves, let alone others like this, who should we think we are?

NOTES

1. Abraham Kuyper, *Calvinism: Six Stone Lectures* (Amsterdam: Höveker & Wormser Ltd., 1899), 1–4. At the recommendation of colleagues in America, Kuyper includes "life-system" among the cognates for "life- and world-view," all translating the Dutch *levens- en wereldbeschouwing* concept (3n1).
2. James D. Bratt, *Abraham Kuyper: Modern Calvinist, Christian Democrat* (Grand Rapids: Eerdmans, 2013), 64.
3. Bratt, *Modern Calvinist*, 380.
4. Bratt, *Modern Calvinist*, 380–81.

5. Mark A. Noll, *American Evangelical Christianity: An Introduction* (Malden, MA: Blackwell Publishers, 2001), 19.

6. I have worked to fill out some of the references to Hegel's philosophy throughout this chapter, but the reader may find a refresher on his thinking helpful. For this purpose, I recommend Matt Qvortrup's brief article "G.W.F. Hegel: An Introduction," *Philosophy Now* 140 (2020), accessed January 29, 2021, https://philosophynow.org/issues/140/GWF_Hegel_An_Introduction.

7. Bratt, *Modern Calvinist*, 32.

8. Kuyper, *Lectures*, 16.

9. Kuyper, *Lectures*, 260. Cf. Abraham Kuyper, *Encyclopedia of Sacred Theology: Its Principles*, 1894, ed. and trans. J. Hendrik de Vries (New York: Charles Scribner's Sons, 1898), 118.

10. Abraham Kuyper, *The Problem of Poverty* (1891), ed. and trans. James W. Skillen (1991; reprint, Sioux Center, IA: Dordt College Press, 2011), 35–36.

11. Kuyper, *Lectures*, 19–20.

12. Kuyper, *Lectures*, 20. Cf. Allan Boesak, *The Tenderness of Conscience: African Renaissance and the Spirituality of Politics* (Stellenbosch, South Africa: Sun Press, 2005), 213, 213n428.

13. Kuyper, *Lectures*, 21.

14. Kuyper, *Lectures*, 31–33.

15. Kuyper, *Lectures*, 19.

16. Kuyper, *Lectures*, 261.

17. Kuyper, *Lectures*, 46.

18. Kuyper supports this conception with reference to a variety of social commentators (*Lectures*, 6–9).

19. Kuyper, *Lectures*, 14.

20. Kuyper, *Lectures*, ch. 1; cf. 112 and 238–43.

21. Kuyper, *Lectures*, 18 and 21.

22. Roger D. Henderson, "How Abraham Kuyper Became a Kuyperian," appendix to Kuyper, *Problem of Poverty*, 92.

23. Kuyper, *Lectures*, 46; cf. 246–49. Kuyper uses the metaphor of a superior mirage in "Modernism: A Fata Morgana in the Christian Domain," 1871, in James D. Bratt, ed., *Abraham Kuyper: A Centennial Reader* (Grand Rapids: Eerdmans, 1998), 96–104.

24. See the text and notes in Kuyper, *Lectures*, 239–46; and Abraham Kuyper, "Modernism," 87–124. Some contemporary interpreters have made like arguments about the Christian (i.e., Puritan) character underwriting the perceived successes of liberalism during and after the Enlightenment—character that liberalism itself cannot replenish but must draw parasitically from "voluntary associations" like Christianity. See, for instance, Larry L. Rasmussen, *Moral Fragments and Moral Community: A Proposal for Church in Society* (Minneapolis: Fortress Press, 1993), and Elizabeth M. Bounds, *Coming Together/Coming Apart: Religion, Community, and Modernity* (New York: Routledge, 1997).

25. James W. Skillen, introduction to Kuyper, *Problem of Poverty*, 12.

26. Kuyper, *Problem of Poverty*, 42n7; cf. 53.

27. Kuyper, *Lectures*, 178–79 and 244.
28. Kuyper, *Problem of Poverty*, 61.
29. Abraham Kuyper, "Common Grace," 1902–04, in Bratt, *Centennial Reader*, 175. Cf. Kuyper, "Our Instinctive Life," 1908, in Bratt, *Centennial Reader*, 275.
30. Abraham Kuyper, *The Work of the Holy Spirit*, trans. and ed. J. Hendrik de Vries (New York: Funk & Wagnalls Co., 1900), xii–xiv.
31. Kuyper does make one exception that I have noticed, referring positively to "the old Evangelical Faith" in his final Stone lecture (*Lectures*, 248).
32. See Kuyper, *Lectures*, 11, as well as Bratt's discussion of this minimal Calvinism in *Modern Calvinist*, 80–82.
33. For a helpful review of these emphases, see Richard J. Mouw, *Abraham Kuyper: A Short and Personal Introduction* (Grand Rapids: Eerdmans, 2011).
34. Kuyper, *Lectures*, 261.
35. As Bratt explains, Kuyper specifically uses *palingenesis* as a term "to remind pious readers that being 'born again' entailed renewal for the whole creation and not just individuals" (*Modern Calvinist*, 210).
36. Kuyper closes his Stone Lectures with this image (*Lectures*, 274–75).
37. Cf. Henderson, 74.
38. Kuyper's conceptuality around terms like (self)consciousness, subject and object, and spirit emerges from a philosophical context particular to his time, place, and education. I will note some such factors—especially his connections with Hegel—only briefly at intervals throughout this chapter and its notes, but I intend to address this material more systematically in a future essay. In the current project, I am more (but not solely) focused on the psychological elements in Kuyper's theory.
39. Kuyper, *Encyclopedia*, 264.
40. Kuyper, *Encyclopedia*, 264.
41. Kuyper, *Encyclopedia*, 83.
42. Kuyper, *Encyclopedia*, 264–65.
43. Kuyper, *Encyclopedia*, 270.
44. Kuyper, *Encyclopedia*, 269.
45. Kuyper, *Encyclopedia*, 271ff.
46. Kuyper, *Encyclopedia*, 272.
47. Kuyper, *Encyclopedia*, 274.
48. Kuyper, *Holy Spirit*, 264; cf. 310–14. See also Kuyper, *Encyclopedia*, §43, §49.
49. Kuyper, *Encyclopedia*, 129. Cf. Kuyper, *Lectures*, 173–74; and Kuyper, *Holy Spirit*, 385–86.
50. Kuyper's concept of "faith" is not the generically religious phenomenon (as in Friedrich Schleiermacher's starting point) that Hegel was eager to move past, but the *one* faith that actually reaches a different object (i.e., revelation). Cf. Kuyper, *Encyclopedia*, 310–11.
51. Kuyper, *Encyclopedia*, 114–15.
52. Kuyper, *Encyclopedia*, 110. Cf. Kuyper, "Our Instinctive Life," 258–69; and Abraham Kuyper, "It Shall Not Be So Among You," 1886, in Bratt, *Centennial Reader*, 130.

64   Chapter 1

53. Kuyper, *Encyclopedia*, 93–95. Cf. Kuyper, "Our Instinctive Life," 267.
54. Kuyper, *Encyclopedia*, 95.
55. Kuyper uses abnormal manifestations of gender roles as an example: "Even the classification according to sex frequently suffers shipwreck upon effeminate men and mannish women" (Kuyper, *Encyclopedia*, 93–94).
56. Kuyper, *Encyclopedia*, 97. Cf. Abraham Kuyper, "Perfectionism," 1878, in Bratt, *Centennial Reader*, 147.
57. Kuyper, *Encyclopedia*, 99.
58. Kuyper, *Encyclopedia*, 266.
59. Kuyper, *Encyclopedia*, 108. Cf. Kuyper's description of political theory and government in the fallen world in *Problem of Poverty*, 23–24.
60. Kuyper, *Encyclopedia*, 112.
61. Kuyper, *Encyclopedia*, 154. Cf. Kuyper, *Lectures*, 174ff.
62. Kuyper, *Lectures*, 17. Cf. Kuyper, *Holy Spirit*, 281, 497.
63. Kuyper, *Lectures*, 70.
64. Kuyper, *Encyclopedia*, 275.
65. Kuyper, *Encyclopedia*, 263.
66. Kuyper, *Encyclopedia*, 347.
67. Kuyper, *Encyclopedia*, 357–58.
68. Kuyper, *Encyclopedia*, 281. In the original English translation, the word in brackets here is "psychical," which is related to the Greek root *psyche* (soul) but has fallen out of use for the intended reference, namely, "spiritual" or "psychological" matters.
69. On the indivisibility of the soul, see Kuyper, *Holy Spirit*, 281.
70. Kuyper, *Encyclopedia*, 580.
71. Cf. John Calvin, *The Institutes of Christian Religion*, 1559, ed. John T. McNeill and trans. Ford Lewis Battles, 2 vols. (Philadelphia: The Westminster Press, 1960), I.15.7.
72. Kuyper, *Encyclopedia*, 580–81.
73. Kuyper, *Encyclopedia*, 281.
74. Kuyper, *Encyclopedia*, 266.
75. Kuyper, *Holy Spirit*, 481.
76. Kuyper, *Holy Spirit*, 314.
77. Kuyper, *Holy Spirit*, 46; cf. III.1.12.
78. Kuyper, *Holy Spirit*, 312.
79. Kuyper, *Encyclopedia*, 375–76; cf. 345.
80. Kuyper, *Encyclopedia*, 113.
81. Kuyper, *Encyclopedia*, 557. See also Kuyper, "Perfectionism," 147.
82. Kuyper claims the process of subjectively appropriating theological knowledge proceeds more or less unconsciously in many people, who do not really register much of what is lost or displaced in their mental worlds as it happens (*Encyclopedia*, 560).
83. Kuyper, *Lectures*, 69; cf. 175–76. Kuyper relates this truth autobiographically: "Oh, what my soul experienced at that moment I fully understood only later. Yet, from that moment on I despised what I used to admire, and I sought what I had dared to despise" ("Confidentially," 1873, in Bratt, *Centennial Reader*, 54).

84. This epistemological shift is behind Kuyper's juxtaposition of "instinctive life" and "reflective life" in "Our Instinctive Life," 258–59. Cf. Kuyper, *Encyclopedia*, 280.
85. Kuyper, *Encyclopedia*, 280; Kuyper, *Holy Spirit*, I.4.13.
86. Kuyper, *Encyclopedia*, 267.
87. Kuyper, *Encyclopedia*, 273–74.
88. Kuyper, *Encyclopedia*, 289; cf. 567–68.
89. Kuyper, "Our Instinctive Life," 268.
90. Kuyper, *Encyclopedia*, 327–28.
91. Kuyper, "Our Instinctive Life," 268.
92. Kuyper, *Encyclopedia*, 223.
93. Kuyper, *Encyclopedia*, 586–87. Cf. Kuyper's reference to logic in *Lectures*, 87.
94. Kuyper, *Encyclopedia*, 66.
95. Kuyper, *Encyclopedia*, 581.
96. Kuyper, *Encyclopedia*, 569.
97. Kuyper, *Encyclopedia*, 283. Christian philosophy building from the proper first principle should even be capable of "lead[ing] to unity of interpretation within the circle of regeneration" (614–15).
98. Kuyper, *Encyclopedia*, 575.
99. Kuyper, *Encyclopedia*, 574–75.
100. Kuyper, *Encyclopedia*, 569.
101. Kuyper, *Encyclopedia*, 570.
102. Kuyper, *Holy Spirit*, 309.
103. Kuyper, *Holy Spirit*, 350.
104. Kuyper, "Our Instinctive Life," 260–61.
105. Kuyper, *Encyclopedia*, 340.
106. Kuyper, *Encyclopedia*, 580.
107. Kuyper, *Encyclopedia*, 580–81.
108. For a sense of how Kuyper inserts mystery into the relationship between human practices and habits and the work of the Holy Spirit, see *Holy Spirit*, 482ff.
109. Kuyper, *Encyclopedia*, 286–88 and 583–85.
110. Kuyper, *Encyclopedia*, 581.
111. Kuyper, *Encyclopedia*, 586.
112. Kuyper, *Encyclopedia*, 586.
113. Cf. Bratt, *Modern Calvinist*, 224.
114. Kuyper, *Problem of Poverty*, 44.
115. Kuyper, *Problem of Poverty*, 45–46 (including 46n12).
116. Bratt, *Modern Calvinist*, 226.
117. Bratt, *Modern Calvinist*, 274.
118. Bratt, *Modern Calvinist*, 277.
119. Skillen, 14.
120. Kuyper, *Problem of Poverty*, 27n7.
121. Kuyper, *Problem of Poverty*, 60.
122. Kuyper, *Problem of Poverty*, 49.
123. Kuyper, *Problem of Poverty*, 59.

124. Kuyper, *Lectures*, 33.

125. Bratt, *Modern Calvinist*, 200.

126. Kuyper, *Lectures*, 33–40. For a different taste of this thinking, see Kathryn Tanner's excellent history in *Theories of Culture: A New Agenda for Theology* (Minneapolis: Fortress Press, 1997), ch. 1.

127. Kuyper, *Lectures*, 37, 40.

128. Abraham Kuyper, "The South African Crisis," 1900, in Bratt, *Centennial Reader*, 331. Cf. Bratt, *Modern Calvinist*, 293. Anyone familiar with the history of race relations under colonial conditions or systems of slavery is aware of such self-serving and patently false claims about sexual contact.

129. For a helpful review of nineteenth-century race theories (in the United States), see Eboni Marshall Turman, *Toward a Womanist Ethic of Incarnation: Black Bodies, the Black Church, and the Council of Chalcedon* (New York: Palgrave Macmillan, 2013), ch. 3. On the "Curse of Ham" in American conversations about race in this period, see Edward J. Blum, *W. E. B. Du Bois: American Prophet* (Philadelphia: University of Pennsylvania Press, 2007), 65–67. Blum goes on to discuss later pseudoscientific developments as well.

130. Kuyper, *Lectures*, 37. Kuyper seems to be working with a "monogenesis" theory in which all races had remote ancestors in common and, thus, would see some key differences as abnormal developments in the context of sin even as God's election determines such realities. See also Bratt, *Modern Calvinist*, 100ff.

131. Kuyper, *Problem of Poverty*, 62.

132. Kuyper, "South African Crisis," 339. Cf. Mouw, *Personal Introduction*, 82.

133. Cf. Bratt, *Modern Calvinist*, 292–96 and 381. A more detailed study of the relationship between Kuyper's neo-Calvinism and South African politics might begin with André du Toit, "Puritans in Africa? Afrikaner 'Calvinism' and Kuyperian neo-Calvinism in late nineteenth-century South Africa," *Comparative Studies in Society and History* 27 (1985): 227–34.

134. Kuyper, "South African Crisis," 339–40.

135. Kuyper, "South African Crisis," 340.

136. Kuyper, "South African Crisis," 340.

137. Kuyper, "South African Crisis," 340.

138. Kuyper, *Lectures*, 34; cf. 107. Kuyper seems to theorize less on the qualities of this supposed inferiority than did Hegel, whose treatment of African history entails claims like the following: "In Negro life the characteristic point is the fact that consciousness has not yet attained to the realization of any substantial objective existence" (*The Philosophy of History*, 1892, trans. John Sibree [New York: Dover Publications, 1956], 93). See also Ronald Kuykendall, "Hegel and Africa: An Evaluation of the Treatment of Africa in The Philosophy of History," *Journal of Black Studies* 23, no. 4 (June 1993): 572–73.

139. Kuyper, *Lectures*, 34. Historians like Oswald Spengler and Arnold Toynbee were routinely rejecting such metaphors by the early to mid-1900s, as highlighted in Samuel P. Huntington, *The Clash of Civilizations and the Remaking of World Order* (New York: Simon & Schuster, 1996), 55. Much about Huntington's world-viewish, civilizational analysis is amenable to Kuyper's; however, one is left to guess as to

whether Kuyper would have seen any wisdom in rejecting "the assumption of the unity of history."

140. Kuyper, "Common Grace," 198–99. Cf. Kuyper, "Uniformity: The Curse of Modern Life," 1869, in Bratt, *Centennial Reader*, 43; and Bratt, *Modern Calvinist*, 203. Kuyper analyzes a nation state in Hegelian fashion as "an integral whole, an organism . . . in connection with the life of centuries past that put its stamp on it and shaped its character"—things like public holidays, national anthems, driving social forces, and currently influential ideas (Abraham Kuyper, *Guidance for Christian Engagement in Government: A Translation of Abraham Kuyper's Our Program*, trans. and ed. Harry Van Dyke [Grand Rapids: Christian's Library Press, 2013], §48). For a greater sense, §44–48.

141. Cf. Kuyper, *Lectures*, 9–10.

142. For instance, in his Stone lecture on politics, Kuyper rehearses a litany of early American documents and records to demonstrate a ubiquitous acknowledgment of God's ultimate sovereignty over the United States (i.e., the Calvinist first principle), notably in direct opposition to the spirit of the French Revolution (*Lectures*, 110–13). See also Kuyper, *Our Program*, 51; and Kuyper, "Calvinism: Source and Stronghold of Our Constitutional Liberties," 1874, in Bratt, *Centennial Reader*, 289–92.

143. Kuyper, *Lectures*, 274.

144. Kuyper, *Lectures*, 273.

145. Kuyper, *Lectures*, 269; cf. 107.

146. Bratt, *Modern Calvinist*, 382.

147. Kuyper, *Lectures*, 123.

148. Boesak, 213.

149. Boesak, 213n428.

150. Vincent E. Bacote, *The Political Disciple: A Theology of Public Life* (Grand Rapids: Zondervan, 2015), 8.

151. James K. A. Smith, *Letters to a Young Calvinist: An Invitation to the Reformed Tradition* (Grand Rapids: Brazos Press, 2010), 97.

152. Smith, 98.

153. Bratt, *Modern Calvinist*, 329.

154. Blum, 67.

155. I see neither Bratt nor Mouw connecting, as I would, Kuyper's racial essentialism with his extensive, essentialist arguments about gender complementarianism and women's role in the various spheres (e.g., opposing women's suffrage in the Netherlands). For a taste of Kuyper's thinking on gender, see Bratt, *Modern Calvinist*, 360–63.

156. J. Kameron Carter highlights the way Christianity is severed from its Jewish roots and reattached to a Greek stump in this shift from the historical-particular to the universal-rational, and he connects this shift with the colonial race logic that read Europeans as representative of the latter and denigrated everyone else. See his *Race: A Theological Account* (New York: Oxford University Press, 2008), 108, 115, and 117.

157. Willie Jennings has masterfully argued this case in *The Christian Imagination: Theology and the Origins of Race* (New Haven: Yale University Press, 2010), ch. 6.

Central to his reading is the idea that whiteness entails a "fail[ure] to read Israel's story as in part a struggle against internalized Gentile identity precisely because we have read their story as Gentiles who have forgotten that we read as Gentiles" (258). Compare this with Dietrich Bonhoeffer's conversation about Jewish Christianity as a religious category in "The Church and the Jewish Question," in *Berlin: 1932–1933*, English ed., Dietrich Bonhoeffer Works (Minneapolis: Fortress Press, 2009), 12:368–70. In terms of my project, we might see thinkers like Kuyper who imagine a kind of "cosmonomic" clarity (to misplace an idea from Kuyper's student Herman Dooyeweerd) within a quasi-theocratic vision for their own modern nation-state (i.e., a variety of supersessionism) as actually seizing and universalizing one version of Israel they are finding within Scripture—and at that, a version that represents more *a temptation for* than *a fulfillment of* the people identified and sustained by the living God.

158. Bratt grants that, given the particularity of God's election, the objects of study here are "not virtual or notional but real persons" for Kuyper (Bratt, *Modern Calvinist*, 105). The *concrete upshot* of his reasoning, however, creates space for skepticism.

159. See Clifford J. Green's commentary on Dietrich Bonhoeffer's criticism of German Idealism in *Bonhoeffer: A Theology of Sociality*, Rev. ed. (Grand Rapids: Eerdmans, 1999), 32.

160. For more on Kuyper's Romanticism, see Bratt, *Modern Calvinist*, 33 and 98.

161. It would be relevant to explore the concept of other spirits that might animate a person, as some contemporary scholars (perhaps most notably Walter Wink) have done in studies of "the principalities and powers" in biblical language.

Chapter 2

A Contemporary Psychological Discussion of Selfhood

A harbinger of the 1940s evangelical movement that would emerge from America's fundamentalist corners, Abraham Kuyper traced the problems of soul and society to the battle for world-viewing truth. Nearly a century on, inheritors of this spirit polemicize against postmodernism and "relativism" as the late-stage evolution of what Kuyper identified in the godless first principle of Modernism. As the scientific method has addressed old questions and raised new ones based on increasingly sound empirical evidence, moral and religious programs proceed under heightened scrutiny of their epistemological foundation and susceptibility to human power dynamics—like justifying Kuyper's racist, colonial framework. We might hope to see an earnest focus on understanding the material of these historical problems and why so many propped them up so that we might improve how we hold our convictions, reflect on them, and attempt to influence the surrounding world through them. But mainstream evangelical voices have more often expressed concern about the highly critical, deconstructive mood in "secular" circles questioning the relationship between power and ways of knowing. On this dreaded train of thought, a person or group only ever justifies their moral judgments relative to their own intellectual framework and not the foundational order of the universe itself. And among theologically oriented social critics, a consensus appears imminent: as traditional sources of selfhood have been losing their purchase in Western societies, the aberrant notions of identity coming out the other side entail rootlessness, disjointedness, and superficiality.

But Kuyper felt justified in his convictions and lived practices, and the way he supported his grizzly historical positions as not only logical but also Christian simply does create problems for how we think religious or moral truth, especially how individual human beings come to know and hold such truth. Many current projects in theology—including those in the line of

Kuyper—are concerned about protecting and promoting what they take to be the good bones of their traditions while shrugging off problematic historical particularities. And motivated at least partly by a pastoral concern for people in need of guiding light in a bewildering world of densifying pluralism, theologians have consistently asserted the importance of integrating one's sense of identity and selfhood within such a view—as a matter of truth as well as psychological wellbeing. While some variety of integration may well be what we need, the targeted form of wholeness tends toward a monolithic, structural unity that oversells the individual human on just how complete their Christian enlightenment already is. In other words, it is all too easy to assume that one's way of thinking about the world is Christian in all the important ways without having to seriously question the unity of our minds' contents, the singleness of our most important identities, the coherence our way of seeing the world and our place within it. Whether conserving traditions or pastoring persons, continuous insistence on world-viewing has meant evading the deeper questions about the world-view concept's epistemological limits and, as this chapter will examine, its fit with current psychological theory.

Over the last century, psychology has expanded as a scientific discipline into more serious clinical and other empirical investigations, increasingly disambiguating itself from the abstract and speculative theories of human minds in modern philosophy and theology. Among more recent developments, various subdomains of psychology are converging to destabilize normative assumptions about what should be understood as a simple or "unified" whole in a human's cognitive space. In Kuyper, we encountered a theologian projecting his theological-anthropological theory into a world that was just starting to hear from the pioneers of modern psychology; William James's *The Principles of Psychology* hit the shelves in 1890, and Sigmund Freud started pumping out books that same decade. As such, we can understand why Kuyper might fall short in this domain. But even along what many consider the cutting edge of theological anthropology today, a silo effect keeps theologians oblivious to fundamental shifts in psychological theory.[1] Whether in the postliberal form of "narratives" or the evangelical form of "world-views," one's own world-view is subjectively understood as an adequate and honestly formulable self-description of the most basic, the most influential, or even the only story one lives by. With partisan political battles and questions of unreflective whiteness in my mind as I write, this chapter will explore the psychological conditions that allow so many white American evangelicals (but not only them) to think of themselves as paradigmatically "Christian" first and foremost and, further, that their politics, social views, and other judgments flow from or at least fit with their biblical world-view.

I will begin with a study of W. E. B. Du Bois (1868–1963), whose sociological work was grounded in the lived experience of souls who do not share in the easy self-normativity of Kuyper and other powerful, colonial subjects. His account of a "double consciousness" in individual African Americans' psyche cracks open the door for a less unified expectation for healthy identity psychology in a world of strife. Then, I will explore how contemporary psychological research says, we process, store, and operationalize self-defining experiences and ideas. This cognition includes the variety of formative and aspirational elements that complicate what Kuyper simply conceived as the "instinctive life" of faith that underlies all intellectual developments and motivates all human living. Moving forward with a more honest take on self-complexity, I will explore the unifying stories people tell about themselves as they make meaning in life and reveal their inner life to others. While there is a deep connection between the world-view concept and "the stories we live by" (to anticipate one approach studied below), we may discover that the impulse to tell a coherent story also drives us to overlook the disharmonies in our lives. By chapter's end, I will use the conceptual tools we gather to describe how the world-viewing impulse operates and to challenge both the truth and the usefulness of the world-view concept as Kuyper and many evangelicals after him have expounded it. In the final section, I will propose some constructive prospects for a viable theology of identity that honestly grapples with the multiplicity within that we so often deny out of deference to our theological preconceptions.

W. E. B. DU BOIS: A BRIEF CASE IN COUNTERPOINT

W. E. B. Du Bois was the first African American to receive a doctorate from Harvard University. During his studies, he took a fellowship in Germany at the University of Berlin, and his work, like Kuyper's, shared in a philosophy of history that coursed downstream from G. W. F. Hegel, who had been philosophy chair and (eventually) rector at Berlin.[2] As a founder of modern sociology, Du Bois broke ground with studies of race in the United States founded on statistical data—as with *The Philadelphia Negro* (1899)—rather than mere philosophical speculation or the pseudoscience of those wrapped up in the colonial enterprise.[3] His collection of essays entitled *The Souls of Black Folk* was first published in 1903, but the opening essay, which famously applies the concept of "double consciousness," was first published in the August 1897 issue of *The Atlantic* as "Strivings of the Negro People"—hitting the stands more than a year before Kuyper delivered his Stone Lectures. So, on the right day, in the right house, during his visit to the United States, Kuyper could have been confronted by Du Bois's work. From the outset, we may wonder whether Kuyper could have comprehended this man whose very existence would throw his social theory into question: Du Bois describes having "a flood of Negro blood, a strain of French, a bit of Dutch, but, thank God! no 'Anglo-Saxon.'"[4]

Du Bois came of age in a world structured by the religion of people like Kuyper—not his particular neo-Calvinist program but the instinctive "form for life" that took shape among white, American Protestants. In an especially poignant passage in *The Souls*, Du Bois broached the subject of his racialized social context, "Between me and the other world there is ever an unasked question: unasked by some through feelings of delicacy; by others through the difficulty of rightly framing it. . . . How does it feel to be a problem?"[5] Yet his conflicted experience of selfhood—"What, after all, am I? Am I an American or am I a Negro? Can I be both?"—and his extended reflection on the origin and nature of this inner struggle revealed a silver lining in the pall of twoness.[6] This second consciousness afforded him unique insight into the so-called social question or crisis around the turn of the century. It enabled him to identify not only different sources for the threat of Mammonism (e.g., whiteness and "the color-line") as well as new threats to American life (e.g., African Americans' internalized oppression and a negative spiritual wage of whiteness) but also a previously untapped source of likely solutions: the spiritual inheritance of Black folk. Below we will examine these ideas and concepts as counterpoints to Kuyper's thinking in themselves and, at another level, in pursuit of a richer understanding of human consciousness and identity.

Though we have seen Kuyper extol the heights of common grace in Western civilization, the concrete outworkings of white religion look(ed) different from the perspective of Black Americans whose forbears had been treated as chattel and who continue(d) to be shut out of the progress. Du Bois challenged the white supremacy of Kuyper's American counterparts, asking, *Which is more fundamental to the rise of rank materialism: godlessness or whiteness?* Put differently, he explored how white supremacy—underwritten by Christians citing the Bible chapter and verse—was more basic to the world-view that trades in materialism than avowed godlessness.[7] For Kuyper, the problem was that once you have unseated God as the sovereign over each heart and each society, the despotic individual will rise to claim sovereignty, and this situation can yield to either egoism or reach its more "natural" end in collectivism. For Du Bois, the problem was that white people had simultaneously (a) attached judgments about divine blessedness and moral virtue to human beings' skin color and (b) reduced dark-skinned persons to chattel to keep the economy humming.

The social crisis, with its unbearable labor practices and unbelievable disparity between the rich and the poor, was bound up with liberal individualism and free-market capitalism. And while poor whites did not reap the same benefits as their upper-class counterparts, who increasingly dominated the ostensibly free market, they seemed to benefit psychologically from their whiteness. However bad their material lot may have been, they could assume membership in the supreme race with its moral and civilizational progress to their credit.[8] This "spiritual wage" made poor whites more susceptible to seeing the doctrines of liberal individualism and free-market capitalism as vital to "the American way," even when these ideas materialized in ways that cut against their own class interests (and perhaps what truth there was in "the American Dream"). More to the point, Du Bois argued that white Americans were locked into a way of inhabiting the world that is obsessed with material gain, and their treatment of other human beings *as material* was both a symptom of this obsession and the cause of a spiritual wound that would require inner transformation and deep repentance to heal. While Kuyper might have protested that Protestants who were, in effect, materialists diverged from the straight paths of Calvinism, he would have needed to rewrite much of his social theory to exorcise the white supremacy and colonialism from his own world-view.

As we have seen, an avowed first principle of God's sovereignty could underwrite a racial system for moral evaluation, not least because the prevailing interpretation of Scripture buttressed the white supremacy that turned out to be the deeper, more determinative principle. Historian Edward Blum highlights Du Bois's judgment that this "spiritual wage of whiteness (and the alleged spiritual bankruptcy of Blacks) led white Americans to displace the true Christian God with a deity made in their own image."[9] The ideas that the white race was superior in terms of cultural achievement and that God elected persons' particularity (including skin color) facilitated a sense of moral achievement or virtue that cohered with one's skin and that simultaneously aided the base desires of whites who stole persons to serve their material interests. As we will explore in chapter 4, associating skin color with both civilizational progress and personal virtue happened in the early moments of encounter between the white European colonizers and the unfortunate souls of color they encountered on foreign soil. From within their own particular view, the former intuited the latter's existence as carnal, heathen, and so on. This was and is a key moment in the (re)production of whiteness: the powerful subject never questions whether their view can take in and explain all persons, places, and patterns they encounter.

Not only did Du Bois have a different read on the social crisis and its primary source, but he also noticed additional threats to American life. On the one side, for example, is a *negative* spiritual wage of whiteness—something like "the wages of sin" the Apostle Paul identifies in Romans 6. Du Bois saw that "Christianity had been undermined by women and men who warped the spirit of Christ for their own economic and psychological gain."[10] In the ongoing attempt to assert the vaunted moral status of whites qua whites without attending to the demands of moral growth, any real virtue withers amid the persistent vice of objectifying and abusing persons of other races. And white Christianity is corrupted by the backflow: "I fear the atrophy of soul which this teaching must bring. Both mentally and morally white folk today are suffering from this attempt to transmute a physical accident into a moral deed—to draw unreal distinctions among human souls."[11] In a different key, Wendell Berry has surveyed this wage as "the hidden wound," a mirror image in the white soul of the harm inflicted on the Black neighbor.[12] On the other side is the psychological wound within the soul of the colonized, who internalize the white gaze and its oppressive assessment of the Black self, generating a secondary consciousness that can manifest as an inferiority complex (as African-Caribbean psychiatrist Frantz Fanon diagnosed the situation).[13] In the fallout of colonialism, one effect of white Europeans exerting a singular identity is the doubling of Black Africans' sense of self as they realize they have been structured out the powerful subjects' self-ascribed identity blessing.

What Du Bois identified as "double consciousness" finds its conceptual origins in two distinct streams of influence: the poetic-figurative writings of folks like Phillis Wheatley and Ralph Waldo Emerson and then-developing medical-psychological theories, not least in the work of William James.[14] In the first stream, Wheatley and Emerson were in themselves dramatically different. Wheatley spoke from within the experience of a soul torn from her native Africa as a child and coming of age within the white, Christian household of her servitude. Emerson's romantic sense of twoness centered on "the downward pull of life in society—including the social forces inhibiting genuine self-realization—and the upward pull of communion with the divine."[15] Du Bois's writing stands out in the field of sociology for its unique wedding of scientific craft and poetic style into a form that could move his audience toward justice. Essays like "Strivings of the Negro People" exhibit *a radical, transformative aesthetics* intended to engage citizens for the sake of social change—to see and engage the world differently.[16] And Du Bois's description of double consciousness itself participates in this aesthetics:

> It is a peculiar sensation, this double-consciousness, this sense of always looking at one's self through the eyes of others, of measuring one's soul by the tape of a world that looks on in amused contempt and pity. One feels his two-ness—an American, a Negro; two souls, two thoughts, two unreconciled strivings; two warring ideals in one dark body, whose dogged strength alone keeps it from being torn asunder.[17]

But exercising poetic license, he did not always employ the double consciousness language family when highlighting the concept. As historian Dickson Bruce explains, the concept of double consciousness in Du Bois's work has at least three layers:

(1) "the real power of white stereotypes in black life and thought" such that racialized others internalize, and (might) feel compelled to live relative to, the white gaze;
(2) an awareness of the lived reality of a racialized society, namely, that one is "both an American and not an American"; and
(3) the conflict within Black Americans between their alternate states of consciousness—the "African" and the "American."[18]

Du Bois believed the African sensibility could cure the rank materialism of mainstream America, making this third sense the most significant in his constructive ambitions. He had in mind African Americans experiencing the "unhappy consciousness" about which Hegel wrote—that acute, internal conflict between two identities, two objective spirits, two sets of values and ways of thinking.[19] When such conflict rises to the level of conscious anguish, and when the person becomes *aware* of the mismatch between the spirits that shape their values, then that awareness can become a motivating factor in their social actions.

Now, we might return to discuss the medical-psychological stream from which the concept of double consciousness flowed into Du Bois's thinking. *Fin-de-siècle* discourse allowed for little equivocation about double consciousness: it is pathological. "As a medical term 'double consciousness' already had a long history by the 1890s, having been the subject of rather extensive experimentation and debate for at least seventy-five years."[20] For example, the early 1800s account of one Mary Reynolds yielded a proto-diagnosis of what we might now call dissociative identity disorder but was then understood as "a duality of person in the same individual."[21] In any case, the educated lay audience of *The Atlantic* would have been aware of this background of meaning, which Bruce points out would have

> further reinforced what Du Bois had emphasized as the genuinely alternative character of African American ideals. In the classic cases of double consciousness, the dual personalities were not just different from each other but were inevitably in opposition. . . . Double consciousness thus entailed a real opposition between the two consciousnesses confined within a single body.[22]

Bruce goes on to say, "As earlier writers had made plain, in classic cases of double consciousness, although the condition itself was clearly abnormal, it could not be said that either personality was more obviously 'normal' or functional than the other."²³ So, even though this overall condition was interpreted as pathological, identifying the more "normal" personality presented something of a challenge. Thus, Du Bois opened the possibility of warring ideals within a person under the standard of discrete identities that flag not only self-relevant information but also sources of conviction and values. While he knew the *occasion* for double consciousness was not positive for Black Americans, Du Bois claimed the differentiation of an African spirit within could be a boon for themselves, America, and the human race. In his immediate context, he saw the potential contribution of Black folk to the health of human civilization (particularly in the United States) as multifaceted.

Disillusioned by the fruit of white religion in America and often interpreted as areligious as a result, Du Bois held out the possibility that Christian faith rising within the Black soul in revulsion against de facto Mammonism could prophetically call all who heed the gospel of Jesus into "an attitude of humility" and a "willingness to suffer persecution for right ideals and in general for love not only toward our friends but even toward our enemies."²⁴ He pictured Black Africans as essentially religious prior to the arrival of European colonizers, already living palpably more spiritual and religious lives than their supposedly enlightened oppressors. And here Du Bois saw an early glimpse of how distinct the souls of Black folk were and thus insisted that Africans were not the carnal heathens the white Europeans made them out to be; in fact, given their fixation with the black bodies they were stealing, the latter appeared to be grotesquely savage.²⁵ He knew that being enslaved shook the faiths of Black Africans, many of whom came to connect with Christian Scriptures, especially the images of the Exodus and the crucified Christ, which fill numerous spirituals.²⁶ Du Bois pointed to these soul-hungry songs as emblematic of African American strength and inner freedom; moreover, he argued these were the people "whose subtle sense of song has given America its only American music, its only American fairy tales, its only touch of pathos and humor amid its mad money-getting plutocracy."²⁷ In the crucible of the transatlantic slave trade, Black Africans had become true inheritors of the gospel, which could be brought to bear on the perverse "practical religion" of American society. As Blum explains, "By juxtaposing the historical poor and oppressed Jesus against modern-day conceptions of Christ as Anglo-Saxon, and by connecting the violence committed against Jesus with that against other minority groups, Du Bois provided yet another example of his challenge to the spiritual wage of whiteness and his efforts to redeem men and women of color."²⁸ He drew parallels between the lot of poor, Galilean Jews and the enslaved and otherwise oppressed African Americans, maintaining that the poor and meek were those blessed by the nearness of God—running out ahead of liberation theologies in expressing a preferential option for the poor.

In both streams—the poetic-figurative and the medical-psychological—the path to resolving the felt problem of double consciousness is seen as one of anguish, given the difficulty of structurally integrating one consistent consciousness.[29] "Du Bois obviously did not break from such a treatment. For him the essence of double consciousness was its problematic character as a symptom of the difficulty that lay in the realization of any true self-consciousness, of any sense of self beyond the problematic sense conveyed in the dilemma as such."[30] Instructively, James "had speculated on the possibility of a real cure for alternating consciousness involving not the victory of one over the other but a process whereby 'the dissociated systems came together,' resulting in a third, new Self, 'different from the other two, but knowing their objects together.'"[31] Du Bois had studied under James at Harvard, so there is little surprise that he inherited something of James's speculation, looking for the African American "to merge his double self into a better and truer self" without losing either of the old selves.[32] Below we will see how these speculations have come to fruition in contemporary theories about the multiplicity of self-representations and the complexity of one's self-concept.

CURRENT DISCOURSES IN PSYCHOLOGY

As psychological conceptuality catches up with the sociological realities that Du Bois began mapping, his take on double consciousness as a gift of sorts to those forced into hybridic identities seems to be vindicated. In fact, while more clearly delineating what counts as pathological, the discourse has created more room for understanding the sense in which human identity and self-consciousness are normally plural. Current psychological theories of the self hold not *self-plurality* (or multiplicity) but *self-fragmentation* (or dissociation) alone to be pathological.[33] To this end, Léon Turner, a researcher at the intersection of theology and human sciences, traces a structurally "unified" self through major theological projects and criticizes their most articulate forms for making selective use of psychological vocabularies without due (or any) consideration of conceptual advances in psychology.[34] He argues that an improved cross-disciplinary conversation would prove fruitful for theology without threatening the variety of selfhood that remains important to Christian theology. So, with Turner's work as a guide in this section, I will chart some of this theologically significant terrain in the psychological realm.

Before exploring some specific psychological streams, I should briefly situate the "selfhood" language and conceptuality that will be vital to what follows. Terms like *self, person, ego,* and *identity* are notoriously slippery, lending themselves to idiosyncratic uses, a lack of clarity, and unstated assumptions—both among laypersons when these terms are used in nonscientific (or pseudoscientific) ways and across the hierarchy of sciences when disciplines develop in relative isolation.[35] For what follows, two sets of distinctions will become increasingly important. First, how our minds grasp, deal with, and structure self-relevant information, which occurs at and beneath the level of conscious awareness, can be distinguished from how we experience and make our selves in the course of our lives in the world. This is one way of putting the distinction between *representational* and *experiential* theories of the self. Second, we might distinguish between a person's sense or experience of selfhood over the course of time as they integrate the many episodes of human living and their sense or experience of selfhood at any given moment. Such is the distinction between *diachronic* and *synchronic* analyses of selfhood, respectively. While early modern psychology centered on fostering an integrated sense of selfhood over the course of a life (i.e., diachronic experiential singularity as a feature of the ego), late-modern/postmodern psychology has turned to investigate the plurality of selves fighting for expression at any one time (i.e., synchronic representational multiplicity). These more recent psychologies are also marked by a transition from dualist theories of human nature (like Kuyper's) to various physicalist ones, in which the self is understood not as "a single static essence or underlying substrate of being" but as a dynamic and multifarious system organically interlaced with, and not necessarily reducible to, a person's bodily life.[36]

Representational Theories of the Self

Cognitive psychologists have theorized about the structures for how people process, store, recall information—and put it to use—in numerous ways. Some examples include "scripts" to describe the event sequences of routine activities (borrowing language, for better or worse, from computer science) and "schemas" to represent how different kinds of knowledge are clustered and organized. Social psychologist Hazel Markus uses the more specific concept of *"self*-schemas" to illuminate how human minds organize ideas and feelings about themselves and the ways those structures in turn "guide the processing of self-related information contained in the individual's social experiences."[37] They are flexible, adaptive, and multilayered "dispositional structures" that (1) represent relationships between specific ideas and conceptions and (2) "direct and regulate self and behavioral processes. They develop as individuals attune themselves to their significant social contexts, and they provide solutions to important existential questions such as *who am I, what should I be doing, and how do I relate to others.*"[38] If an answer to these questions is to become self-definitional or "schematic"—meaning, it forms "a consistent pattern with the individual's other judgments, decisions, and actions"—then it must actually derive "from a well-articulated generalization about the self."[39] One need only think of their own childhood to grasp how some "selves" are relatively short-lived, but others endure as durative, meaning-making, and interpretive structures that lend coherence to life experiences.[40] Self-schemas are often apparent in a person's sense of identity (how they define themselves) and serve as the basis of their self-esteem, and some of the most significant ones will loom large in a person's memory, including examples or cases and practiced feelings toward these ways of defining the self.[41] Each of these self-representations has a particular history with(in) the individual, has certain feelings attached to it, is tied in with less self-specific information (e.g., self-as-Christian links into what one knows about theology), and is thus irreducible to the information it represents.

In a wealth of coauthored works, Markus advances and elaborates this theoretical self-structure, partly by developing and deciphering its empirical basis.[42] She works to predict how people deal with self-relevant information differently based on such self-schemas, looking specifically at whether they help subjects judge incoming information with relative ease, retrieve evidence for (i.e., justify) those judgments, predict their own future behavior on that basis, and resist counter-schematic feedback.[43] Social psychologists focused on self-multiplicity have sometimes illustrated their perspective with the image of a person with numerous social roles, "each of which entails the activation of situation- and role-specific schemata dedicated to the performance of particular behaviors."[44] Also, throwing back to object relations theory (at least for some theorists), close personal relationships are understood to have a particularly strong influence on self-representation as these persons are partially assimilated to the self.[45] Early in the development of self-schema theory, the test areas tended to reflect relatively bland self-representations (e.g., "self as a good student"), personality traits (e.g., conscientiousness, openness, and extraversion), characteristic adaptations (e.g., desires, aversions, coping mechanisms), and more or less stable motivational dispositions.[46] But theorists have gradually come to see self-schemas as underlying more contentious selves as well (e.g., "self as Christian" and "self as [African] American"). Given the relatively simplistic naming of these selves, I should note that a lot of specific ideas, memories, sensations, and feelings can be bundled with or otherwise tied to these selves. The very notion of a schema suggests a person mapping out connections with a schematic diagram.

Self-schema conceptuality could give us a handle on what contemporary social or political theory tends to conceive as discrete "identities," referring to our communities and other aggregate groups. "Every individual participates in a variety of significant sociocultural contexts that constitute the self. In the United States, these contexts might include specific collectives in addition to the nation of origin, such as the family or workgroup, as well as contexts defined by gender, ethnicity, race, religion, profession, social class, birth cohort, and sexual orientation."[47] In her work on cultures and selves, Markus keys on "how psychological processes may be implicitly and explicitly shaped by the worlds, contexts, or sociocultural systems that people inhabit."[48] To this point, Tiffany Brannon (who earned her doctorate under Markus) studies self-schemas as a way of understanding Du Bois's double consciousness—and the two-ness identified by others like Frantz Fanon and Ralph Ellison.[49] Thus, Brannon, Markus, and others have also undertaken empirical research to explore the cognitive impact of these sociocultural identities, including selves tied to various forms of the American identity, for instance, comparing racialized American identities.[50] Such self-schemas appear to provide additional (sometimes competing) solutions to those essential existential questions named above (i.e., who am I, what should I be doing, and how do I relate to others).

A plural self-system framework cuts against theories about the development, discovery, or implantation of *the* self (or a *true* self) even as it preserves a space for something like a *palingenetic* "new man."[51] The research suggests we should distinguish between (a) those self-schemas that are more or less grounded in social reality as past and present selves and (b) those possible selves that we desire (e.g., the successful self, the influential self, or the Christlike self) or dread (e.g., the impotent self, the lonely self, or the damned self).[52] While they differ from racial, gender, or other like varieties of self-knowledge, "possible selves" derive from "the individual's particular socio-cultural and historical context and from the models, images, and symbols provided by the media and by the individual's immediate social experiences."[53] The nature of these hopes and fears as *self*-representations suggests they are made unambiguously individual and personal, even if they have distinct social correspondences or counterparts. Importantly, they "are images of the person actually having achieved a goal, as such, they are both specific and personalized, qualities which may enable them to regulate behavior."[54] The hypothetical or idealistic nature of possible selves unfetters them from material constraints, that is to say, they need not be evident in a person's material life to shape that person's mental life.[55] In short, we may define possible selves as "the cognitive manifestation of enduring goals, aspirations, motives, fears, and threats" that represent both individual creativity in self-making and the effects of socialization (e.g., in generating ideals).[56]

As much as each human being is consistently one self (i.e., the same person) as they live and move in the world, every person's inner life also shifts based on numerous realities—ranging from whether we have eaten well to what has come up in our day so far and with whom we find ourselves at the moment. Markus and company use the term "working self-concept" to refer to the set of self-schemas that is presently active and operating, and thus lending "structure and coherence to the individual's self-relevant experience."[57] And this self-concept is "working" in a second sense, namely, that it is a revisable work-in-progress—"a continually active, shifting array of available self-knowledge" subject to any number of affective, motivational, and environmental conditions.[58] Even as multiple self-representations sometimes vie for expression (much like Du Bois narrated), it is also typical for some number of them to be more or less "offline" at any given moment. We can reasonably expect a consistent showing from that core bundle of selves within the "now-self" (i.e., "the self that is very much a part of the public domain") for a variety of reasons, including "invariances in social feedback, in the targets of social comparison provided by the environment, or a result of individuals' needs to present themselves in a consistent fashion."[59] And this starts to touch on the storied nature of what Drew Westen identifies with the self-*theory*: "the prototypic, generalized representation of self that most people verbalize when asked to do so."[60] A healthy self-theory will basically comport with the way others would describe the person, and one can hope their self-theory is "accurate, useful, logical, and parsimonious, although it is [still] subject to several cognitive and motivational biases."[61] But any working self-concept, now-self, or prototypical self-theory can only be a constellation of selves that trades both in one's historical thinking-feeling-behaving and in one's current experience of who they are.

Westen vigorously and convincingly advocates for bringing the vital, experimentally derived resources of cognitive psychology into contact with psychoanalytical theories that emerge from clinical experience, not least a broader theory of personality.[62] Of particular interest to Westen is the question of motivation. While he affirms that self-schemas function as *perceptional* guides (i.e., people do, in fact, process information through them), Westen denies that these schemas directly motivate action. Considering the emotions that may be involved, for example, one may either pursue the potential pleasure of fulfilling, or seek to avoid the possible pain of failing to reach, any given possible self, ideal standard, or set-goal, which implies more inner activity than mere "cognitive processing."[63] Too many thinkers have naively assumed a particular kind of will (e.g., the supernatural goading of the Spirit, the desire to obey God, or even just knowing what is good) is the consistent basis of one's motivation (i.e., character), operating in the intuition-perception-cognition center with no hint that a more complex interaction may be taking place in one's innermost place where their "loves" (in Augustine's parlance)[64] are formed and ordered. In light of current psychological research, suffice it to say that we must ask better questions about the complexity involved in these elements, which are online and operative (whether the subject is conscious of them or not) as a person views and engages their surrounding world.

With Markus's work on possible selves active in his mind, Westen explains that self-schemas simply do not motivate action on their own. Cognitive or behavioral motivation around such self-representations involves a "cognitive-evaluative mismatch" that moves someone in proportion to the emotional investment or the affective "charge" associated with an ideal self-schema or a dreaded one.[65] So, a person's thoughts and behavior depend on the nature and depth of the feeling they get when noticing the difference between who they are and who they (do not) want to be and as they anticipate attaining (or avoiding) a possible self. "Wishes are mismatches between desired and cognized states; fears are mismatches between undesired and cognized (usually potential) states."[66] For example, the perception that one has acted immorally (i.e., a mismatch between a cognized self-representation and an ideal one) might tap some central elements in the self-system and produce more intense affective reactions. Yet what precisely the person does with this motivation depends heavily on their character, which includes coping and defense mechanisms.[67] Not all motivation is motivation to know, to be, or to do *better*. Since the overall cognitive process also involves structuring information about *others* and groups of others, these other-schemas may also have desired or feared schemas that tie into the same goals, values, and ideals as the subject's possible selves.[68] Moreover, cognitive-evaluative mismatches vis-à-vis others can activate motivational processes that will depend on character, much like intrapersonal motivational processes.

Bringing clinical perspectives into the picture complexifies the self-theory in some other crucial ways as well. Westen calls attention to the unconscious nature of most cognitive processing, which means some active self-schemas will be unavailable for scrutiny by the conscious mind. Furthermore, "conscious and unconscious working representations need not be similar and . . . can be polar opposites," and even the "unconscious working representations active at a given time are also likely to be diverse and contradictory."[69] Emphasis on the unconscious becomes particularly important when considering the many possible discrepancies between the working self-concept and whatever a person verbalizes or even consciously accesses as a self-theory. For instance, "the notion of self-enhancement motives may imply a view of conscious representations of self as transformed versions of unconscious representations that may be considerably more negative but are nonetheless active and play a role in creating their 'touched up' conscious derivatives."[70] So, self-report data may not be all that reliable. Moreover, Westen argues that given the emotional and motivational investment people have in themselves—their sense of self—self-reports "about self-relevant information are probably the least to be trusted in all of psychology."[71] Apart from the issues of self-enhancement, he also argues that self-reflection and introspection are unlikely routes for people to consciously access all that is going on in their

A Contemporary Psychological Discussion of Selfhood 83

cognitive-schematic processes anyway, as a matter of both motivation and cognition. Psychoanalytic theory provides the helpfully messy conceptuality of "compromise formations," each of which is "a psychological process or product (typically a thought, behavior, or pattern of functioning) that reflects a compromise among several psychological processes, particularly wishes, fears, affects, defenses, and efforts at veridical information processing."[72] Such compromises certainly have something to do with self-schemas, which Westen describes as affectively charged to varying degrees and not infrequently in conflict with each other at an unconscious level. At the bottom, the complexities of human personality are not only cognitively schematized; some number of personality elements are always online, operating unconsciously, and thus affecting what a person reveals about themselves in the lab, in the clinic, and in the wider world.

All this complexity, with all its liabilities, is directly linked into the space of world-views in Westen's wider imagination. He hopes to see both psychoanalysts and cognitive psychologists expand their working theories by thinking more critically and more comprehensively. Probing the philosophy of science, Westen sets his sights on how a broad-ranging theory (in a very loose sense of the word) fills out the psychological profile in a full-orbed world-view.

> The theoretical superstructures or paradigms from which specific hypotheses are derived are not, themselves, strictly speaking, empirical, yet they are the wellspring of the questions that scientists even think to ask and the hypotheses they test. Paradigms (or more broadly, "perspectives," in fields such as psychology, which are still preparadigmatic in the Kuhnian sense) are intricate intellectual garments or tapestries, woven with a delicate blend of conjecture, inference, and data.[73]

I see here a striking resemblance to Kuyper's approach to the intuitive faith-function of the soul relative to the "spiritual sciences." And Westen exhibits additional parallels as he continues:

> Between the context of discovery, in which the scientist is playfully observing and forming hypotheses, and the context of justification, in which he or she is submitting these to empirical test, is a context of committed belief, that is, a schematic structure, partially collective and partially idiosyncratic, that the scientist uses to understand reality, to generate hypotheses, and to evaluate rival hypotheses and research.[74]

Importantly, scientific beliefs are like other products of the human mind in that they are compromise formations and can be self-definitional. To apprehend most psychological events—including the theories produced by even the best and most self-aware thinkers—"requires an understanding of the way multiple motives are synthesized (efforts at self-presentation as both decent and intelligent, protection of professional identity and valued beliefs, expression of aggression related to petty rivalries, etc.), consciously and unconsciously, to produce a response."[75] This assessment heavily implicates those beliefs and convictions that are affectively charged to a high degree by their schematization with cherished, highly elaborated self-representations (e.g., who I am professionally) constellated in our prototypical self-concept.

Distinguishing Healthy Multiplicity from the Pathological

Although the pluralization of self-theories is a relatively recent development, some degree of multiplicity is now widely understood as a psychological *given* outside of theological discourses. It is no mere figment of the current, prevailing social climate, and admitting this does not mean giving way to radical rejections of self-stability.[76] Instead, I hope it can prompt serious theological and moral reflection on the sources of self-stability in human lives characterized by the inner complexity named above. If there is no *structural* unity to the individual's cognition except that the individual has but one body, one mind, one *being*, then many conceptions of human identity are too fixed to use in thinking about concrete persons whose daily lives require a certain plasticity. There is bound to be some muddiness around the language of structural unity, singularity, and the like. But I hope to make clear: there is no intuitive space in the human mind that is so deeply unified, so single in its origin and direction, as to be immune to the ongoing influence of numerous cognitive-affective structures that might rightly be described as "identities." Many self-representations play into our working self-concept, so even if one's most cherished self-schema is an ideal *self-totally-identified-with-one-commitment* (i.e., as a Christian), it will descriptively always be in constellation with others—some operating at an unconscious level and even chronically unbeknownst and inaccessible to the ego. We would land nearer the mark if we saw that a number of self-representations codevelop over time and constellate in the prototypical self-theory, which is what we tend to express when we reveal ourselves to others. Some self-schemas are more used than others (we might call them *core* or *chronic* self-schemas), but there is no single, unchanging core or true *self*.

Returning for a moment to the double consciousness of Du Bois's analysis, I contend that while an experience punctuated by forced changes from one working self-concept into another truncated, other-selected self-concept is indeed a social-psychological pathology, the more basic reality of multiplicity can reflect psychological health and even promote resilience. This is not to downplay the harm of having one's state of consciousness and self-actualization scuttled, but these generally represent something more like subpersonalities, which can be painful when disunified, rather than whole discrete personalities, as in dissociative identity disorder. Contemporary theory represents further developments in the conversation about how one can be conscious of multiple different, even warring, inheritances. Those who become aware of their multiplicity can be quite distressed by it, sometimes taking it in at an unconscious level and dealing with it by way of self-deceit. It is hard to realize that you are more than just the one thing—because the world-view feels like one thing—but realize it you may, and then you have to deal with it or drive it down. What Fanon would argue is pathological about this twoness is the way others determine the self and hamper one's agency and the accompanying sense of nonbeing.[77] Moreover, and cutting the other way, the privilege of mythical normativity experienced by white heterosexual male Americans entails being (mostly) unknowingly buffered from this experiential punctuation, facilitating an unhealthy experience of self-unity and the projection of a false self- and other-defining integrity—all of which are defining features of whiteness. As such, the speculation that double consciousness may be resolved into a new self-identity that integrates the others turns out to be a step in the right direction, but mental health on either side of this problem does not mean unhindered, singular experience or being able to define yourself without social input.

Across the growing body of research on possible selves, theories point to their potential as devices for self-growth but also for self-*deception*. Possible selves can function as "incentives for future behavior (i.e., they are selves to be approached or avoided)" and as additional evaluative, hermeneutic, or meaning-making structures for the experiencing subject.[78] The Christian moralist rightly sees the motivation for growth facilitated by an ideal "self as a faithful follower of Jesus" that engenders continuous repentance whenever it is online in the working self-concept.[79] But the preceding discussion (including the case of Abraham Kuyper) must also be read to caution against naively overidentifying a *desired* self with the whole working self-concept or even with one's well-articulated religious self-schema. We must recognize that "an unrealistic conception of the self in a particular domain, or a failure to consider the targeted behavioral domain as centrally self-defining, can have important consequences on a person's ability to initiate and sustain the desired behaviors."[80] Bear in mind Markus's predictions for individuals' behavior relative to self-schemas: they will resist feedback that indicates they are not who they think they are. And, as Westen adds, they may be motivated (even if unconsciously) to avoid the pain of cognitive-evaluative mismatches.[81] This avoidance can manifest in a number of predictable behaviors, including (1) attempts to enlist others to validate the ideal self as the now-self (e.g., "I belong" or "I am Christlike" or "I hold the biblical world-view"), (2) an unwillingness or inability to confess transgressions of this ideal, and (3) a higher likelihood of relying on external signs and symbols to bolster this self-image.[82] Add into this mix the strength of one's commitment to certain possible selves—for instance, the lofty ideal self of one's real or imagined faith community—and we have a recipe for both self-deception and, over time, the disfigurement of genuine community.

While the term "multiplicity" is scarcely used to indicate pathology in psychological discourse, for too many Christian thinkers it seems to connote "duplicity" and a lack of integrity. Certainly, Kuyper would have resisted the suggestion that we carry multiple self-representations, for he gainsaid even the playful manyness of actors taking on different characters as a regrettable "moral sacrifice" because "the constant and ever-changing presentation of the character of another person" ultimately hinders the development of personal character.[83] But research is showing that persons who understand themselves to be complex (i.e., "have a complex self-theory") demonstrate an improved ability to weather criticism of any particular self-schema. "Failure in a single self-domain does not imply failure in all domains. Complexity thus permits maintenance of positive self-esteem despite specific failures."[84] And the opposite is also true; consistently monitoring successes to the exclusion of failures relative to well-articulated self-representations actually decreases one's performance.[85] So, a degree of counter-schematic feedback becomes crucial for growth within any given self-schema—awareness of a mismatch can motivate the process of change and growth not only in behavior but also in one's self-concept (i.e., in a clinical context).[86] The more complex we know ourselves to be, the greater the likelihood we will be able to receive and integrate self-critical information. Personal criticism can then be perceived not as an attack on the one identity we believe ourselves to be at the core (my *true* self, my *total* world-view) but as addressed to one element in our confident, plural self-concept. And looking outward, a plural self-concept might helpfully figure into a world that is increasingly aware of not only its pluralism but also the social problems that arise in the consolidation of power in certain uncritical identity constellations, and it could contribute to the decolonization of psychological theory—not least within theological anthropologies—and to the dislocation of whiteness and the relocation of persons in their places and times.

Moreover, one might identify a kind of pathology in the unquestioned structural integrity of the self among those who live through privileged, normative status (e.g., as a white heterosexual male American), especially when their self-theory is conceived under a single salient identity (e.g., evangelical). Quite contrary to normative Christian expectations, Turner explains, "What begin as distinct sub-personalities may nevertheless become pathological when they become the sole focus of a person's life."[87] He refutes any unified central processing unit and argues that no self-schema achieves independence or rises to become a supreme leader; they own each other.[88] In one sense, this confirms Christian expectations: idolatry, as typically conceived, is a unified focus on one creaturely aspect of life or another; but in another sense, this disconfirms the proposed solution: not even God's indwelling presence irresistibly (re)orients all of our imaginings and strivings toward the kingdom. While we can and should interpret human sin through this self-plurality, we must resist identifying sin with this self-plurality. This mistake paradoxically and invariably entangles the Christian in an unrepresentatively (i.e., self-deceptively) unified self-concept. Misplacing the concreteness of a confessed unity in one's prototypic self-concept offers us too much confidence in our inner unity and leaves us less open to the ways the world, others, and even our selves do not conform to our neat ideals; in fact, it can even motivate us to avoid acknowledging this sometimes painful reality.

An Experiential Theory of the Self

Questions about how the prototypic self-concept functions in our lives even as our minds are comprised by many various and sometimes conflictive strands for self-definition lead us to look at experiential theories of the self. In our experience of our lives, "diachronic singularity" continues to be a basic presupposition of mental health. People can and often do tell stories to connect their distinct and sometimes disparate senses of self they experience over time—like when their cognitive patterns shifted or when their character changed for better or worse. The basis of narrative identity theory is neither a structural unity of the self with all the pieces fitting nicely together like a jigsaw puzzle nor the consistent possession of a single, unchanging sense of who one is. Rather, the possibility that a person might narrate their own life-story is about their experience of being one person over time while living through many self-states. Defining mental health in this way provides an option between radical postmodern social constructionism (e.g., Zygmunt Bauman's image of the self as a palimpsest) and modern confidence in a stable, essentially unified sense of self (e.g., an abstract, idealist construct).[89] But it is worth noting from the start that whenever a person tells their story, they synthesize various self-representations into an autobiography that plays to the intended audience—a function of the working self-concept vis-à-vis the prototypic one.[90] This notion is consistent with what we have learned about current self-representation theory: any given telling of one's life-story will still only be one representation among many. The self-stories we tell offer insight into how we are *experiencing* life and especially how we *construct meaning* out of our life-materials; but as unifying structures, stories also tend to conceal the impact and misfit of important self-schemas by sublimating any discord.[91] And these conclusions directly bear on the way influential theologians like Kuyper understand themselves and depersonalize their own thought-worlds as archetypes for everyone else.

Marking the difference between representational and experiential approaches to personal identity, developmental psychologist Dan P. McAdams argues, "Knowing something about [a person's] life story may give you no more than a weak clue as to what her actions will be. If you want to predict her behavior, you would do better to know her traits. But if you want to know how she makes sense of her life, you had better know her story."[92] He uses a variety of language to name a person's life-narrative, including the poorly termed "personal myth." McAdams's intention is not dismissive, as this phrase might imply; rather, he is highlighting the relationship between *history* understood as an objective account of what really happened and the *stories* people tell to make meaning of their lives—these are "the stories we live by," according to his popular book's title.[93] Current conversations in many domains, including theology and psychology, center on the central role of story in human life. Yet while theological ethicists are concerned with the extent to which a person can and does live into the idealized story of their faith tradition, psychologists focus more on the extent to which a person *is* the stories they tell about themselves. According to McAdams, the ongoing activity of self-narration is a matter of "psychological and social *responsibility*" in a world that "can no longer tell us who we are and how we should live."[94] As meaning-making devices, myths play a more aesthetic or poetic role in the course of human living, and we need not be fully cognizant of our personal myths to be living by them.[95]

Marking some important boundary lines between psychological theories of self and narrative theology as a method, Turner expressly warns that we must distinguish between personal myths and communal narrative traditions.[96] This concern owes partly to the way communal narratives are commonly packaged together in our social worlds (as part II will study more closely), individuals actually draw from multiple traditions in narratizing their own lives. Some self-schemas might correspond to schematized knowledge of one's faith tradition, personalizing and internalizing official, communally held (hi)stories, but those shared (hi)stories themselves are *not* in the foreground here. Further, we must note some tension between individual creativity in meaning-making, the impact of socialization, and a particular community's life together. We tell personal narratives that reveal our identities to be of a different sort than "objective replays of the past. Research in cognitive psychology shows conclusively that episodic memory is highly selective. . . . To a certain extent, we *make* our stories. Within limits, we *decide* who we are, who we were, and who we may become."[97] However, we do not begin to narrate a self ex nihilo.

We each tell our story with language and imagery made available within the working self-concept and the social relations that contribute to it. And a fair amount of rhetorical smoothing and self-service can transpire as we bring the prototypical self-concept and idealized communal narratives—like the biblical world-view or, in other words, "the Great Story"—to expression.

Connecting with Markus's possible selves, McAdams explains how a variety of self-representations "give voice to individual and cultural values" and even "personify those beliefs and standards that society as a whole (or a significant segment of society) holds in greatest esteem."[98] These personified images of the self, which he calls "imagoes," are neither people in themselves nor a person's whole storied identity, but they include aspects of many internalized others and may be modeled on particular figures in our lives (positive and negative).[99] Yet considering what these imagoes contribute to a coherent narrative of who one is or what one is doing with their life, McAdams notes, "As we seek to become many different things, we appear to be pulled in the opposite direction as well, to become one thing upon which, as William James once put it, 'we can stake our salvation.'"[100] Westen refers to identity as "the most complex amalgam of self-elements," given that it

> includes this subjective sense of self, particularly the sense of continuity over time, as well as several other features: an integrated self-concept, an investment in standards and goals that make life meaningful, a weighting of the importance to oneself of various aspects of self, meaningful efforts to actualize one's ideal self-representations, a commitment to a worldview, and some recognition by the social milieu that one is indeed who one thinks one is.[101]

Corresponding with the working self-concept, the process of narratizing one's self is an ongoing process—the person is never *just* born (or born again).[102] Because unity is a predominant cultural value—strongly suggesting that we narratize our multiplicity into a coherent, diachronically singular whole— "integrating and making peace among conflicting imagoes in one's personal myth is a hallmark of mature identity in the middle-adult years."[103] But this process, Turner tells us, "does not structurally unify self-representations into a coherent whole or unify senses of self from moment to moment"[104]; rather, narrative coherence depends on the "systematic interpenetration of the various possible life-stories."[105] As such, a self-story may yet reveal the tension among various social roles, schematized expectations, and motivational dispositions.

Though I am more interested in describing adults in this chapter, some sense of the developmental theory behind narrative identity may prove helpful. We are not born storytellers. Apt as the binomen *Homo narrans* may be for contemporary persons, the mental capacity for appreciating and telling a good story develops in the course of life against the backdrop of other ways of seeing and reasoning. According to McAdams, a "narrative tone" emerges during the first two years of life as a child integrates feedback into their intentional pursuits, establishing "an unconscious, pervasive, and 'enduring belief' concerning the extent to which wishes, intentions, desires, and dreams are 'attainable.'"[106] Children then begin to thematize human intentions and develop motivational dispositions—McAdams points especially to the competition between the two great themes of power or agency and love or communion.[107] Themes and motives are the stuff of our earliest short stories and become constituent elements in narrative identities, and changes in our motives over time can correspond to identity changes.[108] Identity first emerges as a task in adolescence, as one "notices incongruities between who he or she was at one time and who he or she is now."[109] These years see the ebb of narrative modes of thought (with their moral and ideological ambiguity) and the flow of "paradigmatic" pursuits (à la Jerome Bruner)—the search for "Truth."[110] As such, one of an adolescent's primary feats is consolidating an "ideological setting" that provides "a backdrop of belief and value upon which the plot of [one's] particular life story can unfold."[111]

This stage of development should give the theologian pause. McAdams invokes Erik Erikson's famous exploration of Martin Luther's "identity crisis" to introduce the ideological setting. Given the interconnections with the world-view concept, Erikson is worth quoting at length here:

> We will call what young people in their teens and early twenties look for in religion and other dogmatic systems *ideology*. At the most it is a militant system with uniformed members and uniform goals; at the least, it is a "way of life," or what the Germans call *Weltanschauung*, a world-view which is consonant with existing theory, available knowledge, and common sense, and yet is significantly more: a utopian outlook, a cosmic mood, or a doctrinal logic, all shared as self-evident beyond any need for demonstration.[112]

In these terms, we might see how Luther's Reformation resulted in the disunion of a broad, societal world-viewing consensus and how it, thus, triggered the ascendance of personal identity as a matter of serious deliberation, especially for the well-educated.[113] McAdams claims that ideology functions as the grammar of identity-speech. We can scarcely say who we are without reference to "what I believe to be true and good, false and evil about the world in which I live," including "that the universe works in a certain way, and that certain things about the world, about society, about God, about the ultimate reality of life, are true."[114] To say that we "consolidate" such beliefs into an ideology is to recognize the variety of influences pushing and pulling on an individual as they explore and learn about the world into which history has thrown them.

What normally feels to the individual like a single, coherent world-view derives from a constellation of numerous (self-)schematized sets of knowledge, conviction-sets, and compromise formations. "We come to understandings about truth, beauty, and goodness through conversations with friends and family, in classrooms, playgrounds, and workplaces," McAdams writes. "Very few of us go off to the mountains for three years to figure it all out by ourselves."[115] And when we start to ask about the well-lived life, we set out to make our lives with many socially provided resources and forms. A person will find their world-view easier to generalize (and its assumed unity reinforced) as core conceptions are similarly schematized by significant others and more broadly shared in everyday social settings (this anticipates chapter 4).[116] In other words, the more time we spend with others whose personal myths share an ideological setting, the more the corresponding self-schemas underlying those stories will remain online and unchallenged at an intuitive level and, thus, feel like a coherent, shared world-view. Thus, the stories we live by can mask even the possibility of tension in motives and directions in life while packaging up all of our ideas, no matter their source, as a singular world-view that manifestly represents our most vaunted tradition(s). Recognizing the liabilities of this situation tempts one to fall back on one's conscious intentions, but this recourse can only take us so far in the direction of repentance and growth in Christlikeness, of genuine communion with diverse others.

When he analyzes the personal myths of Americans who most nearly resemble the cultural ideal of the highly generative, "redemptive self," McAdams provides a poignant example of the limited self-descriptive potential of intentions vis-à-vis concrete human lives. But to access this example, I must briefly review his theoretical framework for this particular genre of personal myths. To start, he defines "generativity" (after Erikson) as "an adult's concern for and commitment to promoting the well-being of future generations" and as "a broad category that includes many things we adults do and feel as we strive, consciously and unconsciously, to pass on to posterity some aspect of our selves."[117] And McAdams defines redemption as "a deliverance from suffering to a better world" (casting the notion in more general and material terms than many evangelicals would).[118] He expands, "Redemptive stories are not simply happy stories; rather, they are stories of suffering and negativity that turn positive in the end."[119] The conventional, American "rags to riches" story is an easy example here. Experientially, living out such a hero-myth plays well for both the individual and society: for the individual, this trope provides a way of making sense and creating meaning (even if not happiness); for society, those who live the grand societal narratives support and advance the prevailing generative agenda and thus reinscribe those sociocultural narratives.[120]

Now we might be equipped to see the example. McAdams confesses his surprise that high generativity also corresponds with *low degrees of self-reflection* regarding the unity and coherence of one's own ideological setting—or what we might call their "world-view," if qualified by the arguments above. Highly generative Americans "believe that their values are clear, consistent, and coherent and have pretty much always been so," and this "even though they tolerate others' points of view."[121] McAdams does not suggest these Americans "are any more narrow-minded, dogmatic, or arrogant" than others; rather, he claims, they tell life-stories featuring a lead character who has been chosen for goodness and who is steadfast and confident, which does not require frequent, depth-oriented introspection or even openness to the disconfirming feedback of others.[122] Nor does he believe these Americans do not grow or learn (and I insist that the Christian must always hold out that hope). McAdams does say, however, that self-evaluation and thus perceived growth normally occur *within* one's ideological setting and *without* considerable reflection upon or adjustment to that setting.[123] In other words, we gauge our own transgressions (or progress toward sanctification) against this backdrop, such that any sense that one has been or done something wrong will likely implicate the self with reference to already-held beliefs rather than implicating the schematized knowledge itself as problematic or sinful.[124] And we evaluate the faults of others similarly, often with gut-level approval or revulsion.[125] Applying this directly within my project, I might point out that highly generative theologians like Kuyper are not immune to any piece of this evaluation, and the theologies they offer from within their own world-views could even signal where this evaluation touches the ground.

CONCLUSIONS ABOUT WORLD-VIEWING SELVES IN VIEW OF KUYPER

I understand the temptation of Kuyper's contemporary disciples to terminate the troubles of white supremacy and colonial ambition in a sociopolitical criticism of the way his time afflicted the details of his view. And for a similar reason, we would do better to describe Kuyper's labors to depersonalize his own world-view and draw others into its meaning-making orbit with McAdams's theory of narrative identity and observations about generativity than Kuyper's own speculative account. McAdams does not expect highly generative individuals to spend much time deliberating upon their ideological setting. With his ideological setting consolidated, Kuyper was unlikely to question the details of his world-view as he brought the whole to expression—perhaps doubly so, given that much of Kuyper's generative work entailed putting his world-view out there. When he did reflect on these details, his express ambition was to demonstrate the logical coherence of his point of view and then make it appear as though he was merely stringing the harp of God's self-revelation. But the reality that Kuyper was so deeply wrong, so strongly convinced he was right, and did not think to look for hanging threads that might unravel what he inherited from and reinforced within his historical milieu is largely a matter of human psychology as it relates to epistemology—the branch of philosophy dealing with how we justify what we think we know.

Current psychological theory does provide some confirmation that the world-viewing impulse is, in fact, a "natural" human phenomenon, and the criticism that follows should not be read to suggest that narrating one's life-story or bringing one's world-view to expression are signs of pathology. I affirm these actions as reflections of mental health and acknowledge we have good cause to experience (or want to experience) our mental worlds as unified—not least those who have not enjoyed social status and instead experienced the jarring double consciousness that Du Bois narrates. But something like Hume's guillotine is in play here; accurately naming the situation does not yet tell us where we *ought* to go, especially as followers of Jesus. Human beings take in stories that are already compromised, we consolidate an ideological setting that lightens our cognitive load as we move through a complex world, and each of us otherwise has multiple convictional sources that fill out our minds. We make meaning through world-views and build community around and within world-views, but we also deceive ourselves into thinking we have a corner on truth in our view of the world. The many factors that play into our sense of self, the multiple motivations that drive our actions, and other such complexities should make us suspicious about the unity we feel between what we might narrate as our world-view (whether individually or as a group) and the fundaments of the universe itself. We may not know enough about where our thoughts have come from to really know the balance between the multiplicity in our minds and the compromises already made within specific self-schemas. For example, my strong, well-articulated notions of what it means to be an American could deeply impact my world-view alongside my faith, or I could have taken up my whole life a Christianity already compromised from the start, or both to some degree. In sum, what we describe as features of mental health for humans striving toward self-actualization may not indicate the moral trajectory of a person trying to uncover features of their cognitive landscape that prevent genuine communion with God and others.

What we might articulate as our personal world-view is equivalent to an ideological setting in narrative identity theory; it is the grammar one uses to tell their story and make sense of their life and its distinct episodes. And the pervasive cultural sense that the "texts" we produce by telling our stories or depersonalizing our world-views ought to be unified will, whether consciously or not, guide our cognitive process to produce a unified story when communicating with each other. In both storytelling and world-view casting, the subject draws from their many cognitive resources—as well as available social resources—to make meaning in life. And both speak to a person or group's convictions, motivations, and desires. An increasingly conscious attempt to draw together one's cognitive resources into something like a coherent world-view might result in a well-articulated self-representation that includes numerous convictions related to what it means to be and think like a Christian. That representation would descriptively be a compromise formation, but for his part, Kuyper was not particularly concerned with his knowledge having a single origin as long as it glittered in its capaciousness and, in the end, its biblical clarity. And once we have embraced the personal sense of security that comes with a solid world-view in a world of difference, we are likely to conceive of change and growth over time as filling out more of our world-view's details and living into that view more perfectly.

Even if we formally accede to the notion that we might be wrong about something, we may rest assured that we are thinking rightly and doing good, assume any errors will be trivial, and instinctively defend ourselves against counter-schematic feedback. Because Kuyper's omnicompetent, regenerate self is conceived, considered, and applied from within an individual's mental world where an abstract concept like the radical antithesis can seem rather clear-cut, impressions of one's own thought-world coherence and the unity of one's knowledge, its sources, and other cognitive elements can pass untested. And leading *wrongologist* Kathryn Schulz has observed, being wrong feels like being right. She describes the problem by analogy with the Looney Tunes coyote that regularly chases a roadrunner right off a cliff. The bird can fly, of course, but

> what's funny—at least if you're six years old—is that the coyote's totally fine too. He just keeps running—right up until the moment that he looks down and realizes that he's in mid-air. That's when he falls. When we're wrong about something—not when we realize it, but before that—we're like that coyote after he's gone off the cliff and before he looks down. You know, we're already wrong, we're already in trouble, but we feel like we're on solid ground.[126]

While Kuyper's approach to world-viewing has undeniable rhetorical force, the radical-antithetical construct of human beings in his own world-view— which paints one's position in the antithesis as the all-determinative quality of their identity and, ultimately, their world-view—fails to honestly describe any actual human beings, beginning with himself. Whatever is going on in the controlling center and cognitive life of a human person, it is consistently more complex than a concept like "world-view" could hope to describe. Better are contemporary psychological theories that map human cognition as land with peaks and valleys and weather systems, which together represent the relation of various sets of knowledge to affect, motivations, and character.

Another piece of this puzzle is the tension between modern Western ways of constructing an identity that assume individuals' independence in the identity-making process and more interdependent, social forms of identification like Du Bois saw in the idealized African consciousness.[127] Kuyper fixated on regeneration as a formal-structural change in the individual's psychology, setting the biblical world-view into motion on a restored pivot within a reunified cognitive center. He imagined that being born again reversed the formal impact of sin on human cognition (often referred to as sin's "noetic" effects), literally restoring the mind's original-creational functions—not changing one's natural gifts (geniuses arise on both sides of the antithesis) but restoring them to use for divine purposes. Or, in the case of folks raised within the church context as believers, one may chart continuous growth without ever noticing a dramatic change. In either case, knowledge and identity are bound up together, and practicing piety would draw the theologian into increasing affinity with the object of their studies (namely, God); high-grade regenerate thinkers like himself could improve the collective understanding that would be mediated to others who shared the same mind. Without the Hegelian overtones in twenty-first-century American thought, many simply see themselves as self-made—choosing their own identity configuration with clearheaded resolve—such that one knows what they are doing when they espouse the evangelical world-view. But is being born again formal changes to the structures and abilities in individual human minds? A new Christian will surely internalize and schematize new elements throughout their conversion process, somewhat consciously filling out ideas and feelings about Jesus, biblical knowledge, church connections, and self-as-follower-of-Jesus. This will also mean adding elements to their prototypical self-theory and increasingly (we may hope) one's working self-concept. However, being reborn is more like a change in affect, intention, and attention like one experiences at the start of a cherished relationship—one is made new by this great love. We narrate our lives with reference to a new reality, yet God and the church as God's people and the story of their relationship in time and space all remain bigger than us—drawing us story and all *into their orbit*. This is an ongoing, relational change with psychological ramifications. I do not underestimate the challenge of making this leap in our thinking, especially among white American evangelicals, because an emphasis on being and belonging in communion has not really been idealized in the omnicompetent individualist imagination.

Furthermore, openness to change in the context of relationships requires more (and more continuous) cognitive effort than grasping an objective standard and trying to apply it to oneself and others.

Inventorying our self-descriptions and the influence of other realities that we might prefer not to notice, we do better to honestly catalog our complexity and open questioning processes with self, others, and God to see where convictions may be wrongheaded. McAdams's research prompts a conversation about the impact of various sociocultural stories on our sense of self, including even how we evaluate qualities like healthy development, maturity, virtue, and generativity. Self-evaluative criteria like these are shaped by cultural assumptions—including subcultural influences like race, class, gender, and sexuality, among others—and applied in contextual (or sometimes plainly idiosyncratic) particular ways. For his part, McAdams is quite clear that we rarely call these concepts into question.[128] Kuyper was well aware of the "severely Dutch stamp" on his way of thinking—he expressed as much in his own English-language introduction to his *Encyclopedia of Sacred Theology*.[129] But he imagined many of his own historical particularities to gracefully cohere with the contours of the biblical world-view and the logical order of the universe itself. Thus, what he seemed to think he needed was sanctification, not enlightenment. Kuyper's personal sense of piety and normative social power afforded him the ability to be naive about the results of his logical action in a way that Du Bois simply could not be. He influenced the world through his ideas with an unearned sense of virtue that emerged from the reality that he was on top, in power. Before the concept of "virtue" was the Greek "arete," which meant moral perfection but also excellence more broadly. And Kuyper's hardly contestable excellence in his social context afforded him the assumption of his own virtue, his own logical thought world, his vocation of leadership. He experienced his life as pious, reasonable, unified (except maybe in moments of weakness), thus he could assume his world-view was unified, rational, biblical. And he could participate in the social evils and validate them because he shared the colonial mentality and believed intuitively in his own virtue as one who embodied not a problem but a world-transforming problem solver.

Kuyper's gesture toward a practice of piety—without further detail as to what this might look like and where/how one might receive rebuke or other corrective feedback at the level of understanding/world-view—could represent a symbolic route to closure. The juxtaposition of rigorous logical activity to test whether one's convictions fit together, on the one hand, and the pious sense of connection with the one true reality and its divine source, on the other, could result in a kind of false sense of security about what one believes—particularly when their convictions, even really bad ones, are widely shared in their local church. This is one reason mystification and vagueness around the enlightenment process are so problematic. Kuyper seemed to lack any awareness of the possibility that many motivations and other dynamics (e.g., power) operated within his own cognition or, further, that claims to faultless logic would conceal those factors rather than neatly explaining them. With an ideal self-as-unified-world-viewer representation of oneself operating not only within his working self-concept but as a *conscious filter* for what he thinks, Kuyper would be even less likely to notice when various sources of knowledge have come online to assist in and facilitate his interpretation of Scripture—to help him fill in the blanks where he might not have known anything otherwise. In fact, he might even be (unconsciously) motivated to bury them. Part of what is going on in the garden variety of epistemological idealism is a commitment to a mental world that is fundamentally truer and more determinative than the physical one we encounter. The Christian whose identity has been steeled in the contemporary *Weltanschauungskampf* tends to appreciate something like a biblical world-view as an adequate self-description of the most basic, the most influential, or even the only story they live by. The supposedly singular world-viewer will be more prone to resist counter-schematic feedback (e.g., "That is not a biblical view; it is racist, colonial garbage") and simultaneously prone to seek symbolic routes of closure—like enlisting others to affirm one's sense of self. We do not know our minds well enough to know what we need to repent of, and if we are not open to that possibility, what can we say for ourselves?

As we tug at this thread, we cannot help but notice that the unquestioned sense of self-normativity and unearned virtue among powerful white subjects are connected with the problematic notion of self-unity (i.e., the theological-anthropological principles) that facilitates self-deception. The assumption of unity and the lack of consciousness-doubling experiences are both very understandable under the social conditions many white Americans regularly experience. McAdams argues, "opportunities and identity resources are not distributed equally over the lifespan and across the socioeconomic and cultural spectrum. I repeat: In life and in myth, we cannot transcend our resources."[130] In this sense, we may be able to see a paradox in the wealthy, white, educated, heterosexual American (or Dutch, in Kuyper's case) male whose privileged life has scarcely occasioned any sense of double consciousness—any strong realization that a previously understated self-schema is, in fact, highly influential in their modus vivendi. This status often means both a richness in the ability to make a life as whoever one already imagines oneself to be and, ironically, a poverty of self-critical resources to tell one's story in relatively clear and all-encompassing knowledge of what one is doing.[131] With a better understanding of human cognition and personality based on current psychological research across several subdomains, we can see how naive and self-serving theological claims about formal cognitive differences between the regenerate and the rest promote self-flattery and perpetuate self-deception. Practicing seeing ourselves, as humans, as necessarily multifarious in terms of identity materials and influences can alert us to the likelihood of compromises in our most cherished identities, narratives, and overall worldview. This was certainly what Du Bois was hoping would happen as African Americans became aware that they did not belong the way they thought they might in white folk's materialist American dream. The African mentality—with its emphasis on interdependence and a deeper sense of religion—could prompt conversation about what passes as generally American without unseating a sense of hope and loyalty around that shared identity. Such a contrast would sound like "I have something to add here," not "I want to replace this with my own comprehensive vision."

In Du Bois's thinking, while double consciousness may have a recognizable place in the liberation process, it originates in the soul-harm of whiteness as an identity-defining structure. To be clear, the problematic consciousness of the two is the internalized whiteness of the African American, not the African spirit that arises within to confront the oppression. And also, to imagine any possible benefits, we must back away some from the variety of alternating consciousnesses that would be deemed pathological in a clinical setting. According to current clinical psychological discourse, there is no continuum between normal and pathological dissociation nor between normal and pathological experiences of self-plurality.[132] It bears attending to Du Bois's expressed concerns in making use of this conceptuality (e.g., an inferiority complex). He was also concerned that whiteness (marked by greed) would again prevail in the colonized mind even as degrees of freedom and prosperity were attained; for example, in the process of developing Black culture, leaders might be tempted to abandon their spiritual ideals and pursue money instead of righteousness.[133] And if Du Bois was right about the resolution of the kind of twoness he is naming, there is no guarantee as to how each individual will achieve a sense of self-integrity. Furthermore, as womanist theologian Eboni Marshall Turman has argued, myopic fixation on the color-line can allow the structures of the white gaze, which attempts to define others within the all-determinative reality of the powerful self, to be reproduced within communities of color on the basis of other social parameters (e.g., gender).[134] So, there are problems not only in its origin but also in the consciousness it can yield as a kind of reflection of the origin. I will be arguing throughout this project that the unquestioned structural integrity of one's consciousness—conceived under a single salient identity (e.g., evangelical)—in many white persons is, in itself, a kind of social-psychological pathology.

The world-viewing impulse and the attendant sense that its goal is attainable seem to drive people who assume their most basic loyalty is to God and their most basic identity is Christian toward a high degree of confidence in the world-view to which they adhere. Contemporary evangelical patterns of thinking and speaking have locked in a "unified self" concept, but I submit that evangelicals are poorly served by rhetoric and discipleship practices that lead them to overstate their desired selves of *single-minded* devotion as the actual stuff of the now-self (i.e., "I am a Christian and little else matters about how I see or engage the world"). While the healthy ego experiences life over time as a single person, we need to survey the distance between hoped-for possible selves (e.g., the single-minded devotion of Kuyper's *palingenetic* "new man") and the selves we are in real time. The Christian whose self-story centers on single-mindedly worshipping God is, at best, confessing their hope in a possible future that is true in some proleptic sense but remains materially unreliable and experientially in progress. Notwithstanding the genuine piety one may practice within such a view, to operate as if this were true about our mental lives is to risk a slothful lack of self-examination and an ongoing ignorance as to our ignorance. At worst, the overidentification of this singly desired self with a structurally unified self-concept conceals where a person has baptized whatever else is in their self-system and works to convince others of their truth. When we do turn to ask about where we come short of our ideal, we risk judging ourselves merely according to our own ideological setting—our own knowledge of good and evil—without openness to the possibility that our problems start with elements in our ideological setting itself. For some, being evangelical in twenty-first-century America has more or less come to mean *sinning within the right world-view*. I wager this is a key reason it has become so easy to look past the personal moral failings of leaders who champion the cherished world-view. Emphasizing conversion to a unified way of seeing the world, a person continues to be identified with the faith (i.e., seen as enlightened) even if they are routinely too weak to live into the ideal (i.e., as a matter of sanctification). If we become emotionally invested in a unified, world-viewing self-as-Christian, our "world-view" can become an idol that we worship, trust, and *defend* ahead of (or worse, instead of!) the living God who approaches us in our complexity with a mixture of comfort and confrontation.

PROSPECTS FOR A VIABLE THEOLOGY OF IDENTITY[135]

The problems I have flagged in part I should not produce a negative sentiment about human complexity or the status of plural selves in the eyes of God. For one thing, the good news spreads at the scale of real human lives, and the Christian's many facets can become angles for genuine human connection. More broadly, awareness of the multiplicity within can make us more resilient when we are drawn to question key self-defining ideas and identities even as it keeps us open to the reality that our many identities and self-representations compound the process of growth, making it uneven. Practicing self-awareness through a new self-conception that registers and even values, to some extent, the many facets of our identity can foster humility about our place within and enlightenment about a story that is much bigger than we are and help us embrace our radical contingency as creatures of God who exist in and through our relationships. Our various and sundry identities and self-representations do have their liabilities and dark regions, which may remain inaccessible to us until brought to light by genuine encounters with others who provide counter-schematic feedback. And while this may mean directly questioning certain beliefs tied into what we think of as a Christian world-view, it seems more likely that this will consist of becoming aware of the tension between elements of Jesus's teaching and our convictions and values that are rooted in other identities—other self-definitional cognitive schemas. All identities and social power axes are drawn into the disciple's following-after Jesus such that they become obstacles in their impenitence or instruments of the kingdom by way of their reorientation down to the details of their practice.

With this in mind, we should continue to consider and elaborate possible selves (i.e., dream about who we might become) on the understanding that these selves always and only operate in constellation with a number of other selves within us and typically at some distance from our working self-concept, that is to say, with appropriate humility. We need more guidance in mapping our inner lives than the "old man, new man" dichotomy provides. Jesus does not call us to imagine a new, better person or true self and then to struggle our way forward in actualizing that ideal as our end goal (or in continuous mourning at our failure to do so). Human beings are ever constellations of such persons, and we must recognize the inescapable and unpredictable impact this fact has on our perception, thinking, and behavior. As we are held in a relationship of grace, our faithfulness and progress are measured in relational terms: Are we attending to others' self-revelations (even counter-schematic ones) as reliable sources of knowledge? Earnestly looking for ways to grow? Adjusting our practice(s) for the good of others? The fullness of life is not a synonym for inner peace owing to a sense of self-unity relative to an abstract, universal sensibility of created perfection. God approaches us from beyond our selves and graciously draws us out of ourselves into a genuine unity—one that is never fully "haveable" but always securely held in the contingency of an ongoing relationship. As we will explore more directly in chapter 6, the heart of the image of God is not Kuyper's analogy of being that places the value on the human's unique consciousness; rather, it seems more likely that the proper analogy emphasizes the way we are held in this world by relationships—with God, with others, with the rest of creation. Our radical contingency is more than just an idea; it is the stuff of lived faith in a living God that invites us to recognize our ongoing self-plurality, be honest in the context of grace, relinquish control, and accept our weakness as the path to our security in Christ.

I will not pretend this kind of shift is either simple or easy. A lesson from Dietrich Bonhoeffer's *Discipleship* comes to mind. When he is unpacking Jesus's teaching on the hiddenness of prayer, he names the possibility that even in private, we can turn prayer into a performance. "It is even more harmful," Bonhoeffer maintains, "when I make myself the observer of my own prayer, when I pray before myself."[136] Our own ideas of what God expects of us, not least in terms of self-unity and single-minded devotion, can get in the way of our honest seeking after transformation, even in our own self-reflective time. We need more concrete strategies for practicing openness to the Holy Spirit and seeking continuous repentance—not least for those areas we remain not only ignorant but doggedly attached to ideas and ideals for which the kingdom of God is not the clearest source or goal. A certain kind of piety can exacerbate the problem, so part of this growth must be consciously working on getting our ideas of God and God's will for us out of the way so that we might fully live. In Kuyper, we saw vague piety focused on God's sovereignty and a lofty ideal supposed to motivate Calvinist virtue, but this was all wrapped up in real vice amid the assumed virtue of whiteness. Part of what it means to be in relationship with Jesus and, further, in communion with that diverse body of folks who have been called out by God to be church together is to be drawn into a grace-bathed space where identities and commitments can safely be reexamined and questioned without threatening one's sense of belonging.

So, the real starting point, if we are prioritizing matters in good evangelical fashion, is inviting a fresh encounter with the Jesus we meet in the gospels so that we might hear personally the call to follow, to move from the place we are currently standing in, and, if we dare, to discover where we are called to die and live next. When considering new life in a person who has come to know and follow Jesus, we can imagine how (a) a new, ongoing relationship fosters openness to the influence of an "other"; (b) one might partially internalize this other person in reference to ideals and goals, but also as someone whose makes us a responsible agent in view of their needs or desires; (c) a corresponding *self*-schema might idealize a prediction of "self as Christlike"; and (d) all of this contributes to the working self-concept and to the prototypical self-story. But Christians tend to get ahead of themselves in thinking they understand who Jesus is and what he is about, taking on his example in their lives to the extent that they can, and engaging others in and through a new set of lenses—serving the poor, for instance, or otherwise helping the disadvantaged. The risen Jesus, however, enters into the lives of would-be contemporary followers in much the same way he did with the first disciples. As such, no one can start out thinking they can rightly identify Jesus, however thick he may be. We can encounter him as one who speaks truth, be identified by him, and then seek to learn what we can in relationship. Jesus's call makes the same claim on all people in a limited sense, but his claim on each person or community is quite particular. We may identify (with) Jesus only as he shows/tells us here and now who he is, who we are, and who others are to us, that is, how we relate to ourselves and others, beginning with Jesus. Part of this "telling us who we are" entails the uncomfortable variety of self-revelation that would classify as counter-schematic feedback. Jesus encounters the priests and teachers of the law with the message, *You do not belong in the way you think.* Thus, the concept of consciousness-doubling (or more) in a somewhat confrontational way should not be surprising to those who have studied Jesus's interactions with the people around him.

Christian faith and witness do not center on the development and promulgation of a comprehensive world-view, and the solution to the world-viewing problem is not better world-viewing. When God entered the world in Jesus, he came not as the master world-viewer and not even as the conductor—like the classical world might expect—to whip us into shape. The incarnate God was and is a master player, joining us on the stage and beckoning us to respond, to learn rhythm and harmony so that our lives might reflect a truer counterpoint to God's melody.[137] Jesus embraces his embodied particularity (as opposed to sterile universality) to engage concrete persons, in a way that dignifies the oppressed and humbles the powerful. Jesus encounters all people with a certain love and affection; and meeting each person in their particularity and contingency, the good news he brings fits their need at the time, every time. For those whose daily experience, whose disposition and affect, are ostensibly enriched at the expense of these others, Jesus meets them with resistance, disrupting their comfortable patterns of knowing and transforming their social statuses into sites for kingdom work—humbling, even humiliating, the powerful who must turn their allegiances inside out. For those whose daily experience is often very near to death, who assert their dignity in the face of those who would deny it, Jesus affirms their dignity by joining them in solidarity (as in his own incarnation and death) and offers restoration: God is with you, in it, working on your behalf to redeem the mess and honor your dignity. Jesus's call is always a real-time, concrete ask of humans. And meeting us in our complexity, Jesus will undoubtedly deploy different moves or combinations of these moves over time. But Jesus does not exert control, even over his own identity before others; he uses what he has been given and exemplifies a faithful, creaturely life from within God's great composition that draws us all into its life. Moreover, as the central player, he introduces a new melody into the polyphony of our selfhood, such that we begin to properly arrange our lives and loves.

NOTES

1. Exceptions include some process and expressly postcolonial theologians doing more interesting work in this domain. See, for instance, Catherine Keller, *From a Broken Web: Separation, Sexism, and Self* (Boston: Beacon Press, 1986); and Laurel C. Schneider, *Beyond Monotheism: A Theology of Multiplicity* (New York: Routledge, 2008). But such explorations yet prefer philosophical and cultural theory discourses over psychological research.

If philosopher David Naugle represents the heights of evangelical worldview theory in recent years, as endorsers of his *Worldview: The History of a Concept* (Eerdmans, 2002) suggest, then it is telling that he does not choose even slightly interesting (or recent) psychological sources to fill out his interdisciplinary summary. Instead, he curates from Sigmund Freud and Carl Jung an affirmation of the worldview concept and its central function in human minds.

2. The Hegelian contours of Du Bois's approach to "race" are on full display in "The Conservation of Races," 1897, in *The Oxford W. E. B. Du Bois Reader*, ed. Eric J. Sundquist (New York: Oxford University Press, 1996), 38–47. That said, his perspective yields a different typology of world-views or civilizations than either Hegel or Kuyper (especially regarding African contributions), demonstrating not only some of the idiosyncrasies of such heuristic devices but also the absolutely unnecessary nature of some connections Kuyper makes within his own world-view. See also Du Bois, *Darkwater*, 1920, in Sundquist, *Du Bois Reader*, 484–85.

3. Edward J. Blum, *W. E. B. Du Bois: American Prophet* (Pittsburgh: University of Pennsylvania Press, 2007), 64.

4. W. E. B. Du Bois, *Darkwater*, 488.

5. W. E. B. Du Bois, *The Souls of Black Folk*, 1903, in Sundquist, *Du Bois Reader*, 101.

6. Du Bois, "Conservation," 43.

7. Cf. Blum, 7–8.

8. Cf. Blum, 15.

9. Blum, 16.

10. Blum, 103; cf. 108–9.

11. W. E. B. Du Bois, "The Souls of White Folk," *The Independent*, no. 69 (August 18, 1910): 342.

12. Wendell Berry, *The Hidden Wound* (New York: North Point Press, 1989).

13. Du Bois, *The Souls*, 106 and 147. Frantz Fanon, *Black Skin, White Masks*, 1952, trans. Richard Philcox (New York: Grove Press, 2008), ch. 4. Cf. Blum, 123; and Dickson D. Bruce Jr., "W. E. B. Du Bois and the Idea of Double Consciousness," *American Literature* 64, no. 2 (June 1992): 301.

14. Eric J. Sundquist, "Introduction: W. E. B. Du Bois and the Autobiography of Race," in Sundquist, *Du Bois Reader*, 14. Cf. Bruce, 299–300.

15. Bruce, 300–301.

16. On this point, and with the specific language of "a radical, transformative aesthetics," I was particularly impacted by a discussion at the Annual Meeting of the American Academy of Religion (San Diego, CA, November 2019) around the following papers to which Edward Blum responded: Mark S. Cladis, "Du Bois: The Poet-Sociologist," and Hannah Garvey, "The Form of the Color Line: Du Boisian Charts, Antiabsorption, and the Strange Meaning of Being Black."

17. Du Bois, *The Souls*, 102.

18. Bruce, 301.

19. G. W. F. Hegel, *Phenomenology of Spirit*, 1807, trans. A. V. Miller (New York: Oxford University Press, 1977), §207ff. To be clear, in keeping with my treatment of Hegel earlier in this project, he had not imagined any dark-skinned Africans as self-conscious in the first place.

20. Bruce, 303.

21. Bruce, 303. For the current clinical diagnostic criteria, see American Psychiatric Association, *Diagnostic and Statistical Manual of Mental Disorders: DSM-5* (Arlington, VA: American Psychiatric Association, 2013), 300.14. For a brief discussion of dissociative identity disorder in the context of healthy self-multiplicity, see Léon Turner, *Theology, Psychology, and the Plural Self* (Burlington, VT: Ashgate Publishing Company, 2008), 90–95.

22. Bruce, 304.

23. Bruce, 304–5.

24. Du Bois quoted in Blum, 101; cf. 126–31.

25. Du Bois, *Darkwater*, 512. Cf. Blum, 83 and 122–25.

26. Blum, 83–84.

27. Du Bois, "Conservation," 44. Cf. Blum, 63.

28. Blum, 126; cf. 139–40.

29. Bruce, 306.

30. Bruce, 306.

31. Bruce, 306. Quotations from William James, *The Principles of Psychology*, vol. 1 (New York: Henry Holt and Company, 1890), 399.

32. Du Bois, *The Souls*, 102.

33. See Pastoral theologian Pamela Cooper-White's good conversation about what is (not) pathological or normative regarding multiplicity in *Braided Selves: Collected Essays on Multiplicity, God, and Persons* (Eugene, OR: Cascade Books, 2011), ch. 8.

34. Turner, 36 and 45.

35. Turner, 67–71.

36. Turner, 77–78. Cf. Cooper-White, 196. For an introduction to the theological conversation around nonreductive physicalism, see Warren S. Brown, Nancey Murphy, and H. Newton Maloney, eds., *Whatever Happened to the Soul? Scientific and Theological Portraits of Human Nature* (Minneapolis: Fortress Press, 1998); in this volume, I find Ray Anderson's comments on "contingent monism" particularly interesting in light of chapter 6 in my project. On Kuyper's preference for dualism as a Calvinist trait, see his *Encyclopedia of Sacred Theology: Its Principles*, trans. and ed. by J. Hendrik de Vries (New York: Charles Scribner's Sons, 1898), §54.

37. Hazel Rose Markus, "Self-Schemata and Processing Information about the Self," *Journal of Personality and Social Psychology* 35, no. 2 (February 1977): 64.

38. Tiffany N. Brannon, Hazel Rose Markus, and Valerie Jones Taylor, "'Two Souls, Two Thoughts,' Two Self-Schemas: Double Consciousness Can Have Positive Academic Consequences for African Americans," *Journal of Personality and Social Psychology* 108, no. 4 (2015): 587. Cf. Turner, 79–80.

39. Markus, 65.

40. Turner, 79–80 and 85.

41. Karen Farchaus Stein and Hazel Rose Markus, "The Role of the Self in Behavioral Change," *Journal of Psychotherapy Integration* 6, no. 4 (December 1996): 351.

42. For the sake of readability, I will discuss these coauthored works in the main body of this chapter primarily with reference to Markus's name; the notes will do better to track and credit the several others who have worked these fields by her side.

43. Stein and Markus, 351.

44. Turner, 81–83.

45. Drew Westen, "The Cognitive Self and the Psychological Self: Can We Put Our Selves Together?" *Psychological Inquiry* 3, no. 1 (1992): 8.

46. Hazel Rose Markus and Shinobu Kitayama, "Culture and the Self: Implications for Cognition, Emotion, and Motivation," *Psychological Review* 98, no. 2 (April 1991): 226–27. Cf. Turner, 84.

47. Hazel Rose Markus and Shinobu Kitayama, "Cultures and Selves: A Cycle of Mutual Constitution," *Perspectives on Psychological Science* 5, no. 4 (July 2010): 423; cf. Markus and Kitayama, "Culture and the Self," 230n3.

48. Markus and Kitayama, "Cultures and Selves," 422. Later, Markus suggests that self-schematization is not totally confined to the beliefs and values "packed in the head of each individual member of the cultural group"; rather, "cultural beliefs and values—especially those that are important and, thus, have constituted each culture's practices, institutions, and its ways of life—are, by definition, inscribed into these practices, institutions, and ways of life" (Markus and Kitayama, "Cultures and Selves," 426).

49. As in the article cowritten with Markus and Taylor, which presents some of Brannon's dissertation research.

50. See, for instance, MarYam G. Hamedani, Hazel Rose Markus, and Alyssa S. Fu, "My Nation, My Self: Divergent Framings of America Influence American Selves," *Personality and Social Psychology Bulletin* 37, no. 3 (March 2011): 350–64.

51. Cooper-White helpfully delineates unified language like "core self," "nuclear self," and "true self," observing that each is connected with particular theorists and studies (i.e., their usage is frequently idiosyncratic) and that none of them were intended to function with the simplistic ring they have in the ears of laypersons (ch. 9).

52. Turner, 84. Cf. Westen, "The Cognitive Self," 4.

53. Hazel Rose Markus and Paula Nurius, "Possible Selves," *American Psychologist* 41, no. 9 (September 1986): 954–55. Cf. Hazel Rose Markus and Elissa

Wurf, "The Dynamic Self-Concept: A Social Psychological Perspective," *Annual Review of Psychology* 38, no. 1 (February 1987): 307.

54. Markus and Wurf, 321.
55. Cf. Cooper-White, 49.
56. Markus and Nurius, 954.
57. Markus and Nurius, 955. Cf. Stein and Markus, 350–51.
58. Markus and Nurius, 957. Cf. Markus and Wurf, 306 and 314ff.; Westen, "The Cognitive Self," 8; and Turner, 80.
59. Markus and Nurius, 964.
60. Westen, "The Cognitive Self," 7. The language of "self-theory" comes from Seymour Epstein, whose forerunning theoretical work is manifest in both Markus and Westen.
61. Westen, "The Cognitive Self," 3.
62. In the first two major sections of "The Cognitive Self," Westen provides a helpfully brief historical overview of developments in theoretical concepts of the self since the 1950s, including ample references to some of their most pivotal players and summaries of the clinical-observational or experimental-empirical basis for the various theories.
63. Drew Westen, *Self and Society: Narcissism, Collectivism, and the Development of Morals* (New York: Cambridge University Press, 1985), 111n1. Cf. Westen, "The Cognitive Self," 8.
64. I am thinking of Augustine, *City of God*, trans. Henry Bettenson (1972; repr. New York: Penguin Books, 2003), XV.22; and *On Christian Doctrine*, trans. J. F. Shaw (Mineola, NY: Dover Publications, Inc., 2009), I.27–28.
65. Westen, "The Cognitive Self," 8–10. Cf. Westen, *Self and Society*, 111n1.
66. Westen, "The Cognitive Self," 9.
67. Westen, *Self and Society*, 119 and 123–24.
68. Westen, "The Cognitive Self," 10.
69. Westen, "The Cognitive Self," 8.
70. Westen, "The Cognitive Self," 6
71. Westen, "The Cognitive Self," 6; cf. 11. Notice Westen confirming some elements in Kuyper's understanding of the (fallen) psyche and self-reporting—but without an escape hatch for those who also report being piously in tune with who God says they are.
72. Westen, "The Cognitive Self," 2.
73. Drew Westen, "Personality, Culture, and Science: Contexts for Understanding the Self," *Psychological Inquiry* 3, no. 1 (January 1992): 79.
74. Westen, "Personality, Culture," 79.
75. Westen, "Personality, Culture," 80.
76. Such rejections might range from David Hume, *A Treatise of Human Nature*, 1739–40, (repr., New York: Penguin Books, 1986), 1.4.6, to Kenneth J. Gergen, *The Saturated Self: Dilemmas of Identity in Contemporary Life* (1991; repr., New York: Basic Books, 2000).
77. Fanon, ch. 5.
78. Markus and Nurius, 955–56.

79. This research has implications for how we understand Christian conversion, that is, what it takes to adopt a new "Christian" self-schema and fill it out such that it becomes a vital and chronic core self. See indications in Westen, "The Cognitive Self," 9; Stein and Markus, 371 and 376–77; and Markus and Nurius, 963–64.
80. Stein and Markus, 372.
81. Cf. Markus and Kitayama, "Culture and the Self," 240.
82. Markus and Wurf, 322. Cf. "Another category of self-representations is *fantasied self-representations*. These are representations that the person knows are unrealistic but nevertheless manipulates to obtain pleasure or escape psychological pain" (Westen, "The Cognitive Self," 9).
83. Abraham Kuyper, *Calvinism: Six Stone Lectures* (Amsterdam: Höveker & Wormser Ltd., 1899), 92.
84. Westen, "The Cognitive Self," 4. Cf. Stein and Markus, 363; and Patricia W. Linville, "Self-Complexity and Affective Extremity: Don't Put All of Your Eggs in One Cognitive Basket," *Social Cognition* 3, no. 1 (1985): 94–120.
85. Markus and Wurf, 313–14.
86. Markus and Wurf, 303.
87. Turner, 117.
88. Turner, 110–11.
89. Cf. Turner, 99.
90. Turner, 108. Cf. Markus and Wurf, 316.
91. Turner, 102.
92. Dan P. McAdams, *The Redemptive Self: Stories Americans Live By*, Rev. ed. (New York: Oxford University Press, 2013), 284.
93. Dan P. McAdams, *The Stories We Live By: Personal Myths and the Making of the Self* (1993; repr., New York: The Guilford Press, 1997), 34; cf. 55.
94. McAdams, *Stories*, 35.
95. McAdams, *Stories*, 264; McAdams, *Redemptive*, 62–63. McAdams claims, "Although its intended function is to gather data on lives, our life-story interview may also serve to help people *identify* the personal myth that they have been *living* all along" (McAdams, *Stories*, 253).
96. Turner, 106–9. Turner is thinking here of narrative theologians (e.g., Hans Frei and George Lindbeck) as well as philosophers (e.g., Alasdair MacIntyre).
97. McAdams, *Redemptive*, 66.
98. McAdams, *Stories*, 128–29. "We select from competing stories, and we modify those stories we choose to fit our own unique life, guided by the unique circumstances of our social, political, and economic world; by our family backgrounds and educational experiences; and by the dispositional traits and characteristic adaptations that also make up our individuality. . . . *Self and culture come to terms with each other through narrative*" (McAdams, *Redemptive*, 285). Cf. Dan P. McAdams, "The Psychological Self as Actor, Agent, and Author," *Perspectives on Psychological Science* 8, no. 3 (May 2013): 284–86.
99. McAdams, *Stories*, 130–31.
100. McAdams, *Stories*, 117–22; cf. McAdams, *Redemptive*, 62.
101. Westen, "The Cognitive Self," 11.

102. Turner, 114. Cooper-White suggests, "To the extent that we can come to recognize some of the elements within [our own internal landscape], we can make choices about what makes the most mature sense to us" (22).
103. McAdams, *Stories*, 37; cf. 78–79. See also Turner, 113.
104. Turner, 114.
105. Turner, 117.
106. McAdams, *Stories*, 47.
107. McAdams, *Stories*, 68–73.
108. McAdams, *Stories*, 74–75.
109. McAdams, *Stories*, 76; cf. 78.
110. McAdams, *Stories*, 29; cf. McAdams, *Redemptive*, 56.
111. McAdams, *Stories*, 67.
112. Erik H. Erikson, *Young Man Luther: A Study in Psychoanalysis and History* (1958; repr., New York: W. W. Norton and Company, 1993), 41. Cf. McAdams, *Stories*, 81 and 179–86.
113. McAdams, *Stories*, 83–84. See here one version of declinist social criticism. Cf. McAdams, *Stories*, 187.
114. McAdams, *Stories*, 81.
115. McAdams, *Stories*, 84; cf. 82 and 165.
116. See the way Westen talks about political "master narratives" in *The Political Brain: The Role of Emotion in Deciding the Fate of the Nation* (2007; repr., New York: PublicAffairs, 2008), ch. 7. Cf. Jonathan Haidt, Jesse Graham, and Craig Joseph, "Above and Below Left-Right: Ideological Narratives and Moral Foundations," *Psychological Inquiry* 20, no. 2/3 (April 2009): 110–19.
117. McAdams, *Redemptive*, 31. Cf. Erik Erikson, *Identity and the Life Cycle* (New York: W. W. Norton and Company, 1959).
118. McAdams, *Redemptive*, xiv.
119. McAdams, *Redemptive*, 27.
120. McAdams, *Stories*, 265; cf. McAdams, *Redemptive*, 55–60.
121. McAdams, *Redemptive*, 136; cf. 125.
122. McAdams, *Redemptive*, 217–18.
123. McAdams, *Redemptive*, 139.
124. Cf. McAdams, *Redemptive*, 268.
125. Cf. Jonathan Haidt, "The Emotional Dog and Its Rational Tail: A Social Intuitionist Approach to Moral Judgment," *Psychological Review* 108, no. 4 (October 2001): 814–34.
126. Kathryn Schulz, "On Being Wrong," filmed March 2011 in Long Beach, CA, TED video, 17:36, https://www.ted.com/talks/kathryn_schulz_on_being_wrong.
127. Over time, Markus has contrasted elements of self-schema theory that focus on Western, individualist concepts of self with a more interdependent view of selfhood. See Hazel Rose Markus, "Who Am I? Race, Ethnicity, and Identity," in *Doing Race: 21 Essays for the 21st Century*, ed. Hazel Rose Markus and Paula M. L. Moya (New York: W. W. Norton & Company, 2010), 359–89; and Hazel Rose Markus and Alana Conner, *Clash!: How to Thrive in a Multicultural World* (2013; repr., New York: Plume, 2014).

128. McAdams, *Stories*, 96–97. Cf. McAdams, *Redemptive*, ch. 7.

129. Kuyper, *Encyclopedia*, ix. In fact, as he explains, "Being an enemy to abstractions, and a lover of the concreteness of representation, the author could not do anything else than write from the environment in which he lives." One can easily imagine why Kuyper, confident as he is in his folk's cultural supremacy, does not hesitate to embrace concreteness while also naming what he takes to be the defining features of creational order itself.

130. McAdams, *Stories*, 110. Cf. McAdams, "The Psychological Self," 288.

131. Cf. McAdams, *Redemptive*, 180–81.

132. Turner, 116.

133. Cf. Du Bois, *The Souls*, 142.

134. Follow Eboni Marshall Turman's argument from her analysis of Du Bois's "double consciousness" and "the Veil" (ch. 3) through her deconstruction of gender formation within the Black church (ch. 4) to the constructive/prospective conclusions (chs. 5–6) in *Toward a Womanist Ethic of Incarnation: Black Bodies, the Black Church, and the Council of Chalcedon* (New York: Palgrave Macmillan, 2013).

135. Some elements in this section appeared previously in Jacob Alan Cook, "Toward an Incarnational Theology of Identity," in *Justice and the Way of Jesus: Christian Ethics and the Incarnational Discipleship of Glen Stassen*, ed. David P. Gushee and Reggie L. Williams (Maryknoll: Orbis Books, 2020), ch. 2.

136. Dietrich Bonhoeffer, *Discipleship*, English ed., Dietrich Bonhoeffer Works (Minneapolis: Fortress Press, 2001), 4:153.

137. Here I am riffing on a concept Bonhoeffer was mulling in some of his letters from prison. For a sense of the meaning here, see Andreas Pangritz, *The Polyphony of Life: Bonhoeffer's Theology of Music*, ed. John W. de Gruchy and John Morris, trans. Robert Steiner (Eugene, OR: Cascade Books, 2019), chs. 5 and 7.

Part II

SOCIAL REVELATIONS

Chapter 3

The New Evangelical World-View of Harold Ockenga

"The kingdom of hell is at hand," prophesied pastor-scholar Harold John Ockenga in his 1943 presidential address to the newly formed NAE.[1] By that time, the threats beyond the United States' borders seemed clear to all: "On the decaying ruins of Western civilization have risen such systems as Nazism, Fascism, Communism, and other ideologies challenging democracy for world rulership."[2] But Ockenga was concerned about the many Americans who seemed undisturbed by the internal threat to American society posed by alien flows of thought. These menacing ideas included the rationalism, materialism, and scientific naturalism dubbed "Modernism" by his fundamentalist ilk as well as a range of socialisms—big government following the Great Depression, perceived encroachments of Communism from abroad, and the social agendas of both Roman Catholicism and liberal Protestantism.[3] Ockenga saw the United States (and the whole West more broadly) as increasingly vulnerable to such ideologies due to the falling stock of Christian presuppositions like "the belief in God, the existence of absolute moral law, the infinite value of man, and the responsibility of man according to divine law."[4] Standing before the NAE crowd, he charged, "At times men have acted from principles based on a world view or a *Weltanschauung*. Today such world views are largely absent from social movements, and human leaders are taking their place in the demand on the loyalties of men. Men no longer have a map to tell them the direction of their travel. They are in a fog."[5] To seat the human mind in authority above the one biblical word and world-view is, as he explained, to open individuals to a materialism that abets numerous deleterious trends, including the debasement of persons as "nothing but conditioned reflexes," a subjective relativism that upholds the ultimate authority of autonomous selves, and the inflow of other essentially secular "-isms" driven by authoritarians appealing to the appetites of the rootless masses.[6]

Ockenga felt duty-bound to battle against the many godless world-views and the social evils they fostered, and he championed a *new evangelicalism* as the frontline in higher learning, political reform, and cultural renewal. Accompanied by folks like Carl F. H. Henry and E. J. Carnell, he believed the best (and perhaps the only) way to gather a people for the work of preserving the Christian heritage of the West before the watchful eyes of a broken world was to steel American evangelical minds with a full-orbed biblical mindset.[7] Ockenga occupied many prominent posts, including his lengthy pastorship of Boston's Park Street Church (1936–1969) and his founding presidencies of the NAE (1942–1944), Fuller Theological Seminary (1947–1954 and 1960–1963), and the unified Gordon-Conwell Theological Seminary (1969–1979). From these heights, he cut the American evangelical figure as an adept biblical world-viewer with keen insight bearing on faith and public life. To capture how Ockenga stimulated a neo-evangelical movement, I will synthesize enduring fixtures in his thought and register some correspondences with and pertinent deviations from Henry's public voice during roughly the same period—the 1940s through the early 1970s. In the background are the Great Depression and the US federal response, World War II, the Cold War and anxieties about socialism, and the civil rights movement, alongside many significant cultural shifts, not least in the 1960s. This history precedes the Moral Majority era of organized-but-contested evangelical political engagement, and so it reflects, at least partly, the effort that made possible later evangelical "identity politics"—if we find that concept pertains here. Given the nature of his labors, what follows is no high academic treatment of public theology but chiefly an examination of Ockenga's proclamations to and on behalf of American evangelicals. Such material promises a view to how sympathetic hearers might have (been) identified with the world-view he put forth.

This chapter will begin with a review of how Ockenga presented the world-view concept and filled out the evangelical world-view's most important details. His strategy was similar to Abraham Kuyper's, as studied in chapter 1, in wanting to identify and embolden a broad, Spirit-infused movement with hopes of clarifying the impact of faith on all sectors of life and seeding the impulse for extensive social reform. But Ockenga operated more on the general notion of world-view floating around in public discourse relative to World War II–era ideologies than a rich philosophical treatment of idealist world-view conceptuality. After examining these general contours, I will investigate the slippage between the few confessed fundaments of the "evangelical" world-view and the more specified activism of one who speaks into American public life "as an evangelical." More specifically, I will examine what Ockenga's world-viewish analysis of specific social issues and his political activism reveal to be key features of his world-view, including a partisan political and economic agenda and the status quo of white authority—over against civil rights legislation and efforts to hasten desegregation. Seeing him deploy the world-view concept to stimulate and marshal religious impulses toward specific sociopolitical ends should raise questions about the ease with which Ockenga could assume the evangelical spirit would support his agenda without ever feeling the need to scrutinize his social location. Through the case of Harold Ockenga, I will demonstrate how supposedly neutral evangelical world-view rhetoric took shape within a relatively homogenous social network that allowed convictions and commitments from numerous social groups and aggregate interests (e.g., affluent, conservative, white, Republican) to hide within what he nominalized as the commonsense evangelical perspective. While his strategy and agenda raise issues that correlate meaningfully to twenty-first-century American life, Ockenga's peak influence is a distant enough memory that we might be sufficiently dispassionate to evaluate his ideas and activism honestly. Because he is willing to name his commitments to Christian nationalism, free-enterprising capitalism, and some degree of racial segregation, he reveals even as he resists what it means to generate religious energy *within a particular, historical container.* The meaning of and motivation for that resistance, which continues to characterize much of American evangelicalism, will be especially significant as part II unfolds.

PLACING OCKENGA IN HISTORICAL CONTEXT: A VERY PRESENT HELP IN TROUBLE

The ominous, capital-I Ideologies marching self-confidently onto the global scene in the first half of the twentieth century occasioned stateside conversations about *Weltanschauungen,* and Ockenga seized the moment to claim the neo-evangelical world-view as the best candidate for strengthening American society.[8] As he told the story, there was a time "when most Americans were theists, or at least deists," including most of the Founding Fathers.[9] Ockenga sometimes elided this claim with his sense that evangelicals had provided the activation energy for US representative democracy, and he maintained the conventional wisdom "that there is no value in democracy without a Christian condition to undergird it."[10] According to historian George Marsden, Ockenga and his many neo-evangelical associates were "Republicans of the sort who supported Robert A. Taft" (not more progressive "Rockefeller Republicans"), who "would add to the critique of other Republicans . . . the opinion that the real source of the ominous direction of contemporary America was its forsaking of evangelical Christianity."[11] Mainline Protestants had maintained a more robust image and influence in the public square during this period through ecumenical organelles like the Federal Council of Churches and

The Christian Century as well as bastion institutions like New York City's Union Theological Seminary and Riverside Church. So, below we will notice how Ockenga casts his vision in contrast with other influential Protestant voices. For example, he defined the "new evangelicalism" in contradistinction to other expressions of Christianity he found inadequate: versus liberal Protestantism, "accept[ing] the Bible as the authoritative Word of God"; versus neo-orthodoxy, "accept[ing] the Word of God as written, rather than something which was divorced from and above the written Word"; and versus fundamentalism, "believ[ing] that we had a responsibility to society in our day."[12] Retrieving genuine social concern within an intellectually rigorous world-view was of central importance to those raising the neo-evangelical standard, especially those emerging from, or at least sympathetic to, Christian fundamentalism.

When Ockenga analyzed the first few decades of the twentieth century, he found that fundamentalist Christians in the United States maintained the high ground of theological orthodoxy in the face of Modernism but regularly forsook its application to the social situation while continually splintering over nonessential doctrines.[13] Moreover, as historian Mark Noll explains in his landmark book *The Scandal of the Evangelical Mind* (Eerdmans, 1994), "Public reverses for fundamentalism in the 1920s seemed to signal the end of intellectual vitality among conservative evangelicals."[14] So, Ockenga's generation of young and restless fundamentalists rose with hopes of fostering "a 'new evangelicalism' that would value scholarship and take an active interest in society while maintaining traditional Protestant orthodoxy."[15] Introducing Carl Henry's *The Uneasy Conscience of Modern Fundamentalism* (Eerdmans, 1947), Ockenga framed his commitment to American society this way: "If the Bible-believing Christian is on the wrong side of social problems such as war, race, class, labor, liquor, imperialism, etc., it is time to get over the fence to the right side. The church needs a progressive Fundamentalism with a social message."[16] Henry, for his part, stressed "appl[ying] the genius of our position constructively to those problems which press most for solution in a social way."[17] In addition to his fundamentalist compatriots, Ockenga also called to arms those who already shared a biblical world-view and genuine social concern but lacked a sense of fellowship with others in political engagement—those who mourned the ground lost to better-organized others (e.g., the Federal Council of Churches) but felt like "lone wolves" in the struggle for America's soul.[18] So, he labored to recollect a shared history, generate a sense of solidarity, and muster social and political willpower under a shared identity. Although he was hesitant to embrace the kind of organizational unity he saw in the Federal Council of Churches, Ockenga did seek some kind of concord in the guileless, organic unity of "biblical Christians" (a synonym for "evangelicals" that continues to circulate in the twenty-first century).[19]

Leading up to the NAE's creation, Ockenga invoked the feeling that a *kairos* moment was dawning under God's providential guidance. At the 1942 gathering that generated a mandate for establishing something like the NAE, he predicted "decisions which will affect the whole future course of evangelical Christianity in America," and he likened the assembly to the Jerusalem Council narrated in Acts 15.[20] Ockenga believed the nascent organization represented "a very large minority, perhaps a majority, in America, which is discriminated against because of the folly of our divided condition."[21] Furthermore, he declared that the hour greatly needed identifiable "evangelicals" to band together across denominational lines under the umbrella of historical orthodoxy.[22] Ockenga appropriated "faithful remnant" language from Scripture to describe neo-evangelical early adopters and invoked the legendary headship of "an Elijah, or a Daniel, or a John the Baptist, or a Paul" as exemplifying the galvanizing leader that they needed, which turned out to be Ockenga himself.[23] Issuing the call for a united evangelical front, he displaced the boundaries of faithfulness and Christian identity from those of historical traditions (and fundamentalist splinter cells) onto plain-sense evangelical ones—the radical antithesis between "those who believe in Christ and the Bible, and those who reject Christ."[24] Out of fidelity to their shared vocation, Ockenga pressed NAE members to sacrifice other historical or organizational loyalties when necessary. With war raging in Europe and the United States aiding the Allies, Ockenga cast a forward-looking, Christian nationalist vision for the founding NAE membership in 1943:

> I believe that the United States of America has been assigned a destiny comparable to that of ancient Israel which was favored, preserved, endowed, guided, and used of God. Historically, God has prepared this nation with a vast and united country, with a population drawn from innumerable blood streams, with a wealth which is unequaled, with an ideological strength drawn from the traditions of classical and radical philosophy, with a government held accountable to law, as no other government except Israel has ever been, and with an enlightenment in the minds of the average citizen which is the climax of social development.[25]

What destiny had God assigned the United States? "To diffuse the knowledge of God and truth through the Gospel unto the world. Apparently, the last great privilege of ministering to mankind was committed to this particular nation."[26] Before American society reached the point of no return, its many Christian citizens could reclaim the nation's divinely bestowed identity as an evangelical agent of God's will for the good of the world.

Diverging from the many forking paths of their fundamentalist forebears, the "new evangelicals" would advance a united front to enable biblical

Christians to live faithfully within all sectors of life (i.e., family, economy, and state) and thereby launch an assault on global evils. "Let us learn something from the Soviets and the Nazis," Ockenga preached. "It is time for the children of the light to open their eyes and learn how to carry on God's work.... Personally, I am just as tired of defensive tactics in ecclesial matters as Americans are tired of defensive tactics on the part of the democracies of the United Nations."[27] A good neo-evangelical *offense* could restore confidence in the United States and its proud democratic achievement as a viable home for the faith. This work would entail reperforming American history as a chosen people struggling toward an all-encompassing vision of freedom against totalitarian powers. Ockenga located the hope of genuine social change in individuals prepared to do "the rethinking and the restating of the fundamental thesis and principles of a Western Culture. There must be today men who have the time and the energy and the inclination and the ability and the support to be able to redefine Christian thinking and to fling it forth into the faces of these unbelievers everywhere."[28] Forecasting the NAE's potential, Ockenga called those who maintained their deep roots in orthodoxy to branch out and meet society's greatest needs by way of *this organization.* It would be the vanguard of a movement promoting a spiritual world-view to compete with godless, alien alternatives and reinvigorate the American (evangelical) way of life. Overall, the neo-evangelical strategy would depend on concerted leadership from "the brain trust of the evangelicals" dispersed in various organelles throughout society (e.g., media outlets, an organization for colleges and universities, the schools themselves, a clearinghouse for missionary work, and organized political lobbies) to facilitate the development and broad dissemination of their world-view over the long haul.[29]

From the immediate post–World War II period through the Cold War, Ockenga consistently sounded the alarm: "According to the percentage that we reject the *foundations* of our society, we shall also see the *forms* of society change."[30] In his first convocation address at Fuller Seminary in 1947, he exhorted his audience to get about the work of God while they had time. With the world on fire, urgency pressed the opening of such a school to do what they could "before another holocaust takes place that everybody is predicting now."[31] Over the years, Ockenga grew increasingly concerned with Americans' defense against the threat of Communism—both foreign (e.g., in Korea, Vietnam, and Cambodia) and domestic. Warning of a cataclysmic showdown between two worlds, he preached that obedience to the Great Commission (Matthew 28:16–20) would factor into just how long America could stay the apocalypse.[32] Ockenga was particularly concerned about social *forms* like the civil rights movement's social engineering agenda and the protests and general rebellion against authority (not least in the area of sexuality) of college-aged Americans in the 1960s and 1970s. He imagined Communist agitators under the spell of Russia, Cuba, and the like were stoking much of this rebellion. Whether these efforts led immediately in the direction of anarchy or some form of socialism, these insurgents were inevitably paving the way for godless, authoritarian ideologues.[33] Ockenga routinely and openly worried about the endless sense of revolution and change (associated with Marxism) and deconstruction (during the advent of postmodern philosophy), and he professed the need for an indubitably solid foundation. He urgently coached the American public, especially its sizeable Christian population, toward repentance for national sins, including injustice (e.g., issues of chattel slavery and unequal opportunity in the past), the pride of enduring prejudice, lawlessness (e.g., rejecting retributive justice), atheism, drunkenness, (sexual) immorality, and prodigality (e.g., excessive federal welfare).[34] Nevertheless, these vices were only so many outward signs of the more central crisis of character: displacing God as the *foundation* of one's world-view.

THE WORLD-VIEW CONCEPT IN OCKENGA'S THEOLOGY

While modern streams of thought were sweeping many Americans downstream, Ockenga sought to plant new evangelicals in a life-orienting *"Weltanschauung*—truly one much opposed to the other views which still survive, but a powerful and a sufficient ground for our action. That world view binds us together as men cannot otherwise be united."[35] This section will focus primarily on the unfolding of Ockenga's world-view concept, especially what he sees as the fundamental principles of an evangelical world-view and, thus, the generative structure for real-time political engagement. So, here I will give more space to the general and systematic, then in the next section, I will take up the particulars of judgments on specific occasions or issues. Drawing from our learning in part I, I should also name here the tendency to think in terms of general principles and their particular applications as a temptation to be avoided. Bridging this section with the next, we will get the distinct sense that the general and the particular are bound up with each other, especially if what we are talking about is something like a "world-view." As such, we might start to see "evangelical" and "world-view" as floating signifiers and, furthermore, to understand how these concepts come to facilitate public claims to representation while masking over a large degree of diversity.

The Fundaments of Biblical Theism

If we were to begin with the simple question, "Where shall we find the kind of unity the Lord seeks?" Ockenga would respond, "Obviously in his revelation, the Bible."[36] As he extended his view of Scripture throughout his career, he both appealed to its authority and expounded upon its utility. Recounting the story of the Reformation and the first common language Bible translations, Ockenga argued, "Once the people began to read the Bible, they immediately recognized the distance which the church had departed from primitive Christianity in simplicity, sacrifice, and service"—he hoped for the same in his "New Reformation."[37] The individual believer's "right of the private interpretation of Scripture" was a mark of Protestantism's genius, predicated on the belief that each believer "possesses[es] the gift of the Holy Spirit for the purpose of interpreting the Word of God."[38] Accordingly, regenerate Christians can recognize one another across denominational lines using a shared (biblical) language, for "the Spirit blows where it pleases."[39] In contrast to such unforced and organic unity among evangelicals, the organizational union sought by liberal Protestants in the Federal Council of Churches (or by Roman Catholics under the Pope's headship) was not only undesirable but tyrannical and antithetical to biblical principles. Ockenga sometimes framed his philosophy of life as "Biblical Theism," signifying a thin set of convictions "accepted by all evangelical Protestants" and encompassing "the controlling teachings of the Word of God."[40] On these few fundamentals, assent would need to be exacted despite the noetic effects of sin, but beyond these principles, difference should be anticipated and borne with patience.[41]

All the same, "Evangelicals champion the authority of the Bible," Carl Henry maintained, "and are critical of pluralism in theology."[42] And according to Ockenga, insistence on "the authority of the Bible alone *uninterpreted by traditions*" is another mark of Protestantism's genius.[43] According to these erstwhile fundamentalists, Modernism itself had become an interpretive tradition for many. To correct for its assumptions and prejudices, the neo-evangelicals began "with what is surely known about the earliest followers and ambassadors of Jesus Christ."[44] Henry articulated the apostolic world-view in greater systematic detail than Ockenga, including convictions about the God-givenness of the orders of creation, the conjunction of justice and justification in the gospel, the present fullness of life in a personal relationship with Christ, and the future culmination of human life in the resurrection.[45] We can get a sense for the perceived force of uninterpreted biblical revelation by listening in on Henry's criticism of Reinhold Niebuhr, who

> stressed that man's reason is always partial and infected by self-interest, and that all value judgments are conditioned by one's social context. . . . Power and life, Niebuhr argued, will always transcend reason. . . . It was Niebuhr's rejection of final truth, in the interest of dialectical tension, and his relativizing of the entire content of man's knowledge, that supplied a major basis of evangelical critique. . . . Seen from the perspective of historic Christianity, Niebuhr elevates

man's corruption to a final principle of interpretation, and on this basis, rejects the orthodox view of revelation (and sin); Biblical Christianity acknowledges revelation as definitively explanatory of sin and does not regard sin as rendering revelation ambiguous.[46]

Niebuhr insisted that sin and self-interest will always impact human interpretations of anything, including Scripture. However, Henry, Ockenga, and company insisted that regeneration constrains sin's effects on human knowing such that Christians can and must see the world through Bible-tinted glasses.[47]

Appeals to reason and rationality were also prevalent in the neo-evangelical conversation. But in contradistinction to the bald human reason elevated in Modernism, Ockenga claimed, "Through the Gospel reason is re-enthroned. Men are transformed from being subject to passions, prejudices, and practices of sinful action to being subject to the will of God as far as they know it."[48] Significant in this particular way of putting the matter is Ockenga's implicit concession that Modernists may be right about the role of reason, unaided by traditions of human opinion, even while identifying the crux of the issue as the moral character of the one who is applying it.[49] Describing the restoration of reason vis-à-vis Scripture, Carl Henry explained, "Special revelation lifts the reason of man to the lofty knowledge which the turning aside to sin made impossible."[50] Ockenga too insisted that the human intellect was fallen, incapable of knowing rightly, and "not willing to receive the revelation."[51] So, the doctrine of regeneration was essential to his world-view theory as "a change which can take place at the core of one's being which will counteract the noetic effects of sin."[52] With reason restored, the biblical world-view becomes the map Christians use to discern their way through the fog with increasing confidence that their path is good and true. As more details are charted on the biblical map, however, the differences and dissent one is willing to tolerate may become fewer and farther between.

With so much emphasis on awakening and nurturing evangelical minds, Ockenga and company sought to concretize their concerns for intellectual responsibility largely through institutions of higher education. In the context of university education, he imagined that a thoroughly Christian school could operate with "a governing ideology" that integrates all the various disciplines of study such that a biblical world- and life-view sets the limits of academic freedom for the faculty.[53] At the neo-evangelical institutions of Ockenga's dreams, the reigning ideology "holds together in the mind of God," so faculty and students could engage in all their academic pursuits with confidence that their labors could uncover and detail God's revelation structured into the cosmos.[54] Carl Henry contended, "The Western concept of popular education has its legitimate rootage in the determination of the church to indoctrinate the masses in the major doctrinal essentials of the Christian world-life view."[55] As part of the public arena of *Weltanschauungen*, Ockenga explained, "our educational system must compete with the Communist's system which subordinates education to the goals of world revolution and the liberation of the masses," and it must contrast with "the prevalent relativism in truth, ethics, and progress."[56] In his view, the evangelical university would provide space for students to gain confidence and guidance while building from the philosophy of Biblical Theism. The graduate would develop "a commitment to patriotism as he sees the areas in which Christian truth has governed the life of this nation. . . . He will make a commitment to a philosophy of life."[57] Ockenga hoped, from there, the world-view would trickle through the churches in which these individuals lived and worked to "reverse the trend of fragmentization within churches and communities."[58]

Numbering among the fundaments of Ockenga's world-view, though seldom, if ever, named in institutional statements of faith, was the principle of free enterprise, which cut across the religious, political, and economic spheres and loomed large in his educational paradigm. George Marsden rightly identifies an American, individualistic entrepreneurial spirit deep in the neo-evangelical marrow, and it really goes hand in hand with the presumptively nontraditioned approach to Scripture.[59] In the background, we may notice the pervasive influence of modern, individualist notions of the human person and distrust of human traditions as avoidable assemblages of opinion. Together with the practical demands of a diffuse, nonorganizational movement across numerous established denominations, these notions encouraged the trend to see churches as comprised of individual converts, free agents exercising direct, personal responsibility to God, and thus Christian identity as individually grasped.[60] In the context of this weak ecclesiology, Ockenga and others engaged the American spirit of free enterprise and founded their own supra-denominational schools, evangelistic agencies, and networks. This activity made them de facto "separatists" even if they disavowed separatism as a formal doctrine and also, ironically, "progressives" (i.e., not seeking the conservation of existing institutions).[61] Historian Matthew Sutton sharpens the point here, identifying Ockenga and company as "savvy religious innovators" who offered "a third way between liberal Protestantism and creedal, churchly conservatism."[62] In his address calling for the founding of the NAE, Ockenga confessed, "I have very few things which I can unreservedly support except my own independent church and its one-hundred percent evangelical program."[63] And when he spoke to and for "unvoiced multitudes," Ockenga was thinking of an ideal church comprised of all born-again individuals who believe in Christ and love the Bible—and this within the policeable boundary of a few core convictions partially outlined in statements of faith for the NAE, Fuller Seminary, and so on.

The free-enterprising, entrepreneurial nature comes to matter for the neo-evangelicals in several ways. The first is just the sense that it is possible to innovate and establish new organizations. A second is the free-enterprising competition between increasingly visible leaders of emerging evangelical institutions and organelles looking for support to keep their work going, in terms of followership and sponsorship. But a third reflects how the traffic runs two ways, as manifest in the enshrining of free enterprise values—and, in the interest of full disclosure, as a connection point with key donors (e.g., J. Howard Pew and Herbert J. Taylor) interested in projects supporting their overall world-view.[64] Historian Curtis Evans highlights the relationship between the entrepreneurial aspect of evangelicalism—particularly in drumming up the financial resources to make their institutions work—and the *gospel of free enterprise* crafted as the heart of evangelicalism. For example, "Fuller Seminary, with Pew's support, initiated a series of lectures (beginning in 1954) on the 'Christian Heritage' of America, which emphasized protecting free enterprise against communism."[65] So, even before we finish our study of neo-evangelical world-viewing fundaments, we find Ockenga maintaining that Christian colleges have a responsibility to the communities in which they exist that includes "undergirding the conviction of free enterprise."[66] More systematically and in almost-Platonic fashion, Ockenga projected a trichotomous model of the human person onto human society: "body being the economic structure of society, soul being the political form of society, spirit being the religion dominant in society."[67] Filling out this model, he prescribed for the United States, "first of all, capitalism as the economic form, second, democracy as the political form, third, Christianity as our religious form."[68] In another metaphor, Ockenga described capitalism as a river, with democracy and Christianity as its two banks; the threat to American society was manifest in the erosion of Christianity on the one bank and the frenetic overcompensation of the government on the other. We might ask, however, why would capitalism be the river flowing in this metaphor? Moreover, do *all these details* hold together in the very mind of God?

As Ockenga's world-view continues to unfold below, we might also begin to reflect more critically on the sources of its basic principles and more specific deliverances: which are biblical and which are partisan-political or otherwise sociocultural? Drawing on his Keswick holiness background, Ockenga attributed his personal clarity and seriousness to an experience of the second blessing, "the critical coming of the Holy Spirit in His fullness whereby the New Testament level of spiritual life became a reality" to him.[69] In terms of the diverging paths of knowledge and the centrality of personal piety to proper knowledge, Ockenga seems to share many of Kuyper's sensibilities about what is happening in the arena of world-view struggle. Yet, answering *"sola scriptura"* to questions about moral sources and authorities settled the perennial hermeneutical issue of sinful self-interest only ideologically, not concretely.

On Social Stability and Change

Speaking directly of political order and civil authority in the wake of 1960s unrest, Ockenga argued that God established human government after the Noahide flood as a check on human evil and remains sovereign over all its concrete forms. As such, resisting civil authorities means resisting God, and God's judgment for this resistance comes through the state itself (cf. Romans 13).[70] The command to obey civil authorities is nearly absolute, not least in times of war, but in principle, divine law does supersede any human laws and must be obeyed at all costs. Ockenga set forth three basic options for Christians living between God's law and civil law: (1) honor and obedience insofar as the laws do not conflict; (2) participation in social change efforts (i.e., "prayer, petition, and legislation"); and (3) revolution, "which is man's right when God's law is violated," though what may count as a violation per se remains unclear.[71] Given the implicit sociopolitical context of his comments alongside his view of the United States as the chosen inheritor of God's promise, Ockenga assumed the first two options would be sufficient domestically. In America, evangelicals could "regain" unparalleled influence, unseat or convert non-evangelical civil authorities, and revive the national soul.

The way Ockenga framed other Christian streams of social theory and activism reveals the depth of his commitment to a particular constellation of religious and political ideals. For example, he openly lamented the sizable role that Roman Catholicism (called "Romanism") played in America, not least in his city of Boston. In the 1940s, he stated, "I am chagrined, chagrined, that we have allowed Romanism to step in with a social program that will make Romanism the challenging religious factor in . . . the United States."[72] Specifically, Ockenga narrated the Catholic influence behind growing government oversight and increasing social welfare programs—both steps in the wrong direction in his book.[73] For another example, he identified the same strategy in liberal Protestants, who strove for "social justice through labor laws, old age assistance, medical care, assistance to the poor, the underwriting of education, public housing, and a program of social change."[74] Given its theopolitical agenda, "that terrible octopus of liberalism" was to Ockenga (as to his mentor, J. Gresham Machen) a different religion from biblical Christianity and, thus, an altogether different world-view.[75] The social agenda of those who pursue direct social change through the church tends to carry them beyond the recognizably Christian fold into community with those more fundamentally identified as "socialist."[76] He connected Modernism with the social gospel agenda, which together comprise socialism as against "supernaturalism" (another thin term for Ockenga's Biblical Theism). While socialism tries to force social change, supernaturalism elicits change through reforming individuals' character.

All this attention on social agendas and the world-views that animate individuals raises the question of whether social structures can, in themselves, harbor sin. Ockenga observed the "emergence of a new set of gods who have taken the place of the absolute Jehovah revealed through the Lord Jesus Christ. Those gods consist of blood, power, sex, money, hunger, strong men, and strong weapons. They are worshiped by the masses."[77] And he recognized these not as mere idols, fashioned by human hands—though there is undoubtedly a human imprint on these creatures—but as "heathen demons" that have "invaded our lives again."[78] Rather than accepting a world disenchanted by Modernism, Ockenga pushed his audience to see evidence of activity on a spiritual plane as well. But his enchanted world-view maintained boundaries around this devilry: "The Bible teaches that Satan's sphere is individual; he leads men to do his will, but he does not have kingdoms to give. When Satan's emissaries control the state, the laws may conflict with God's law, but Satan's kingdom is under God's sovereignty."[79] While some sins may be visible corporately, sin is categorically constrained to the realm of individuals; thus, we should not see particular social orders as themselves bedeviled even if some category of sin is palpable throughout one or another.[80]

Having absolved all (American) social structures from harboring supra-individual sin, the neo-evangelicals reasserted a corollary doctrine in *the biblical estimate of man* as a sinner in need of saving. They saw liberal Protestants' focus on societal change as a dangerous misdiagnosis of the problem. In Carl Henry's analysis, "By the 1960s, . . . the stance of nonevangelical Protestantism had now become so anti-metaphysical and anti-intellectual that truth was subordinated to unity. . . . Instead of personal evangelism and the spiritual regeneration of individuals, they advocated changing the social structures by the Church's direct engagement in political controversy."[81] Tersely put, he charged, "The neo-Protestant view . . . substitutes the notion of corporate salvation for individual salvation."[82] Henry claimed such Christians do not care to think of their sins, have no time for worship or pursuits of holiness, and only want social activism. Such strategies simply would not address the heart of the matter, namely, individual sin and the urgency of not common but *saving* grace. Henry would argue only this starting point "is sufficiently realistic to make at all possible any securely-grounded optimism in world affairs."[83] Personal conversion follows *an individual's intimate experience of God*, which prioritizes respectable apologetics and evangelism.[84] The long-term strategy for individual change also includes a vibrant pastoral and teaching ministry that will furnish the believer with "the full doctrine of Christian faith . . . across a series of years."[85] Such catechesis alone (in the church and additionally in the university) will fill evangelical minds with the full range of Christian principles they would need for social criticism and engagement.

Ockenga saw social change as an effect of Christian individuals voluntarily applying their convictions to the day's most pressing social issues, reading and responding to them through the biblical world-view. We do not have both a personal and a social gospel, he argued, but the one gospel "is personal with a social outreach."[86] For the good news to have some "carryover" into society, the faithful must go on *to exert themselves faithfully upon society*. Ockenga's logic here flows from a stream of evangelicalism that understands the breaches most in need of repair as those "of individual religious life caused by the resurgence of heathendom. Only thereby can the foundations of democracy be made safe. . . . Our first line of defense consists of righteousness in the individual soul."[87] Breaking it down, Ockenga argued, "[The] means of changing social conditions, then, comes through regeneration of the individual. This has an effect upon family, industry, education, recreation, and every aspect of society."[88] Such an approach to individual and social change has been the lynchpin of white American evangelical proclamation. The more evangelicals we have (i.e., the greater the population of regenerate individuals applying their consciences), so the reasoning goes, the more righteous actions and reasonable policies will prevail. Nevertheless, Ockenga insisted that we not trust the simple equation that if you get persons saved, you will solve all social problems—"it just doesn't happen that way."[89] Thinking about racism, he thought one could well be saved in the religious sense while having a long way to go in the realm of personal pride and prejudice. To address those social issues on which some Christians have blind spots (e.g., racial prejudice, economic oppression, and war), churches would need to continuously inculcate the biblical world-view and transform individual Christians' habits.[90]

POLITICS IN THE NAME OF "EVANGELICALISM"

Notwithstanding the priority of personal evangelism and conversion, individual evangelicals may yet have cause for direct political action, including solidarity with nonevangelicals (even non-Christians). Carl Henry insisted that, if evangelicals are in the majority of a social context in which good reforms arise, they should simply support the reforms. In such situations, evangelical convictions about saving grace (what Henry sometimes called the "redemptive reference") versus the common grace improved by social action will be sufficiently clear. But when evangelicals are in the minority of a reform coalition, Henry urged them to make their protest known, "insisting upon the regenerative context as alone able to secure a permanent rectification of such wrongs" even if, admittedly, "how to express such a protest in a positive rather than a negative way, beyond a minority committee report, remains to be studied."[91] In many cases, especially in the early years of the neo-evangelical movement, the explicit social agenda remained rather vague even in more detailed works (e.g., "faithful Christian living, serving, and if necessary, dying" within the all-encompassing world-view).[92] For example, in one of the more concrete suggestions of *The Uneasy Conscience of Modern Fundamentalism*, Henry wrote, "Is there political unrest? Seek first, not a Republican victory, or a labor victory, but the kingdom of God. . . . Then there will be . . . political rest."[93] Among others, Henry faced criticism from their contemporaries for not risking a more concrete Christian social agenda.[94]

But for all his emphasis on personal transformation, Ockenga did not blush at the prospect of a far-reaching social agenda even from early on, and he frequently lifted his voice on political matters as a representative of the new evangelicals. Looking back from the early 1970s, he painted the emerging American landscape as a world on fire. College students protesting across the nation knew "nothing of the cataclysmic upheavals of the first world war, of the giant depression, of the New Deal, of World War II, or even of the Fair Deal."[95] Ockenga had already suffered three full terms (and the start of a fourth) of Franklin Roosevelt's presidency. FDR secured two of his three elections on the perceived merits of his active approach to the Great Depression, which differed from Herbert Hoover's approach especially on the point of voluntarism in public-private cooperation versus government regulation of business. In any case, Ockenga opposed FDR's pursuit of an unparalleled *third* term, literally rattling sabers: "To your tents, to the battle, O Americans, we will have no part in dictatorships."[96] Then during FDR's third term, he numbered among the conspiracy theorists who feared the Communist long-game takeover of the United States, noting of the president among others: "Communistic influence has permeated this nation to a degree thought unbelievable."[97] Ockenga's views were representative of the Park Street pulpit; his predecessor, A. Z. Conrad, had used his station to blast the New Deal as "socialistic and dictatorial."[98] And in the early years of the NAE, Ockenga openly opposed FDR's *fourth*-term campaign, citing his blatant disregard for the American way of life characterized by evangelical Christianity, participatory democracy, and free enterprise.[99] Furthermore, Ockenga observed in the Roosevelt orbit other signs of immorality that exemplified biblical, end-times prophecies like "the president's perceived inaction on growing sexual licentiousness in the forms of 'homosexuality, fornication and adultery' and Eleanor Roosevelt's support of interracial marriage."[100] Following Roosevelt's death, Ockenga then had to endure nearly two full terms of Harry Truman, whose domestic "Fair Deal" agenda consciously built upon FDR's legacy. Overall, so much Democratic administration in these years (from 1933 to 1969, only eight years of Republican presidency) signaled dark times for a Taftite Republican like Ockenga.

There were moments when Ockenga's sense of responsibility to represent the evangelical position in public theology led him into open conflict with other Christians' political activism. For instance, reacting to the preaching of Riverside Church's famed founding pastor, Harry Emerson Fosdick, during US engagement in World War II, Ockenga intoned, "Protestant Christian patriotism endorses and supports the use of force to free the world of the menace of German militarism and Japanese barbarism. We want the men at arms to know that the church is praying for their complete victory."[101] He also eschewed Christian pacifism more generally, preaching on Romans 13, "In a matter of war, we must admit that the ministers of the State become our conscience before God. What the rulers decree we must obey. We do not have the right to sit in judgment."[102] As another illustration, Ockenga vocally supported Richard Nixon's presidential candidacy beginning in 1959. In the run-up to Nixon's 1960 loss to John F. Kennedy, Ockenga pledged "anything I can do in the advancement of your candidacy" along with "the loyal support of thousands of people in our own constituency."[103] One thing he did was public theology at an event billed as an open conversation about the impact of "religion" on the presidency. The event included no Roman Catholics and was exposed by the press as a thinly veiled denigration of JFK's faith meant to stoke Protestant concern.[104] And as a third illustration, Ockenga criticized Lyndon B. Johnson for his unwillingness to drive the war in Vietnam to a prompt and victorious end. Speaking "as a Christian," Ockenga preached, "I believe we must stand against Communism in Southeast Asia," and in this effort, he wrote to President Johnson urging him to use "whatever weapons and firepower necessary to win."[105]

While conflict with someone like Fosdick who represented a different theological tradition was inevitable, Ockenga was also destined for trouble with members of his own identity groups (not least *evangelicals*) who disagreed with his public opining.[106] If nothing else, advocacy around the Nixon campaigns critically exposed this reality. For his part, Ockenga was refreshed and hopeful in the 1968 and 1972 campaign cycles. He gave Nixon full-throated support during his 1972 reelection campaign. Even as details of the Watergate scandal spilled into public view, he vouched for the "high moral integrity" of his "personal friend" in a newspaper article published just before the election.[107] But by this time, a group of young, progressive evangelicals (including Richard Mouw, Ron Sider, and Jim Wallis) had emerged to challenge the politics of Ockenga's particular neo-evangelical bloc. These progressives expressed concern over Nixon's record on race relations, including his benefiting from whites' backlash against a politicized sense of social unrest (i.e., his "law and order" rhetoric) as well as Nixon's economic policies that further disenfranchised poor Americans. In turn, Ockenga chastised "Evangelicals for McGovern," who supported Nixon's opponent, Sen. George McGovern (D-SD). With (likely genuine) puzzlement, he wrote to them, "I for one cannot understand how any of you men of evangelical conviction can back Mr. McGovern."[108] McGovern was the son of a fundamentalist Methodist minister but had pursued a Wesleyan strand with a greater sense of "prophetic zeal" for social "issues such as poverty, war, ecology, racism, and hunger."[109] Ockenga and other Republican evangelicals looped him with the social gospel millstone. But in the final analysis, evangelical conviction qua "evangelical" never produced the consensus around even a thin political platform that Ockenga presumed.[110] (This story continues in chapter 5.)

On Race and Integration

Preaching in the 1970s on the conditions for "national healing," Ockenga named racism among the United States' "national sins"—manifest as slavery, but also problems in equal education, fairness in housing, and employment opportunities. He seemed consistently concerned with eradicating oppression and improving the situation of minority groups, and he referred to "the rise and expansion of the white race" as one of the "most sordid chapters in human history."[111] Within his principled world-view, Ockenga interpreted national sins as visible corporately yet committed *individually*; as such, national healing was predicated on *individual* repentance and conversion.[112]

Following the passage of the Civil Rights Act of 1968 (more on his approach to the civil rights movement in the next subsection), he did not think any of the abovementioned sins of racism endured. Historian Charles Marsh relates this sensibility through a story about a mid-1960's incident at Gordon-Conwell Theological Seminary. When he caught wind that John Perkins had "criticized free-market capitalism in a lecture," Ockenga made a public statement to the board, saying "I don't think there's any exploitation of the black race in American today."[113] For Ockenga, the real ongoing manifestation of America's race problem was personal pride and its attendant prejudice: "We must confess that with many of our people there is a prejudice against minorities of race and color. There is the attitude 'We are the people.' Since the advantages of being white Anglo-Saxon Protestant background are ours, we have discriminated against others."[114] Even here, real progress had been made, he thought, but problematic dispositions linger in individuals here and there. Giving about as much detail as he ever did on the subject, Ockenga summarized social change in the area of race like this in the early 1970s:

For decades we have seen the black man making great progress legally and socially and economically in the nation. His protest against discrimination, prejudice, injustice and limitation is a legitimate protest and has achieved definite ends. The movement has now progressed beyond reformation to revolution. Emphasis on black separation, on reparations for blacks, on partiality for blacks in employment practices and on group dominion illustrates the transformation in attitude. Even the most mild blacks have turned into militants.[115]

Ockenga appears unaware of the size of his paintbrush as he overidentifies Black Americans with Black Power revolutionaries. And one struggles to imagine how such speech would invite or maintain a dialogue with Black *evangelicals*.

If we can set aside the scope of his claim for a moment, we might dig a bit deeper to see how Ockenga's analysis is substantively tied into his longstanding theory of race vis-à-vis his reading of the Bible. In an early 1940s sermon series on Ephesians, we see him tackle the issue of "racial animosity," beginning with his interpretation of the hostility between Jew and gentile and the tearing down of the dividing wall in Ephesians 2.[116] Ockenga called the salient portion of this chapter "a racial discussion and a revelation involving racial conditions," and later slipped into an analysis of Black-white relations in the United States.[117] He interpreted Jesus's breaking down of the dividing wall ecclesiologically. In the church, no one is privileged based on race or otherwise, and he describes this reality as "an extremely radical theory then, . . . no less radical now."[118] Commenting on "the social question," Ockenga expressly addressed the inestimable value to God of "every soul, whether black or white, male or female"—speaking not to material conditions but spiritual ones.[119] He used this discussion to degrade Nazi *Übermensch* ideology, concluding, "The color line must be removed among believers. That does not mean that all classes and races of men have the same opportunity, but it does mean that they are equal in value before the Lord. Hereby we see that the Church is the solution of many of the social problems which the radicals are attacking."[120] Studying the interpretational history of this passage in Ephesians, pastor-scholar William Rader explains the exceptional nature of Ockenga's categorical call among *conservative* American Christians.[121]

Knowing the Federal Council of Churches and several more progressive denominations were already working to desegregate churches and society by this time, we may yet wonder about the material implications of Ockenga's ecclesiological interpretation of this passage. Rader questions Ockenga's lack of specificity about the removal of the color-line: "He only says that it 'does not mean that all classes and races of men have the same opportunity.' As a description of the contemporary situation in church and society in the United States, the statement is correct. But up until this sentence, Ockenga had not been describing the situation; he had been demanding that it be changed."[122] Rader finds a resolution to this tension when Ockenga, speaking of liberty within the context of order and freedom under the law, reasoned:

> Let us recognize that the freedom or liberty which we prize as an ideal must be within certain limitations. The first limitation is race. Race distinctions are honorable and are recognized by God in Scripture. The Lord distinguishes among Shem, Ham, and Japheth with a Divine purpose in mind. The Lord distinguishes between the descendants of Shem and the descendants of Japheth just as much as he distinguishes between the descendants of Japheth and the descendants of Ham.[123]

Here, Ockenga invoked an archaic argument from Genesis 9 to establish race distinctions—including the authority of white rule—as a part of God's ordering of creation, grounded in the curse of Canaan owing to the sin of his father.[124] And further, given the divine conferral of these distinctions, he submitted, "To attempt to abolish racial distinctions would be folly and is impossible."[125] Again, what *precisely* this means remained uncertain. For one thing, it was unquestionably a judgment on white folk's sinful treatment of Black persons during the years of chattel slavery (God "will hold the sons of Japheth responsible for the rule which He committed to them over their brethren").[126] But regarding the ongoing, divinely justified limitations on freedom or liberty, we are left in the dark. Rader concludes, "Ockenga emphasizes that the natural order is God's creation, and that it must not be disregarded. From what he considers the nature of God's created order, he derives the ethical command to maintain the identity of the white race," and this without explaining how this might relate to the Ephesians passage itself in terms of the removal of the color-line.[127] Even those who would stop short of Rader's conclusion should recognize here a particularly conservative white sociopolitical agenda in the world reified by *Plessy v. Ferguson* (1896).

Driving closer to the point, the language Ockenga used to frame the problem reveals his perspective's poverty, coming from a position of power with an air of superiority. In his commentary on Ephesians, he argued, "Men are rejecting the status of servants. They are demanding security, equality, and a larger share of the material goods of this world. The colored races have become self-conscious, resentful, and the problem of dealing with them fairly is at the forefront."[128] Ockenga goes on to observe the misuse, even abuse, of "liberty" language by these liberated servants who fused the concept of liberty with *equality* and who had begun to demand top-down legislative fixes for issues like discrimination in employment and housing—and concomitantly to threaten civil society with turmoil (e.g., the 1940s race riots in places like Detroit and Los Angeles).[129] In principle, he sought to preserve practical distinctions between liberty, equality, and fraternity—referring to the French Revolution slogan—and he invoked Herbert Hoover's definition of liberty.[130] The danger of those who push legislation to equalize social conditions was "the want of some common denominator which can turn equality into the principle of identity. As soon as men attempt the leveling process, whether in position or possession or person, they destroy one of the foundations of society," namely, the liberty of those who have earned their status and possessions.[131] In practice, Ockenga argued, biblical teaching "falls back on general principles and doctrines fruitful in developing a Christian conscience on a particular subject, so that it [in this case, *manumission*] is voluntarily dealt with."[132] *So, this was how Ockenga expected the biblical world-view to function.* The solution to the race problem could only be the individual's relationship with God, which can remove "his hates, his antipathies, his pride, and his rebellion."[133] The answer to all social problems must be Christ manifest in each soul, servant or master, individually redeemed and carrying the faith over into the contexts in which one is found and called.[134]

During the civil rights movement, Ockenga was not alone in his long-held belief that gradualism led by voluntary actions on the part of individuals in the private sphere was the right way forward relative to racial integration. As historian David Swartz points out, northern evangelicals tended this direction, though they were not particularly outspoken about it and hoped the very public struggle would just go away.[135] Proposals to drive social change from a legislative angle, push integration, and open the possibility of race becoming less defining within society were the essence of "socialism" in some sectors of midcentury evangelicalism. Socialism was a broad term that betokened opposition to libertarian individualism in any matter (e.g., free-market capitalism and voluntary segregation). So, rather than encouraging those in his orbit to pursue integration more earnestly and forthrightly, Ockenga proclaimed to a 1957 NAE gathering, "There is nothing Biblically, nothing morally, nothing legally against it, but it is not wise, that is all, for expediency's sake because it is selfish."[136] But his orbit would have included people like medical missionary and father-in-law to Billy Graham, L. Nelson Bell, who favored "voluntary" segregation, and Southern Baptist preacher W. A. Criswell, who was promoting the mutual benefits of keeping social institutions (e.g., churches and schools) segregated in the same timeframe.[137] And Ockenga would have been careful to avoid over-association with the cause of those "integrationists" who received criticism from the fundamentalists Ockenga hoped to drag along with him in the general movement. Too much silence here leaves room for all manner of speculation. In any case, Ockenga's comments on the matter do not appear to be the fruit of a mind seriously looking for efforts to integrate—or even looking for occasional conversation with Black evangelicals.

Law, Order, and Civil Disobedience

Ockenga's approach to law and order is given flesh in his interaction with the civil rights movement. Before the Civil Rights Act of 1964 (pushed by both JFK and LBJ) passed into law, Martin Luther King Jr. and others from the Southern Christian Leadership Conference joined local leaders for demonstrations in St. Augustine, Florida. There they protested, among other things, the sluggish progress of integration following the Supreme Court's decision in *Brown v. Board of Education of Topeka* (1954) during the Dwight Eisenhower administration.[138] Together, movement leaders in St. Augustine called for volunteers to join demonstrations that April, and among the recruits was Mary Peabody, the 72-year-old mother of then-Massachusetts governor Endicott Peabody (Dem.). Her arrest as part of an integrated group made front-page news, incensing Boston's prominent pastor, Harold Ockenga, who numbered among those chagrined by her (and others' similar) engagement. Ockenga chided northern whites involved in demonstrations there as "doing more harm than good.... The whole situation is rapidly deteriorating. If we break the law by forcing the situation [i.e., integration], we are going to encourage the extremist groups. We ought to be careful what we do."[139] As it happened, those demonstrations helped end a drawn-out filibuster of the Civil Rights Act.

By the time of Nixon's administration, Ockenga was concerned that revolution was indeed on its way to America. For some background here, historian Howard Zinn cites a survey by the Urban Research Corporation, according to which, "for the first six months of 1969 only, and for only 232 of the nation's two thousand institutions of higher education, showed that at least 215,000 students had participated in campus protests."[140] During the 1969–1970 school year, "the FBI listed 1,785 student demonstrations, including the occupation of 313 buildings."[141] Prior to Ockenga's preaching cited below, Nixon's order to invade Cambodia in the spring of 1970 prompted a student demonstration at Kent State University in Ohio (May 4), where National Guardsman fired into the crowd and killed four students. "Students at four hundred colleges and universities went on strike in protest. It was the first general student strike in the history of the United States."[142] Later that year, four young people bombed a science building at the University of Wisconsin-Madison, protesting the university's involvement in military research.[143] Preaching at the 1971 "Jerusalem Conference on Biblical Prophecy," Ockenga's outlook on the situation was dire: "A philosophy is active in the world, under the Communist theory, that aims at revolution.... Students throughout the world are set on changing the structure of the nations and are calling their activity *revolution*. They are resorting now to violence, to riot, and to destruction in order to smash the present system and to bring about a new one. The masses are in ferment."[144]

Such was the societal atmosphere when, in a sermon entitled, "Will We Have Anarchy in America?" Ockenga reacted to student demonstrations at a representative handful of universities (referring mostly to New England schools, but also Northwestern in his home state of Illinois). Summarizing the students' actual complaints, he named the administrations' depersonalization of students in the education process and lack of interest in minority student needs as well as student opposition to the war in Vietnam. Without addressing the substance of these complaints, Ockenga spoke of the ratio of "revolutionaries" to students as being about one in one hundred, including a "hard core of insurrectionists."[145] This core group was due the lion's share of the blame for making unrealistic demands of university administrators and intentionally provoking a response, including police action and the inevitable clashes. In the same breath, Ockenga spoke of "black revolutionaries [who] make speeches calling for violence" and connected this with the campus demonstrations and other efforts to block "legal activities of industry, of military recruiting, and of education."[146] Further, he bemoaned that many in authority even encouraged the students' protestations, affirming the justice of their causes. Ockenga saw the Black cause and the Communist cause as closely linked.

So, Ockenga rebuked the students' assessments. Their actions violated "every value, every conviction, every code of conduct."[147] He referred to the Civil Rights legislation passed from 1954 to 1968 to support this claim and asked whether these safeguards were somehow insufficient.[148] Now defending these policies, Ockenga fell back on his belief in voluntarism, invoking the "good faith of much of the business and political communities" in their efforts to include minorities in their practices properly.[149] He thereby denied the legitimacy of the demonstrators' claims of an evil imbuing the social order itself—or of systemic injustice—locating the agitators' real motives in their affinities for the Communist world-view and ties to foreign agencies.[150] In a proclamation hauntingly current in view of the 2010s #BlackLivesMatter movement, Ockenga asked, "Must we expect violence in race relationships? Is the charge of brutality against police officers who seek to maintain order justified? Or, are some of these devices of Communist strategy intended to demoralize the people and weaken our nation? What answer does the Bible give to these questions?"[151] He was drinking from the same well as Nixon, whose 1968 election was buoyed by disillusioned white southerners heartened by his "law and order" rhetoric (also hauntingly current).

To the question of how the Bible answers the problems created by Communists agitating for anarchy throughout the United States, Ockenga responded within the same sermon: (1) God has ordained the government to maintain law and order; (2) personal change, not legislation, is *the* key (a claim he supported with other claims about North Korean POWs who became acceptable citizens when Christianized); and (3) our Christian responsibility (i.e., standards and attitudes) must carry over into human relations at all levels.[152] Through this simple, ostensibly prudential counsel, Ockenga exhibited his essential comfort with, and trust in, the status quo. One might also wonder if he was unable to see the potential of civil disobedience short of revolution as service to God's will, in general, or if his criticism applied specifically to either the concrete forms of protest or the stated aims of those protests that he was witnessing or both. At bottom, the world-viewing impulse generated commitments within Ockenga's mental life that blinded him to the genuine Christian faith in the hearts of many civil rights leaders—and among those evangelicals whose sense of Christian responsibility compelled them into demonstrations for African Americans' rights.

While Henry's record has some notable positive points of divergence from Ockenga, Evans sees the same basic approach as other visible leaders in midcentury neo-evangelicalism, namely.[153] Part of the question here has to do with when he said what. Henry clearly heard and learned from his Black evangelical contemporaries (e.g., Bill Pannell) at some point, and he noted the ongoing need for both legislative and cultural changes to address racism. He, too, believed that evangelical churches had made "large strides in the realm of interpersonal relations between races," but Henry also claimed, "It remains for Evangelicals to identify themselves conspicuously and publicly with Negroes and others in the struggle for equality before the law."[154] Henry's emphasis in this arena remained on personal attitudes and conduct, which he could imagine carrying over into direct political engagement and public displays of solidarity: "It is the duty of Christians to advocate and support good laws and to lead the way in obeying them."[155] But he stridently rejected any suggestion that the church, as an institution or as a separate sphere of social life, should exert itself on the political sphere.[156] In the case of civil rights legislation, he vaguely registered some reservations and described the role of government as protecting rights, not compassion or charity.[157] All the same, these more direct comments on race and social structures appear in his *Evangelicals at the Brink of Crisis* (Word Books, 1967), which reflect some shifts in his approach as he engaged critical feedback—as in his 1966 exchange with Fuller Seminary ethicist Lewis Smedes in *The Reformed Journal*. And as we will see in chapter 5, Henry did connect in some ways with the more progressive wave of younger evangelicals in the years that followed.

PRELIMINARY CONCLUSIONS

In light of Ockenga's public theology and activism, we would do well to reflect on the historical problems of (a) how to identify "evangelicalism" as a spiritual stream or spirit in the first place and (b) whether one could genuinely speak on behalf of a group identified as "evangelicals" in public. George Marsden casts doubt on the coherence of a distinct "new evangelicalism" in the more expansive evangelical sea that came into view in the 1970s.[158] He is thinking of specific historical developments like the breakthrough of racially diverse evangelical voices, the rise of Pentecostalism, and also the emergence of political progressives making counterclaims to Ockenga's white fundamentalist-evangelical brand. Scholars more in touch with nonelite, rank-and-file evangelicals (e.g., Donald Dayton) have regularly questioned whether the ambitious, highly visible neo-evangelicals of Ockenga's build could truly represent "evangelicalism"—theologically, politically, or otherwise.[159] Putting a different spin on these problems, Molly Worthen frames "how to act publicly on faith after the rupture of Christendom" as a typological *question* with which evangelicals wrestle.[160] This strategy enables her to look beyond those who have shared a narrowly conceived "evangelical" consensus. There she finds, for example, numerous Anabaptists and Wesleyans who contributed to key conversations about the meaning of evangelicalism from early on and yet remained on the fringes as the mainstream cohort of neo-evangelicals united around a chiefly Calvinist, politically conservative platform. Similarly, Matthew Sutton traces the diversity of "fundamentalists" (in his terminology), providing an especially illuminating juxtaposition of Black and white fundamentalists' apocalyptic interpretations of prevailing social conditions.[161] He also spotlights long-standing political disunity among those who maintained fundamentalist theological convictions, owing at least partly to other significant demographic features (e.g., geography and class).[162]

Though they foregrounded fundamental theological beliefs and a certain spiritual mood as they identified with evangelicalism in the flow of church history, I find that Ockenga and company's new evangelicals reflect a *historically comprised and compromised social group* more so than the heights of some generic, ideal type. In making this claim, I mean to sit askew the debate among historians like Mark Noll and David Bebbington about whether "evangelicalism" is merely a helpful conceptual tool for organizing historical data, an ideal type that exists prior to specific historical persons and groups in which it appears, or some kind of essence discernible in the same real-world data.[163] Whatever one might come up with while studying along those lines, Ockenga and his cohort were no *mere* evangelicals. And the same is indisputably true of anyone self-identifying as or ascribed an identity as such. The sense that a new evangelical (or fundamentalist reform) movement was possible and necessary in the first place emerged from congenial conversations among a relatively small number of American religious leaders and sponsors. To be more specific, as Marsden notes of the folks organizing Fuller Theological Seminary, they all shared a "classic American, rugged individualist outlook. All, for instance, were conservative Republicans. They represented . . . those who characteristically had struggled through the [Great D]epression but who had maintained their pride and firm attachments to the traditional Protestant American values of hard work and self-help."[164] In fact, the early neo-evangelical brain trust shared a good many other overlapping identities: as Christians, Protestants, and evangelicals *indisputably*, but also as straight, white, affluent, male Protestants (to suggest a twenty-first-century spin on the old WASP acronym). This small number of folks shared a (hi)story and a set of convictions sufficient to envision and work toward the same goals, but given these numerous similarities, we cannot effortlessly determine which or how many parts of their consolidated identity structure sparked the movement.

We do know the neo-evangelicals *nominalized* their cherished religious identity as the essential difference between them and the various threats they perceived—from the godless, influential liberal to the revolutionary, Black student. And folks like Ockenga used this identity for cultural engagement and political activism that, in truth, exemplifies the vulgar sense of "identity politics" as a zero-sum war of cultures. This trajectory carried through the Moral Majority era and later the George W. Bush administration made "evangelicalism" a household name in America. In their day, early neo-evangelical leadership framed a storied response to the falling stock of Christian faith and the attendant social degradation together with an attempt to name the broad orthodoxy they imagined "unvoiced multitudes" to share.[165] But they failed to even register the possibility that more than one nerve (e.g., spiritual, theological, racial, and partisan-ideological) could have been pinched by the perceived assaults. And when a group operates in public space under the assumption that it is always already under siege and in need of defense, insiders are much less likely to comprehend the complexity or its dilemma. Thus, they could narrate a history of Christian nationalism even though they felt their illustrious tribe was embattled, and they could push to legislate their own morality while decrying the creep of an octopus-like state—all within the assumed normativity of their superior, all-ordering world-view.[166] The relative homogeneity of Ockenga's social network enabled him and other insiders to continue thinking of themselves as evangelical Christians first and foremost.

Yet without feeling the need to *name* them among the sources of their core beliefs, the neo-evangelical leaders *voiced* many "other" salient social factors within their public-facing world-view. And while they did this, they conceived of the evangelical individual generically and thus maximally in their image—as holding eminently to what they claimed as biblical world-view principles that cashed out in shared political commitments. This process was aided by the appearance of voluntary association with the evangelical cause; anyone sharing the stated convictions was presumably welcome to join. But some number of individuals were excluded in practice because visible leaders made clear (if in the style of dog-whistle politics) that factors like race and political ideology indeed limited recognized membership and because, partly for that reason, the leadership structure did not include them from the start. The principles that Ockenga outlined as the most important, and thus as supposedly precipitating moves in the more detailed platform, were thin enough to seem as though they allowed some latitude even as the unspoken rules and convictions of the social group served an inhibitive function. Describing how the embedded and (mostly) unconsidered commonalities named above started to matter, Marsden explains, "The fundamentalist wing of evangelicalism was a church without a formal creed, but with many informal ones. Standards of the informal creeds could be enforced by appeals to popular opinion. Before that court, even more than before a formal ecclesiastical court, the truly fundamental was difficult to distinguish from the peripheral."[167] And Ockenga is a clear case study in how the notion of a "biblical world-view" invoked in representative advocacy "as an evangelical" can somewhat quietly balloon with other categories' convictions. The history of neo-evangelicalism reads less like a voluntary association gathering around a spiritual-theological ideal and more like a social group trying to revise its history and clear its path to hegemonic power.

The totalizing narrative about an "evangelical" identity inhibited any sense of solidarity with those who shared the stated principles of the neo-evangelical movement and appreciated the general goal of social action *yet differed from the establishment* in the details of their socially structured reality or, more simply, of their world-view. For instance, Ockenga flatly rejected the emphases of Black evangelicals while conserving the salience of racial difference as God-ordained, which, taken with the analysis above, reflects a white supremacist posture even if somewhat unintentionally. White Christians need to assess such identity politics (visible and hidden) with eyes wide open, starting with the identity-based power dynamics at play in their own churches, denominations, and cherished parachurch institutions, and they must stop (I should say, "*We* must stop") uncritically imagining that any other identifiers either fall below the Christian one hierarchically or gracefully cohere with it. After reviewing some of Ockenga's particular social pronouncements "on behalf of" this constituency, one might pessimistically conclude that he learned too much from his perceived world-viewing opponents (here the Federal Council of Churches), who had "proven by their official acts that they will not tolerate dissent in their membership in reference to the support of missionary and benevolent enterprises. Human nature is such that, given the opportunity to exercise such power, oppression of dissenting minorities would again arise."[168] In this conclusion, applied to Ockenga himself, is some truth. For aside from his *intentions*, one might see him living in isolation from (and insulation against) any real, evangelical "others."

All the same, these evangelicals did not amount to a conventional "social group" either. What would it mean to identify, address, represent, and oversee a movement of people who share some beliefs and sensibilities (i.e., a Weberian ideal type) but no formal union or organizational structure encompassing enough to allow for shared discernment and accountable leadership? Recall Ockenga's claim, "I have very few things which I can unreservedly support except my own independent church and its one-hundred percent evangelical program." He was calling on the many individuals dissatisfied with their real-life local communities to join in the wish-dream of a church unified in his Biblical Theism such that they would sacrifice other loyalties when necessary to support the general community of the faithful. Ockenga capitalized on the libertarian, free-enterprising views of individual actors to weaken local ecclesial ties while imagining himself as pastor-leader of unvoiced multitudes joined in an ideal church organization in the vanguard of a broad cultural movement. Part of what has long made the image of "evangelicalism" as an identifiable social movement plausible is that its constituent audience is such a broad, abstract, genuinely nonexistent "community" comprised of individuals who may or may not regularly engage, let alone commit to, a local church of real human beings. This state of affairs facilitates a lack of accountability (except to donors) on the part of highly visible leaders like Ockenga, and it simultaneously gets people thinking of Christianity primarily as beliefs—specifically, about the consonance of what they hear in church, through media, and so on with their own inner unity of ideas. When individuals practice a preference for such abstract ideals, they become untethered from historical traditions that might contextualize and cast in relief the constellation of social factors in their own cognition; and this untethering in turn encourages the consumerist trend of church shopping, such that a person can pack up, leave, and find a church that seems "more truly evangelical" any time their current community makes or supports any notion that disturbs their sense of inner unity. Real, historical community where actual, local accountability is engendered (sometimes in genuine, inescapable disagreements) is thus undercut, further ensconcing the unaccountable individualism that is so characteristic of certain sectors of American public life.

So, what should we say about evangelical identity politics? Does "identity politics" as a mode of activism work to describe evangelicals like Ockenga? We might do well to set the concept in this landscape as a mode of social group activism that originates in analyses of prevailing power arrangements that uncover oppression—ranging from marginalization and powerlessness to exploitation and overt violence—on the basis of a common nominal social parameter (e.g., race, gender, sexuality, and/or religion).[169] To engage in identity politics, then, means to claim such a parameter from within and to assert its salience as a basis for solidarity and consciousness-raising in order to end the oppression of *this* identifiable group, at the very least. More ambitious goals include disrupting the various forms of power (e.g., political, economic, moral) consolidated against those who share in this identity and securing a power distribution that is neutral to or more advantageous for the same. Sometimes a combination of parameters is taken up (e.g., womanism), especially when the visible leadership of mainstream single-identity politics (e.g., feminism or Black liberation) fails to account for the actual lives of those who are oppressed on the basis of more than one parameter. Poet-activist Audre Lorde named this issue quite clearly when she described something of an impulse among those who stand somehow outside the consolidated power of a "mythical norm" to isolate and emphasize a single social parameter by which they differ from that norm and to "assume that to be the primary cause of all oppression, forgetting, and other distortions around difference, some of which we ourselves may be practicing."[170] As an example, Lorde names this in the feminist movement, which at least then tended to "ignore differences of race, sexual preference, class, and age. There is a pretense of homogeneity of experience covered by the word *sisterhood* that does not in fact exist."[171] Consequently, much of the contemporary criticism of identity politics is leveled at either the naivety or the totality of such narratives, especially when conceived as a zero-sum game in defiance of the original meaning explored by the Black feminists of the Combahee River Collective (i.e., as a way of saying: if life looks better for Black women, it will look better for everyone).[172] This is the case when whites get up in arms about the #BlackLivesMatter movement, responding to a straw man (i.e., *only* Black lives matter) with an "all lives matter sentiment."[173] For the Combahee River Collective, the #BlackLivesMatter movement, and many other identity-political groups, the idea is not to promote the welfare of one aggregate or association or social group over all others; it is to recognize the problems specific to people who share life at a particular intersection of social parameters and to name how those identities matter as a basis for pursuing a more just and sustainable reality for all.

Neo-evangelicals imagined themselves as orthodox Christians whose forebears had been instrumental in American progress but whose ilk had been branded "socially withdrawn" and "anti-intellectual" and thus had been gradually displaced from political power and disparaged by influential liberal Protestants and secular Modernists. Taken as an uprising against this perceived mistreatment, Ockenga and company's agenda of reawakening American society by forging tough evangelical minds and promoting a united front for evangelical political action might be analogous to identity politics.

But as we have seen, if Ockenga and company were, in fact, playing identity politics *as evangelicals*, their agenda was also influenced by their whiteness, US patriotism, Republican partisanship, sexuality, and so on—the stuff of their Christian tribalism. Power had in no way been consolidated against the neo-evangelicals; indeed, they incarnated Lorde's "mythical norm."[174] More than that, these folks thrust their political identity into public space partly as a gasp of frustration about the unquestioned, intuitive sense that their perspective had been and should continue to be normative in society and politics. This twentieth-century protest was born out of a sense of privilege and omnicompetence, never once considering the liabilities of social location, and it has continued as such into the twenty-first century. So, to push the analogy between neo-evangelicalism and identity politics too far would be misappropriation at best but probably just farce.

In Ockenga's story, we can clearly grasp something we might be tempted to call a "world-view," but I would not say it is overwhelmingly "evangelical" as if that were the most prominent descriptor or even sufficient in any way to name the bundle of convictions he articulates as "biblical." His race, gender, class, nationality, partisan ideology, and more come through in what he articulates without him given direct attention to these features—the true unvoiced multitudes. White evangelical resistance to the civil rights movement in the 1950s and 1960s is a clear example of how Ockenga's social network was captive to the surrounding culture, preaching the status quo as part and parcel of the evangel.[175] So, we might say the language of world-view is interesting and helpful as far as it gets us, but it is also profoundly misleading. Our convictions come to us from a variety of sources such that a singularly nameable, shareable "world-view" fails to do us justice. For Christians living within the complex field of relations that comprises American society, James Wm. McClendon Jr. cautions, "Our true sociality is called church, yet that does not end the matter: we find ourselves, as did Jesus, engaged by a world that enters us—as temptation, if we are like him; or when we fall short of his graceful stance, as constitutive reality."[176] Many worlds course around but also *through* Christians, and thus their churches, exerting formative power upon individual lives and communal histories and myths. Perhaps the more substantive point here is that such power not only shapes human ways of seeing the world but structures the social world into which history throws us, without regard for whether we see it as such. Willie Jennings calls this "the dual operation of the way the world is imagined and the way social worlds constitute the imagination."[177] From the early days of the new evangelicalism, leaders like Ockenga impressed upon their institutions a life- and world-view hypothesis that shrouds this social constitution of their imaginations, the imagination involved in their theologizing, and the contingency of all obedience. And we may also begin to ask how the social groups beneath his other statuses and commitments come to benefit from the more visible and ostensibly more virtuous identity politics (namely, evangelical) as they begin to pass unnamed. Ockenga represents a kind of historical bridge character in that he (a) articulates the white identity politics more explicitly in keeping with past generations (b) within the seemingly more neutral form of omnicompetent world-viewing that renders the operations of whiteness more transparent in and to later generations.

While he seemed to be aware of the need to observe and tolerate dissent among identifiable evangelicals, Ockenga seized upon a usefully empty signifier (namely, "world-view") to use rhetorically with shifting and underdeveloped content to fit whatever polemic or insecurity he and his social network felt at the moment. When speaking of what was required for evangelical consensus and mutual representation, Ockenga named only thin theological principles, as represented in official statements of faith. But when speaking to and on behalf of this constituency, he pushed a more specified social agenda that he more or less genuinely imagined flowing naturally from his principles. When he spoke politically on issues of partisan politics, warfare, economics, race, and civil rights, he descriptively did not speak on behalf of many who shared his stated evangelical convictions.[178] And it is precisely the relative emptiness of the named world-view itself that makes it so full of bad power and serviceable to all kinds of things that go unrecognized or at least understated. The conviction that the principles settle the whole world-view is just that, a conviction; from outside the ideological power center and its normative membership, it appears as though the social group settles the comprehensive world-view by constellating the fundamental religious convictions, including principles of interpretation, with a number of others. But again, a focus on individual adherence to a stated world-view, with emphasis on conversion and conscience, untethers individuals from accountability to actual churches or even persons unless they are already predisposed to agree with the judgment coming their way—accountable *within* the affirmed world-view, but accountable to no one *for the world-view itself*. This is true from laity to leadership. Had Ockenga been held to account for the details of his world-view, had he been able to hear those who could be identified as "evangelical" by NAE statement of faith standards, then he might have encountered folks like Bill Pannell (who will appear in chapter 4) in their opposition to his racialized politics—and in so doing he might have had a fruitful consciousness-doubling experience that would also make demands of his posture toward his social context(s).

While the NAE continues to broadcast its "influence for the good" over the largest identifiable population of "evangelicals" (i.e., according to core beliefs), the politics of 2016 and beyond have put mainstream evangelical organizations' feet to the fire. Given the wide range of moral deficiencies, troubling rhetoric, and cruel policies and actions put forward by candidate and then president Donald Trump, the reality that he enjoyed the support of roughly 80 percent of white evangelicals in the 2016 presidential election (and 76 percent in 2020) has at least superficially raised existential questions among the leadership of many mainstream evangelical institutions.[179] And partly to combat the problematic optics of white evangelical Trump supporters, some insiders have revealed their temptation to play up the diversity of those who share the stated theological convictions (e.g., 44 percent of Black Americans and some number of mainline Christians and Roman Catholics).[180] As Ed Stetzer explains, "Perhaps most important, this belief-centered approach includes evangelicals who are commonly missed by other studies. Although African American Christians have historically aligned with evangelical beliefs, they use the identifier language less frequently."[181] But think of what such strategy means in terms of deflecting responsibility and conscripting the unwilling service of historically excluded others. As I hope becomes clear by the end of part II, the history of American evangelicalism, including the role of the NAE—as distinct from the National Black Association of Evangelicals, founded 20 years later to promote biblical *and cultural* integrity—can and does make sense of the white evangelical Trump supporter even as the NAE statement of faith cannot. Worse, long-standing mainstream organizations' circumscription of diverse and, in many cases, "anonymous" evangelicals could be cynically interpreted as keeping with the neo-evangelical entrepreneurial tradition of using data selectively to preserve their relevance and legitimacy—without reflecting deeply (or theologically) about all of this or seeking institutional cultural reform.[182] In the earlier days of evangelical counting by Gallup, Inc., based primarily on self-identification throughout the 1970s and 1980s as they began inquiring during Jimmy Carter's 1976 presidential campaign, Ockenga and other evangelical leaders would claim the larger numbers to boost their credentials when they spoke "as evangelicals" in public, pushing a less representative agenda, even as they policed institutional membership according to a larger battery of tests, including racial and political ones. Contemporary leaders may claim to be defined by a theological evangelicalism that reflects a more diverse population rather than being confined to a particular sociocultural history and thus try to contest their share in the embarrassing politics of the many white evangelicals.[183]

I wager that the greatest threat to contemporary Christian faithfulness is the ongoing insistence not only on the *existence of* but on *my people's and my personal adherence to* "the biblical world-view." Such a perspective rarely helps us live more honestly or bear authentic witness to the world around and within us; on the contrary, this insistence subsumes powerful, less-than-Christian interests and loyalties within the Christian imagination, setting barriers to Christian recognition of and repentance from these powers. In the world we know, we would be hard-pressed to identify anything like "pure Christianity" that stands over and against the practices of this world. Christianity itself comes to us *in and through the world*. At worst, attempts to say otherwise veil the desire to re-create others in one's own image, to write one's own perspective across the whole of Christendom. From this trajectory, we must turn. We must unremittingly critique even our most cherished communal myths precisely because they inform group identities that are *real* to the extent that they have real consequences. Many react against the real or perceived authoritarianism in and of faith communities with a commitment to secularism, which suggests that the world-view strategy for responding to the storied threat of godless Modernism is precisely the wrong approach.[184] Neo-evangelicals located one precipitating problem in modern thought—the abandonment of the biblical God as the first principle—and those who react against its authoritarian reassertion in the form of an exclusionary, comprehensive, and secular world-view locate the problem in one precipitating principle: the biblical God. Both are wrong. The problem is the botched witness of those who cannot recognize their w(h)it(e)ness—in other words, the evangelicalism of Ockenga and company could only conceive of Christian witness with some silent letters. Now we must ask: Why?

NOTES

1. Harold Ockenga, "Christ for America" (presidential address, meeting of the National Association of Evangelicals, Chicago, May 4, 1943), in National Association of Evangelicals, *United . . . We Stand: A Report of the Constitutional Convention of the National Association of Evangelicals, May 3–6, 1943* (Boston: NAE, 1943), 11 and 13.

2. Ockenga, "Christ for America," 12.

3. Ockenga, "Christ for America," 11. Carl Henry named "the ultimacy of nature" as concurrently (a) the "central postulate of the modern mind" and (b) a fundamental "denial of special divine revelation" (*The Drift of Western Thought* [Grand Rapids: Eerdmans, 1951], 41). He saw "the genuine alternates [as] the biblical revelation or a naturalistic emptying of the meaning of life and the voiding of the significance of history" (75).

4. This way of phrasing the presuppositions is consistent with Ockenga's thinking in this period but comes from a later sermon published in *Faith in a Troubled World* (Wenham, MA: Gordon College Press, 1972), 49. Cf. Harold Ockenga, "The Challenge to the Christian Culture of the West" (presidential address, opening convocation of Fuller Theological Seminary, Pasadena, CA, October 1, 1947), accessed March 9, 2020, https://fullerstudio.fuller.edu/the–challenge-to-the-christian-culture-of-the-west-opening-convocation-october-1-1947/; and Carl F. H. Henry, *Evangelicals at the Brink of Crisis* (Waco, TX: Word Books, 1967), 115.

5. Ockenga, "Christ for America," 9.

6. Ockenga, "Christ for America," 12. Cf. Ockenga, *Troubled World*, 4–6 and 48–49; and Henry, *The Drift*, 54 and 62. Ockenga was partly rehearsing Christian fundamentalist assessments of what happened to Germany around World War I, as the US propaganda machine painted Germans as devolving into barbarity and thus threatening the Western way of life. For Christian fundamentalists, it was expeditious to tie this civilizational breakdown to the embrace of Modernism (historical criticism of the Bible, evolutionary science, etc.), but in my analysis, Ockenga's interpretation of ideologies like Nazism as utterly secular is indefensible. Not only did Nazism deal in premodern Teutonic mythologies, but its propagandists borrowed extensively from Christian language and imagery (see chapter 6).

7. Mark Noll prominently credits these three names with this intellectual endeavor in *American Evangelical Christianity: An Introduction* (Malden, MA: Blackwell Publishers, 2001), 19.

8. In the mid-1960s, Henry claimed, "Only three formidable movements insist that man can know ultimate reality," namely, Communism (esp. in its cooptation of Hegelian idealism), Roman Catholicism, and evangelicalism (*Brink of Crisis*, 7).

9. Ockenga, *Troubled World*, 4.

10. Ockenga, "Christ for America," 12. Cf. Ockenga, *Troubled World*, 18; Ockenga, "The New Reformation," *Bibliotheca Sacra* 105, no. 417 (January–March 1948): 101; and Henry, *Brink of Crisis*, 78. One would do well to read historian Mark Noll's account of early evangelical presence and the flows of influence in the United States (*American Evangelical*, 183–85 and 191–200).

11. George Marsden, *Reforming Fundamentalism: Fuller Seminary and the New Evangelicalism* (Grand Rapids: Eerdmans, 1987), 62.

12. Ockenga, *Troubled World*, 31; cf. 76–77. Cf. Harold Ockenga, "The New Evangelicalism," Societal Questions and Problems, Part 5 (sermon, Park Street Congregational Church, Boston, MA, January 5, 1958), accessed August 10, 2015, http://www.parkstreet.org/library/sermons/speaker/Harold-Ockenga; and Henry, *Brink of Crisis*, 54–55.

13. For a snapshot of these fundamentalists, see Noll, *American Evangelical*, 16–18.

14. Mark A. Noll, *The Scandal of the Evangelical Mind* (Grand Rapids: Eerdmans, 1994), 213.

15. Noll, *Scandal*, 213. Cf. Noll, *American Evangelical*, 18–19.

16. Harold Ockenga, introduction to *The Uneasy Conscience of Modern Fundamentalism*, by Carl. F. H. Henry (1947; repr., Grand Rapids: Eerdmans, 2003), xx. Marsden clarifies here that Ockenga's use of "progressive" here applies to the fundamentalism but not to the social message (81).

17. Henry, *Uneasy Conscience*, xvii.

18. Harold Ockenga, "The Unvoiced Multitudes," in *Evangelical Action!* (Boston, MA: United Action Press, 1942), 20–21. For more on the history of the transition between dominant modes of Protestant Christianity in the United States, see Robert P. Jones, *The End of White Christian America* (New York: Simon & Schuster, 2016), 30–37.

19. Harold Ockenga, *Our Evangelical Faith* (Grand Rapids: Zondervan, 1946), 70.
20. Ockenga, "Unvoiced Multitudes," 19; cf. 21–24.
21. Ockenga, "Unvoiced Multitudes," 27.
22. Ockenga, "Unvoiced Multitudes," 20–21.
23. Ockenga, "Unvoiced Multitudes," 37–38.
24. Ockenga, "Unvoiced Multitudes," 33.
25. Ockenga, "Christ for America," 10. Comparing the mainline Protestant vision with evangelicals' more defensive midcentury approach, Jones argues, "Instead of confidently ushering in 'the Christian Century' with a vision of international cooperation with all people of good will, their [evangelicals'] goal was to restore and protect a distinctly Protestant Christian America, which would then allow the United States to fulfill its divine mandate in the world" (37).
26. Ockenga, "Christ for America," 10. Cf. Owen Strachan, *Awakening the Evangelical Mind: An Intellectual History of the Neo-Evangelical Movement* (Grand Rapids: Zondervan, 2015), 61–62.
27. Ockenga, "Unvoiced Multitudes," 25.
28. Ockenga, "Challenge."
29. Ockenga, "Unvoiced Multitudes," 35–37. Cf. Henry, *Uneasy Conscience*, 69ff; and Henry, *Brink of Crisis*, 43–46.
30. Ockenga, *Troubled World*, 76; emphasis added.
31. Ockenga, "Challenge."
32. Ockenga, *Troubled World*, 81–82.
33. Ockenga, *Troubled World*, 36 and 39. Cf. Carl F. H. Henry, *A Plea for Evangelical Demonstration* (Grand Rapids: Baker Book House, 1971), 37–43.
34. Ockenga, *Troubled World*, 87–89. Cf. Harold Ockenga, "Fulfilled and Unfulfilled Prophecy," in *Prophecy in the Making*, Messages Prepared for Jerusalem Conference on Biblical Prophecy, ed. Carl F. H. Henry (Carol Stream, IL: Creation House, 1971), 304–5.
35. Ockenga, "Christ for America," 9. Henry invoked James Orr's Kerr Lectures (mentioned in the Introduction) and counseled, "Christianity, if it is to make good its claim to universal and perpetual significance, must relate itself to the other views of God and the world" (*The Drift*, 76–77).
36. Harold Ockenga, "The Unity Christ Seeks," *The Christian Century* 73, no. 9 (February 29, 1956): 266. "The basic requirement to any understanding of unity is the presupposition that the will of God has been mediated to men through a divinely inspired company of prophets and apostles" (266).
37. Ockenga, "New Reformation," 91.
38. Ockenga, "New Reformation," 92.
39. Ockenga, "Unity Christ Seeks," 267.
40. Ockenga, "Unity Christ Seeks," 266–67. For a fuller sense of what Ockenga has in mind here, see *Our Protestant Heritage* (Grand Rapids: Zondervan, 1938), 129–30. This explication was in the neo-evangelical air; Henry freely used this terminology too, as in *The Drift*, 46 and 55. See also Ockenga, "New Evangelicalism," Ockenga, *Our Evangelical Faith*, 70, and Ockenga, *Troubled World*, 9, 27–29, and 52–53.

The New Evangelical World-View of Harold Ockenga 147

41. On the interplay of fundamentals and difference, follow Ockenga's approach in *Our Evangelical Faith*. Early in his career, Ockenga even mounted a vigorous defense of the Christian dissenter's rights as another virtue of Protestantism, as in *Our Protestant Heritage*, chs. 7–8. Cf. "Finite perspective and personal interest prevent Christians from enjoying agreement on the details of Christian revelation. Christians must be willing to learn from one another in the spirit of love as they discuss and appropriate God's truth" (Ockenga, "Unity Christ Seeks," 266–67).

42. Henry, *Brink of Crisis*, 97.

43. Ockenga, "New Reformation," 91; emphasis added.

44. Henry, *A Plea*, 45. Henry notes of Christian alternatives to the neo-evangelical world-view, "Modern prejudices so dominate the contemporary spirit that it seems to many inconceivable that anything else should have motivated the first Christians" (45). And while it may be true that "no religious community is able wholly to divest itself of dependence upon the culture of its day," Henry contended, "Protestant orthodoxy must nonetheless bring driving criticism to bear upon the existing social order by insisting both on the social consequences of the fall and on the need of supernatural divine redemption" (42).

45. Henry, *A Plea*, 45–47.

46. Henry, *A Plea*, 36.

47. Henry did note the importance of "Niebuhr's insight that group behavior has massive possibilities of self-deception," but, in Henry's final analysis, Niebuhr had misapplied it to suggest that immorality does not originate in the unregenerate individual (*A Plea*, 34). It is now widely known that Niebuhr later mused that a more accurate title might have been *Immoral Man and Even More Immoral Society*, but even had *this* understanding been driven throughout Niebuhr's text, the score with Henry still would not have been settled.

48. Ockenga, *Troubled World*, 43.

49. For more on the variety of Modernism being discussed here, see Alasdair MacIntyre's account in *Whose Justice? Which Rationality?* (Notre Dame, IN: University of Notre Dame Press, 1988), ch. 17.

50. Henry, *The Drift*, 107; cf. 110–11 and 117. Cf. Ockenga, *Our Evangelical Faith*, 24, 43, and 64.

51. Ockenga, *Our Evangelical Faith*, 25; cf. 17 and 49. Cf. Ockenga's assessment of God's sovereignty in transferring a person from a realm of freedom only to sin to one of freedom to obey in *Our Protestant Heritage*, 57–58.

52. Ockenga, *Troubled World*, 54.

53. Ockenga, *Troubled World*, 50; cf. 56.

54. Ockenga, *Troubled World*, 54–55, 59.

55. Henry, *Uneasy Conscience*, 68.

56. Ockenga, *Troubled World*, 60–61.

57. Ockenga, *Troubled World*, 13.

58. Ockenga, *Troubled World*, 14.

59. Marsden, 17 and 28–29.

60. Marsden, 2 and 29. In a late 1930s sermon series, Ockenga called for a "vigorous Protestantism emphasizing individualism, dissent, liberty, and tolerance" (*Our*

Protestant Heritage, v). Note the irony of these emphases, betokening as they do the modern turn in history, given Ockenga's flat disparagement of "Modernism"—conceived as a threat totally outside evangelicalism. We might notice how Kuyper's concerns about "Methodism" as discussed in chapter 1 find their fulfillment here; perhaps not incidentally, Ockenga's own upbringing was, indeed, in the Wesleyan stream.

61. Marsden, 2, 5, and 7. Strachan suggests that Machen's route out of the Modernist conflict at Princeton Theological Seminary in the late 1920s (i.e., cofounding a new seminary) alerted Ockenga to entrepreneurial possibilities (42).

62. Matthew Avery Sutton, *American Apocalypse: A History of Modern Evangelicalism* (Cambridge, MA: The Belknap Press, 2014), 4.

63. Ockenga, "Unvoiced Multitudes," 21.

64. See references to J. Howard Pew in Marsden, 156ff., Curtis J. Evans, "White Evangelical Protestant Responses to the Civil Rights Movement," *Harvard Theological Review* 102, no. 2 (2009): 271–73, and Frances Fitzgerald, *The Evangelicals: The Struggle to Shape America* (New York: Simon & Schuster, 2017), 188–90; to Herbert J. Taylor in Darren E. Grem, *The Blessings of Business: How Corporations Shaped Conservative Christianity* (New York: Oxford University Press, 2016), ch. 1.

65. Evans, 272.

66. Ockenga, *Troubled World*, 62; cf. 75–78.

67. Ockenga, "Unvoiced Multitudes," 28.

68. Ockenga, "Unvoiced Multitudes," 28.

69. I do not see him saying this bit out loud in many places, but this sentiment is found in his "Who's Who" application, as quoted in Strachan, 30.

70. Ockenga, *Troubled World*, 37–38.

71. Ockenga, *Troubled World*, 41.

72. Ockenga, "Challenge." Cf. Ockenga, "Unvoiced Multitudes," 26–29.

73. Ockenga, *Troubled World*, 6–7.

74. Ockenga, *Troubled World*, 76.

75. Ockenga, "Unvoiced Multitudes," 26–27; and Ockenga, *Our Protestant Heritage*, v. Cf. Strachan, 40.

76. Ockenga, "New Reformation," 94.

77. Ockenga, "Christ for America," 12. Cf. "Under [Satan] we have many antagonists which are called evil spirits or demons, and which have various ranges of authority and power among themselves. They are called princes, authorities, world rulers. . . . The iniquities of our day are largely demon-inspired, so that men are worshiping them as such, by which we mean sex, blood, power, strong weapons, strong men, even human theories marshaling nations for war" (Harold Ockenga, *Faithful in Christ* [New York: Fleming H. Revell Company, 1948], 243).

78. Ockenga, "Christ for America," 13.

79. Ockenga, *Troubled World*, 37–38. Notice the door this opens for directly naming who Satan's emissaries are (i.e., demonization), believing that one can tell by observing their policies and public arguments down to the detail.

80. Ockenga, *Troubled World*, 86.

81. Henry, *Brink of Crisis*, 56–57.

82. Henry, *Brink of Crisis*, 74. Henry lamented the state of "evangelism" in the Western world, where its "isolation . . . from the New Testament evangel" and its direction away from "spiritual-redemptive" and toward "secular-political" foci had redefined the Church's task in the world: "The mission of the Church, we are now told, is the revolutionizing of social structures, not the salvation of sinners" (*Brink of Crisis*, 35).

83. Henry, *Uneasy Conscience*, 13.

84. Ockenga, *Our Evangelical Faith*, ch. 4.

85. Ockenga, "Challenge." Cf. Ockenga, "New Reformation," 99–100; and Henry, *Brink of Crisis*, 113.

86. Ockenga, *Troubled World*, 30. Cf. Ockenga, "New Evangelicalism."

87. Ockenga, "Christ for America," 15.

88. Ockenga, *Troubled World*, 30. Cf. Henry, *Brink of Crisis*, 73.

89. Ockenga, "New Evangelicalism." Evans calls attention to this same sentiment in E. J. Carnell, who explicitly rejected the sense that conversion to belief in Jesus Christ would necessarily lead to a robust sanctification (256).

90. Ockenga, *Troubled World*, 30. Cf. Henry, *Brink of Crisis*, 72.

91. Henry, *Uneasy Conscience*, 79–80. Cf. Ockenga, "New Evangelicalism."

92. Ockenga, *Troubled World*, 44–45. Cf. Henry, *A Plea*, 122–24.

93. Henry, *Uneasy Conscience*, 84–85.

94. David Swartz names Henry's *Uneasy Conscience* "a call . . . without a well-defined program," and he recounts Lewis Smedes's criticism of Henry as lacking concreteness and indicating, "Evangelicals do not yet have a social ethic" (*Moral Minority: The Evangelical Left in an Age of Conservatism* [Philadelphia: University of Pennsylvania Press, 2012], 21; Smedes quoted in ibid.). This criticism is especially important given Henry's derision of so-called American Protestant orthodoxy (naming Union Theological Seminary) whose representatives were proving incapable of producing a "unified social ethics or program of evangelical social action," instead promoting "successive and competitive theories characterized by repeated revision" (*A Plea*, 23).

95. Ockenga, *Troubled World*, 3.

96. Harold Ockenga, "Rehoboam, a Nation's Dictator—or—The Civil War of a People," (sermon, n.d.) quoted in Sutton, 259.

97. Harold Ockenga quoted in Sutton, 270.

98. H. Crosby Englizian, *Brimstone Corner: Park Street Church, Boston* (Chicago: Moody, 1968), 221.

99. Cf. Ockenga, *Troubled World*, 78.

100. Sutton synopsizes these points from Harold Ockenga, "The American Way of Life and Its Substitutes" (sermon, May 28, 1944) on page 290. Cf. Ockenga, *Troubled World*, 5–6. Sutton argues that white fundamentalist preaching and literature during the interwar period made clear: "at the root of their racial anxieties was a deep-seated fear of intermarriage" (134). Cf. William E. Pannell, *My Friend, the Enemy* (Waco, TX: Word Books, 1968), ch. 7.

101. Harold Ockenga, "Letter to the Times," *New York Times*, March 6, 1944, quoted in Sutton, 277.

102. Harold Ockenga, "The Christian as a Member of the State" (sermon, October 20, 1940), quoted in Sutton, 277.

103. Shaun Casey cites a letter from Ockenga to Nixon dated March 2, 1959, in *The Making of a Catholic President: Kennedy vs. Nixon 1960* (New York: Oxford University Press, 2009), 220n48.

104. Casey, 252.

105. Harold Ockenga quoted in Sutton, 331.

106. "Evangelicalism" as an identity has political heft in the early twenty-first century that it did not have in the prime of Ockenga's public theology. Partly for this reason, and partly because Ockenga and company imagined their New Evangelicalism as a movement to renew the broader Protestant spirit through the public energy of the all-encompassing biblical world-view, representatives sometimes identified themselves as "Christian" or "Protestant," rather than "evangelical."

107. Harold Ockenga, "McGovern vs. Nixon," *Hamilton-Wenham Chronicle*, November 2, 1972, quoted in Swartz, 174–75.

108. Harold Ockenga to Walden Howard, October 13, 1972, quoted in Swartz, 175.

109. Robert G. Duffett, "The Gospel according to George McGovern," Sojourners (March 2014), accessed January 25, 2021, https://sojo.net/magazine/march-2014/gospel-according-george-mcgovern.

110. Swartz describes the political landscape among evangelicals even before the 1960s as basically incoherent, with geographic and occupational differences factoring in heavily (14; cf. 25).

111. Harold Ockenga, "Race Prejudice," quoted in Garth M. Rosell, *The Surprising Work of God: Harold John Ockenga, Billy Graham, and the Rebirth of Evangelicalism* (Grand Rapids: Baker Academic, 2008), 167. Cf. Sutton, 136–37.

112. Ockenga, *Troubled World*, 86.

113. Charles Marsh, *The Beloved Community: How Faith Shapes Social Justice, From the Civil Rights Movement to Today* (New York: Basic Books, 2005), 263n126.

114. Ockenga, *Troubled World*, 87.

115. Ockenga, *Troubled World*, 7–8. Swartz demonstrates the partial truth of Ockenga's claim regarding Black evangelicals who moved from moderate positions to separationist ones in the 1970s (189–95). Also, even relatively sympathetic white evangelicals were concerned about aspects of the civil rights movement, threatened by perceived leadership ties to Communism and/or agenda tendencies toward socialism (Swartz, 39).

116. William Rader has provided a brief but helpful analysis of Ockenga's series in *The Church and Racial Hostility: A History of the Interpretation of Ephesians 2:11-22* (Tübingen: J. C. B. Mohr [Paul Siebeck], 1978), 238–41.

117. Ockenga, *Faithful in Christ*, 123; cf. 147ff. See also Rader, 238.

118. Ockenga, *Faithful in Christ*, 148.

119. Ockenga, *Faithful in Christ*, 231; cf. 235.

120. Ockenga, *Faithful in Christ*, 148. This distinction between varieties of equality resembles that of Billy Sunday, who preached in Philadelphia in 1922: "There will never be social equality between the white and the black. . . . The black man is entitled to civic equality. . . . When you are out on the highway with your Pierce-Arrow

limousine you have got to give half of the road to that darkey with his tin lizzie. Civil equality is all right. Social equality is another proposition" (quoted in Sutton, 135).

121. Rader, 239. Garth Rosell agrees with this assessment, but ties Ockenga's conviction back to John Wesley and Charles Finney (167–68). Rosell does not deal with any sources that might complicate this image of Ockenga; rather, he sticks with the official analysis along the lines of Ockenga's own intentions, that is, an emphasis on the individual nature of sin. Further, Rosell mistakenly equates the views of Carl Henry and Ockenga as both "seem[ing] to understand the nature of evil in corporate as well as individual terms" (173). I do find this true of Henry, but not of Ockenga; as this chapter demonstrates, the broad neo-evangelical emphasis on social *engagement* does not necessarily foster a belief in the social *nature of sin*.

122. Rader, 239.

123. Ockenga, *Faithful in Christ*, 232.

124. We have already encountered this interpretation of Genesis 9 as a fundament of Kuyper's white supremacy in chapter 1. For a sense of Ockenga's interpretive continuity with his fundamentalist forebears, see Sutton, 133–34. Willie Jennings notes some medieval and early modern theological sources for such a discussion of "Noah's sons and human ancestry," including Hugo Grotius, John Gill, Granville Sharp, and John Clarke (*The Christian Imagination: Theology and the Origins of Race* [New Haven, CT: Yale University Press, 2010], 190 and 329n55).

125. Ockenga, *Faithful in Christ*, 232.

126. Ockenga, *Faithful in Christ*, 232.

127. Rader, 240.

128. Ockenga, *Faithful in Christ*, 230.

129. Ockenga, *Faithful in Christ*, 232.

130. Ockenga, *Faithful in Christ*, 230.

131. Ockenga, *Faithful in Christ*, 234.

132. Ockenga, *Faithful in Christ*, 231. For context, this commentary was published the year after Jackie Robinson broke the color-line in Major League Baseball and in the same year that Harry Truman ordered the integration of the armed forces.

133. Ockenga, *Faithful in Christ*, 236.

134. Ockenga concludes this chapter with a poignant story illustrating the value of a Christian servant becoming the best servant he can be, winning the favor of the master and praise for God. The punch line of the story is a Polish prince saying to Ockenga, "If that is the kind of work the evangelical Christians are doing in Poland, I am willing to support it" (*Faithful in Christ*, 237).

135. Swartz, 26.

136. Harold Ockenga quoted in Strachan, 62.

137. Cf. Evans 263; and Jones, 167ff.

138. Dan R. Warren, *If It Takes All Summer: Martin Luther King, the KKK, and States' Rights in St. Augustine, 1964* (Tuscaloosa, AL: University of Alabama Press, 2008), ch. 4.

139. Harold Ockenga quoted in Warren, 70.

140. Howard Zinn, *A People's History of the United States*, new ed. (New York: Harper Perennial, 2010), 490.

141. Zinn, 490.
142. Zinn, 490.
143. Ockenga, "Fulfilled and Unfulfilled Prophecy," 306.
144. Ockenga, "Fulfilled and Unfulfilled Prophecy," 304.
145. Ockenga, *Troubled World*, 33–34.
146. Ockenga, *Troubled World*, 34.
147. Ockenga, *Troubled World*, 34–35.
148. Ockenga, *Troubled World*, 35.
149. Ockenga, *Troubled World*, 35.
150. Ockenga, *Troubled World*, 36.
151. Ockenga, *Troubled World*, 36.
152. Ockenga, *Troubled World*, 37–45. Willie Jennings identifies something of an *ordo salutis* in the long Western history of justifying white colonialist activity as "Christian," matching Ockenga's observation regarding North Korean POWs (20).
153. Evans, 265–68.
154. Henry, *Brink of Crisis*, 71. Cf. "Dare we look for interracial teams of evangelists who will circuit the earth in courageous confrontation of whole communities and nations torn apart by racial strife?" (Henry, *Brink of Crisis*, 118).
155. Henry, *Brink of Crisis*, 72. Cf. Henry, *A Plea*, 60 and 67–69; and Henry, *Uneasy Conscience*, 77ff.
156. Cf. Henry, *Brink of Crisis*, 97.
157. Carl F. H. Henry, "What Social Structures?" 1966, in *The Best of the Reformed Journal*, ed. James D. Bratt and Ronald A. Wells (Grand Rapids: Eerdmans, 2011). Cf. Swartz, 23.
158. Marsden, 9 and 230.
159. See Douglas Sweeney's helpful account in, "The Essential Evangelicalism Dialectic: The Historiography of the Early Neo-Evangelical Movement and the Observer-Participant Dilemma," 1991, in *Evangelicals: Who They Have Been, Are Now, and Could Be*, ed. Mark A. Noll, David W. Bebbington, and George M. Marsden (Grand Rapids: Eerdmans, 2019), 56–73. Cf. Marsden, 49–50.
160. Molly Worthen, *Apostles of Reason: The Crisis of Authority in American Evangelicalism* (New York: Oxford University Press, 2014), 6.
161. See, for instance, Sutton, 62–66, 109–12, 210–11, and 335.
162. Cf. Noll, *American Evangelical*, 14.
163. See their respective contributions to the roundtable on Bebbington's now-canonical "quadrilateral" for defining evangelicalism in Noll, Bebbington, and Marsden, ch. 6.
164. Marsden, 29.
165. In Ockenga, we see an early application of the trope casting evangelicals as a latent majority while also being a beleaguered minority. And his "unvoiced multitudes" rhetoric (1942) predates Richard Nixon's "silent majority" (1968) by a quarter-century.
166. As a complement to the more theological Bebbington quadrilateral, Michael Hamilton has named a "white evangelical political quadrilateral" that amounts to: (1) *Christian nationalism*, these folks believe the United States is to be a Christian nation, mostly in supersessionist terms; (2) *Christian tribalism*, the sense of loss in

contemporary American moral culture that masks what whites hope to conserve or restore in society; (3) *political moralism*, the government should promote Christian values; and (4) *antistatism*, a smaller state is better in the wake of FDR's run in the early twentieth century. See his "A Strange Love? Or: How White Evangelicals Learned to Stop Worrying and Love the Donald," in Noll, Bebbington, and Marsden, 221.

167. Marsden, 152.

168. Ockenga, *Our Protestant Heritage*, 137–38.

169. I am thinking here of Iris Marion Young's "five faces of oppression," as in *Justice and the Politics of Difference* (1990; repr., Princeton, NJ: Princeton University Press, 2011), ch. 2.

170. Audre Lorde, "Age, Race, Class, and Sex: Women Redefining Difference," 1980, in *Sister Outsider: Essays and Speeches* (1984; repr., Berkeley: Crossing Press, 2007), 116. In a larger conversation around the mythical normal and the intersectionality of identity-based power dynamics, another important conversation partner would be Elisabeth Schüssler Fiorenza, whose concept of "kyriarchy" will come up in the conclusions of chapter 5. Cf. Elisabeth Schüssler Fiorenza, *Wisdom Ways: Introducing Feminist Biblical Interpretation* (Maryknoll, NY: Orbis Books, 1970), 118–22.

171. Lorde, 116.

172. Combahee River Collective, "A Black Feminist Statement," April 1977, in *Capitalist Patriarchy and the Case for Social Feminism*, ed. Zillah R. Eisenstein (New York: NYU Press, 1979), 362–72.

173. Barna Group researchers found evangelicals to be the most likely group to respond like this in "Black Lives Matter and Racial Tension in America," May 5, 2016, accessed January 5, 2021, https://www.barna.com/research/black-lives-matter-and-racial-tension-in-america/.

174. Speaking of her US context, Lorde observed, "This norm is usually defined as white, thin, male, young, heterosexual, christian, and financially secure" (116).

175. Jones, 170.

176. James Wm. McClendon Jr., *Ethics: Systematic Theology, Volume 1*, Rev. ed. (Nashville: Abingdon Press, 2002), 163–64.

177. Jennings, 248.

178. Richard Mouw named something like this in the late 1970s; see his "Evangelicals in Search of Maturity," *Theology Today* 35, no. 1 (April 1978): 43.

179. For the polling data, see Frank Newport, "Religious Group Voting and the 2020 Election," Gallup, Inc., November 13, 2020, accessed January 25, 2021, https://news.gallup.com/opinion/polling-matters/324410/religious-group-voting-2020-election.aspx. On the existential questioning, see for example, Mark Labberton, ed., *Still Evangelical?: Insiders Reconsider Political, Social, and Theological Meaning* (Downers Grove: InterVarsity Press, 2018).

180. Ed Stetzer, "Defining Evangelicals in Research," *Evangelicals* 3, no. 3 (Winter 2017/18): 12–13.

181. Stetzer, 13.

182. Compare Stetzer with Mark A. Noll, "One Word but Three Crises," in Noll, Bebbington, and Marsden, 7.

183. See the insistence on theological self-definition over against political, social, and cultural definitions in the NAE-sponsored "An Evangelical Manifesto: A Declaration of Evangelical Identity and Public Commitment," May 7, 2008, page 4, accessed February 23, 2021, http://www.ntslibrary.com/PDF%20Books/Evangelical_Manifesto.pdf. More on this document in chapter 5.

184. See, for instance, the survey data on reasons those who identify as nonreligious cite for their unaffiliated status in Pew Research Center, "Why America's 'Nones' Don't Identify with a Religion," August 8, 2018, accessed February 27, 2020, https://pewresearch.org/fact-tank/2018/08/08/why-americas-nones-dont-identify-with-a-religion/.

Chapter 4
A Sociohistorical Analysis of White, American Evangelicalism

When they set out to gather and galvanize a people under the "evangelical" banner in the 1940s, Ockenga and company envisioned fundamentalist orthodoxy swelling into a movement to recast the United States as a conservative Christian nation. And they flew their standard in public as representatives of such a movement as though the silent majority of Americans were already behind them. Political punditry from the 1970s through the turn of the century started picking up on their rhetoric and, in their gestures toward evangelicals as a more or less unified voting bloc, seemed to vindicate the founders' assumptions and validate their impact. And as polling data began to reflect the heft of an identifiable evangelical populace, all the more credence was lent to the image of the evangelicals as a political force to be reckoned with. Given the high-profile activism of some evangelicals since those days, the general public along with many rank-and-file evangelicals suppose a simple form of contemporary "identity politics" is afoot. But despite the efforts of some highly visible leaders in the mainstream evangelical establishment (including Richard Mouw, to be studied in the next chapter) to turn the evangelical tide against Donald Trump in the 2020 US presidential contest, a large majority of white evangelicals doubled down on their commitment to, if not the president, the Republican party.[1] Clearly, the expressed positions of key, mainstream evangelical leaders and the survey and exit poll data on white rank-and-file evangelicals are at variance.

In this chapter, I will analyze the relationship between whiteness and evangelical world-viewing, including current sociological resources shedding light on racialization in American churches. As we will discover, the whole "world-view," or even the total politics, of any group operating in a highly differentiated social space can hardly be spelled out by way of a single identifier, that is, whatever "identity" *this* people understands to be most significant. And when that identity is cherished and allowed to exert a totalizing effect on its members, this difficulty is compounded—all the more when the identity group is portrayed as, and feels like it is, besieged. Relatively few white American evangelicals, including those in visible leadership positions, have either the skill or will to discern with any clarity the numerous social factors impinging upon and structuring their lives in the world. And still less are willing to entertain the possibility that their claims to Christian orthodoxy, at times, conceal the interests of more particular communities and social groups (their churches included). Below I will analyze the social liability of an evangelical world-view relative to whiteness and the Christian nationalism and tribalism that attend it, using language and concepts current with sociologists, political and cultural theorists, and theologians who make use of these categories. I will particularly explore how "whiteness" has operated as a transparent social imaginary within mainstream evangelical institutions and churches since, if not by, their design. Of course, this has rarely been an explicit element in the rhetoric of evangelical leaders—though we have seen it in Ockenga. But diagnosing the contemporary problems accurately requires exploring the formative impact of nonvoluntary social parameters and experiences. As a matter of description, if not intention, single identifiers like "evangelical" or "biblical Christians" can mask other social factors that significantly affect the social group gathered under that banner. So, the concepts channeled into more direct criticism throughout this chapter will prove helpful only to the extent that they reveal how a multiplicity of social parameters can and do operate behind such identifiers, masking their operation from those who claim and maybe even those who narrate that identity.

I will open with the case of William E. "Bill" Pannell (1929–), whose social criticism defied Ockenga's attempt to represent publicly all who hold the explicit evangelical convictions (i.e., the NAE's statement of faith). He openly identified the marriage of conservative, partisan, wealthy white interests to the "evangelical" program, and he contested the claim that his own evangelical convictions must lead to the same detailed, "psycho-political" world-view. Much of what follows this vignette will amount to spotlighting this problem's rippling effects in the present and layering on new language and conceptuality for the problems that Pannell saw and named so clearly. First, current sociological studies will put numbers and theory to the real problems of racialization and lagging integration among twenty-first-century American evangelicals. Even in the growing number of multiracial churches, the forms of whiteness that characterize evangelicalism continue to exert a surprising and somewhat hidden influence. Framing this reality within current theory will help us picture how Ockenga and others could perform evangelicalism within racialized structures without necessarily intending it—and why reforming these structures presents an uphill battle. Then, I will demonstrate how the impulse to imagine the whole world and all of its people(s) at once through "the biblical world-view" has been bound up in the racial framework of the modern West since its arrival as a global reality. The world-viewing impulse itself is embedded in a history that involves the globetrotting quality of "whiteness," as I will underscore by engaging Willie Jennings's masterful work on this phenomenon. And finally, I will bring all this analysis to bear on the history of white American evangelicalism since the World War II era. In my closing pages below, I will suggest some viable pathways for a theology of identity that truthfully accounts for the multifaceted realities generated by humans' indelibly social nature and that decenters human attempts to secure our place in the world by way of increasingly comprehensive world-viewing.

WILLIAM E. "BILL" PANNELL: A BRIEF CASE IN COUNTERPOINT

Bill Pannell became Fuller Theological Seminary's first Black trustee in 1971, joined the faculty in 1974, and has since carried many titles throughout the seminary.[2] Considered by many to be "the father of Black evangelicalism," Pannell found his footing in a space that others (both Black and white) struggled even to see.[3] (And many still struggle to see it, as a supermajority of Americans who self-identify as "evangelical" are white.[4]) Reflecting on a life devoted to the good news of Jesus and the work of reconciliation, Pannell recalls the oddness of the space he has occupied. Describing the mostly white audiences from his days as an itinerant evangelist, he recounts, "Some were reluctant to take me seriously because I was a black person, but they felt obliged because I sounded just like them, believed as they did, was evangelical as they were."[5] Meanwhile, Pannell found members of major Black church denominations to be "uncomfortable with the term 'evangelical' because they see it as a denotation of white culture. It's more than that, but folks rarely realize that. . . . If an African American pastor were to ask, 'Pannell, what church are you with?' and I replied, 'I'm with the Plymouth Brethren,' he would say, 'Huh?'"[6] In his ground-shaking 1968 book, *My Friend, the Enemy* (Word Books), Pannell underscored his "own personal hang-up" as relating to *both* Christianity *and* Black people.[7] And this kind of existence primed Pannell to see the need for diversity in the theological classroom—without it, "you're not going to get the full range of what it means to be evangelical. It's still too lily-white, too middle American Presbyterian."[8]

But Pannell did not always see the situation in such a textured way. Throughout his writings, he describes how he began to discover within his own patterns of thought signs that whiteness had colonized his mind. Pannell would say of himself (a graduate of mostly white Fort Wayne Bible College) and of other Black evangelicals he knew, "From a cultural and theological perspective we were white men."[9] Having been raised *to think whitely* and further trained in Bible school by white fundamentalist Christians, Pannell could speak as an insider to white American evangelicalism. Taught to focus the key doctrines of a world-view that was negative toward "the world" and perceived idolaters, he recalls, "I could not have given you a good reason for many of my views. But no matter since 'orthodoxy' was all-important."[10] A crucial, if often overlooked, insight came to Pannell later in his career as he looked back on his Bible school experience: "We were behaving socially, but we didn't understand, nor were we taught, that men are social creatures by nature, by creation, by God's design. We conceived of lost men in terms of individuality."[11] In other words, the essentially white evangelical ghetto in which he lived and moved from his growing up years through Bible school fostered a particular identity politics for which, given its self-understanding, the community itself could not account.

In one article from the early 1970s, Pannell opened with the confession, "Like most Evangelicals who are black, I came to the issue of power rather late. . . . The question of power vs. powerlessness was never raised, since we felt we were in touch with the only real power—the Gospel of Jesus Christ."[12] When he did come to speak about the "power-orientation" of the American social system, he began with the history of Polish Americans, Jewish Americans, and Italian Americans using identity politics to secure their share of "white power."[13] Such power had benefitted white American evangelicals at least as much as anyone; however, inextricable from this sensibility was the reality that now "white men in North America play power games continuously without realizing it."[14] Further, Pannell daringly avowed, "When a Negro begins to operate on the same historic assumption, when he shows signs of aggressive responsibility, the first shouts of 'foul play' rise from my conservative friend."[15]

Following a string of experiences in the 1960s, particularly the 1963 bombing of 16th Street Baptist Church in Birmingham that killed four young Black girls, Pannell awakened to the power dynamics affecting evangelicalism. He confessed that he was initially critical of the civil rights movement but came to see the disparity between the "good news" preached by predominantly white revivalists and the social scene that they were inept at addressing. In those days, Pannell's view of Jesus and his work on the cross was radicalized (vis-à-vis other evangelicals) as he began to see its parallels in the experience of Black persons in America.[16] Pannell described the whiteness of his own education and socialization processes alongside the internalization of Black inferiority and the damage to Black children's psyches.[17] He named a mentality, forged in slavery years, that endured and sat behind white American fears (including fear of interracial marriage). And at the same time, he described the difficulty of naming the *whole* problem of race in America, for the prevalence of belief in Black folks' inferiority throughout US history had created an *atmosphere*.[18] As such, Pannell deployed the biblical language of the "principalities and powers" (Eph. 6:2) to describe both Jesus's confrontation on the cross and the Black church's existence amid bedeviled social structures.

The titular conservative white evangelical *frenemies* were disappointed in Pannell upon hearing of his newfound sympathy for "all this rioting."[19] And he recalled the pain inflicted by these friends who wanted to talk about human rights but felt no compulsion to get involved in the struggle of Black folk, instead citing the "violence these marches incite" and their feeling that such activity set back the "growing toleration and good will" of white Americans.[20] Pannell criticized how "most people committed to evangelism in the evangelical sense of the word are also committed to a conservatism that identifies the *status quo* with the will of God."[21] Growing from this ideology, the typical white evangelical criticism of the civil rights movement bewailed its "excesses" and supposed socialist or even Communist sympathies. Such friends would remind Pannell of *the biblical estimate of man*, which cannot be changed by legislation—to change society, one must change persons. Without denying this sensibility, he rejected the logic that

> nothing can be done until that happens. In fact, were I imprisoned in Cleveland's Hough area and all you offered me was forgiveness, I'd very happily tell you where to go. . . . If I'm hungry and naked, jobless because uneducated, uneducated because the educational establishment is more dedicated to tradition than to people, don't offer me a changed heart. That's not where the problem is. . . . What right has the oppressor to demand that his victim be saved from sin? You may be scripturally and evangelistically correct, but you are ethically wrong.[22]

White evangelicals' desire to return to the preaching of the gospel of Jesus as a response to the civil rights movement and its demonstrations was a false kind of conservatism that, in effect, conserved an exploited underclass within the protected society to which all citizens were expected to submit.[23] That state of affairs is the definition of hegemony.

In a particularly poignant analysis following our case study of Harold Ockenga, Pannell argued, "This false conservatism which characterizes most of the evangelical movement, reveals a theological perspective which sees the benefits of our Lord's passion as aimed at solving personal rather than systemic ills. It is virtually blind to corporate iniquity."[24] He called this "the failure of the Evangelical to understand the nature of institutional power and its relationship to the personal sin of racial bigotry."[25] Further dealing with the social aspect of sin, Pannell quoted feminist theologian Rosemary

Radford Ruether to say, "A concentration on individualistic repentance has led in Christianity to a petty and privatistic concept of sin which involved the person in obsessive compunction about individual (mostly sexual) immorality while having no ethical handle at all on the great structures of evil which we raise up corporately to blot out the face of God's good creation."[26] Pannell might as well have been speaking directly to Ockenga when he named the "conservative brother who refuses to link my social needs with his preaching of the Gospel" and goes on to lobby for prayer in schools and against "fluoride in the water" and "pornographic literature" and to decry the encroachments of socialism and the Communist menace.[27] Once you step into the realm of society's inhumanity toward Black folk, Pannell said, "These crusaders begin mumbling about sin."[28] *Fine*, says Pannell, *but whose sins shall we talk about?*

Importantly, Pannell identified the racial overlays on the American values of "democracy" and "free enterprise." As for democracy, he said, "The problem is that one's internal commitment to democracy has little to do with one's treatment in this democracy. When you are judged by your color before you can open your mouth, the republic has become a pigmentocracy."[29] Of the economy, Pannell boldly charged, "The mentality that produced and prospered the system of slavery is still with us. Today, we don't own slaves, we rent them, and for the non-white this system of enterprise is anything but free."[30] Furthermore, speaking of the "freedom" advocated by American patriots, he named its "limited or parochial" application in the United States, and thinking of the war in Vietnam, he asked whether Americans could really "export what we do not fully possess at home."[31] A thorn in the side of many white evangelicals of Ockenga's variety, Pannell said of Communists abroad, *At least they worked out their ideal in concrete forms.* Elsewhere, Pannell cited a then-current commentary on race in America, to say, "Americans do not think of their country as 'white,' but they are very careful to keep it that way."[32] And he linked this directly to the social context of Nixon's 1968 election, his "law and order" rhetoric, and his administration's "almost unbelievable . . . insensitivity to continued outrages."[33] Pannell reported that, among Black Americans, Nixon's following became subject to the aphorism: "Blessed is the black man who expects nothing from the Nixonians. When it comes, they shall not be disappointed."[34] Pushing a layer deeper, he also doubted Christian conversion's material efficacy among those who think like whites and listen only to white fundamentalist or evangelical preaching.[35]

When Pannell talked about the competition of world-views in history, he described a shift away from the geopolitical basis of classically understood world-views (i.e., G. W. F. Hegel's state-cultures or Samuel Huntington's civilizations) toward a "psycho-political" basis.[36] Connecting social issues to the theopolitics of white American evangelicalism, and sounding a bit like Du Bois in chapter 2, Pannell mused, "My white brother . . . taught me to sing 'Take the World but Give Me Jesus.' I took Jesus. He took the world and then voted right wing to ensure his property rights."[37] He learned to see the theopolitical tradition into which he was initiated in Bible school as "perpetuat[ing] the myth of white supremacy" as well as "associat[ing] Christianity with American patriotism (it's called nationalism when we criticize its manifestation in Africa), free enterprise, and the Republican party."[38] He turned Ockenga's social analysis on its head: "For if the failure of America is its capitulation to secularism and a lot of other 'isms,' then it seems to me that the failure of the church is its capitulation to America. The church *is* America. One can scarcely tell where piety leaves off and patriotism begins."[39] In this regard, he cited Carl Henry as having a slightly clearer view of the problem. He quoted Henry as criticizing "Institutional Christianity" for losing its evangelistic edge and cozying up to "reactionaries and revolutionaries" while trying to present "an attractive public image."[40] But while Henry selectively applied his reproach to Protestant liberals, Pannell saw the critical edge cutting both ways: "If the National Council [of Churches] has sold itself to revolutionaries and reactionaries, some of us black people get the impression that the National Association of Evangelicals has sold itself to patriotism, conservative politics, and the preservation of the good old American way."[41] With a wry bit of humor, he continued, "I am not so sure, gentleman, that from a historical point of view you can support the idea that Jesus Christ was an American, much less an evangelical."[42] In Pannell's analysis, "our sin as a church in America today is not that we are un-American or not even that we are just pro-American, but simply that we are more American than Christian!"[43] And to work this problem out, history needs to be "de-honkified," which includes learning to distinguish one's Americanness from one's holiness or belonging to the peoplehood of God.[44]

However, Pannell's reader should not take his ambivalence toward specific manifestations of American patriotism as a criticism of American ideals. Like Ockenga, he felt a personal concern for a lost and sick American society, and he, too, believed evangel(ical)ism could heal the nation.[45] And Pannell harbored some concern that the small but vocal minority of Black revolutionaries would succeed in upsetting the whole American project.[46] He continued to believe that America would heal only "when we begin to live up to our ideals as Americans and as Christians."[47] He did not expect abundantly gracious neighborliness from white Americans, qua Americans; instead, "it seems reasonable, on the other hand, to expect those who say they love God to love their brothers."[48] Nevertheless, this prescription called (and still calls) for, "as a first step to evangelism in a racially torn society, a wholesome evangelical fellowship with the courage and humility to confront fellow believers honestly about attitudes that divide them."[49] Pannell said this at least partly as a commentary on white evangelicals' (his friends, the enemies') continuing inability to address the racism within their free-enterprising power structures.[50]

CURRENT SOCIOHISTORICAL STUDIES OF RACE, RELIGION, AND POLITICS

American society was marred in the 2010s by an unrelenting rash of headline-grabbing events that underscored deeply divided outlooks on race relations and social-structural injustice. Since 2015 the Public Religion Research Institute (PRRI) has been tracking changes in American adults' perceptions of such realities according to factors like race, religion, and party affiliation. When asked to choose what was significant within their communities from a list of problems, Black Americans were much more likely to name police mistreatment (64 percent) and racial tensions (60 percent) than white Americans (17 percent and 27 percent, respectively).[51] Since that first data came back, white *evangelicals* have consistently ranked among the most likely to see recent police killings of Black men as isolated incidents (hovering around 72 percent in three different surveys)—more likely than white Americans overall, but second to the largely overlapping demographic slice of white Republicans (80 percent or more depending on the year).[52] For comparison, only 17 percent of Black Americans agreed with that sentiment in 2020, and the number of white mainline Protestants who agree has steadily declined from 73 percent in 2015 to 53 percent in 2020.

In the sea of such studies on evangelicalism and race in America, one can observe a distinction between (a) data on the ground about what is happening in the world and (b) how people see, think, and worry about that world. When PRRI asked whether "today discrimination against whites has become as big a problem as discrimination against blacks and other minorities," the number of white mainline Protestants who agree moved from 55 percent down to 43 percent during the timeframe studied. In comparison, white evangelical Protestants who agree have bobbled around 61 percent since 2015, but only 13 percent of Black Americans agree. Yet when asked about the cumulative effects of slavery and generations of discrimination on Black opportunities to work their way out of the lower class, 7 in 10 white evangelical Protestants (67–72 percent in the years studied) disagreed that slavery and discrimination have limited African American economic mobility. Only about 22 percent of Black Americans disagreed, and the number of white mainline Protestants who disagree has consistently dropped from 72 percent down to 54 percent.[53] In Barna Group surveys from late summer 2019, 75 percent of Black practicing Christians at least somewhat agree that the United States has *a history of oppressing minorities* compared with 42 percent of white practicing Christians. And nearly 8 in 10 (78 percent) Black practicing Christians believe America *continues to have a race problem* while not quite 4 in 10 (38 percent) white practicing Christians see the same.[54]

Now consider the following on-the-ground realities in the United States. (1) The 2019 median household income was $76,057 for non-Hispanic whites compared to $45,438 for Black households.[55] (2) Among young adults aged 25–29 (in 2019), the highest level of education attained also varied by race. Following upon a somewhat comparable baseline of high school graduates (about 96.3 percent of non-Hispanic whites and 90.9 percent of Blacks), roughly 44.9 percent of non-Hispanic whites attained a Bachelor's degree or higher compared to 29.0 percent of Blacks, and 10.3 percent of non-Hispanic whites attained a Master's degree or higher compared to 6.2 percent of Blacks.[56] (3) In a study published in 2012, researchers engaged 6,548 faculty members across 260 US universities with the same email posing as a potential doctoral student to request a meeting the following week, changing only the fictive student's name to signal gender and ethnicity. Versus white men, the likelihood of being ignored increased for white women 12.5 percent, Black men 22.6 percent, and Black women 29.8 percent.[57] The links between educational attainment and income (and unemployment figures) are regularly demonstrated in the general population even before accounting for race. But the way important demographic markers like these covary with race under conditions revealed in this third data point suggests that transparent identity- and status-related realities structure our world and that injustices are unevenly distributed along lines like gender and race.

One missing piece of the white-evangelicals-and-race puzzle seems to be the lack of skill or will to see race in America as a *social issue* in the first place—let alone an issue in which they are implicated. This section will explore signs that mainstream evangelical organizations and churches continue to reflect their knotty history as "white institutional space." We may hope to come to different conclusions about evangelical *potential*, but to do so, we must reckon with the world painted by the best available data and locate ourselves within that world.

American Evangelicalism in Black and White

Concerned that American churches appear to reproduce rather than reform our society's troubled racial dynamics, sociologists Michael Emerson and Christian Smith started exploring how churches fare in a society in which "race matters profoundly for differences in life experiences, life opportunities, and social relationships."[58] The first wave of the National Congregations Study (NCS) conducted in 1998 found that 93 percent of evangelical churches were racially homogenous (comprised of 80 percent or more of the same race).[59] And only 13 percent of all persons attending religious services of any kind in the United States attended "multiracial congregations," in which no single race made up more than 80 percent of the population. This data confirmed what Martin Luther King Jr. had estimated in a sermon three decades earlier: *eleven o'clock on Sunday morning is the most segregated hour in America*. After studying the situation, Emerson and Smith argued that religious congregations in the United States—with evangelicals as a case in point—descriptively could not transform America's racial dynamics because these churches, in fact, instantiated them.

In their book *Divided by Faith* (Oxford University Press, 2000), Emerson and Smith identify the impact of race in America with the term "racialization," which is arguably weaker than "racism" but also carries less personal-intentional freight.[60] Studies like theirs are less interested in protecting feelings than accurately identifying discomforting real-world trends, including what they describe as "the cultural tools and intergroup isolation of evangelicals" that "lead them to construct reality so as to individualize and minimize the problem."[61] Even as they cast doubt on the sense of progress claimed by Ockenga and company, Emerson and Smith warned that the average white American evangelical would resist the notion that "we need not intend our actions to be discriminatory for racialization to occur."[62] Studying the relatively hidden layers of racialization that ensnare even those who mean well is not to discount the overt racism in pockets of America—or within evangelicalism. It is, instead, to probe further into how and to what degree white folks who think of themselves as beyond such problems still perpetuate race-based inequalities and divisive ideology.

While more recent studies have superseded their quantitative data, much of the conceptual system that Emerson and Smith advanced in 2000 continues to hold currency in sociological studies of race in American evangelicalism. Specifically, they commonly found three convictions about human sociality enmeshed with white evangelicals' theology (e.g., definitions for sin, gospel transformation, and social action) in the white American evangelical "cultural toolkit."[63] When Emerson and Smith's team of researchers directly raised questions about the ongoing problems of race, the following convictions proved to be normative:

(a) an *individualism* in which persons are seen as independent from structures and thus fully responsible for their own actions;
(b) a *relationalism* that reduces social problems and their solutions down to individuals' sins and interpersonal relationships; and
(c) a coalescence of these two in an *antistructuralism* that villainizes even the suggestion of structural social differences as shifting the blame from the true problem, individual sin.

As an example of how such elements might begin to appear in an interview, Emerson and Smith quoted an interviewee explaining how to make progress on race discrimination and de facto segregation: "The only way you're going to do it is through prayer. But we also have a moral obligation to speak out whenever possible. Let them know where you stand. And not be a part of it. Don't lend a hand to the situation."[64] Processing their extensive interview data, Emerson and Smith explained the impact of this toolkit:

> Much research points to the race problem as rooted in intergroup conflict over resources and ways of life, the institutionalization of race-based practices, inequality and stratification, and the defense of group positions. These are not the views of white evangelicals, however. For them, the race problem is one or more of three main types: (1) prejudiced individuals, resulting in bad relationships and sin, (2) other groups—usually African Americans—trying to make race problems a group issue when there is nothing more than individual problems, and (3) a fabrication of the self-interested—again often African Americans, but also the media, the government, or liberals.[65]

They may as well have been summarizing Ockenga as they put those words to paper, but we might also hail their prescience in light of the post-2016 political landscape that has seen such views crawling out into the open.

Dreadfully, white American evangelicals tend to flout any data that contradict their ostensibly theological convictions about continuing problems of race and how to resolve them.[66] As Emerson and Smith explain, "the close connection between faith and freewill individualism to the exclusion of progressive thought renders white evangelicals even more individualistic than other white Americans."[67] An understanding of sin plays a key role here. In the faith of many white evangelicals, "sinful humans typically deny their own personal sin by shifting blame somewhere else, such as on 'the system.'"[68] It bears repeating how Ockenga read the situation vis-à-vis human governments: "The Bible teaches that Satan's sphere is individual; he leads men to do his will, but he does not have kingdoms to give."[69] And while God's law and human law may indeed conflict under these conditions, he thought American federal law had established by the late 1960s sufficient civil rights and racial justice at a structural level; furthermore, he maintained that much of the average American's goodwill was already on display in educational institutions, workplaces, and neighborhoods. For white evangelicals like Ockenga, it was (and remains) easier to imagine rogue individuals and their businesses maintaining racially discriminatory policies in the areas of housing or hiring—and even easier to imagine some persons remaining relatively harmless bigots—than any broader or deeper "system" coordinating and conserving such policies across the land.

When Emerson and Smith studied the Black-white socioeconomic gap as a specific area of ongoing inequality and prospective social change, they found that filtering their respondents the strength of evangelicalism scale was a reliable predictor of respondents' perspectives. Many conservative white Christians did not appreciate being asked to explain the Black-white socioeconomic gap at all. But when they did try to explain it, they talked rather meanly about their Black neighbors—suggesting pervasive cultural issues, ranging from family instability and a shortage of role models to laziness and a lack of internal drive.[70] And the strength of evangelicalism variable accentuated this tendency; the more substantial the evangelical steeping, the stronger the association of the socioeconomic gap with at least some Black culture or motivation factors. More recent data on this question suggests that such views continue among about half of all whites (Christian or otherwise) depending on the study and how the question's framing.[71] By contrast, a sizeable majority (i.e., 72 percent and higher) of nonwhite Christians disagreed with such sentiments in 2018 PRRI research.[72] Speaking to the world-viewish quality, Emerson and Smith found that white evangelicals were inclined to imagine Black Americans as violating critical tenets of their faith (i.e., by making structural excuses for their sins and voluntarily relying on social welfare programs rather than helping themselves).[73]

As we might expect, how people see the problems in the first place is deeply connected to the solutions they propose. Barna Group surveys from 2019 reveal that 61 percent of white practicing Christians "continue to take an individualized approach to matters of race, saying these issues largely stem from one's own beliefs and prejudices causing them to treat people of other races poorly."[74] Cutting against the possibility of social-structural solutions for combatting racism, white evangelicals in Emerson and Smith's study tended to propose more nebulous solutions reliant upon individuals—like individuals making friends with people of other races. Emerson and Smith classify such solutions under "the miracle motif," which maintains: "as more individuals become Christians, social and personal problems will be solved automatically."[75] We have seen this motif operating in Ockenga's thought, and it courses through the heart of his stream of evangelicalism as first focused on the conversion of individual persons.[76] Overall, Emerson and Smith found that the stronger the evangelical type, the more likely the person was to offer interracial friendships and congregational integration as *the* solutions to the race problem; this much was true for white and Black evangelicals, but Black evangelicals more strongly support the latter solution.[77]

With questions of racial integration, Emerson and Smith tested responses against a "strength of evangelicalism scale" (gauging the degree of a person's steeping in evangelical "institutional subculture and theology").[78] And more than half of all strong evangelicals thought "integrating congregations" was "a very important method to address racism."[79] However, white evangelicals meant something slightly different than we might expect here, namely, that "their specific congregation is or ought to be open to all people. They did not mean they should consider going to a mixed or nonwhite congregation. No one spoke about that possibility."[80] According to 2014 data from LifeWay Research, "most churchgoers are content with the ethnic status quo in their churches."[81] Among those whom LifeWay surveyed, evangelicals were most likely to say their church is already diverse enough (71 percent), and whites were least likely to say their church should become more diverse (37 percent); by contrast, about half of Blacks (51 percent) said their church needs to become more diverse. When Barna researchers recently asked "how the Church should respond in light of our nation's 400-year history of injustices against black people," they found 33 percent of white practicing Christians selected "there's nothing the Church should do," which is more than double the percentage of Black practicing Christians who feel the same (15 percent).[82] The most common response among Black respondents (33 percent) was "repair the damage."

Looking beyond church walls, Emerson and Smith were astonished by "how racially homogenous the social worlds of most evangelicals are, particularly those of white respondents. Other than an occasional acquaintance, they had few interracial contacts. With a few notable exceptions, none lived in worlds that were not at least 90 percent white in their daily experience. Many commented on this while answering the race questions."[83] This picture is reinforced by 2015 data from PRRI focused on the lack of diversity in Americans' social networks.[84] Taken together, these data suggest something like the "homophily principle" widely invoked in sociological circles, namely, that people tend to connect based on proximity and similarity.[85] But deeper than that, real-world spatial segregation (e.g., neighborhoods and parts of town) along lines like race, as political theorist Iris Marion Young has observed, "enacts or enlarges many material privileges of economic opportunity, quality of life, power to influence actions and events, and convenience. At the same time, it obscures the fact of such privileges from many of their beneficiaries."[86] Given the impact of race and socioeconomic status on where one finds housings, they are also significant factors in what feel like free, associational choices—where one lives, goes to school and church, finds work, and so on—appear to be influenced have nonvoluntary, structural factors.

Reiterating the White Evangelical Toolkit in Multiracial Churches

Along with an array of new research trajectories, Emerson and Smith's seminal work inspired hopes for multiracial churches that could draw attendees to intentionally scrub the human tendency to associate almost exclusively with similar others, breaking down the walls of hostility into which history has structured America's churches. Their data demonstrated that less isolated respondents had indeed begun to interpret reality differently and apply their cultural toolkit differently.[87] In particular, Emerson has supported the vision of multiracial churches through various projects like his *People of the Dream* (Princeton University Press, 2008). By the fourth wave of the NCS, conducted in 2018–2019, only 78 percent of evangelical churches were racially homogenous, and twice as many religious attendees (24 percent) could be found in multiracial congregations compared with 1998 numbers.[88] But as more recent investigations suggest (and Emerson and fellow researchers have acknowledged), the hope we might wish to project into space now increasingly occupied by multiracial congregations may be misplaced. At the very least, the framework for hope needs to address the ongoing, veiled, and underexplored dynamics of whiteness in such settings.

Contributing to our understanding of this gap, sociologist Korie Edwards brings national congregational-level data together with her findings from a firsthand study of attendees in a particular conservative, multiracial Protestant church located in a large, midwestern city. In her study of Crosstown Community Church in *The Elusive Dream* (Oxford University Press, 2008), Edwards found "white attendees were more likely to emphasize ignorance [of racial others based on limited exposure], racial segregation, and discrimination as explanations for racism and racial inequality, [while] African Americans were more likely to provide explanations that focused on power, opportunity, and economic reforms."[89] And fittingly, white attendees also shared a tendency "to see racial integration as *the solution* for racial problems in the United States."[90] At first blush, this data essentially echoes Emerson and Smith's findings on the role of cultural toolkits in interpreting issues of race and imagining their repair. But this is not the whole story.

When asked about racial inequality, Edwards reports, "African-American attendees at Crosstown were actually more inclined to use individually oriented explanations [e.g., lack of motivation among some Black Americans] for racial inequality than were white Crosstown attendees."[91] And while we might question the results of one case study as a sketchy basis for drawing conclusions about the effect of multiracial churches overall, a 2015 study by Ryon Cobb, Samuel Perry, and Kevin Dougherty using a large, nationally representative dataset also found "little evidence that multiracial congregations promote progressive racial views among attendees of any race or ethnicity."[92] In fact, their findings suggest the opposite: "Multiracial congregations may (1) influence minority attendees to embrace dominant White racial frames and/or (2) select on minority attendees who already embrace such frames in the first place."[93] As they demonstrate,

White explanations for racial inequality are not associated with whether they attend a diverse congregation or not. This important finding sheds some light on the supposed potential of multiracial congregations to challenge the racial status quo. . . . Whites in multiracial congregations are just as likely as Whites in predominantly White congregations to question the importance of social structure in accounting for Black/White inequality and emphasize the importance of Blacks' own motivation.[94]

But for Black attendees of multiracial congregations, the conclusions look different:

Blacks who attend multiracial congregations are less likely to affirm structural explanations for racial inequality than Blacks in nonmultiracial congregations. In other words, Blacks who attend multiracial congregations seem to embrace explanations of racial inequality that are more in line with the dominant White racial frame, diminishing the importance of structural factors such as discrimination or lack of access to education.[95]

In short, multiracial churches have not proven themselves effective in reforming the white evangelical cultural toolkit and seem instead to become sites for affirming it amid visible diversity.

Pushing deeper into her analysis, Edwards concludes, "Interracial churches work, that is remain racially integrated, to the extent that they are *first* comfortable places for whites to attend."[96] Suggesting a distinction between (a) real equity for and inclusion of *diverse voices* and (b) what is sometimes called merely *the diversity of faces*, she compares the reality of multiracial churches to a dish of vanilla ice cream with some rainbow sprinkles on top.[97] There simply is not much substantive difference between these churches and predominantly white congregations in the same traditions.[98] Actually, Black attendees of Crosstown named their preference for some of the church's white culture (e.g., shorter church services, informal dress, and expository preaching) as primary in their decision to attend Crosstown.[99] They also tended to appreciate the diversity of the church community, but their preference for aspects of the worship service effectively ruled out more homogenous Black churches as viable alternatives for them. White attendees of Crosstown saw diversity as highly significant in their church experience and came at least partly for this reason. The church had not dramatically changed their social networks or their ability to see their own whiteness, however, and they continued to see more homogenous white churches as viable alternatives for themselves.

The imbalance in Black and white attendees' perceptions of their own options in the local church marketplace represents a power dynamic hidden by what, at the surface level, could be described as voluntary association in a free market. White attendees could think of themselves as experimenting with this church and, thus, as freer to walk if the experience lost its shine, but Black attendees largely felt like they needed *this* church to work given the lack of suitable alternatives. During the tenure of Crosstown's first Black pastor, the church's membership shifted from 70 percent white to 65 percent Black.[100]

> The congregation was fine with the idea of hiring an African American as long as it did not have any major impact on the church. But once his African-American identity became more evident (i.e., that he really was a "brother"), the idea became less attractive. Furthermore, congregants did not hesitate to make their concerns about various practices, styles, or activities known to him and the elders.[101]

Participating in a multiracial church that was predominantly white in culture—from elements in the service to the way direct conversations about race were raised from the pulpit to outsized representation in leadership structures—allowed white attendees to remain comfortable within their ideological setting while ostensibly opening a welcoming space to nonwhite Christians. Unspoken in this dynamic and somewhat transparent to the white attendees are the assumptions that the service would continue to reflect white cultural practices and styles and that church messaging on race and integration would primarily reflect the white evangelical cultural toolkit.

Even the barriers to interracial friendship do not necessarily fall away in multiracial churches the way the average evangelical might expect. For one thing, Crosstown attendees' closest friends in the church tended to be of the same race, and, more broadly, their closest friends did not attend the same church.[102] But for another, interracial friendships may not have the destabilizing effect on race that whites tend to hope they will. In an interview with Krista Tippett, popular young adult author Jason Reynolds offers a helpful perspective on the impact of interracial friendships:

> I have so many women friends who . . . say, if you want to know how a man is going to treat you, just look at how he treats his mother, and then you'll know whether or not he's good or not. And my reply to that is, that is ridiculous, because that man sees his mother as exceptional. That's his mother. [laughs] You're not his mother. [laughs]. . . . He sees his mom as exceptional, and that is the reason why he treats her the way he treats her.
>
> And so, when we think about this idea of the Black friend, it's not that you're not racist, it's that you somehow have aligned yourself with who you believe is an exceptional Black person. And that is the problem. These are Black people

who are convenient for you to love. But the truth is . . . it doesn't matter how many Black friends you have, it's a specific kind of Black person that you're OK with, not Black people.[103]

Reynolds is saying mere friendships do not make people less racist and can reinforce their racism while taking near and beloved others as exceptions to what one otherwise believes to be true. By extension, we might gather that in a church setting where the white racial frame prevails, white attendees could intuitively conclude that Black attendees share their normative outlook on the world and race as a feature in it. White attendees could easily imagine their Black co-congregants as exceptions to the racist attitudes they continue to harbor against Black folks beyond their congregation. At the scale of a church, we can see the status quo maintained through a system that selects, even if unintentionally, for a diversity of faces without really creating space for the influence of, and for wrestling with, a diversity of cultural toolkits.

White Institutional Space

At this point, I will start layering on theory to elucidate what exactly "whiteness" is and how it gets bound up in the fabric of churches or, we might helpfully envision here, parachurch organizations like schools and associations. Here we can start to unpack the meaning of Pannell's comment about learning to think whitely in his Bible college education—and maybe answer his plea for "the courage and humility to confront fellow believers honestly about attitudes that divide them." I am especially interested in developing a framework for grasping the hidden operations of whiteness so that we might better understand the emergence of neo-evangelicalism at the hands of Ockenga and company. How could voluntary associations, institutions of higher education, and other such organizations explicitly gathered around a shortlist of principles packaged as the biblical world-view also reproduce the ordering effects of whiteness within their structures and culture? In their public advocacy? In their sense of what it means to be evangelical?

Edwards uses the notion of "white hegemony" to introduce and frame what she saw unfold at Crosstown Community Church. Hegemony, in general, has to do with the leadership or dominance of one social group over others and thus connotes power dynamics within social relationships and their structures. But in the twenty-first century, a key feature of whiteness is the *hiddenness* of its organizing power—not least as some nonwhite members are enlisted to prop up the hegemony in their own ways. While coercion may be needed at times to gain and maintain power, consent is necessary for long-term power.[104] "Whiteness" in this sense is certainly not about ironing out one smooth fabric of something like white ethnicity—having to do with culture, history, descent, and so on. Few people would suggest that all white people are overwhelmingly alike down to the detail in their actual forms for life or thought (even if they might be tempted to think that way about groups of nonwhite others). And as Pannell, Edwards, and others have expressed, the actual norms (beliefs, practices, etc.) may well be taken up by nonwhite persons. White hegemony, Edwards argues, is created and sustained by three constitutive, interdependent dimensions: white structural advantage, white normativity, and white transparency.[105]

It is challenging to figure out exactly where to begin defining the three constituent elements of Edwards's understanding because they are so interconnected. Teasing out the details of whiteness relative to the American legal system and elite law schools, Wendy Leo Moore has helpfully conceptualized the development and maintenance of "white institutional space" in a way that has clear analogs in churches and mainstream evangelical organizations.[106] Leveraging this conceptuality into an analysis of church dynamics in a cowritten article, Moore boils the problem down this way:

> Simply put, white institutional space is created through a process that begins with whites excluding people of color, either completely or from institutional positions of power, during a formative period in the history of an organization. During this period, whites populate all influential posts within the institution and create institutional logics—norms of operation, organizational structures, curricula, criteria for membership and leadership—which imbed white norms into the fabric of the institution's structure and culture. Although the norms are white, they are rarely marked as such. Consequently, racially biased institutional norms are wrongly defined as race neutral and merely characteristic of the institution itself (e.g., "the appropriate way to act in church"), masking inherent institutional racism. Upon this tacitly racist foundation, institutional inertia and actors build a robust culture that privileges whites by vesting power in white leaders' hands, populating the organization with white membership, orienting activities toward serving and comforting whites, and negatively sanctioning non-white norms.[107]

While this summary already reads like a generic account of what happened in the organizations founded by Ockenga and company, it also helps situate Edwards's three-part conceptuality for white hegemony. Advantages are structured into institutions by way of founding representation and rendered transparent from the start through the normative influence of founders and early adopters, setting in motion a social machine that will invariably strive to maintain homeostasis, to conserve itself amid the push and pull of latecomers. In Edwards's study, the structural advantage was evidenced by features like the outsized presence of white members in higher leadership positions relative to their share of the church membership as well as the dynamic named above with marketplace conceptuality. And the white norms of Crosstown ranged from cultural practices in the church service to ideological components of the white cultural toolkit. All of this was more or less invisible to the white attendees even if they broadly understood that race for their nonwhite co-congregants entailed social-structural inequalities. White attendees assumed their intentionally multiracial church did not participate in those problems.

As we have gathered by this point, much of the racism that actually impacts systems in American society can be read as somewhat unintentional relative to individual agents. Speaking in the context of American law, Moore describes how, once the norms and practices were generated in the absence of diverse actors, the experts can assert the law is "a neutral and impartial body of doctrine unconnected to power relations."[108] I sense a strong resonance between this description and Ockenga's gesture toward "the authority of the Bible alone *uninterpreted by traditions*" as a virtue of evangelical faith.[109] But if you want to know why whiteness is in the air for so many institutions, Moore argues, "attention must also be paid to the historical racial exclusion that . . . provided the context for the uncontested construction of white institutional space that is the foundation for contemporary white institutional norms and policies that reproduce white privilege and power within these spaces."[110] Building intentionally on Young's comments about space earlier, Moore explains, "Racialized spatial segregation becomes a mechanism for the reproduction of racial inequality without regard to the intent of racial actors in different communities. . . . The material and ideological privileges that whites receive as a result of racial segregation get rendered invisible because they require no individual racial animus."[111] In a setting like Crosstown, whatever white congregants may have voiced in terms of support for racial integration in the church, and however much Black members may advocate for specific changes reflecting Black church practices, the space itself was carved out of whiteness. The formal reality that churches are voluntary associations serves to mask the white hegemony within any given institution, not least many churches intentionally branding themselves as mosaic in culture.

At this point, we might pause to name some distinct conclusions about the theoretical solutions that white American evangelicals offer (and have offered since Ockenga's time) to the race problems they are able and willing to see. First, while the personal level may appear to be the most critical, white American evangelicals tend not to have friendships with people of other races because they tend not to have regular, meaningful interactions with people of other races. Even attending a multiracial church does not change this dynamic much. But more to the point, close interracial friendships can reinforce stereotypes by welcoming others as specific exceptions to general conceptions. Second, as Emerson and Smith noted, "intimacy is less important than having a variety of contacts, such as also having black acquaintances and living in mixed neighborhoods."[112] Put in terms of the cognitive schemas of chapter 2, the development and maintenance of positive, generalized schema(s) related to racial "others" requires sufficient data on those others from which to generalize; without such data, we are more likely to fill in the gaps with assumptions or convictions that may unjustly represent actual racial "others." On this point, multiracial churches do seem to add to white attendees' cultural toolkits possibilities for understanding the systemic nature of the problems their minority co-congregants experience. But this notion does not seem to alert white attendees to the possibility that their whiteness participates in the problem. Such is one of the paradoxes in whiteness, especially among those who are more progressive on this issue: understanding how race is a disadvantage for Blacks without registering the advantage of their own whiteness.[113] And third, while there is a great deal of social pressure for whites to diversify their social circles, the prevailing notion that Americans' personal associations are voluntary masks the underlying realities of homophily and hegemony. White folks may embrace diversity as a general principle while only preserving space for racial others who prove to be exceptional and, thus, selecting for diversity managed within white institutional space.[114]

In Edwards's catalog of explanations for the status quo, colorblindness is the most common. While there is something to the vision of all lives mattering equally that serves as the basis of colorblind thinking, equal opportunity let alone footing in the material world has yet to be realized. Under the aegis of twenty-first-century colorblindness, the impact of race remains mostly hidden from view. Because race continues to be a determining factor in how life goes for people, even in the absence of overtly race-based laws and policies, correcting these disparities depends on the work of people who are able and willing to see the impact of color to begin with. Otherwise, white folks' sense of free, voluntary association will shape their conceptions of racial minorities' circumstances and prospects at an intuitive level.[115] Being blind to color is not the same thing as being able to empathize with the texture of someone's experience or even to see their perspective on the world. Colorblindness to the tune of "all lives matter" affirms others' general personhood without getting close enough to affirm any other living person as a person. More than a reference to skin color, "whiteness" is a transparent, self-normative way of being in the world that thrives under social-structural support.

NOTICING A WHITE CHRISTIAN SOCIAL IMAGINARY

Willie James Jennings, a Fuller Seminary graduate and now trustee, has set a poetically moving account of communion over against the operations of whiteness in modern Western history and its performance in the theological register. Much of his book *The Christian Imagination* (Yale University Press, 2010) unpacks the life and thought of individuals who, in their attempts to live Christianly within the spacetime established by colonialism, represent microcosms of its accompanying theological insurgency.[116] In his more recent *After Whiteness* (Eerdmans, 2020), Jennings has the theological academy in his crosshairs as subject and audience, drawing from his own experience in academic administration to offer an account of the academy's entanglement in whiteness and his hope for a more genuine communion. Together, these two books provide immediately significant insights for my project, which turns upon case studies of individuals engaged in intellectual formation— as two of them founded schools with theological faculties (Kuyper: Vrije Universiteit in Amsterdam, Ockenga: Fuller Theological Seminary) and all presided over and taught in such institutions. From Jennings, we may learn the importance of studying complex Christian performances rather than working solely in with sterilized and abstracted theological ideals. A methodological focus on the particularities of faith at the scale of actual human lives also suggests strategies for thinking theology differently from the start (i.e., as opposed to merely correcting the world-viewing form), which will emerge in my constructive comments from the end of this chapter forward.

Describing the advent of whiteness, Jennings names a density of effects that was and continues to be unfathomable. "Four things are happening at the same time," he explains, "first, people are being seized (stolen); second, land is being seized (stolen); third, people are being stripped from their space, their place; and fourth, Europeans are describing themselves and these Africans at the same time."[117] As a window on these happenings, Jennings describes the tears of pity that Gomes Eanes de Zurara, a royal chronicler for Portugal's Prince Henry the Navigator (1394–1460), shed for a group of agonized African slaves being driven from a ship before throngs of people to the site of their auction.[118] But Zurara's sorrow was allayed by an epiphany: this enslavement of black bodies would lead to the slaves' salvation. "The *telos* and the denouement of the event will be enacted as an order of salvation, an *ordo salutis*—African captivity leads to African salvation and to black bodies that show the disciplining power of the faith."[119] This episode represents the nascence of a logic that renders the white observer's position in the world simultaneously normative and invisible as they think order over whole peoples. Before this period in history, white Europeans may have assumed the power and promise of Christian civilization to have a universalizing trajectory; but, in living contact with dark-skinned people from Africa, they intuited their sense of cultural superiority and the significance of human skin color as coterminous. As they were taken with their divinely bestowed position and vocation in the global scale of human cultures, white colonizers automatically (i.e., impulsively) located the virtues of their faith on their own bodies in contrast to the bodies and life-systems of others—with skin color as a visible marker of a person's identity and potential. *This* is the most salient feature; *this* essentially reveals one's estate within God's economy.[120] Even as these supposed virtues were mapped onto bodies, they were simultaneously held to be civilizational achievements, instantly opening a path to cultural comparison and analysis, as well as to calculations about where to prioritize Christian missionary energies (i.e., witness).

Here we begin to see that *to think whitely* is at least partly a matter of *scale*. Before the "scale of whiteness" becomes a hierarchy of races conceptualized as totalized entities (also eventually extended as a gradient of purity in racially mixed children), the concept of scale is architectonic, signifying the white gaze's capacity to locate everything and every body on a blueprint. So, whiteness materializes subtly, "not simply as a marker of the European but as the rarely spoken but always understood organizing conceptual frame. And blackness appears as the fundamental tool of that organizing conceptuality."[121] The concept of scale reflects Du Bois's analysis: "The using of men for the benefit of masters is no new invention of modern Europe. It is quite as old as the world. But Europe proposed to apply it on a scale and with an elaborateness of detail of which no former world ever dreamed. The imperial width of the thing—the heaven-defying audacity—makes its modern newness."[122] The scale itself as a conceptual tool for capturing the whole world "is of the world but not of any specific world. It is tied to specific flesh, but it also joins all flesh. Such identity markers do not establish racial essences as their first work. They quietly, beneath the surface, join human beings and in effect uncouple their identities from specific places."[123] In the voyages of Christopher Columbus (still a boy when Prince Henry died), Jennings identifies the "breathtaking geographic flexibility" of the racial scale that connects the bodies of Africa to those of the Americas while maintaining the hegemony of white European bodies in all spaces. Speaking of those who endeavor to "gather people," Jennings notes that Christians were by no means the first. The powerful "always gathered people together, seeking to verify or solidify their power, convey their dreams, or bring order to their worlds," and this truth should help his judgment sink in: "There is nothing inherently good about gathering people together, but there is something inherently powerful."[124]

Perhaps shockingly, precisely here is a natural point of connection with my project's concern about contemporary evangelical patterns of "world-viewing." Jennings argues that whiteness was "a theological imaginary because whiteness suggested that one may enter a true moment of creation gestalt."[125] Then as now, white world-viewing draws power from a doctrine of creation in which "the inherent instability of creation means that all things may be altered in order to bring them to proper order toward saved existence."[126] The perceived conferral of God's authority to humans—initially mediated by more overt church-state structures, but now typically in more hidden ways—within a creational framework serves as the basis for claiming a "right to reshape the discovered landscapes, their people and their places."[127] Secure in the divine mandate to order creation, the chosen people have only to strategize about doing it. In Jennings's account, the perpetrators of the colonial moment "imagined they could see the peoples of the world better than the peoples of the world could see themselves, and that their insight was key to forming institutionalizing processes that were crucial to global well-being. They were as indispensable as God."[128] They reimagined the whole world as fitting within the framework of their thinking, their epistemology—and, as we will explore shortly, "Western education and modern theological education were formed in this condition without entering into lament over its harmful effects."[129] White American evangelicals (though not only they) are prone to imagine that they can see and touch and think together at once the whole world and all its people, at least in all meaningful ways. Their confidence in this vision is intimately connected to their supposed grasp of God's revelation concerning how and by whom the world is to be ordered.

A central aspect of the Christian identity crisis in Jennings's work is the displacement of land and locality as the primary signifiers of the individual's identity by identities "mapped" onto placeless bodies. This pattern of dislocation corresponds with Pannell's observation that world-views (here as definitive of one's identity) have been shifting from a geopolitical basis to a consolidated psycho-political one, with skin color as a reliable visual marker of one's essential identity.[130] Black bodies were stripped from their ground of being and meaning and bereft of all social relations; when they disembarked in foreign lands, those bodies were dealt with solely on the basis of their aesthetic condition, as determined by the white persons gazing upon them.[131] These white-bodied handlers were self-assured in their total view of the situation, including the possible future of black bodies redeemed by God in the European lands of promise. This expression of white agency "was a theological form—an inverted, distorted vision of creation that reduced theological anthropology to commodified bodies. In this inversion, whiteness replaced the earth as the signifier of identities."[132] Transgressing all known boundaries that would identify Europeans as such, white explorer-missionary-mercenaries propelled themselves into a boundaryless reality, "blowing by and through the specifics of identity bound to land, space, and place and [ultimately] narrating a new world that binds bodies to unrelenting aesthetic judgments."[133] Further explaining how the use of the racial scale was a theological operation, Jennings observes that it "begins with positioning Christian identity fully within European (white) identity and fully outside the identities of Jews and

Muslims."[134] Never mind the theological reality that the church can only exist as unnatural grafts drawing nourishment from the trunk of Israel—of a community called together and called blessed by God's own doing.

This operation set white Christians on a destructive path of imagination that led them to abuse the meaning of God's election, claiming exclusively for themselves the election of a people that superseded Israel as God's chosen.[135] (We might recall Ockenga's expression of God's unique calling on the United States.) "If Israel's election had been the compass around which Christian identity gained its bearings and found its trajectory, now with this reconfiguration the body of the European would be the compass marking divine election. More importantly, that new elected body, the white body, would be a discerning body, able to detect holy effects and saving grace."[136] So, as illustrated by chapter 1's study of Kuyper, "reprobation is not simply the state of existence opposite election; it is also a judgment upon the trajectory of a life, gauging its destiny from what can be known in the moment."[137] Kuyper added another layer to this analysis in that his very standard for assessing the worth of a world-view was its ability to command as much of the world as possible—to make the most significant difference for the most people. As such, he claimed, "the life of the colored races on the coast and in the interior of Africa [represents] a far lower form of existence."[138] European Christians "positioned themselves as those first conditioning the world rather than being conditioned by it. They performed a deeply theological act that mirrored the identity and action of God in creating."[139] And further, "European colonialists in acts of breathtaking hubris imagined the interlocking nature of all peoples and things within their own independence of those very people and things."[140] The social imaginary of white civilization dominated the peoples it encountered and was itself understood as bound for world domination and even eschatological vindication.

The painful-to-acknowledge underlying reality is that the fusing together of Christianity and whiteness in the colonial era has impacted the theological academy at least as much as it has any other sector of Western societies. And absent any intentional and practiced commitments to shifting that dynamic, that has not changed—no matter how diverse the faces get. As Jennings charges, "We theological educators have never reckoned sufficiently with the racial character of institutional life in the colonial West. . . . We are caught in a distorted institutionalizing practice that hinders life-giving institutional performance and that thwarts the development of healthy institutional personality."[141] Churches and their houses of learning alike have been constructed as white institutional spaces, and practical observations about their formation confirm the absence of nonwhite voices amid a wider social reality that is dramatically segregated. But all the same, Jennings observes a fundamental resistance among theologians "to think *theologically* about their identities."[142]

The formal arrival of "integration" as a possibility in the American imagination did not dispense with the historical lack of presence, let alone influence, belonging, or genuine communion. "Theological education in the West," Jennings explains in language that has appeared already above, "was born in white hegemony and homogeneity, and it continues to baptize homogeneity, making it holy and right and efficient—when it is none of these things. 'Hegemony' and 'homogeneity' are words that mean control and sameness, a control that aims for sameness and a sameness that imagines control."[143]

Many, of course, mistake homogeneity in thought to be the goal of higher education, not theological education in the direction of orthodoxy—the effect of the one-mindedness to which biblical authors appeal from time to time. "We live in a defeated conceptual moment when so many have surrendered their imaginations to working inside the ideas of race, religion, and nation as the most rational way to think collective existence and for peoples to know and announce themselves."[144] This is true, for instance, even of some liberation theologies, which may feel the pressure move from a form of liberation that opens into a broader community toward a narrower, totalizing identity politics. But there is the world-wise homogeneity of whiteness that aims to dispel any sense that it is bound to a particular time or place. Its aim is "what is reasonable," smuggling the influence of traditions under cover of neutral reasoning, such that those who come to different conclusions are merely wrongheaded. In Jennings's words, "This is an assimilation that hides itself as assimilation. It can be hidden in such practices as critical thinking, or traditioned reflection, or the repetition that makes for skilled execution of a task, gesture, or performance. This is our curse."[145] One core problem, then, is the tendency to imagine each and every human being as exactly one instance of the same generic thing: *a person who must take up the Christian world-view (as I understand it [above all else])*.

CONCLUSIONS ABOUT NEO-EVANGELICAL IDENTITY POLITICS IN VIEW OF HAROLD OCKENGA

Since Edwards, Moore, and others underscore the significance of specific institutions' particular histories for understanding the dynamics of whiteness within them, we might reflect on the emergence of (neo-)evangelicalism in twentieth-century America under the rubric of white institutional space. By framing their tribalism as the commonsense representation of a more innocent, golden-age-seeking Christian nationalism, Ockenga and company claimed to represent all those who simply wanted America to stand as a city on a hill. But the unspoken factors influencing that vision became more evident over time. As named in chapter 3, mainstream institutions' founding generation enjoyed broad overlap in their social location (e.g., white, heterosexual, male, Protestant, Republican). And Ockenga's public rhetoric around race issues was a representatively clear indication that factors like race and political ideology would indeed limit recognized membership in *their institutions*. As Pannell relays, neo-evangelical conversations did not include Black folks from the beginning, so the implicit rules and everyday practices of those within the fold were descriptively white. Had persons with other perspectives participated earlier in evangelical institutions' histories, key ideas would likely have been set up or cashed out in dramatically different practices and norms. Bill Pannell embodied this possibility as he criticized the political persuasion of folks like Ockenga who shut him and others out—sometimes explicitly, but often by presenting significant political positions so as to encourage the wrong sort to self-select not to get involved. Among others, Black Christians who would have been identified as "evangelical" by their assent to something like the NAE statement of faith were segregated from emerging evangelical organizations. The story of post–World War II American evangelicalism is the story of white institutional space. Evangelical witness and world-viewing are enmeshed with what is relatively transparent to and for the vocal group—what seems like common sense unwittingly (or half-wittingly) entails white norms.

From local churches to larger parachurch organizations, the American sensibility is one of free, voluntary association, and evangelicals have adopted at least this much from their Modernist environs despite their explicit protestations about other modern notions. From the early days of the neo-evangelical movement, leaders knew they would need to compete with their fundamentalist kith for financial resources, and what came to be known as "evangelicalism" is a testament to the power of people voting with their feet and with their wallets. But a purely associational model for assessing at least one's own sociality simply cannot register the many nonvoluntary sociocultural factors that operate within and upon all human associations. In an important sense, social groups are prior to and thus constitutive of individuals; people are socialized into these groups in the ordinary course of human development even as they contribute to the group's shape moving forward.[146] To deny the ontological priority of the individual is not to deny that one can join, leave, or fundamentally change a social group(s). All the same, our most meaningful social groups—we live in and through several, and they are all varyingly complex—tend to be those that emerge most naturally from the complex field of relations into which we are thrown, where we feel we have always shared a living history with others like us. In other words, we assert identities for ourselves that make meaning out of our actual social experiences—even if we do so with incomplete awareness of all "meaningful" factors. And our identities may be politicized and galvanized (in our own minds or on our behalf by "representatives") around just one such group identity such that it masks or melts away other important group commitments. For Young, Edwards, Moore, and others, the unreasonable and plainly prejudicial power dynamics at work in the modern world's highly differentiated societies invalidate the voluntary-associational model taken as the sole (or even the most significant) model of human sociality. The semblance of free, voluntary association among individuals combines with the dogma of colorblindness to mask the operations of whiteness and maintain the hegemony.

Many white evangelicals took up a colorblind approach following the civil rights movement, which only further ensconces elements in the white racial frame—essentially inviting those who look different to come, think, and live the same as I. In a colorblind world, everyone should be free to think and act whitely. However, racialization remains intact, and whites continue to be deeply uncomfortable both with that fact and with the presence of real, cultural difference that challenges the normativity of their ideas. So, given the lack of consciousness-doubling experiences for those whose lives are near the mythical norm, even the basic self-awareness necessary to begin working with one's own self-plurality (let alone the skill or the will) remains rather low. In any case, Ockenga and other white neo-evangelicals might not have seen how their ostensibly religious language and practices instantiated the already-racialized society and certainly could not imagine how an evangelical faith might challenge it. French literary theorist and philosopher Roland Barthes has termed this phenomenon "exnomination," describing the way statuses like class, whiteness, and masculinity do not announce their presence as they exert their power, instead hiding their function as such in order to (a) pass off their ideologies as the norm, (b) conscript others into willing service to this perspective (i.e., assimilation), and thereby (c) conserve their supremacy.[147] But this is also a feature of what Edwards has identified more directly as "white hegemony," a trifecta of structural advantage, normativity, and transparency. Jennings shows up the creation of "race" in European colonialism as a process originating in whiteness's unnamed normativity, which encompassed Christian civilization for the colonizers. And Pannell recalls how the grammar of whiteness had organized his own mind—he had been assimilated. Whatever group presents itself as a voluntary association is experienced quite differently depending on the identity and power dynamics of the organization itself—in its founding and in the forms of its conservation. The ignorant if privileged path is open almost exclusively to those who occupy higher status positions along important identity axes. As such, we must learn how to name with increasing clarity the salience of "other" social factors that pass unnamed in even our most cherished identity groups.

I submit that the evangelical world-viewing concept as described thus far in my project has unwittingly exnominated a central impulse of the whiteness that has characterized Western history from its nascence.[148] In hindsight, its likeness can undoubtedly be identified in the powerful, self-norming subjects who, notably in contact with "others," automatically (i.e., impulsively or instinctively) take themselves to be seeing clearly and assessing reasonably. World-viewers past and present claim to see the whole world clearly and sense a general, divine calling to order its parts according to God's will. And Jennings's comments on white colonizers seem appropriate also in analyzing Ockenga's new evangelicals: they "positioned themselves as those first conditioning the world rather than being conditioned by it," and they "imagined the interlocking nature of all things within their own independence of those very things." Partly because it remains compelling and transparent, especially to whites who have enjoyed hegemony atop so many institutions, the framework of world-scale viewing is deeply embedded in forms of thought and life that continue to shape our realities. And this pertains not only to racialization but also power differentials within many socially significant identities. I would not be surprised to find something of this problem anywhere a person or group claims to have the correct read on the whole world and its peoples comparatively from the posture of the normative (Western, Christian, white, civilized)—for it is only through such wide-angle "judgment" (or *intuition*, as Immanuel Kant's term *Weltanschauung* suggests) that the possibility of a "world-view" even emerges.[149] Looking back to part I, Kuyper grounded his world-view concept in an abstract, universal antithesis in the human community and assumed that his own logic could represent the best available resources of the most positively influential tradition in the history of humankind—not least when compared with his estimate of the limited, provincial views in Africa and South America.

While mainstream evangelical institutions sloughed off a great deal of their overtly racist conceptuality by the late twentieth century, its world-viewing projects have continued to be understood from within as comprehensive and as binding for all people. Addressing the denizens of the United States offered Ockenga a sense of geopolitical groundedness, but his insistence on a "psycho-political" world-view continued the trend of mapping identities onto placeless bodies. And his actual judgments on matters of race (i.e., his "application" of this world-view) betrayed the whiteness of his all-ordering gaze. Criticizing evangelical world-view theory itself as "white" may surprise some of its normative insiders; thus, part II has aimed to uncover both the explicit racism of many white evangelicals (Ockenga included) and to unmask the whiteness ensconced in modern projects of world-viewing, in general. "Whiteness" as a term or concept works symbolically in a way that can be misunderstood in terms of ethnicity or culture. Whiteness is about the ability to disappear into one's perspective; to claim a cool, rational blandness; to assume self-normativity while only superficially registering the world's contestation. Whiteness is the color of modernity, of the sense that culture and history have no bearing on truth. Ironically, this same form of thought has made clear to many nonwhite persons and communities that culture and history do, in fact, matter a great deal—not least, the history and imperial culture of those who can pass as the norm (i.e., whites). As Jennings describes, "Whiteness invites us to imagine that we become invisible to ourselves and others only through its narration of our lives."[150] It does not do this forthrightly, of course, or while flying its own standard but in appeals to common sense, neutral Christian orthodoxy, and the uninterpreted meaning of Scripture.

Even if only by example, people teach each other how to integrate their histories within various social groups and statuses into something livable and coherent, including the *"skill" of inattention to those areas where these stories do not happily meet.* If taken to name such marriages, the social group identification conceptuality developed above parallels and networks into the "self-theories" and "personal myths" of chapter 2. The stories we tell about our most important groups—our "communal myths" for stylistic continuity— may function to name what we think our communities *intend* to be about and how we make meaning amid our shared experiences in the world.[151] Given the impact of consolidation, shared histories around intricate social webs consummate new narrative marriages over time. But as a way of naming how we "make meaning" of our experiences, communal myths and world-views stand in uneasy relationship to both the socially structured world around us and to what might be understood as the permanent, ahistorical matrices of truth, which is how many neo-evangelicals characterized their reading of Scripture (i.e., unimpeded by human traditions). Looking around at the social and intellectual landscape, thinkers like W. E. B. Du Bois and William E. Pannell did not deny something like a world-view was in play. But they were indeed critical of claims from within the views they saw operating that the fundamental, all-determining reality was faith and not whiteness. The case of Harold Ockenga and the "new evangelicals" gathered around him demonstrates how a small, consolidated social network serves to reinforce the sense of obvious unity in what is actually a troubled narrative marriage of multiple sources and layers of meaning. And this marriage serves as the basis for public engagement and other performances of "witness" to the world. Put more controversially, this variety of witness has some silent letters: w(h)it(e)ness.

Developing the skill to name the exnominated social factors that establish and maintain self- and group-serving structures of power and (dis)advantage is only one part of addressing the racism in American evangelicalism and its surrounding society, for many are also genuinely unwilling to see these structures. With this judgment, I mean to criticize not personal-individual willfulness (i.e., having sinful intentions)—though this judgment also may apply in some cases—but the ongoing malformative power of those social realities that structure the world(s) into which individuals are born.[152] Given the free-will individualism in their cultural toolkit and the conviction that regeneration has unclouded their reasoning capacities, white evangelicals are disinclined to receive information that suggests any such thing has affected them without their knowledge ("counter-schematic feedback" in the language of chapter 2). Here is a chicken-or-egg loop between a personal-individual hang-up that enables sinful extra-personal structures that malform individuals. One can participate comfortably in an evangelical faith community and even, as exhibited in Ockenga's case, powerfully fulfill the evangelical world-viewing impulse without really noticing that part of their comfort and experience of plain reasonability comes from also sharing nonfaith group memberships (e.g., race, class, and political partisanship). Because this view of the situation deemphasizes the intentionality of racism in persons and throws paint on transparent structures, it is at odds with typical evangelical social analysis. However, the unvoiced and somewhat nonvoluntary nature of both whiteness and racialization is precisely what makes them so pernicious and intractable.

PROSPECTS FOR A VIABLE THEOLOGY OF IDENTITY[153]

While there is something to appreciate in Ockenga's sentiment about walking in a "New Testament level of spiritual life," such spirituality necessarily entails asking to which of Jesus's first-century contemporaries we are most similar. Ockenga was describing his own spirituality, of course, trying to position himself as a modern-day apostle—one deeply in tune with God's rhythms in this world, pulling back the curtain for others to hear them as well—and in this, he shares in the spiritual swagger we also encountered in Abraham Kuyper. That said, I do believe the risen Jesus enters into the lives of would-be contemporary followers in much the same way he did with the first disciples. So, perhaps living in light of biblical stories means, as Jennifer Harvey advises her (privileged) white reader, testing out different roles in the New Testament reality.[154] For instance, problematizing the question "What Would Jesus Do?" she argues that white folks should more often be asking, "What Would Zacchaeus Do?" In the story of his encounter with Jesus, Zacchaeus acknowledges his sin and, to enter into communion with Jesus and others, he repents and pays reparations. Which worldly forms of security do we grasp for ourselves, and from what might we need to repent in order to enter into such community in our place and time?

As we think through various roles in such gospel episodes, I submit that we should consider Jesus's personal interaction with others in terms of a *disruptive, invitational, reorienting practice*. And this practice plays out differently for those who inhabit social power in ways that oppress others than it does for those seeking a basis for asserting their dignity in the face of those who would deny it. The latter already cannot rely on their identities (religious or otherwise) to secure them social power, to secure their place in the world. As such, those on the margins can reasonably expect Jesus's solidarity, for even he appears as one who embraces worldly weakness through nonviolent direct action and exudes a maddening soul force tapped into the veiled power of the kingdom of God. But Jesus calls the powerful and influential, especially the would-be disciples among them, out of their false world-view security and the unspoken privilege of their ill-begotten identity certainty—they must die to those things—in order to live with the personal God. And those who feel compelled to identify (with) Jesus for others must first hear the other's lament as the voice of Jesus to them—identifying them and their place in the communion of persons. When recognized in their dignity, these voices create the occasion for responsibility, repentance, and restorative action. Such a practice of identification leads to continuous repentance according to the contingent nature of our lives and the accidental nature of our responsibility as we actually encounter others. Following Jesus entails honest and ongoing interrogation of how we and others have been ascribed social power based on race, gender, class, sexual orientation, citizenship, and other categories. In the absence of theological reflection on these identities, social power is routinely transfigured into *theopolitical* power, such that persons and groups that already enjoy social power (e.g., white heterosexual American evangelicals) also become de facto authorities on Jesus's identity, God's will, and so on. And this is true not *in abstracto* but because the follower who appears in the world evangelically is tasked with engaging others amid and through such realities—whether acknowledged or not. As I said in chapter 2, all social identities and power axes are drawn into the disciple's following-after Jesus, such that they become obstacles in their impenitence or instruments of the kingdom by way of their reorientation down to the details of their practice.

Among the would-be followers who have benefitted from various forms of social power ascribed to them, following after Jesus cannot predictably amount to simply (and safely) wielding that power better (i.e., to benefit "the least of these"). But neither can we merely disavow our ascribed social statuses and privileges, however much we may wish we could do so. There is no simple solution to the complex reality that is human life in this world. When he calls us to follow him, Jesus finds us within a constellation of sociopolitical realities that structure our external world and our inner life. We must reckon with such spirited powers in our (hi)story—as they play out in our actual relationships, which make us responsible as agents. Our approach to identity security and the levers of power must be refigured to fit the new reality of God's kingdom power and a new life through death-to-self by a thousand cuts (i.e., to the ways, certainties, and powers of old selves). Following after Jesus in the fashion of the New Testament disciples is a self-involving journey that leads from a specific place along a particular path that prioritizes one's ongoing, holistic identification by and with the Christ in full view of once-similar, socially powerful others, whose response may predictably include disownment. And while abundant, life along this path will almost certainly entail innumerable embarrassing wrong turns and missed opportunities. In Paul's counsel on the subject of self-structuring social realities in 1 Corinthians 7, we hear simultaneously "remain in the condition in which you were called" (v. 20) and let those who marry, mourn, rejoice, live in the world do so "as if they do not" (vv. 29–31)—as if these structures had been shown their value in light of the little time that remains. Let them be turned upside down and inside out for the sake of our ultimate concern. And if we are going to intentionally engage in our social setting, we must regularly ask whether our strategies are consistent with the goals we hope to attain.

Here at the end of part II, we may well be wishing for a clear sense of authority by which we can seize the evangelical project, make definitive claims about the identity for the right side, and thus clean up the problems in the world-view. But I wager that the problem would still be represented here, for the authority available is the same foot-stomping, fatherly "because I said so, dammit" authority that Ockenga modeled. While we may wish to keep the form but fix the details, as we will see Richard Mouw attempt in chapter 5, I will be arguing in the final moves of this book that the form itself is broken. As the concept of world-view reaches over more terrain and broader populations, it turns upon the coercive logic of a world still in free fall but always trying to build a framework to hold itself in the sky. Evangelical thinkers have thus far only come up with patches for parachutes riddled with holes. Waging war against relativism, the many have become convinced they are standing on solid, biblical ground. But this amounts to no more than a vindication of the theory of general relativity: we are so accustomed to plummeting that it has become our unfelt baseline for life. Born into the free fall, we have never known terra firma.

So, in talking about a pattern of identification discernible in gospel stories about Jesus, the temptation would be to establish a new universal and all-encompassing ethic to attempt to live out and judge ourselves against. But this ethic would require more stable, solid ground than the organic communion at the heart of Jesus's ministry in the world through the church, which is his body existing today. There is no universal, one-size-fits-all solution to de facto racialization or the mentality of whiteness except to say that we all must do what we can from wherever we are called. Harvey demonstrates the incompetence of universalist ethics relative to race relations, arguing instead that we need an ethics of particularity that speaks truth over our different situations and helps us relate more honestly to and through our varied histories with racial awareness.[155] And as we may be gathering by this point in my project, the reliability of our own structures for determining the *pattern* we may discern (e.g., in Scripture) for how Jesus interacts with individuals is deeply suspect, given our own tendencies to misplace our confidence and mishandle our power in self-serving ways. We must resist abstracting Jesus into a lean set of principles or a predictable mechanism that doles out whatever judgment conforms to our thickest, most sanctified conscience. In the course of embodied human life, we cannot be helped much by projections from within the theological worlds of confident others who wish we would just take up their total world-view as our own.

And in contrast to whatever else we might want to call "identity," the solidity of Christian identity is always in question. It is not found even in assent to the idea of a Jesus who confronts, liberates, and saves; it is found in communion with the living, biblical, historical Jesus and in an expansive community that incarnates God's grace to us. Neither Jesus's identity nor our own identification with Jesus are "haveable" things we can seize and hold onto any more than we can the hand of another person whom we love. I submit that we need to radically reimagine our place in the world, embracing our lives at the scale of creatures within a world of God's making. At this scale, we can genuinely and honestly engage others whose inner constellation of selves may demonstrate for us more faithful patterns of living amid the principalities and powers that contend with each other to shape our lives. Diverse others can expose for us where our current self-configurations conceal the infidelity of *convictional sins*. And we need to see and test how others navigate their many identities as they become sites for inner turmoil, ethical dilemmas, and bona fide responsibility. As a theological reality, I propose centering on an identity held in relationship with the living God in contrast to supposedly certain knowledge of good and evil and of God (more on this in chapter 6).

To be clear, as Dietrich Bonhoeffer would counsel us, we must also do our best to embrace the nature of church community from the start. "Christian community is not an ideal we have to realize, but rather a reality created by God in Christ in which we may participate."[156] And this means that we cannot approach genuine community with an abstract, idealistic notion of community that we then expect to be realized among the people with whom we are willing to associate.

> Every human idealized image that is brought into the Christian community is a hindrance to genuine community and must be broken up so that genuine community can survive. Those who love their dream of Christian community more than the Christian community itself become destroyers of that Christian

community, even though their personal intentions may be ever so honest, earnest, and sacrificial.[157]

Central to the problem here is the spiritual swagger of those who misplace their wish-dream's concreteness, those who envision themselves building out the kingdom come. Bonhoeffer's words here are particularly harsh:

> God hates this wishful dreaming because it makes the dreamer proud and pretentious. Those who dream of this idealized community demand that it be fulfilled by God, by others, and by themselves. They enter the community of Christians with their demands, set up their own law, and judge one another and even God accordingly. They stand adamant, a living reproach to all others in the circle of the community. They act as if they have to create the Christian community, as if their visionary ideal binds all the people together.[158]

On the contrary, God goes ahead of us, creating not only the possibility of community but the community itself, and we are drawn in as the forgiven who thankfully receive with open hands and without demands. "Is not what has been given us enough: other believers who will go on living with us through sin and need under the blessing of God's grace? . . . Even when sin and misunderstanding burden the common life, is not the one who sins still a person with whom I too stand under the word of Christ?"[159] Before we are too quick to interpret this as a justification for our own angles on identifying sin (i.e., from within our secure world-views), let us remember that, in Jesus's own words, the kingdom is already nearer to those who experience oppression in this world; in fact, he himself is (in some way) freshly incarnate among such persons as made clear in Matthew 25. From his days as a doctoral student, Bonhoeffer had been missing where local church-community could satisfy his conviction that *this* is the body of Christ existing today. And Christian ethicist Reggie Williams argues that Abyssinian Baptist Church in Harlem is where—years before he penned the words above in *Life Together*— "Bonhoeffer found Christ existing as community where historically marginalized and oppressed black people knew Jesus as cosufferer and the gospel spoke authoritatively into all areas of life."[160] We do not get to preselect who partakes in community with us partly because God shows up to us in others to share words we need to hear—words we might not otherwise select for, and even still might struggle to hear and grapple with, ourselves.

What seems like the problem of particularity actually arises when universality is assumed from within a particular perspective, rendering all other perspectives deficient. Particularity with a closed fist becomes imperial in its universality and authoritarian in its self-governance. Yet as we see with white evangelicals in the United States, even an authoritarian, imperializing particularity can be disorganized without centralized leadership and become ineffective when centered on faceless individuals. Racialization in America combined with the spirit of free enterprise has together facilitated the emergence of white evangelical leadership from within contexts that are mostly homogenous, speaking to individuals displaced from any context whatsoever, accountable to no one except their own conscience, which has been formed mostly by homogenous others. (This is to say nothing yet of downward trends in church attendance in general, even as irregular or nonattendees claim beliefs and/or self-identity consistent with evangelicalism.) Jesus is made incarnate to us in particular others, and these others—because they represent a different constellation of realities—can alert us to our self-deception, offer alternative interpretations of the situation at hand, and make us responsible agents in our actual places.

A focus on particularity in our socially constituted lives can restore the possibility of living with God from exactly here, this place, in light of all the many relationships and structures of the world seeking to determine my existence. Jennings argues, "If Christianity is going to untangle itself from these mangled spaces, it must first see them for what they are: a revolt against creation."[161] The way forward cannot be merely the reclamation of creational theology in the forms it has taken within much of traditioned theological discourse (as will be exemplified in chapter 5). Rather, a Christian doctrine of creation centers on and in communion, "the deepest sense of God-drenched life attuned to life together, not with people in general but with the people that comprise the place of one's concrete living and the places (the landscapes, the animals, and the built environments) that constitute the actual condition of one's life."[162] This entails embracing the particularity of identity as tied to place—an actual location from and upon which transformation can be undertaken. Since the increasingly globalized world presents the most pressing problems as massive, atmospheric even, we are likely to continue trying to think up correspondingly massive solutions that pretend to see the whole but misplace the concreteness of our models. We are better prepared to address these powers as we embrace a posture of incompetence to transform the whole world and consciously work on and from our local province.[163] Our attempts to seize integrity for our lives through totalized Christian identities are misguided. While trying to demonstrate the comprehensive scope and complete coherence of our Christian world-views, we conceal the lack of integrity in those views owing to the constriction of powerful practices that we have neither the skill nor the will to identify. As we make the final turn in this project, there is something about this idea of the world-viewing impulse pushing us to seize integrity for our own lives that merits further exploration. In the cases under study up to this point, the exposed world-views have claimed support in logic, Scripture, and the very self-revelation of God. We have explored the fit between the world-view concept, human psychology, and human sociality, but the world-viewing impulse itself has not come under direct scrutiny as a natural facilitator of creaturely knowledge of God. In part III, we will address the philosophical and ultimately theological questions about world-view epistemology and, particularly, how human beings come to know God in our twilight.

NOTES

1. Compare Sarah Pulliam Bailey, "A New Group of Evangelical Leaders Forms in Support of Biden," *The Washington Post*, October 12, 2020, accessed January 25, 2021, https://www.washingtonpost.com/religion/2020/10/02/new-evangelical-leaders-support-biden/; and Frank Newport, "Religious Group Voting and the 2020 Election," Gallup, Inc., November 13, 2020, accessed January 25, 2021, https://news.gallup.com/opinion/polling-matters/324410/religious-group-voting-2020-election.aspx.

2. Pannell's appointment came within two years of Ockenga's departure from Fuller's board. While Pannell's trusteeship was significant in its own right, it also signified a broader shift in the life of Fuller and of the evangelical establishment.

3. See, for instance, Joy J. Moore quoted in Lauralee Farrer, "This Is Then, That Was Now," *FULLER*, no. 1 (2014): 17. Quotations from William E. Pannell in this article are largely found in the extended interview section.

4. Data from the Pew Research Center suggests 76–81 percent of self-identified evangelicals are white (registering Latinos separately) while only about 6 percent are Black ("Racial and Ethnic Composition," Religious Landscape Study, accessed May 20, 2020, https://www.pewforum.org/religious-landscape-study/racial-and-ethnic-composition/).

5. William E. Pannell quoted in Farrer, 19. In David Swartz's analysis, "Despite declaring that he was 'more grateful to SNCC than to Southern Baptists,' Pannell remained within evangelical boundaries, encouraging his tradition to pursue racial justice" (*Moral Minority: The Evangelical Left in an Age of Conservatism* [Philadelphia: University of Pennsylvania Press, 2012], 34). For instance, concluding this retrospection with a brief prospective commentary, Pannell expressed (with true evangelical grit), "My fear is that now that we are in touch with the social dimensions of our responsibilities, we are tempted to think we can solve things without Jesus. Are you kidding me? That's why evangelism is in our DNA at Fuller, for crying out loud" (quoted in Farrer, 22).

6. Pannell quoted in Farrer, 19.

7. William E. Pannell, *My Friend, the Enemy* (Waco, TX: Word Books, 1968), 6.

8. Pannell quoted in Farrer, 21.

9. William E. Pannell, "Evangelism and the Struggle for Power," *International Review of Mission* 63, no. 250 (April 1974): 201. Cf. Pannell, *My Friend*, chs. 1–2; Swartz, 193.

A Sociohistorical Analysis of White, American Evangelicalism   191

10. Pannell, *My Friend*, 50–51.
11. Pannell, *My Friend*, 51. Pannell cites existentialist philosopher Jean-Paul Sartre to say, "almost everything comes to us from others. To be is to belong to someone" (*My Friend*, 35).
12. Pannell, "Evangelism," 201.
13. Pannell, *My Friend*, 67.
14. Pannell, "Evangelism," 201.
15. Pannell, *My Friend*, 68.
16. Pannell, *My Friend*, 5–6 and 55–57; and Pannell, "Evangelism," 202 and 205. Cf. Farrer, 17.
17. Pannell, *My Friend*, 29, 38, and 47–48. See also the discussion of an internalized inferiority complex in chapter 2.
18. Pannell, *My Friend*, 27–28.
19. Pannell, *My Friend*, 57.
20. Pannell, *My Friend*, 63.
21. Pannell, "Evangelism," 204.
22. Pannell, *My Friend*, 64.
23. Pannell, "Evangelism," 204. Here he cites the concept of "false conservatism" as Helmut Thielicke explained it in *Theological Ethics*, vol. 2 (Philadelphia: Fortress Press, 1969), 627. Cf. "Self-promoting, exclusive, evasive. One could passionately wish these words exclusive of the church. But, of course, the church is middle-class, even that section of it called evangelical, and rather than challenge the oppressive system which denudes men of their humanity, the church reflects these majority values" (Pannell, *My Friend*, 33).
24. Pannell, "Evangelism," 204.
25. Pannell, "Evangelism," 204.
26. Rosemary Radford Ruether quoted in Pannell, "Evangelism," 205.
27. Pannell, *My Friend*, 65.
28. Pannell, *My Friend*, 65.
29. Pannell, *My Friend*, 25.
30. Pannell, *My Friend*, 25.
31. Pannell, *My Friend*, 29–30.
32. William E. Pannell, "The Evangelical Christian and Black History," *Fides et Historia* 2, no. 2 (1970): 6.
33. Pannell, "Evangelical Christian," 6–7.
34. Pannell, "Evangelical Christian," 7.
35. Pannell, *My Friend*, 48.
36. Pannell, "Evangelical Christian," 11.
37. Pannell, *My Friend*, 6. Cf. Mark Noll's comments on the Black evangelical experience in *American Evangelical Christianity: An Introduction* (Malden, MA: Blackwell Publishers, 2001), 21. Concretely, Pannell spoke of the 1966 midterm elections, which granted sweeping victories to Republicans in Congress and cleared the way for policies that held back minorities and poor people. And these elections were aided by none other than the conservative white Christian (71–72).
38. Pannell, *My Friend*, 53.

39. Pannell, "Evangelical Christian," 9.
40. Pannell, "Evangelical Christian," 10.
41. Pannell, "Evangelical Christian," 10.
42. Pannell, "Evangelical Christian," 10.
43. Pannell, "Evangelical Christian," 10.
44. Pannell, "Evangelical Christian," 13.
45. Pannell, *My Friend*, 31.
46. Pannell, *My Friend*, 82.
47. Pannell, *My Friend*, 120.
48. Pannell, *My Friend*, 120.
49. Pannell, *My Friend*, 125.
50. Pannell, *My Friend*, 121.
51. Betsy Cooper et al., "Anxiety, Nostalgia, and Mistrust: Findings from the 2015 American Values Survey," Public Religion Research Institute, November 17, 2015, accessed January 19, 2021, http://publicreligion.org/research/2015/11/survey-anxiety-nostalgia-and-mistrust-findings-from-the-2015-american-values-survey/. Cf. Robert P. Jones, *The End of White Christian America* (New York: Simon & Schuster, 2016), 150–55.
52. Public Religion Research Institute (PRRI), "Summer Unrest over Racial Injustice Moves the Country, But Not Republicans or White Evangelicals," August 21, 2020, accessed January 5, 2021, https://www.prri.org/research/racial-justice-2020-george-floyd/.
53. PRRI, "Summer Unrest."
54. Barna Group, "Black Practicing Christians Are Twice as Likely as Their White Peers to See a Race Problem," June 17, 2020, accessed January 5, 2021, https://www.barna.com/research/problems-solutions-racism/.
55. US Census Bureau, "Income and Poverty in the United States: 2019," accessed January 6, 2021, https://www.census.gov/content/dam/Census/library/publications/2020/demo/p60-270.pdf.
56. US Census Bureau, "Educational Attainment in the United States: 2019," accessed January 6, 2021, https://www.census.gov/content/census/en/data/tables/2019/demo/educational-attainment/cps-detailed-tables.html.
57. Katherine L. Milkman, Modupe Akinola, and Dolly Chugh, "Temporal Distance and Discrimination: An Audit Study in Academia," *Psychological Science* 23, no. 7 (July 2012): 710–17.
58. Michael O. Emerson and Christian Smith *Divided by Faith: Evangelical Religion and the Problem of Race in America* (New York: Oxford University Press, 2000), 7.
59. Kevin D. Dougherty, Mark Chaves, and Michael O. Emerson, "Racial Diversity in U.S. Congregations, 1998–2019," October 12, 2020, page 8, accessed January 5, 2021, https://sites.duke.edu/ncsweb/files/2020/10/Racial-Diversity-in-U.S.-Congregations-1998-2019.pdf. This paper has since been published in *Journal for the Scientific Study of Religion* 59, no. 4 (December 2020): 651–62.
60. For an interesting, critical discussion of Emerson and Smith's term "racialization" in the context of a seminar in a multiracial church, see Korie L. Edwards,

A Sociohistorical Analysis of White, American Evangelicalism   193

The Elusive Dream: The Power of Race in Interracial Churches (New York: Oxford University Press, 2008), 48.

61. Emerson and Smith, 89.

62. Emerson and Smith, 9.

63. Emerson and Smith credit Ann Swidler with the "cultural toolkit" language for the concept "that culture creates ways for individuals and groups to organize experiences and evaluate reality. It does so by providing a repertoire or 'tool kit' of ideas, habits, skills, and styles" (75–76).

64. Emerson and Smith, 72.

65. Emerson and Smith, 74.

66. Swartz identifies "taking social scientific studies seriously" as a distinguishing mark of the evangelical *left* as a distinction from the establishment folks like Ockenga (43).

67. Emerson and Smith, 77.

68. Emerson and Smith, 79. Swartz's analysis is shot through with the conflict between Black and white evangelicals on strategies for social change, influenced by individual versus structural conceptualizations of sin (chapter 2).

69. Harold Ockenga, *Faith in a Troubled World* (Wenham, MA: Gordon College Press, 1972), 37–38.

70. Emerson and Smith, 101–2.

71. Compare Alex Vandermaas-Peeler et al., "Partisan Polarization Dominates Trump Era: Findings from the 2018 American Values Survey," Public Religion Research Institute, October 29, 2018, accessed January 8, 2021, https://www.prri.org/research/partisan-polarization-dominates-trump-era-findings-from-the-2018-american-values-survey/, and Pew Research Center, "On Views of Race and Inequality, Blacks and Whites Are Worlds Apart," June 27, 2016, accessed January 8, 2021, https://www.pewsocialtrends.org/2016/06/27/on-views-of-race-and-inequality-blacks-and-whites-are-worlds-apart/.

72. Vandermaas-Peeler et al., "Partisan Polarization."

73. Emerson and Smith do note one slightly discrepant piece of data: strong evangelicals were slightly more likely than weak-to-moderate evangelicals to also cite at least *some* structural reason (106).

74. Barna Group, "Black Practicing Christians."

75. Emerson and Smith, 117.

76. Carl F. H. Henry freely used "miracle" language, noting that after Reinhold Niebuhr, neo-Protestants "would scoff at evangelical enthusiasts who look to the miraculous conversion of individuals for the effective transformation of society" (*A Plea for Evangelical Demonstration* [Grand Rapids, MI: Baker Book House, 1971], 37). In terms of evangelism, the colonialist question remains: To what are individuals to be converted? And to what extent is the entire neo-evangelical world-view the aim?

77. Emerson and Smith, 124ff.

78. Regarding the evangelical scale, interviewers subjectively ranked respondents on a scale from 1 to 10 "based on their adherence to theologically evangelical hallmarks, their strength of connection with evangelical institutions (churches,

colleges, para-church ministries, and strength of identity as an evangelical" (Emerson and Smith, 105).

79. Emerson and Smith, 122.
80. Emerson and Smith, 122.
81. Ed Stetzer quoted in Bob Smietana, "Sunday Morning in America Still Segregated – and That's OK with Worshipers," January 15, 2015, accessed January 21, 2016, http://www.lifewayresearch.com/2015/01/15/sunday-morning-in-america-still-segregated-and-thats-ok-with-worshipers/.
82. Barna Group, "What Is the Church's Role in Racial Reconciliation?" July 30, 2019, accessed January 5, 2021, https://www.barna.com/research/racial-reconciliation/.
83. Emerson and Smith, 80.
84. Cooper et al. Cf. Jones, 159–60.
85. Emerson and Smith, 131.
86. Iris Marion Young, *Inclusion and Democracy* (New York: Oxford University Press, 2000), 196. Cf. Moore, 25.
87. Emerson and Smith, 84–85.
88. Dougherty, Chaves, and Emerson, 8.
89. Edwards, 94.
90. Edwards, 91.
91. Edwards, 96.
92. Ryon J. Cobb, Samuel L. Perry, and Kevin D. Dougherty, "United by Faith? Race/Ethnicity, Congregational Diversity, and Explanations of Racial Inequality," *Sociology of Religion* 76, no. 2 (Summer 2015): 195.
93. Cobb, Perry, and Dougherty, 195.
94. Cobb, Perry, and Dougherty, 195.
95. Cobb, Perry, and Dougherty, 195.
96. Edwards, 6.
97. Edwards, 8.
98. Jessica Barron demonstrates the usefulness of a "managed diversity" model for understanding why urban churches find appropriating certain elements from Black culture appealing in "Managed Diversity: Race, Place, and an Urban Church," *Sociology of Religion* 77, no. 1 (Spring 2016): 18–36.
99. Edwards, 131–33.
100. Edwards, 66.
101. Edwards, 65–66.
102. Edwards, 109.
103. Jason Reynolds, "Fortifying Imagination," interview by Krista Tippett, *On Being*, aired June 25, 2020, on NPR, accessed January 7, 2021, https://onbeing.org/programs/jason-reynolds-fortifying-imagination/.
104. Edwards, 121.
105. Edwards, 10.
106. See Wendy Leo Moore, *Reproducing Racism: White Space, Elite Law Schools, and Racial Inequality* (Lanham, MD: Rowman & Littlefield, 2008), especially ch. 1.

107. Glenn E. Bracey II and Wendy Leo Moore, "'Race Tests': Racial Boundary Maintenance in White Evangelical Churches," *Sociological Inquiry* 87, no. 2 (May 2017): 285.
108. Moore, 27.
109. Harold Ockenga, "The New Reformation," *Bibliotheca Sacra* 105, no. 417 (January–March 1948): 91.
110. Moore, 27.
111. Moore, 25.
112. Emerson and Smith, 131.
113. Edwards, 99–100.
114. Barron's analysis on this point is especially sharp.
115. Edwards, 84. Cf. Moore, 30.
116. Willie James Jennings, *The Christian Imagination: Theology and the Origins of Race* (New Haven: Yale University Press, 2010), 9.
117. Jennings, *Christian Imagination*, 24.
118. Jennings, *Christian Imagination*, 15–17.
119. Jennings, *Christian Imagination*, 20. In loftier theological terms: "Divine immutability yields Christian character—an unchanging God wills to create Christians out of slaves and slaves out of those black bodies that will someday, the Portuguese hope, claim to be Christian" (22).
120. Jennings, *Christian Imagination*, 23.
121. Jennings, *Christian Imagination*, 25. Cf. Willie James Jennings, *After Whiteness: An Education in Belonging* (Grand Rapids: Eerdmans, 2020), 136.
122. W. E. B. Du Bois, *Darkwater*, 1920, in *The Oxford W. E. B. Du Bois Reader*, ed. Eric J. Sundquist (New York: Oxford University Press, 1996), 504.
123. Jennings, *Christian Imagination*, 30.
124. Jennings, *After Whiteness*, 135.
125. Jennings, *Christian Imagination*, 59.
126. Jennings, *Christian Imagination*, 29.
127. Jennings, *Christian Imagination*, 29.
128. Jennings, *After Whiteness*, 137.
129. Jennings, *After Whiteness*, 137.
130. Jennings, *Christian Imagination*, 39.
131. Jennings, *Christian Imagination*, 43.
132. Jennings, *Christian Imagination*, 58.
133. Jennings, *Christian Imagination*, 31.
134. Jennings, *Christian Imagination*, 33.
135. For more on this supersessionism, see Jennings, *Christian Imagination*, ch. 5.
136. Jennings, *Christian Imagination*, 33–34.
137. Jennings, *Christian Imagination*, 34.
138. Abraham Kuyper, *Calvinism: Six Stone Lectures* (Amsterdam: Höveker & Wormser, 1899), 34.
139. Jennings, *Christian Imagination*, 60.
140. Jennings, *Christian Imagination*, 61.
141. Jennings, *After Whiteness*, 84.

142. Jennings, *Christian Imagination*, 7.
143. Jennings, *After Whiteness*, 6–7.
144. Jennings, *After Whiteness*, 137.
145. Jennings, *After Whiteness*, 110–11.
146. Iris Marion Young, *Justice and the Politics of Difference* (1990; repr., Princeton, NJ: Princeton University Press, 2011), 45–47. Young cites Martin Heidegger on "thrownness" to say "one *finds oneself* as a member of a group, which one experiences as always already having been" (46). This does not mean that groups have a substantive essence, nor does it mean that a person cannot join, leave, or fundamentally change a social group.
147. See, for instance, Roland Barthes, *Mythologies*, 1957, trans. Richard Howard and Annette Lavers (New York: Hill and Wang, 2012), 251–62.
148. It bears mentioning that J. Kameron Carter has delivered a powerful account of Western thought as extracting Christianity from it particular, historical Jewish root and grafting it into the stump of universalizing Greek philosophies in *Race: A Theological Account* (New York: Oxford University Press, 2008), ch. 2. A more robust conversation around this point, especially given the implication of "worldview" conceptuality (with the rational human mind as microcosm within the macrocosm), is one product of this historical-botanical nightmare.
149. Kant's universality was also conceived within a racialized framework, as discussed in Susanne Lettow, "Modes of Naturalization: Race, Sex and Biology in Kant, Schelling and Hegel," *Philosophy and Social Criticism* 39, no. 2 (2013): 117–31.
150. Jennings, *After Whiteness*, 137.
151. This compares with what Drew Westen has called the "master narrative" of successful political movements in his *The Political Brain: The Role of Emotion in Deciding the Fate of the Nation* (2007; repr., New York: PublicAffairs, 2008), ch. 7. See also Jonathan Haidt, Jesse Graham, and Craig Joseph, "Above and Below Left-Right: Ideological Narratives and Moral Foundations," *Psychological Inquiry* 20, no. 2/3 (April 2009): 115f.
152. Recall how Pannell connected such power and structure with biblical "principalities and powers" language above. With more space, this conceptuality would be worth exploring in its own right as a potential source of insight into the distinct reality of Christianity as a set of counterformative practices amid such power structures.
153. Some elements in this section appeared previously in Jacob Alan Cook, "Toward an Incarnational Theology of Identity," in *Justice and the Way of Jesus: Christian Ethics and the Incarnational Discipleship of Glen Stassen*, ed. David P. Gushee and Reggie L. Williams (Maryknoll: Orbis Books, 2020), ch. 2.
154. Jennifer Harvey, "What Would Zacchaeus Do?: The Case for *Dis*identifying with Jesus," in *Christology and Whiteness: What Would Jesus Do?*, ed. George Yancey (New York: Routledge, 2012), 84–100. Cf. Jennifer Harvey, *Dear White Christians: For Those Still Longing for Racial Reconciliation* (Grand Rapids: Eerdmans, 2014), 184 and 206–7.
155. Harvey, *Dear White Christians*, 57–62.
156. Dietrich Bonhoeffer, *Life Together*, DBWE 5 (Minneapolis: Fortress Press, 1996), 38.

157. Bonhoeffer, DBWE 5, 36.
158. Bonhoeffer, DBWE 5, 36.
159. Bonhoeffer, DBWE 5, 36.
160. Reggie L. Williams, *Bonhoeffer's Black Jesus: Harlem Renaissance Theology and an Ethic of Resistance* (Waco, TX: Baylor University Press, 2014), 26; cf. 15.
161. Jennings, *Christian Imagination*, 248.
162. Jennings, *After Whiteness*, 13–14. Cf. Jennings, *Christian Imagination*, 248.
163. This language of "atmospheric" problems and a posture of "incompetence" runs through Willis Jenkins, *The Future of Faith and Ethics: Sustainability, Social Justice, and Religious Creativity* (Washington, DC: Georgetown University Press, 2013).

Part III

DIVINE REVELATION

Chapter 5

The Evangelical Calvinist World-View of Richard Mouw

When America elected the outspokenly born-again Jimmy Carter to be president in 1976, *Newsweek* heralded "The Year of the Evangelical." The editors did not feel the need to elaborate on which kind of evangelical. But a lot has happened since then, including: the Moral Majority and the proliferation of evangelical social-and-political activism, the *Left Behind* series and seasons of open cultural warfare, and more than five years beset by Donald Trump's rhetoric and record of activity—including the widely panned stunt of forcibly clearing #BlackLivesMatter protestors to walk to a nearby church with a Bible for a photo op. Amid this era's sociopolitical fog but before we made it to this last leg, Richard Mouw and a committee of other evangelicals drafted and released "An Evangelical Manifesto" with the express ambition of illuminating the evangelical identity and its (mis)uses.[1] Situating themselves as "American leaders and members of one of the world's largest and fastest growing movements in the Christian faith," the signatories stated, "No one speaks for all Evangelicals, least of all those who claim to. We speak for ourselves, but as a representative group of Evangelicals in America."[2] However, this document's "manifesto" element signaled: "We speak only for ourselves, yet not only to ourselves."[3] After a brief warning about the dangers of identity politics in the twenty-first century, Mouw and company insisted, "We ourselves, and not scholars, the press, or public opinion, have the right to say who we understand ourselves to be. We are who we say we are, and we resist all attempts to explain us in terms of our 'true' motives and our 'real' agenda."[4] Evangelicals, they argued, should be defined in *theological* terms, not social, cultural, or political ones.

All the same, the first Trump election felt like a wake-up call to many American evangelical leaders, who asked new questions about the real-world meaning of their cherished identity label and its political impact. Many self-identified evangelicals left the name behind while others resolved to hold on for better times—some advocating introspection and reformation to the tune of "we speak only for ourselves, yet not only to ourselves." As one kind of example, Mouw joined Ron Sider among others to make a stand in the 2020 US presidential election as *pro-life evangelicals for Joe Biden* (a move prefigured by their 1972 support of George McGovern against the incumbent president, Richard Nixon).[5] But the overwhelming white evangelical support for Trump in 2020 (76 percent, down only 4 percent from 2016) suggests, if nothing else, that commentators on evangelicalism (even insiders) ought to be extra careful as they traverse the nexus of ideals, representation, and survey data.[6] But we might also want to know, in terms of both historical realities and theoretical ideals: What do majority opinion or varieties of "consensus" mean for an identity group? How does one speak for or even to "evangelicals"? And where is a "biblical world-view" supposed to be in all of this?

This chapter's case study centers on Mouw, an heir to both Abraham Kuyper's neo-Calvinism and Harold Ockenga's "new evangelicalism." His rise to prominence began in the early 1970s with a group sometimes styled (in those days) as the "young evangelicals" and still sometimes called the "evangelical left" (though the centerline has moved since those days).[7] Mouw's public persona was forged in the heat of advocacy around structural racism and civil rights, fostering just acquisition and distributions of wealth, ending the war in Vietnam, and counteracting the sexual revolution. Tapping into Kuyper's civic energy and systematic public-theological insights, Mouw has striven to harness evangelicals' piety and energy for personal evangelism to the work of "cultural discipleship" with an air of civility. Recognizing not only his ability as a Christian intellectual but also his thoughtful angle on the meaning of evangelicalism for a diverse movement, Fuller Theological Seminary hired Mouw in the 1980s. It installed him as its fourth president in 1993—a position he held until 2013. The following case study includes a systematic reconstruction of Mouw's theology of world-view based on his sprawling (and still expanding) body of work, especially his books and scholarly articles, but also some popular sources that highlight important features of his public theology.

In this chapter, I will study how Mouw argues for evangelical cultural engagement based on his richer Calvinist tradition and, in turn, serves as an evangelical statesman in public theological discourse. Since he identifies himself with both theological streams represented by my earlier case studies, I will first situate his work within that already emerging evangelical (hi)story. And by tracing Mouw's complicated relationship with neo-evangelicalism, including explicit criticism of Ockenga, we will see some of the texture in how he participates in and represents evangelicalism—sometimes in his dissent. I will then focus on the fundamental neo-Kuyperian convictions (i.e., about God's will and how humans come to know it) that inform his concern for a broader "evangelical" cultural engagement. Up to this point, my project has centered more obviously around racism, but this chapter will broaden our view of how the colonial-imperial framework for knowing and organizing the whole world, which we have seen in "whiteness," is manifest in institutions and projects helmed even by those who see the enduring color-line and know it represents structural sin. To be clear, today's American evangelicalism (as exemplified in chapter 4) and even, to some degree, Mouw's legacy as a seminary president (more below) demonstrate the abiding challenges of visualizing and striving after racial equity. However, I will highlight additional sites for omnicompetent self-normativity, in part by reviewing Mouw's public engagement of same-sex marriage. This section will help us see how world-viewing functions in evangelical public discourse today and as prompt wider questions about natural theology and essentialism, the basis for epistemic confidence in evangelical public advocacy, and the sometimes coercive power dynamics of knowledge. World-viewing via abstract, all-encompassing principles ascribed to God's will reinforces our unearned epistemic confidence while helping us distance ourselves from the hard impacts of our coercive judgments, as in the real lives of persons who identify as LGBT+. So, as we explore the broader applicability of this project's analysis moving into the endgame, I will surface a deeper theological reality that calls into question the animus of evangelical identity politics and (I hope) compels us toward a fresh examination of evangelical faith.

PLACING MOUW IN HISTORICAL CONTEXT: EVANGELICALISM THROUGH THICK AND THIN

Baptized as an infant in a Dutch Reformed congregation, teenage Mouw made a decision for Christ during Billy Graham's months-long 1957 evangelistic crusade in Madison Square Garden.[8] Partly under his parents' influence, partly due to personal affinity, neo-evangelical voices (e.g., Ockenga and Carl Henry) were reliable fixtures in Mouw's youth.[9] He attended an evangelical college but, anticipating a career in Christian academia, undertook graduate studies in environments that would "test [his] integrity by spending several years staying away from those specifically Christian scholarly pursuits."[10] Mouw has alternately called this time "a few years trying not to be an evangelical," and each portrayal bears its own significance.[11] Mouw's emergent political concerns (e.g., civil rights, the Vietnam War, and economic justice) triggered "a strong sense of distancing from any association with evangelicalism as a movement," and he wrestled with whether his evangelical inheritance applied to the world he was coming to know.[12] Establishment leaders' allergy to the concepts of structural injustice and corporate sin and their poor record of social engagement vexed him.

As he processed his "new moral convictions," Mouw sought "to ground them in a larger understanding of the way things are."[13] His academic wanderings beyond the evangelical fold covered vast terrain in terms of "worldview" (e.g., Roman Catholicism and liberal Protestantism but also secular philosophies), yet no alternative could "satisfy [him] in the deep places of [his] soul."[14] Furthermore, Mouw sensed that his evangelically formed heart was precisely what animated his social concern, so he resolved to uncover where his evangelical faith held "clues . . . for the broader path of discipleship."[15] He threw in his lot with a theologically diverse, socially engaged circle of younger evangelicals—including Bill Pannell, Ron Sider, Jim Wallis, and John Howard Yoder—who initiated him into a rich theological conversation around a progressive political agenda unified by a common evangelical faith.[16] Notwithstanding, it became clear in their workshops that majuscular theological traditions (e.g., Anabaptism, Calvinism, Lutheranism) and other social identities (e.g., race and gender) not only provided much of the participants' energy for political activism but also colored their arguments about specific agenda items. Mouw and Yoder, for example, debated long and hard about the nature of culture and political order.[17] These experiences of evangelical difference launched Mouw's campaign to develop an "evangelical Calvinist" option and primed him for leading exchanges around the more "generic" (as he sometimes puts it) evangelicalism.

Some older evangelicals sympathized with the younger generation's social concern—Carl Henry even participated in the workshop that produced the Chicago Declaration of 1973—but others were dismissive and still others combative. An honest analysis of this situation must register some difficulty identifying whether the negative responses were primarily theological or social, cultural, or political. For example, in a foreword to Harold Lindsell's *The Battle for the Bible* (Zondervan, 1976), Ockenga blasted young interlopers who "claimed the name, but did not confess the doctrinal position of orthodoxy" and who thereby attracted unfair criticism to the establishment.[18] Young Mouw was incensed that sincere evangelicals like himself had been saddled with "charges of heterodoxy [by] leaders who show no empathy with the quandary we have experienced."[19] He found Ockenga's response "arrogant and self-serving"[20] and called out the old guard for censuring his generation's engagement with neo-orthodox sources that offered greater insight into the looming social issues when the neo-evangelical leaders failed to issue adequate social guidance based on their own biblical hermeneutic.

Instructively, Mouw diagnosed a theological deficiency within evangelicalism that needed treatment, turning the tables on Ockenga, Lindsell, and company. While institutional insiders were policing the evangelical identity with myopic attention to a few ostensibly theological matters, they missed the roll call on pressing *doctrinal* issues like racism. Among the old guard's "very narrow range of issues," the nature of Scripture predominated, but some social issues, like promoting free enterprise and a "zealous nationalism," apparently figured in too (see part II).[21] Mouw outed folks like Ockenga as fiscal "Pelagians" (think: "God helps those who help themselves"), and he charged (channeling Bill Pannell), "While evangelicalism's watchmen on the wall have scanned the horizons for bearers of a Bultmannian hermeneutic, a 'honky hermeneutic' has taken over the city."[22] And he predicted that the evangelical coalition would not last long by deploying watchwords (like a certain take on biblical inerrancy) to "control and limit membership in the orthodox party," so leaders urgently needed to resolve some fundamental internal tensions.[23]

It came to pass that some of the younger evangelicals rose to prominence within the mainstream establishment, and Mouw's reflections from "the other side" will fill out our picture of evangelical identity and clear a path to his Calvinist emphases. Some Christian labels serve two functions, he observes, "They point to a characteristic widely shared among believers of various stripes—but they are also used to single out a subgroup of the larger Christian community."[24] With this second function, Mouw zeroes in on "a loose coalition of groups and ministries that have their origins in various branches of Protestant pietism and pietist-type groups."[25] He goes on to explain,

> We present-day evangelicals, like the pietists of the past, insist that to be a Christian, properly understood, is to experience the regeneration of the inner self, so that the claims of the gospel are appropriated in a very personal way. We want people to know Jesus as a living Savior. The Bible for us is a book that God uses in order to speak to each of us about how we should live our lives.[26]

Notice how he initially styles the subgroup with sentiments that could represent *self-identified* "evangelicals" as well as a sizeable number of non-evangelical Christians who, frankly, resist the politics of evangelicalism. In wider ecumenical or public settings, Mouw traces evangelical history from the fundamentalist-modernist disputes into midcentury neo-evangelicalism, admiring the latter for preserving key "non-negotiable basics" while rejecting fundamentalist anti-intellectualism, other-worldliness, and separatism.[27] Modernist challenges to a biblical world-view had provoked the fundamentalists' response at specific sites, like the nature of Scripture (its inspiration, infallibility, etc.), the substitutionary atonement of Jesus, and the historicity of biblical miracles (e.g., Jesus's virgin birth and bodily resurrection). As Mouw narrates, "We evangelicals see a deeper issue at stake here. The basic question is whether we are willing to accept the worldview of the Bible."[28]

His rhetoric here is significant partly because it manifests a conventional evangelical appeal to *the* biblical world-view as if it were more about piety than doctrinal details. It also sets the signifier up to float and defend other theological convictions as fundaments of that world-view whenever the sociocultural context applies pressure.

At his sharpest, Mouw describes the term "evangelical" as a theological *modifier* to other, *thicker* Christian traditions. While he sees the benefits of a united evangelical front for pursuing a shared vision, he genuinely "worr[ies] about a movement in which the only operative theology is of a generic evangelical variety."[29] Mouw explains,

> A consensus evangelical theology is a weak basis for sustaining biblical orthodoxy. Much to be preferred is an evangelicalism that, sharing some fundamental convictions that are ignored and even explicitly denied in the larger Christian community, eagerly enters into a freewheeling discussion of what we can best draw upon from the "thick" confessional traditions of the past in addressing urgent questions today.[30]

For example, "evangelicals" have no shared ecclesiology (as discussed in part II); however, visible leaders should have much more to say about the church when speaking out of their own rootedness in a historical church tradition. So, Mouw denies evangelicalism status as a standalone tradition or denomination, and a good deal of evangelical engagement occurs in parachurch forms.[31] In his hopeful account, identifying as an evangelical presupposes an individual already situated within an ecclesial context with a richer tradition.[32]

To better understand how Mouw uses "thickness" conceptuality, we might draw on political philosopher Michael Walzer, who develops the term to explain how and why people from different (sub)cultural contexts might empathize with each other and make common cause.[33] Walzer explains that varyingly thick understandings of concepts like "justice" (or, perhaps, "the biblical world-view") do not exist side by side in an individual's mind, each to be applied when appropriate; rather, "the morality in which the moral minimum is embedded, and from which it can only temporarily be abstracted, is the only full-blooded morality we can ever have."[34] Thin, minimalist concepts emerge within genuine exchange, debate, and even confrontation based on thick, maximal expressions. Yet people from different thick social contexts pick up "resonances" in the others' arguments that can become the basis for common effort—no matter the distance between their cultures or traditions. Mouw narrates one such experience from his youth:

> One impact that the personal story told by the black delegate to the church convention had on my teenage self was *empathy*. I began to *care* about whether

folks like that couple got served in restaurants. It made perfect sense to me that I would soon be hearing reports about public efforts to integrate lunch counters in the South—access to cheeseburgers was important to the beginnings of the civil rights movement. Spiritual formation for caring about justice requires stories that create empathy. It requires seeing the faces of our fellow citizens and hearing their voices.[35]

Thus, Mouw knew he needed to hold the significance of corporate sins and systemic change in tension with the value of spiritual formation to root out "doctrines of racial superiority" in our hearts.[36] Such tension fueled his quest to faithfully articulate social justice commitments from within the evangelical world-view—to thicken what he *felt* was true by way of the thin, empathic connection.

Taking the conceptuality in a slightly different direction, "thin" does not mean "substantively minor or emotionally shallow. The opposite is more likely true: this is morality close to the bone."[37] Early neo-evangelical leaders came to the proverbial table with thick, traditioned theological convictions, and there they hammered out a thin description of evangelical piety and theology to energize a shared enterprise; the same is true for Mouw's younger cohort. Even so, a question lingers: What does it look like for evangelicals to represent this thin consensus while maintaining their thick traditions? In Walzer's view, whenever people "give some substantial account of the moral minimum," we should "understand that it is necessarily expressive of [their] own thick morality."[38] People cannot help but draw on the resources of their thick traditions that seem best suited to explaining their empathy for and support of the common cause. So, Mouw is an *evangelical Calvinist*; this compound identity marks out a subgroup within Calvinism, but it also reveals *how* he is evangelical.

THE WORLD-VIEW CONCEPT IN MOUW'S THEOLOGY

Synopsizing what a thick, neo-Calvinism brings to the evangelical table, Mouw names three necessary dispositions that I will unpack in this section. First, one must be willing to see God's designs for human social patterns as woven into the fabric of creation and as reflective of a standing "cultural mandate" incumbent upon humans since Adam and Eve's days in the garden. Second, one must warm to the ideas that creation is positively diverse by design and many manifestations of diversity (though not all) reflect the cultural mandate too. Third, despite sin's "total" effect on human nature, one must maintain a certain "optimism about our ability to discern the proper contours of created culture."[39] With a cultural mandate in Genesis, detailed in terms of sphere-laws, human cultural production and (trans)formation become essential to Christian discipleship under the twofold expectation that the regenerate *can unearth* God's standing ordinances for human sociality and *participate in* them and their wider restoration (i.e., "cultural discipleship"). For American evangelicals, this may mean expanding their normative concerns—otherwise focused on saving souls through personal evangelism—to include cultural duties.

Culture in the Fabric of Creation

Working in the line of Kuyper, Mouw focuses his world-view through the framework of the sovereign God's changeless, all-inclusive, lawlike ordering of the universe. So, the categories introduced here are total in scope, leave nothing out of their ordering significance, and instruct Christians in all the knowable details of God's will for humankind. Neo-Calvinist social and political engagement is rooted in an imaginative construal of the divine instruction to "fill the earth" (Gen. 1:28) as a "cultural mandate."[40] Mouw exposits this command as "not merely a divine request that Adam and Eve have lots of babies. The earth was also to be 'filled' by the broader patterns of their interactions with nature and with each other. They would bring order to the Garden."[41] Given the significance of the *imago dei* in Kuyper's worldview theory, we might do well to note that Mouw situates his approach in the more recent developments of such conceptuality, especially since Karl Barth's well-known treatment of potential analogies for understanding the image (e.g., being, operation, or relation).[42] In the process, Mouw makes a *neo*-Kuyperian move, shifting the basis of the *imago* from a static element in the human's *being* into a combined relation-operation paradigm he terms "covenantal partnership" that reaffirms its connection with the cultural mandate. Covenantal partnership highlights our indelible social nature, which generates deep needs and longings within us, and our mandate to exercise "dominion together" by producing cultural forms consistent with God's designs.[43]

Numerous social patterns have regularly ordered and enriched human life over time (e.g., family and politics) and have thus manifested—or at least gestured toward—the basic structures of this created or commanded "culture." Mouw argues, "God invested the original creation with complex cultural potential, which human beings were then expected to actualize."[44] Taking some additional creative liberties, Mouw (after Kuyper) imagines that God draws human beings to fulfill the cultural mandate through a bundle of discrete "spheres." Neither Kuyper nor his contemporary devotees furnish a complete catalog of spheres, but it would include family, church, government, business, education, and art. Perhaps most importantly, the spheres exhibit the Calvinist's first principle: *"the Sovereignty of the Triune God over the whole Cosmos*, in all its spheres and kingdoms, visible and invisible."[45] God's sovereignty is neither limited to the church sphere (as in the secularist perspective) nor mediated by any one sphere to the others (like the church in the medieval perspective).[46] Rather, each created cultural sphere (a) encompasses a distinct aspect of life, (b) entails structures that regulate its distinct goods, (c) operates under the governance of distinct authorities established directly by God, and (d) aims to foster corresponding virtues and to reach distinct ends.[47] We might think of these four aspects as loosely fitting to the Aristotelian or Thomist causes—material, formal, efficient, and final—if we see God as ultimately above and behind all causes and God's eternal-creational will as the only real standard for human flourishing.[48] Mouw helpfully summarizes:

> Our cultural activity, in both its obedient and disobedient forms, occurs within a creation that is *ordered* culturally, in at least two senses: God created a macro-ordering of diverse spheres of cultural interaction, and he gave to each of the individual spheres its own unique internal orderedness. The fulfillment of the cultural mandate, then, requires the discovery and implementation of God's complex ordering design, both among and within the spheres.[49]

We may notice the spheres in their concrete historical forms, but as eternal-creational patterns for natural human relationships, they truly *precede* and structure human lives. Kuyperians imagine the spheres as the prelapsarian designs by which humans "naturally" relate to one another and produce culture together: marriage structures the relationship between people drawn together by gender complementarity; fruitful human unions grow into family and, in due course, government; "the natural productivity of the potencies of our imagination" create forms of art; and so on.[50] We might see in Mouw something of H. Richard Niebuhr's definition of culture as "the 'artificial, secondary environment' which man superimposes on the natural."[51] But perhaps more precisely, he is expanding Niebuhr's transformationist view of human culture in the fallen world as "corrupted order rather than order for corruption."[52] This phrasing underscores God's original, orderly will for human sociality that continues to underlie human activity; even disobedient cultural activity occurs within a creation structured by this will.

To fill out Mouw's concept of the spheres, we would do well to look briefly behind his work to other Kuyperian thinkers whom Mouw sometimes references. Describing how God's lawlike will extends to even the minutest level, Kuyper himself summarized, "There is a will, a command, an ordinance of the Lord for everything that people can have two opinions about."[53] David Naugle borrows the term "cosmonomic" from Kuyper's student Herman

Dooyeweerd to define our metaphysical situation, arguing, "Divine legislation is total in its application to the physical universe, to religious and moral life, and to the basic domains of human existence. God rules all things through the instrumentality of his law."[54] Albert Wolters (after John Calvin) identifies two "orders" in the world we know: an order of creation and an order of sin and redemption.[55] We can understand the order of creation in terms of "structure," which he defines as "the constant creational construction of any thing, what makes it the thing or entity that it is. Structure is anchored in the law of creation, the creational decree of God that constitutes the nature of different kinds of creatures. It designates a reality that the philosophical tradition of the West has often referred to by such words as *substance*, *essence*, and *nature*."[56] So, naming the cultural spheres and spelling out their substantive details means putting words to the divinely infused essence of each relational structure as directing human beings toward something intrinsically good for them as a matter of actualizing potential or fulfilling the design. And the spheres are ever-present as structures of blessing or judgment in human relations. They are designed to order human lives for the good of the humans involved—literally to convey certain goods to them—and to the extent that the law was given for the benefit of humankind, persons living into these structures increasingly flourish whether they know God or not. This is an aspect of common grace.

Once we have discovered the lawlike spheres' creational essences, we must acknowledge the original essences are not all that fallen humans might understand of these structures. Cutting across the created order, Wolters explains, sin has "establishe[d] an unprecedented axis, as it were, along which it is possible to plot varying degrees of good and evil."[57] Certain conceptions and concrete iterations of the spheres require serious scrutiny, for "anything in creation can be directed either toward or away from God," including social institutions (e.g., schools and businesses) and human functions (e.g., sexuality and reasoning).[58] Calvin's analysis of 1 Corinthians 6 offers a sample directional evaluation:

> The expression, therefore, that they two become one flesh, is applicable in the true and proper sense to married persons only; but it is applied to fornicators, who are joined in a polluted and impure fellowship, meaning that contagion passes from the one to the other. For there is no absurdity in saying that fornication bears some resemblance to the sacred connection of marriage, as being a corruption of it; . . . but the former has a curse upon it, and the other a blessing.[59]

So, the "direction" of concrete forms or real-life functions in the order of sin and redemption (toward or away from God) is manifest in their (dis)obedience relative to the God-breathed structures and spheres that order creation.

For Mouw, the social transformation agenda will involve advocacy and activism that teaches people to live into these relations' true structure as a service to God and the common good. But the current order is one of sin *and* redemption, so we can only see the human condition in the decidedly mixed light of this order.

The Pros and Cons of Diversity after the Fall

In *Pluralisms and Horizons* (Eerdmans, 1993), Mouw develops with Sander Griffioen a heuristic device for assessing the contemporary West's bewildering diversity of world-views. They distinguish between descriptive and normative (i.e., advocating) stances toward pluralism and establish three broad types of pluralism: contextual, associational, and directional.[60] *Associational pluralism* is a rather broad spectrum, including family on the "natural" end but also "voluntary" groups like churches, schools, and businesses.[61] Highly differentiated societies like the United States comprise numerous associational relations, any number of which can make simultaneous claims on individuals. *Contextual pluralism* covers "a variety of cultural and social experiments involving the human spirit," including racial, ethnic, geographic, gender, and class experiences.[62] Most of these categories represent numerous possible expressions, and several "contexts" form each person. *Directional pluralism* involves "ultimate" (e.g., religious or ideological) commitments and thus "the diversity of visions of the good life that give direction to people's lives."[63] Significantly—and this is where the heuristic quality of their classifications comes into play—"the borders that separate these three categories will not always be easy to discern."[64] Nonetheless, Mouw and Griffioen combine the two sets of distinctions into a grid of six possibilities for what "pluralism" can mean.

Only one of those possibilities raises serious *categorical* objections: normative, directional pluralism. Associational pluralism just names the variety of concrete forms that arise within the creational spheres, and we can imagine this variety within a Christian world-view as healthy channels for fulfilling the cultural mandate.[65] Contextual pluralism can be appreciated as the Creator "having distributed different aspects of the divine likeness to different cultural groups, with each group receiving, as it were, a unique assignment for developing some aspect or another of the divine image."[66] Humans even practice and produce theology within specific contexts that "profoundly shape the act and the content," and recognizing this fact "gives new occasion for celebrating the riches, and the universality, of the Christian gospel."[67] For Mouw, it is "quite likely that throughout eternity we will be aware . . . of our cultural, ethnic, and racial identities"—even some emerging from sinful distinctions (e.g., contemporary forms of "race").[68] Directional pluralism, however, evokes the biblical language of "godly and sinful 'ways' and righteous and unrighteous 'paths,'" taken to represent substantive matters and "comprehensive patterns of behavior."[69] So, directional analyses attend to not "marginal issues from a biblical perspective" but "basic orientations, either God-honoring or God-dishonoring, [that] are the steering factors for our life pilgrimages."[70] Such pluralism is descriptively real but not a positive contributor to our reality.

Unpacking the episode of humankind's fall (Gen. 3), Mouw accentuates classic Calvinist motifs for understanding the origin and nature of sin, namely, authority and rebellion. While we cannot escape the laws of biology or physics, humans are unique in creation in that we can exercise our will to obey or rebel against God's moral ordinances (including the sphere-laws).[71] The serpent presented "a set of philosophical alternatives," which boil down to antithetical first principles concerning who is at the center of things: the sovereign God or human beings.[72] Many philosophers over time have followed suit, displacing "God's revelation in the Scriptures as our only reliable authority on the important issues of life" with appeals to human rationality or "an enlightened imagination."[73] Mouw does not deny that humans should use their cognitive powers, but he underscores how humans must *rely* on their basic trust in the biblical God.[74] Some ambiguity remains about locating the line between the directional and the contextual, created culture and contextual diversity, universal principles and historical particulars. For example, in view of my project thus far, we might want to know to what degree and toward what ends race has affected the trajectory of normative theological understandings of what it means to have a basic direction in the first place.

Speaking generally, Mouw interprets directional pluralism through the concept of idolatry. With Griffioen, he notes Augustine's affective (e.g., "love") or spiritual (e.g., "worship") language for portraying individuals' most basic direction.[75] Elsewhere, Mouw refers to the "basic trustings" formed in a person's innermost self (i.e., the biblical "heart" or Kuyper's "controlling center") that direct their life.[76] Going further, he argues that proper reasoning about the things that matter most is itself a component of the human's creaturely dependence on a living, trusting relationship with the biblical God; conversely, a relationship of enmity with God renders one's reasoning faculties unfaithful.[77] Mouw offers a simple evaluation tool: "If your picture [of what reality and goodness are all about] has the biblical God at the center of things, it is an accurate one. If it places something or someone else at the center, it is idolatrous."[78] Following this trajectory to its end, Mouw and Griffioen add that "nontheocentric intellectual perspectives" should also be understood as manifestations of the same root problem: idolatry.[79] Aside from the more obvious directional competition among religions, Mouw and Griffioen also have in mind here how associations and contexts can assume priority in a person's world-view, thus blurring the distinctions among the types of pluralism. "Creature-centered thought is reductionistic in character," they explain, "people will organize their understanding of reality around an 'absolutizing' of some aspect of the creaturely."[80] And Mouw reads Romans 1 within this view, naming how "the apostle describes various ways in which people can be 'given over' to evil passions and projects," which he exposits as "the possibility that we can become 'possessed' by the evil that we flirt with."[81] Mouw and Griffioen did warn us that the boundaries between the types of pluralism would not always be easy to discern.

While the basic directions seem clear enough when registered in highly generalized terms, a major concern arises regarding the biaxial structure-direction paradigm: in a concrete human life, any number of functions or relations may be directed toward or away from God. Mouw and Griffioen concede, "Actual people often seem to be pulled in two directions at once."[82] Elsewhere, Mouw doubts whether humans universally feel the supposed need for a unified world-view: "It may be that we have become quite capable of moving back and forth between diverse, and inconsistent, worldviews with little regard for the question of what it is that ultimately unifies our cultural worlds."[83] Given Mouw's approach to diversity in creation, we should see some dividedness as a mark of human selfhood, but such dividedness becomes a liability in applying the "radical antithesis," that is, the possibility of only two directions of human life, to *people* (cf. chapter 2).[84] It is relatively easy to imagine how "comprehensive patterns of behavior" might direct a person away from God, but what should we say about *partially unsanctified* patterns of behavior or, more relevant for the current project, *partially unenlightened* world-views?

Notwithstanding, we may wonder about the extent of the connections between an individual's *most basic* direction, the evangelical identity, and the comprehensive "biblical world-view" unfolding in Mouw's work. Remember, both Kuyper and Ockenga moved rather rapidly from the pietistic, born-again spirit to an ever-expanding set of claims about the world and humans' roles in it. Mouw's reflections on the "basic directions" of persons and world-views lead him into two different modes of talking about what is happening here. First, when talking about actual persons, he addresses the individual's "basic trustings" in a pietistic and pastoral sense as a function of their relationship with the living God.[85] Misdirection may not account for all of the ways a person could arrive at a different understanding about this or that creational sphere. Mouw warns against placing too much emphasis on the "devilry" of human cultural or social (or even theological!) divisions; otherwise, the Christian may add undue cosmic gravitas to differences with others (literally: "demonization").[86] And he mourns how "many evangelical commentators these days insist that salvation is closely tied to doctrinal clarity."[87] Following Kuyper, Mouw registers a sense of "mystery" around the Spirit's ministry of regeneration and subsequent works of sanctification and enlightenment.[88]

Second, when gesturing toward the stuff of "the real conflict," Mouw argues in an objectivist-philosophical mode that we are examining "differing sets of basic life-guiding principles."[89] Because the "radical antithesis" is largely about epistemes, as Kuyper argued, the issues and the stakes become clearer once theological world-views are *depersonalized*. What is directional in the person is not entirely detached from what is directional about a comprehensive world-view considered impersonally, but we should handle the two differently. Conducting a comparative analysis of world-views from within a Kuyperian schema, Mouw's baseline is a comprehensive, principial system of God's lawlike will, within which all entities and relations have an ideal-essential structure that is directionally "good" when concretized. The neo-Calvinist evangelical presents this system as part and parcel of the biblical world-view, judging any deviation from it as directional—in theory, even if not always corrupting a person across the borderline into badness.

Discovering and Advocating the Contours of Created Sociality

At this point, we may ask to what extent fallen humans in all their complexity come not only to grasp *the* biblical world-view but to fill it out with reliable details of God's original-creational social patterns and structures. For his part, Mouw explains that the Spirit enables the Christian to know God's will and "*appropriates* these matters to our inner selves" (i.e., subjectively).[90] But, of course, we explored this question to some extent (and with unsatisfactory results) in the study of Kuyper in chapter 1. As such, we might anticipate some trouble distinguishing between the defining, essential features of created human sociality's sphere-structures and those qualities that can be blessedly diverse in a person's or community's successful pursuit of a given sphere's necessary goods. Put differently, we are ever searching for a reliable practice for avoiding the moral failures of past attempts (e.g., Calvin's and Kuyper's patriarchy) to distinguish "accidental" qualities from the substantive ones in each sphere. And church historian Charles Partee helps us get right down to the most pressing question: "It would seem difficult, if not impossible, to establish the criteria, whether rational or spiritual, by which individuals and groups are judged to possess sanctified reason and whether their possession is permanent or only occasional."[91]

Mouw takes this "noetic" concern to be a key distinction between Calvinist thought and the Thomist natural law tradition. The latter reflects a "natural" knowledge of God accessible to all humans in large degrees, but Calvin argued that fallen humankind became blind to the "many burning lamps" of creation that could lead to "the pure and clear knowledge of God" or to the *telos* of humankind.[92] Interpreting the first three acts of the "biblical drama" (creation, fall, and redemption), Mouw summarizes:

> In our shared human nature, we have been designed by the Creator to respond in obedience to this lawful ordering of reality. But in our sinful rebellion, our response has become one of disobedience. The redemptive mission of Christ was required to make it possible for depraved sinners to be redirected toward paths of obedience. The moral life that Christ came to inaugurate, then, is on this view not something brand-new. Rather it is the reclaiming and restoring of that which had been seriously marred by original sin.[93]

At this point in the drama, however, the degree to which creation itself persists in its original, revelatory condition versus suffering and groaning for its restoration (i.e., whether creation as *fallen* can mislead humans) is an open question.[94] In any case, salvation history has also entailed the inscripturation of some knowledge of God the Creator, which serves to clarify what has always been on display in creation. And the regeneration that makes salvific knowledge of Christ's work personal also restores access to whatever knowledge of God is immanent in creation. Calvin famously illuminates this relationship on the metaphor of Scripture as a pair of glasses that clarify what we see through our natural capacities, but Kuyper expands the discussion around human noetic capacities, speaking of the grafted tree drawing its life through the original stump.[95]

We must share something of Mouw's noetic concern because, when he speaks of the "creational order," the concept plainly takes in more than is revealed in the biblical creation accounts or the wider body of Scripture. Filling out the neo-Calvinist world-view involves mapping the "lawful patterns" and "lawlike regularities" of the world God has created, disclosing the hidden contours of reality itself. Insiders to such expeditions perceive the internalization of these patterns as central to all Christian formation, their impact on broader social patterns as central to "cultural discipleship." In terms of the Christian condition before God,

> to be childlike in the Christian sense is . . . to see the universe as a friendly place, not because we have set aside our critical abilities, but because we have formed the very adult conviction that when we uncover the lawlike regularities and cause-and-effect relationships of the world in which we live, we are discovering signs of the faithfulness of the One who is at every moment "upholding the universe by his word of power." (Heb. 1:3)[96]

As a matter of method, Mouw and company are not merely *reading* God's revelation as deposited in Scripture. They are doing philosophical work (i.e., reasoning, speculating, and imagining) based on their knowledge of God's historical self-revelation in the pietistic confidence that such work is ultimately "grounded in an experience of the presence and power of the divine Spirit."[97] Yet Mouw is upfront about the first few chapters of Genesis being a rather meager basis for deriving normative content, including about "the human social condition as the Creator intended it"[98] or even about "the *kind* of cultural formation that God intended."[99] One must discover many essential details (or clues to them) in or behind the whole biblical drama, for example, its portrayal of "what was lost or perverted because of the entrance of sin into human affairs."[100] Sometimes this method entails sprinting from select biblical references to sprawling theological constructions that involve generalizations of, and extrapolations from, those passages along with their "readings" of the book of creation and certain assumptions about what each act of the biblical drama might contribute to the authoritative world-picture.

The sphere of government offers a ready example of this reasoning. Mouw argues that political order is a God-willed structure that would have generated concrete forms in due and natural course without the fall.[101] Humans are social beings created to fill the earth, so scalable forms of joint human endeavor and provision for the common good (e.g., traffic lights and sidewalks) are implied in the original creation.[102] By God's design, according to Kuyper, "political life, in its entirety, would have evolved itself, after a patriarchal fashion, from the life of the family," and it would have been markedly different from the political world we know—"Who binds up, where nothing is broken?"[103] Thus, the sphere of government epitomizes the tension between the order of creation and the order of sin and redemption. Under fallen conditions, even the best government takes on some functions relative to the other spheres for which it now must carry the sword; specifically, political authorities have a "threefold right and duty" to (1) adjudicate inter-sphere disputes, (2) defend the weak against the strong in intra-sphere relations, and (3) take necessary actions to coerce trans-sphere solidarity (e.g., in bearing the cost of common goods).[104] Thus, Mouw says, not all coercion is sinful; indeed, some forced compliance (or punishment for noncompliance) is a prerogative of those who wield the sword by the authority of God (cf. Rom. 13).[105] We are to imagine and promote essential political forms that can only, in fact, be *post*lapsarian ideals—God's preserving words for humankind in a fallen world bearing by the sin-restraining quality of common grace.[106] And this reality casts shade on the eternal-creational rhetoric.

At this point, we might wonder what exactly is restored to the person in regeneration to make such a theological method possible for those who inherit the first humans' blindness.[107] As Partee observes, "While Calvin presumes the validity of his inferences from Scripture, he does not more specifically indicate the logical grounds of their legitimacy. In other words,

Scripture has a dominant, almost exclusive, role in the knowledge of God and man, but Calvin *assumes* rather than *explains* the epistemological transition from text to application."[108] The Westminster Confession of Faith fills the gap this way: "The whole counsel of God concerning all things necessary for His own glory, man's salvation, faith and life, is either expressly set down in Scripture, or by good and necessary consequence may be deduced from Scripture" (1.6). In his commentary on this passage, Partee pulls no punches: "The claim is that the necessary consequences are not located in the mind of the deducer but in the text itself! Thus, theological affirmations can be drawn from Scripture exactly without adding to or diminishing from its meaning."[109] But what does this say about all the creative and particular interpretive activity that occurs in the space between what is in Scripture and what is deduced from it "without adding to or diminishing from its meaning"? Partee identifies the corner into which we are backed:

> The ontological relation between source and deduction requires expansion into an epistemological context containing individuals and communities who possess rectified, regenerate, or sanctified reason, as the Westminster divines recognized. Interestingly, the Westminster Confession precisely defined the first two parts of this sequence (Scripture and deduction) but left the latter two (sanctified reason in individual and community) without careful analysis.[110]

As such, we have no criteria for judging whether theologians, traditions, or churches possess *sanctified reason* as a reliable cognitive faculty that will produce true theological formulations. Such criticism also applies to Kuyper, who theologized "enlightenment" as the equivalent of sanctification for the person's faculty of understanding without adequately naming or addressing the not-so-humble implication that his own enlightenment was quite advanced while the pious, equally erudite Methodist would necessarily be less pure in their knowledge of God the Creator. Mouw notes that Kuyper and his followers "say surprisingly little" about their grounds for believing in the sphere sovereignty framework, "choosing for the most part to explicate rather than provide a rationale for their scheme."[111] And he confesses, "We Kuyperian Calvinists have regularly erred in not being clearer about where the lines fall in our thinking between revelation and speculation *about* revelation."[112] So, we must ask what grounds we have for claims about God's eternal-creational will for all humankind and, in addition to that, cause for the energetic work of transforming culture and pressing our society into what we know of its "creational" mold.

In recent writing, Mouw has emphasized (borrowing phrases from Arthur Holmes) the tension between "epistemic humility" and "epistemic hope" in Christian lives.[113] Put briefly, "we confess that only the Creator has a clear and comprehensive knowledge of all things. This should inspire in us a deep humility. But we also have received the promise that God will eventually, in the end-time, lead us into that mode of perfect knowing that is proper to us as human creatures."[114] Both the finitude and the fallenness of human beings should sustain "a humbly modest approach to human knowing," but the promise of the fourth act (namely, the coming age) should impel us to keep exploring.[115] Mouw understands that Kuyperians' bold and sweeping claims about the contours of created culture may not play well in the wider community—Christian or otherwise. And reflecting his ultimate confidence in the sphere-laws framework for grasping and living within God's lawlike will, he advises his cohorts,

> In explaining this process to others, we need to be clear about the fact that we have been captivated by a very imaginative way of charting out God's designs in the revealed drama of creation, fall, redemption, and eschaton. And when we encounter disagreement and dissent, as we surely will, we cannot fall back on pronouncements. Rather, we must explain as best we can why we are deeply convinced that all of this is, while surely a speculative exercise, the product of sanctified imaginations.[116]

Mouw has also expressed some reservations about the "packaged feel" of what many contemporary Christians mean by "world-view"—suggesting "it" is something that we can definitively "possess" and wield over and against others.[117] He sometimes shifts to *engaging in world-viewing* language, which I have appropriated throughout this project. Mouw sees this posture as better reflecting the individual's dynamic transformation by God's grace. He talks about nurturing "reality lovers" who search and see deeply into the created reality, reason about its features, but also grow attached to its goodness and feel its points of pain.[118]

Directly addressing the cliché, "We ought not to identify our own specific political programs with the will of God," Mouw responds, "To speak and act in the name of the Lord is, of course, a difficult and fearsome thing; for to think that we could legitimately do so would be pretentious were it not for God's announced intention that he *will* speak and act through the faithful people he has chosen."[119] On the one hand, "there is room for genuine disagreement among Christians about the details of public righteousness"— Mouw offers approaches to war and peacemaking as an example.[120] On the other hand, where the complex witness of the Bible is debated and discussed as nonideologically as possible, "we can often be fairly confident about the merits of specific strategies and programs."[121] Note Mouw's reference to the context of debate and the implication of consensus, which reflects the "young evangelical" consensus that *this* war (namely, in Vietnam) was unjust. While

Mouw has clearly found some theologians' world-views mistaken in the details—the social gospel (e.g., Walter Rauschenbusch), equating God's kingdom with the "American way of life" (e.g., Carl McIntyre but maybe also Harold Ockenga), and certain "radical" (read: liberation) theologians—concrete failings point only to the "*general* difficulty of knowing God's will with respect to specific matters."[122] This should not engender passivity; God is merciful and blesses the faithful *intentions* of those who engage in political activism, even if they are not always in the right. "Our comfort in God's sovereign purposes in history must be intimately related to the active *trust* with which we seek to do his will."[123] Clear pronouncements on specific issues may be made based on Christian principles if following Mouw's recommended "hard and fast rule: *the Church must only pronounce on specifics when there is a threat to the Christian faith, witness, and life.*"[124] At least once, however, he ominously remarked that an open-eyed analysis of the surrounding world would find that such threats "are not rare," and he mused that an adequate assessment of human society might conclude that we are in a constant, general state of emergency.[125]

POLITICS IN THE NAME OF "EVANGELICALISM"

This section will review Mouw's public-theological commentary on marriage and family with a view to same-sex relationships, so we might do well with some observations around his pastoral-theological concern in this specific discussion. For starters, writing directly about civility, he confesses, "Given my strong convictions on the subject, it really is rather difficult for me to be civil about sex."[126] His rhetoric tends toward a *love the sinner, hate the sin* posture,[127] certain moments reveal a depth to this love. Mouw takes the desire of same-sex partners to partake in marriage covenants as "evidence that we're sort of designed that way."[128] And speaking positively of the people involved, he claims the "conservative-evangelical community" could take a constructive step by recognizing "there can be grace in relationships that may not measure up to what, when we read the Bible, . . . we see God requiring of us there."[129] Building from an argument common among Roman Catholics, Mouw says, "Genital intimacy in a committed same-sex relationship is an instance of *disordered friendship*. But the fact of the *disorder* should not keep us from ignoring the value of the intimate *friendship*. To affirm this value is to be willing to explore difficult—but highly significant—pastoral territory."[130] More than once, he questions whether labels like "straight" and "normal" are apt for describing any human's sexuality in a fallen world.[131] Taken together, such considerations should prompt Christians to practice self-criticism, avoid oversimplifications, "curtail irrational fears" (while preserving rational ones), remember the actual evils committed against LGBT+ persons, and cultivate empathy.[132] Moving forward, I am less interested in the merits of Mouw's claims about marriage than what his public theologizing reveals about the world-viewing impulse and evangelical identity politics.

On the Sphere of Marriage

Nowhere in print does Mouw offer a detailed treatment of marriage, biblical or otherwise—ostensibly because his typical audience already shares his "traditional" definition. What *they* need, he thinks, is coaching in the cultural mandate and the practices of convicted civility.[133] Mouw's fundamental understanding of marriage and family is undoubtedly supplied by his *thick* neo-Calvinist sphere-law framework, which ironically comprises a rather *scant* set of hermeneutic principles and a moral platform abstracted from Kuyper's historical-particular world-view.[134] Mouw made the bare basics of his position clear early in his career, advocating for "the biblical view" of marriage and maintaining "sexual intimacy cannot be properly experienced apart from a context of covenant faithfulness—which is properly realized in monogamous, heterosexual relationships characterized by lifelong fidelity."[135] Signifying this conviction's fundamentality, he urged, "Departures from this commitment to the norm of marital fidelity must be considered as serious 'breaches of faith.'"[136] Mouw lamented over Protestants impotent "to confront contemporary sexual culture with those liberating themes of judgment and healing which are central to the biblical address to human sexual relationships."[137]

Filling out "the biblical world-view," Mouw points to creation for sexual norms and Romans 1 for the noes. Within his tradition, one might expect him to run with the concepts of "being fruitful and multiplying" (Gen. 1:28) and finding a "suitable helper" (Gen. 2:18). These texts suggest two God-given goods that marriage structures: procreation and a supportive, mutually complementary relationship. "Sexuality is a very important feature of our created nature" and performs "a basic role in the human drama" (i.e., in procreation).[138] In contrast to Calvin and Kuyper, however, Mouw abandons the *gender-role* complementarianism that has often attended "biblical" and "traditional" claims about the natural, essential structures of marriage and family (and government, etc.).[139] And in a fallen world, marriage also provides a third good: a sanctioned context for sexual intercourse to hedge against the sin of fornication.[140] Speaking the noes inferred from Romans 1, Mouw expounds,

> I really do think that it refers not just to a certain kind of group of promiscuous homosexuals or temple practices of homosexuals. I think it's talking about

what is *natural*. And once you take that view, as I do, then you go back to all those other passages, and . . . even though by themselves they don't make the case, there's a kind of pattern there that we see. And that's been the traditional consensus of the Christian churches.[141]

Note Mouw's appeal to the category of "naturalness," which may find conceptual footing in Kuyper's radical antithesis.[142] When asked whether God could somehow surprise him in support of same-sex marriage, Mouw points back to Romans 1:

> If I could be convinced that I was just misunderstanding God's intentions in inspiring the writer to write those words, I would be very open to that kind of surprise. But to me, it really is struggling with those texts. . . . I'm a Calvinist, and [I know that] we are so capable of self-deception, and that means that I may be guilty of self-deception in accepting the traditional reading of those texts, but it also may mean that I'm allowing my good feelings about experiences and things that I see to influence me in such a way that I'm refusing to hear what God is saying, and I think that's a real danger.[143]

The other texts and passages to which he keeps referring would include commands concerning same-sex sexual intercourse in the moral-legal context of Leviticus 18:22 and 20:13.[144] In view here is the moral law's didactic function, which Calvin saw as its predominant meaning for Christians. This instructive element registers the law's primacy as not only *the* authoritative body of teaching for Christian living but also God's express will for all human beings. In this vein, Mouw claims, "God's prohibition of homosexual sex is good for people; we might want to explain that the Bible hasn't given us arbitrary restrictions. In this view, we would argue that even if you don't accept the Scriptures, somehow you ought to be open to the possibility that this is a better way to live, that people were created to live this way."[145] Mouw regularly gestures toward the flourishing available through the biblical worldview; humans are happier when living closer to God's will, whether they acknowledge the living God or not.

In a world marred by sin and rebellion, we must ask how God's people should maintain and mend the marital sphere. Establishing some ground rules, Mouw argues that the strictures of Christian community are not coterminous with what Christians should expect of their surrounding cultures.[146] For example, while there is "a sense in which Christians ought to promote 'Christian standards' in the larger society," they cannot legitimately or justly advocate "legislative bans on certain kinds of sexual behavior" (i.e., "sodomy laws").[147] Since Christian social engagement "must not be motivated by a desire to manipulate others, . . . we are justified in promoting legislation only when it is aimed at a more equitable distribution of rights and opportunities."[148] Mouw's deeper principles pertain here: "A concern to promote justice must be based on a desire that human beings be free to pursue the interests and projects that flow from their fundamental life commitments, *however regrettable those choices may be from a Christian point of view.*"[149] And considering the biblical norm of justice, he proclaims, "It is a terrible matter when Christians attempt to exercise a pattern of coercive lordship which God himself has refused."[150] In terms of direct political action, three strains of Mouw's advocacy invite our attention: (1) some positive rights for same-sex "unions"; nevertheless, (2) a public definition of "marriage" that recognizes the *essential* nature of two biological sexes; and (3) the Christian's right to discriminate and otherwise to maintain a dissenting world-view within Christian entities throughout the various spheres.

On Public Definitions

Joining a conversation about public definitions early in his career, Mouw noted that political philosophers had a methodological shift thrust upon them. He explained that political-philosophical theories had traditionally developed through responding to a series of *general* but essential questions. But now very *specific* sites emerging within American life were pressing the guild for consideration. Instead of structural questions like "What is a marriage? What is a family? What is a church?" many thinkers were fielding questions in the concrete forms of "gay marriages, the commune, and house churches."[151] In response, Mouw argued that contra the "frantic and faddish" investigations prevalent in society, such matters are properly addressed through serious theological (read: generalizing and essentialist) work.[152] Regrettably, as noted before, if he has personally engaged in the work of detailing subjects like marriage, family, and sexuality, his arguments have not been made publicly available.

When asked about a constitutional ban on same-sex marriage in a 2006 interview, Mouw hedged his view by questioning the definition and scope of an "amendment."[153] Speaking of the anger on various sides of the issue, he compared a constitutional ban on one extreme to those "willing to break the law in local situations" to solemnize same-sex marriages on the other, and he claimed, "We really have not had an adequate public debate about this."[154] Juxtapose this line of thought with Mouw's approach shortly after the 2008 ballot initiative in California known as Proposition 8 passed, *amending* the state constitution's "Declaration of Rights" with one definitional sentence: "Only marriage between a man and a woman is valid or recognized in California."[155] Addressing the uncivil air around Prop. 8 for *Newsweek* with his "best shot"[156] (in about 750 words), he flatly stated, "I voted for the ban," and he justified both his position and his activism by merely declaring, "As an evangelical, I subscribe to the 'traditional' definition of a marriage, and I do not want to see that definition changed."[157]

With no further explanation to the general-public audience of *Newsweek*, Mouw insisted that his advocacy did not mean that he wanted to impose his personal or religious convictions on others, and he concluded his piece by asking (in reference to the "adequate public debate" mentioned above), "Can we talk?"[158] Reflecting on this article later, he insisted, "I don't see myself as motivated by a desire simply to impose my religious views on everyone else. In this case, though, I said that I worry about what permitting same-sex marriages would mean for the overall health of society."[159] Mouw represents numerous evangelicals who have seen mainstream cultural trends on issues of sex and reproduction as "a threat to the Christian faith, witness, and life" that warrants dissenting public statements and activist endeavors. On this escalating threat, Mouw offers some backstory:

> We evangelicals began to feel an intensified cultural desperation as secularism and the 'sexual revolution' began to dominate the public arena. As pornography, homosexual rights, abortion-on-demand, rising divorce rates, and sex education in the schools became increasingly prominent on the cultural agenda, it became difficult to think of ourselves as a remnant group capable of protecting ourselves from cultural forces. The very fabric of family life, even within our sheltered communities, was now threatened by these new trends.[160]

The sexual revolution and all its supposedly constituent parts materialized powerfully in a relatively brief historical moment, the intensity of which has colored conversations about any of the parts. The felt anxieties of a fast-changing social landscape make it all too easy for social critics of all stripes to rhetorically bind whatever they see as the leading problems of the day together as the fruits of godlessness. For his part, Ockenga clearly tied civil rights advocacy together with anxieties about socialism in the 1960s and 1970s. White evangelicals' hostility toward the #BlackLivesMatter movement bears this sensibility and style of argumentation, criticizing the explicit affirmation and inclusion of LGBT+ individuals, which is especially true in some specific locales but also reflects the lived, intersectional reality of key founding voices.[161]

Mouw bundles the struggle for "homosexual rights" with an entirely negative battery of initiatives destroying family life and grating on evangelicals' identity. How exactly the increasing prominence of same-sex relationships could destroy family life on its own—that is, outside of the revolutionary bundle—remains untold.[162] Perhaps most tellingly, Mouw's *Newsweek* article tagged a complex of genuine fears:

For many of us, "normalizing" same-sex marriage comes down to deep concerns about the raising of our children and grandchildren. What will they be taught about sexual and family values in our schools? How will they be affected by the ways the entertainment media portray people with our kinds of views? And will we even be allowed to counter these influences in our homes and churches without being accused of "hate speech"?[163]

So, the *cost* society imposes on those who dissent from "official" (i.e., legal and cultural) definitions of marriage is the categorical threat to Mouw's community as it defends its understanding of "the common good." In one sense, this cost is calculated in social capital, legal standing, and a sense of belonging. Mouw urges civility even in disagreement and allows no room for such violence against minorities, but what he means by "counter these influences" does include "religious freedom" to call same-sex relationships "sinful" and discriminate against others who do not conform to their sexual ethics in matters of hiring and service. Just how many spheres this "freedom" should cut across seems open for debate, but the final walls of defense are those of churches and homes. Mouw also recognizes how civil law forms virtues in its citizens, and as the costs to evangelicals rise, he fears that even the most strident defenders of marriage's "traditional" definition will feel compelled to capitulate. As much as defending the legal status of that definition is some evangelicals' cross to bear, if opposing same-sex marriage really *felt like a cross*, this aspect of cultural discipleship may be forsaken. But in a more literal sense, Mouw is also concerned about the financial cost of educating children within a world-view that is at least neutral toward Christian faith.

On Sexuality and Education

Early in his career, Mouw predicted that dissenting Christians would need to "become more aggressive in demanding a fair trade-off for our willingness to allow others to pursue their preferred lifestyles," including "the right to have alternative modes of educating our children, without experiencing unjust economic burdens in the process."[164] The problem presents itself in the form of "sex education," among other areas. On the grounds of what world-view will such matters be taught? Before the sexual revolution, many concerned parents "had taken it for granted that a strong family life could inoculate their children against whatever secularism might be at work in public education. Now they began to suspect that public education had itself become a chief propagator of values that were too powerfully antithetical to many of their most cherished convictions."[165] Add to this the perceived weakening of the familial sphere, and Mouw sees cause for the church to take up some *emergency* functions to "compensate for that weakness, at least as a temporary remedial strategy."¹⁶⁶ The long-range strategy may be partially evident in the account above, but Mouw summarizes in a rather open-ended way, "The necessary remedies, then, will require both sphere repair and worldview nurturing. These, in turn, require patient work within civil society, in a variety of spheres, including an address to issues in public policy, a focus on various vocations, specific kinds of marriages, family counseling, and so on."¹⁶⁷ Perhaps here we find a concretization of the constant state of emergency that Mouw mused about in some of his earliest published thoughts. In any case, for Calvinists who see all knowledge as "of a piece" with the basic worldview, allowing children to be immersed in an *anti*-Christian world-view would be negligent and unfaithful. While certain segments of society may be permitted to "go to hell" (Mouw's words),¹⁶⁸ Christians must not allow their children to join that field trip.

Mouw has consistently expressed a qualified sympathy for a public education system that distributes equitable funding to several different educating bodies (including religious ones), reflecting how Kuyper and others established a plural, "pillarized" school system in the Netherlands a century ago.¹⁶⁹ With the pledge that "the government should maintain a position of impartiality toward these various worldview 'pillars'"—namely, social-democrat, Protestant, Catholic, and liberal/neutral—all schools in the Dutch education system remained "public," and each *major* pillar's schools received equal legal recognition, public funding, and so on.¹⁷⁰ In fact, Christians under such a system "are obligated . . . not only to ask the state to allow them to work out the implications of their own comprehensive vision of life," but also to "demand that the state grant the same rights to other worldview groups, even if Christians disagree seriously with the content of those alternative perspectives on life."¹⁷¹ Mouw has remained skeptical about translating this model into American life for at least two reasons. First, he cogently argues that Christians who "take seriously our obligations to live sacrificially on behalf of, and for the sake of, those who are victims of injustice" would best secure the wellbeing of disadvantaged children by sticking with public schools—even when the government has not adequately attended to Christians' world-view rights in public education.¹⁷² Mouw is primarily concerned about the poor, but he also observes how the Christian rush to establish private schools in the wake of the sexual revolution concealed, for some, anxiety about the accelerated pace of racial integration in public schools. (Remember the bundling effect of felt anxieties discussed above.) Second, the changing landscape of "pluralism" raises important questions about what counts as a world-view pillar when finer degrees of diversity come to be acknowledged.

Mouw noted a concrete assault on the Dutch settlement pattern in 1982 when legislation was introduced to prohibit some pillarized institutions (e.g., Christian schools, but *not* churches) from "discriminat[ing] against homosexuals and 'cohabitating' unmarried couples."[173] He began analyzing the situation by imagining normative acceptance of diverse sexual expressions completely outside the once-mainstream world-view pillars, dramatically escalating the importance of sexuality: "Now there are new pillars being built—homophilia, cohabitationism, feminism—which necessitate a rearrangement of the older structures."[174] What is worse, in Mouw's view, is legislation "insist[ing] that persons of these persuasions have the right to work *within* the traditional pillars."[175] He asks, "Doesn't there come a point where new expansions and new patterns of toleration destroy the social entity which is allegedly being expanded?"[176] In cross-examination, one might ask whether these concrete social entities (including the world-views of real persons and communities) could possibly be expanding their patterns of toleration on grounds *internal to those entities.*

An Evangelical Manifesto

Returning to the 2008 "Evangelical Manifesto" introduced above, when they turn to address "issues" with clear political, social, and cultural implications, Mouw and company risk overextending their representational reach after the fashion of Ockenga and company.[177] (In fact, numerous evangelical leaders took issue with various elements of the framework—some Baptists with the notion that "evangelical" means archetypical "Protestant," some conservatives with what seemed to be a desertion of political activism.)[178] Speaking of the need to "reform our own behavior," the drafters make needed gestures, including a denunciation of de facto segregation in churches and a confession that Christian identity should transcend any contemporary identity politics.[179] Yet in the same breath, they turn toward two highly politicized issues (namely, abortion and marriage), noting the need to expand evangelical concern without "back[ing] away from our biblically rooted commitment to the sanctity of every human life, including those unborn" or "deny[ing] the holiness of marriage as instituted by God between one man and one woman."[180] Here, if not before, we are reminded that theological terms are never politically, socially, or culturally innocent, even as the committee claims to address these issues as *essentially* theological (and therefore not directly political, etc.). Moreover, spoken into this cultural moment without any theological argumentation about these issues, these claims seem to serve not theological ends but *only* political, social, and/or cultural ones.

As a manifesto, this document partly addresses what Mouw dramatized a few years prior as a "new sense of a cultural crisis threatening *the very fabric of evangelical identity.*"[181] More recently, lamenting the shift in public policy and cultural sentiment since the short-lived "victory" on California Prop. 8, he penned in *Evangelicals* magazine, "The cultural tide has turned against us," and "biblical Christianity is increasingly under attack."[182] In line with this analysis, Mouw has also identified a "'post-evangelical' trend that features the rejection of the substitutionary atonement along with long-held evangelical convictions about sexual morality."[183] In the same breath, he criticizes the new "young evangelicals" weaving strands of several theological traditions into what he sees as "designer" theologies rather than working primarily from the thick, comprehensive traditions upon which true evangelical consensus is supposedly predicated.

PRELIMINARY CONCLUSIONS

Mouw acknowledges that evangelicalism, inasmuch as it represents a thin consensus, should not stand on its own. But the leading phrase "as an evangelical" in his *Newsweek* article seems to stand in for an argument already made or a consensus already reached. Shorthand like this could be useful in arguments where one can assume what has already been justified elsewhere in order to arrive at novel findings sooner; it means: "see my previous argument about what this means." But Mouw has made no argument sufficient to substantiate how he's using the evangelical identity. And in this, he is ironically representative of American evangelical arguments around same-sex marriage. Mouw has operated on assumptions from within his thick tradition and whatever consensus he reached with some other insiders in his political activism on this issue. That identifying phrase stands in for *whatever I think evangelicals must also think given their basic trust in the biblical God*. The term is not totally vacant, of course, but when the many do share something thin, close to the bone, visible leaders can seize or otherwise appeal to that for support as they engage in more specified (and thus not exactly representative) action and advocacy. And this exemplifies how useful empty or "floating signifiers" are, *absorbing rather than emitting meaning*.[184] The path to success in contemporary evangelical life runs through the competitive culture established in the warp and woof of this movement. Rhetoric like this is something of a convention in the Wild West of evangelical public theology, but problems accrue when the thin identity does not have its own intellectual resources to justify such claims.

With no unified institutional structure, in-house contentions (or, more nearly, guerrilla battles) about what it means to be evangelical tend to spill into tendentious public representation, which generates new problems within a public that cannot discern when claims "as an evangelical" are disputed. I do not want to give too much away, however, to the already-mistaken notion that either popular vote or genuine consensus about much of anything actually defines evangelicalism. The lack of focused, biblical-theological attention to the details of social arguments was so common in early neo-evangelicalism that young Mouw could feel the spiritual energy around issues like civil rights and wonder why his people had not shown up. In their 1973 Chicago Declaration, the young evangelicals' central objective was connecting Jesus's lordship over all of life with their shared social justice causes. Opening with the familiar appeal "as evangelical Christians," the drafters wasted little time before calling for action in specific areas: naming and working against structural racism, fostering just acquisition and distribution of wealth, and marking the critical distance between church and state to stave off the violence of war (as in Vietnam).[185] While Ockenga claimed to represent the silent majority as he projected his vision for biblical social concern, these younger evangelicals were painfully aware that they did not represent many evangelicals—as Ockenga himself made clear—yet they claimed the biblical and moral high ground. Leading with their evangelical identity signaled a prophetic seizure of the label itself as they proclaimed a message of repentance to the wayward folks who *self*-identified by this name. And even their consensus was a product of its time, coalescing specific people for a particular, shared challenge—even as it consciously subverted the neo-evangelical powers. At bottom, any thin consensus is constrained by the limited purpose(s) for which it was forged and, thus, has no inner resources to serve as a general or stable source of authority.

Through many changes of the guard, mainstream evangelical leaders have learnt to use their own positions—derived from their own thick traditions and perhaps shared with some others grounded in other traditions—as "watchwords" that define and limit access to evangelical branding. Too often, the result has been dismissing out of hand well-articulated theological positions offered by characters living within evangelicalism, whether defined in terms of particular history or a more generic piety. And while we might not agree with one another's thick theological arguments, we may yet balk at such power plays, especially when differing on a topic that has been framed as "identity-defining" only in recent history. More to the point, perhaps evangelicals should engage in more genuine debate around Christianity's "traditional" commitment to nonviolence, which seems more fundamental to a posture of creaturely trust in God relative to a fallen world's coercive strategies for social engineering (or, more crassly, the brazen will to power). Coercion need not materialize in threats of physical sanction when regulatory appeals to the divine are sufficient to close ranks and quash dissidence. For example, by proclaiming same-sex marriage antithetical to the biblical worldview, some options are predetermined "out" on the basis of a presumably overwhelming "traditional" case against them. Yet here is a site for genuine debate and, perhaps, an agreement that one simply cannot speak "as an evangelical" on some matters. Of course, some have self-selected not to get or remain involved with evangelicalism once they realized the implicit agenda of key standard bearers on this issue, as did many Black evangelicals in the 1960s or exvangelicals in the 2010s. But when some highly visible evangelicals have taken a "nontraditional" approach, a preponderance of others have derided them as *no true Scotsmen*. Such leadership should send up red flags for those who have fought this kind of battle before and rankle those who believe in dissenters' right to argue their case in good faith instead of being muscled out of the conversation before reaching the table.

Over the years and in various ways, Mouw carved out and occupied space within each of his inherited traditions or movements, often as a dissenting insider. Even before throwing in with the young evangelicals, he tried but could not stop identifying with the evangelical movement:

> When I marched for civil rights during my graduate school years, I helped to organize "ban the bomb" marches and protested the Vietnam War. I was clearly out of step with much of the evangelicalism of the day.
>
> When one key evangelical leader suggested that the Rev. Martin Luther King Jr. was being used by the Communists to undercut American values, I came close to resigning from the movement. But when I realized I had nowhere else to go theologically and spiritually, I simply hung on and hoped for better days.[186]

He added social issues like racial and economic justice as considerations of orthodoxy over and against Ockenga and company, though he did not deny their evangelical identity. And Mouw's antiwar advocacy was met with painful criticism and a sense of isolation from his family and wider fundamentalist home community.[187] There is also an element of dissent (albeit in a different key) in his embrace of Kuyper. Let us not forget that Kuyper's "traditional" definition of marriage included both patriarchy and the relatively homogenous skin tones of those wed, with the traits of gender and race contributing *substantive* elements to the relational structure. And with such embarrassing details in mind, Mouw coaches his sympathetic reader, "We do [Kuyper] no favors by focusing too much on his own practical applications for the purposes of evaluating his overall scheme."[188] Perhaps surprisingly, Mouw seems willing to look past flagrantly misdirected and sinfully ignorant aspects of Kuyper's world-view and to conclude that Kuyper's theology was "thoroughly orthodox" and his faith was warmly "evangelical."[189] As such, Mouw joins the chorus we heard dissipating the *directional* force of the error and sin in and of Kuyper's world-view in chapter 1.

The world-viewing impulse produces equivocation. One can claim insider status, even representative power to chart the faithful course for whole traditions and movements, while both dissenting from positions maintained by other insiders (whether visible leaders or even a perceived majority of the rank and file) and denying the social group identity to still others who dissent on different issues. But despite his generosity toward Kuyper and Ockenga, a new doctrinal myopia had prevented Mouw from extending like grace, or even just genuine recognition, to evangelicals who disagree with his view of same-sex relationships—no matter their thicker tradition. In his discussions of Prop. 8 and the need to shore up "religious freedom," Mouw expressed his desire that civil authorities would recognize a legal right to dissent from the expanded social and legal definition of marriage. In moments of pastoral theology, he expresses tolerance for persons who identify as evangelical and LGBT+, provided they are willing to practice his sexual ethic in the concrete specifics (i.e., remain celibate, reject sex reassignment surgery, and otherwise prevent their sexual desire from materializing). But when it comes to how other evangelicals *think* about same-sex relationships—when they support a different sexual ethic, even if grounded in other theological traditions—he can abide no dissent. Mouw borrows from Ockenga's playbook when he deems "*post*-evangelical" (that is one way to say, "beyond the fold") those who do not confess the doctrinal position of orthodoxy (e.g., on the nature of atonement) or disagree with his sexual ethics. And now in his twilight years, Mouw has expressed the return of his dissenting insider sentiment in the wake of the 2016 election cycle that shattered the optics of progress on key issues—or, perhaps, revealed the challenge of really moving the needle in such a diffuse movement.[190]

Along with his enlightened judgments on gender equality and civil rights, we might hope Mouw would directly address the methodological errors that make supposedly biblical world-viewing perfectly compatible with misogyny, white supremacy, and other such problems in practice. Since, as they say, "the devil is in the details," we cannot accept a detail-independent approach. But alas, Mouw regularly slaps away criticism with language borrowed from H. Richard Niebuhr, saying corrupt historical instances of the lofty ideal structures represent "evil as perversion, and not as badness of being," and he applies the same logic to the natural-creational theology that props them up.[191] He tries to position the neo-Calvinist option as a viable third way between a natural law/theology angle and the Barthian "Nein!" to natural theology. Yet Mouw fails to register that Barth was not merely concerned about noetic access—such that sinful minds are bound to get some details wrong—but also the way Christians embrace theoretical frameworks for life that structurally evade Christological scrutiny—from the doctrine of revelation to what they do with it. Throughout this project, we have witnessed a "badness of being" that continuously absolves the world-viewing impulse in advance (given its good intentions) as it engenders speculative, systematic knowledge of good and evil. Whatever goes wrong under these conditions is written out of the greater (hi)story as a superficial blemish on an otherwise illustrious set of basic principles. Mouw offers no principles or practices for avoiding either the excesses of the past or their justification as the results of "sanctified imagining," particularly when those results can be tied to biblical grounds somehow. As we saw with Kuyper, mystification (i.e., of the process by which one arrives at the norms they use to order others' lives) is the grammar of bad power.

Scrubbing the most glaring manifestations of historical sins without scrutinizing the underlying principles effectively renders the coercive structures transparent and allows their machinations to shift shapes within the optics of diversity. A story might help illustrate the point here. Within a few years of Mouw's 2013 retirement from the Fuller Seminary presidency into an endowed faculty role, minority graduate students mounted a vocal campaign to draw the next administration's attention to the representation of diverse voices and stories at every level (from the board of trustees to the curriculum), retention problems around minority faculty members, and the broader issues of institutional culture and climate.[192] The students' disillusionment boiled over into protests both in digital forms (e.g., stories and concerns attached to the #ToxicFuller hashtag) and on the ground during Spring 2018 commencement events. As one student wrote during that season, "We're fighting centuries of deceit and denial wrapped up in a smiling white jesus that Mary never birthed. Still this jesus exists and he exonerates all violence exacted by whiteness. This holy whiteness does not even need to wear gloves to commit a crime. It hides in plain sight and declares its violence divinely ordered, nothing but a faithful response to 'WWjD?'"[193] And all of this despite structures like a Center for Asian American Theology and Ministry, a Centro Latino, a Korean Studies Center, and what is now called the William E. Pannell Center for African American Church Studies. An institution can affirm "diversity" or "inclusion," but one only discovers what such words mean for *this* people as they use them. And structures of whiteness can be maintained even while intending to foster diversity and social justice because the meaning of these terms differs depending on where you are in the overall power dynamic. The Mouw administration represented an approach to inclusion that, in effect, limited actual power-sharing—that is, in setting the agenda and tone for cultural discipleship—as well as representation *within* the curriculum (rather than as an optional adjunct to it). In other words, he preserved white institutional space even while inviting diverse faces to share in the logic of whiteness. Recognizing the faith of theological others can express a kind of humility, but *sentimentally* acknowledging others often conceals, even ennobles, the act of trampling them.[194]

As such, Bill Pannell's analysis holds: thinking evangelically too often means thinking whitely. Whiteness names something specific in terms of a racialized, world-scale episteme within which transformation is sought, but it also participates in a wider, multivalent reality of coercive, dominating, and otherwise bad uses of power in a fallen world. Here we might benefit from Elisabeth Schüssler Fiorenza's concept of "kyriarchy" (or lordship), which names patterns of submission, oppression, and domination.[195] In her words, "we inhabit structural positions of race, gender, class, and ethnicity, [and] one of them might become privileged so that it constitutes a nodal point. While in any particular historical moment class may be the primary modality through which I experience gender and race, in other circumstances gender may be the privileged position through which I experience race in class."[196] The result is not so much a fixed hierarchy as a shifting and complex pyramid system with those who embody the prevailing norms at the top and others aggregating oppressed statuses to form the expanding base. The kyriarchal spirit thrives through cognate concepts like sovereignty and headship, which are thick in the Kuyperian tradition. Mouw's approach to resolving the tensions around same-sex marriage carries the marks of whiteness as both world-scale-viewing and the omnicompetent individual's ability to visualize and maybe actually transform the world after God's design. Of course, world-viewing exerts its influence upon the world and its inhabitants under the auspices of God's eternal-creational will with the best of intentions. But there is nothing polite or pious about the damage this kind of thinking has wrought and continues to wreak in our world. To name this problem is not to deny "the kingdom, the power, and the glory forever" to God; it is to inquire about their qualities, how they operate, how the God we see incarnate in Jesus goes about his work in, around, and through humankind.

Mouw's whole theoethical method ultimately turns on an epistemology with an unresolved tension, an insecurity at its very core. The entire biblical world-view hinges on the essence of marriage in a way that is presupposed and nonnegotiable for Mouw, and this makes conceding or even sharing the power to define marriage unbearable. Marriage is *the* social sphere that Scripture seems to portray most explicitly (in its accounts of creation, no less), making it the most plausible ground for the whole sphere-sovereignty, creational-political scheme. On the surface, neo-Calvinists like Mouw are epistemological and moral *realists*, describing truth and moral order as structures within our material reality itself. Human beings in their right mind are presumably able to reason out its details (thus the recent trend toward analytic philosophy among Calvinist thinkers). But sin has broken human minds and brought creation down with them, so true knowledge of God's willed structures for the natural world, human sociality, and all the rest can only really *exist* in the mind of God. Mouw's thick tradition claims the Holy Spirit operates within the regenerate mind and restores its capacity to reflect reliable knowledge of God and of good and evil. Without proper attention to the tension here, the claim to sanctified knowledge becomes a house flag for those who think they have the clearest connection to God and, thus, the most refined vision of God's will (descriptively speaking, an *idealist* perspective). Like Kuyper and Ockenga, Mouw operates with epistemic confidence (or "hope" as he might style it) without a satisfactory explanation for why he is so confident in the degree to which (some) intelligent Christians can have, hold, and logically act upon key sources of revelation—or why dissenting insiders should come around and assent to the products of the others' sanctified imaginations. This confidence has not been earned by way of solid argumentation; in fact, it has no grounds whatsoever if not for the supposed prestige of Mouw's thicker theological tradition.

The very act of depersonalizing or abstracting my world-view facilitates the process of imagining *my* view as simply *God's will*, which ripples into numerous problems. For one thing, such a perspective allows me to distance myself from failures to live up to my own standards in order to claim the manifest truth of my better principles. Where I turn out to be right, it is the product of a sanctified imagination; where I am wrong (even sinfully wrong), it is the product of human depravity. Here, "world-viewing" is sanitized to mean *merely living and moving and having my being under the aegis of God's-law-as-I-know-it*. Too often, this means we are not genuinely looking to be corrected, looking for where we need to repent in our thinking; to the contrary, we see the world stage as a competition of such general views—and one that we want to win. The nature of the principles' basicness is truly expressed in the particulars of human life; without that concrete form, the concept (e.g., structures of reality and sphere-laws) and the claim (e.g., pious, biblical, and evangelical) tend to serve as rhetorical cover for some bundle of propositions and practical commitments and habits, and thus to serve contradictory and distorting uses. We risk enshrining our concrete intellectual sins as biblical ideals and the structures of reality itself. Improving the details handed on by past generations, we think *this much* must be part of the eternal-creational framework (e.g., marriage as a lifelong relationship characterized by monogamy, heterosexuality, and fruitfulness *but not* patriarchy or skin color).

By invoking God's will as the basis for the detailed ideals for human living that we have discerned for ourselves, we can at least partly evade our own responsibility for the concrete moral traditions that we generate. By hanging our most difficult judgments of other human beings' complicated lives on God's will or the Bible or our Tradition of interpreting the two, we let ourselves off the hook as simple messengers—we need not "own" the troubles that our messages generate for others. More than that, as we seek to institutionalize our knowledge of good and evil and of God in public structures, we may organize and superintend the lives of other humans without looking them in the eye. By seeing the whole world through abstract categories allows the idealist to imagine how their world-view applies to all humans without carefully considering the lives of actual persons, and certainly without having to own our responsibility for our judgments. Distancing oneself from one's judgments like this can be traced to the categorical relegation of some folks to less-than status to make it easier to treat them as material without thinking about it, without owning it (as in the transatlantic slave trade). Although the details change, the form's deep theological errors remain. And supposedly, so long as we do not set out with the raw *intention* to coerce others, our coercive actions and advocacy can be given the benefit of the doubt, courtesy of the doctrine of double effect. But those concrete others have the right to ask a deeply theological question: What gives divine force to the mandate assumed by humans? If Christian thinkers have not adequately accounted for their epistemological confidence in terms that even other insiders can recognize, what warrants their move beyond that community as its supposed representatives to the world?

As this project turns into the final chapter, I will add another layer of interpretation to the white evangelical project we have been following. By the end, we must ask whether the world-viewing impulse itself participates in the original-sinful cognitive rebellion that Mouw has narratized into his thick evangelical Calvinists world-view. I submit that the ideal world-view stands in for exactly no historical community and only inadequately or dishonestly represents the mind of the powerful evangelical world-viewer who invokes or produces it (and probably not even that). Idealized, essentialist views of human nature fail to describe real persons, yet they have rarely failed to aggrandize the thinker who generates them. Our constitutions, as humans, simply are not so singular and resolute, even at their best—certainly not in any universal sense as totally in line with and knowledgeable of God's eternal will. We must back up to think carefully and theologically about the fallen noetic situation in part because personally grasped knowledge of good and evil (i.e., what we take to be "God's will"), in the context of humans trying to be *sicut deus*, is the original temptation itself. There is no reliable way to tell the difference between sanctified imaginations or unsanctified ones by their products in a way that is not already self-serving. Claiming ownership of our world-views might become more important to us if we start to register how evading responsibility for the details undercuts our pious pursuit of communion with the living God.

NOTES

1. "An Evangelical Manifesto: A Declaration of Evangelical Identity and Public Commitment," May 7, 2008, page 2, accessed February 23, 2021, http://www.ntslibrary.com/PDF%20Books/Evangelical_Manifesto.pdf.

2. "Evangelical Manifesto," 2.

3. "Evangelical Manifesto," 19.
4. "Evangelical Manifesto," 4; cf. 8.
5. See Sarah Pulliam Bailey, "A New Group of Evangelical Leaders Forms in Support of Biden," *The Washington Post*, October 2, 2020, accessed February 22, 2021, https://www.washingtonpost.com/religion/2020/10/02/new-evangelical-leaders-support-biden/.
6. Frank Newport, "Religious Group Voting and the 2020 Election," Gallup, Inc., November 13, 2020, accessed January 25, 2021, https://news.gallup.com/opinion/polling-matters/324410/religious-group-voting-2020-election.aspx.
7. David R. Swartz, *Moral Minority: The Evangelical Left in an Age of Conservatism* (Philadelphia: University of Pennsylvania Press, 2012), 2 and 205–6.
8. Richard Mouw, *The Smell of Sawdust: What Evangelicals Can Learn from Their Fundamentalist Heritage* (Grand Rapids: Zondervan, 2000), ch. 4 and p. 153.
9. Richard Mouw, *Adventures in Evangelical Civility: A Lifelong Quest for Common Ground* (Grand Rapids: Brazos Press, 2016), 145.
10. Mouw, *Adventures*, 37.
11. Mouw, *Sawdust*, 39. Cf. Richard Mouw, "Despite Trumpism, I'm Not Quitting Evangelicalism," *Religious News Service*, December 13, 2016, accessed June 4, 2020, https://religionnews.com/2016/12/13/richard-mouw-despite-trumpism-im-not-quitting-evangelicalism/.
12. Mouw, *Adventures*, 59; and Richard Mouw, "Evangelicals and Political Activism," *The Christian Century* 89, no. 47 (December 27, 1972): 1316–17.
13. Mouw, *Sawdust*, 40.
14. Mouw, *Sawdust*, 40.
15. Mouw, *Sawdust*, 13. Cf. Richard Mouw, *Political Evangelism* (Grand Rapids: Eerdmans, 1973), 7.
16. Mouw, *Adventures*, 59–61.
17. Richard Mouw, "Weaving a Coherent Pattern of Discipleship," *The Christian Century* 92, no. 27 (August 20, 1975): 729–30; and Mouw, *Adventures*, 61ff. Cf. Swartz, ch. 10; and Richard Mouw and John Howard Yoder, "Evangelical Ethics and the Anabaptist-Reformed Dialogue," *The Journal of Religious Ethics* 17, no. 2 (Fall 1989): 124ff.
18. Harold Ockenga, foreword to *Battle for the Bible*, by Harold Lindsell (Grand Rapids: Zondervan, 1976), 12.
19. Richard Mouw, "Evangelicals in Search of Maturity," *Theology Today* 35, no. 1 (April 1978): 46.
20. Mouw, "Evangelicals in Search," 46.
21. Mouw, "Evangelicals in Search," 47–48. Cf. Mouw, *Sawdust*, 138.
22. Mouw, "Evangelicals in Search," 47–48.
23. Clark Pinnock quoted in Mouw, "Evangelicals in Search," 43–44 and 50.
24. Mouw, *Sawdust*, 20.
25. Mouw, *Sawdust*, 21. In early Pietism, Mouw finds concern for "both the church and the larger social order" ("Life in the Spirit in an Unjust World," *Pneuma* 9, no. 2 [September 1987]: 115).
26. Mouw, *Sawdust*, 21.

27. Mouw, *Sawdust*, ch. 7; cf. Mouw, *Adventures*, 145ff.
28. Mouw, *Sawdust*, 72–73.
29. Mouw, *Adventures*, 146.
30. Mouw, *Adventures*, 147. Cf. Mouw, *Sawdust*, 23.
31. Richard Mouw, *Restless Faith: Holding Evangelical Beliefs in a World of Contested Labels* (Grand Rapids: Brazos Press, 2019), pp. 145–47 and ch. 13.
32. Mouw, *Sawdust*, 23.
33. Michael Walzer, *Thick and Thin: Moral Argument at Home and Abroad* (Notre Dame, IN: University of Notre Dame Press, 1994). In *Adventures* (233n1), Mouw cites cultural anthropologist Clifford Geertz's popularization of the term.
34. Walzer, *Thick and Thin*, 11.
35. Richard Mouw, "How to Change Hearts on Race," *Religious News Service*, January 23, 2018, accessed June 4, 2020, https://religionnews.com/2018/01/23/how-to-change-hearts-on-race/.
36. Cf. Mouw, *Restless Faith*, ch. 13.
37. Walzer, *Thick and Thin*, 6.
38. Walzer, *Thick and Thin*, 9.
39. Richard Mouw, "Some Reflections on Sphere Sovereignty," 1998, in *The Challenges of Cultural Discipleship: Essays in the Line of Abraham Kuyper* (Grand Rapids: Eerdmans, 2012), 55; cf. 50–56.
40. See Mouw, "Some Reflections," 41; Richard Mouw, "Creational Politics: Some Calvinist Amendments," 1993, in *Challenges*, 108–9; Richard Mouw and Sander Griffioen, *Pluralisms and Horizons: An Essay in Christian Public Philosophy* (Grand Rapids: Eerdmans, 1993), 126; and Richard Mouw, *Abraham Kuyper: A Short and Personal Introduction* (Grand Rapids: Eerdmans, 2011), ch. 2. For a larger discussion of the "cultural mandate," Mouw often points to Henry R. Van Til, *The Calvinistic Concept of Culture* (1959; repr., Grand Rapids: Baker Book House, 2001).
41. Richard Mouw, *When the Kings Come Marching In: Isaiah and the New Jerusalem* (Grand Rapids: Eerdmans, 1983), 16.
42. Karl Barth, *Church Dogmatics III.1: The Doctrine of Creation* (Edinburgh: T&T Clark, 1958), 183–95.
43. Richard Mouw, "The *Imago Dei* and Philosophical Anthropology," *Christian Scholars Review* 43, no. 3 (2012): 259.
44. Mouw, "Some Reflections," 41. Cf. Mouw, *When the Kings*, 65; and Richard Mouw, *Politics and the Biblical Drama* (Grand Rapids: Baker Book House, 1976), 138.
45. Abraham Kuyper, *Calvinism: Six Stone Lectures* (Amsterdam: Höveker & Wormser, 1899), 99.
46. For helpful charts and descriptions of various authority models, see Mouw, *Personal Introduction*, 40–42.
47. Cf. Abraham Kuyper, "Sphere Sovereignty," 1880, in James D. Bratt, ed., *Abraham Kuyper: A Centennial Reader* (Grand Rapids: Eerdmans, 1998), 461–90; Kuyper, *Calvinism*, ch. 3; and Mouw, "Some Reflections," 37–38. Michael Walzer made a similar but independent argument on nonreligious grounds in *Spheres of Justice* (New York: Basic Books, 1983). Kent Van Til has fruitfully compared the

two models in "Abraham Kuyper and Michael Walzer: The Justice of the Spheres," *Calvin Theological Journal* 40 (2005): 267–89.

48. Cf. Paul Helm, *John Calvin's Ideas* (New York: Oxford University Press, 2004), 99–101. As we draw nearer to the issue of epistemology and human ways of knowing God's will, we will find the Thomist connection less helpful. In Mouw's words, "the disagreement with the natural law tradition is not over the 'ontic' but about the 'noetic'" ("Law, Covenant, and Moral Commonalities: Some Neo-Calvinist Explorations," 2010, in *Challenges*, 82).

49. Mouw, "Some Reflections," 42. Cf. Kuyper, *Calvinism*, 33.

50. Kuyper, *Calvinism*, 117–18. See James Bratt on Kuyper's pronounced patriarchalism in *Abraham Kuyper: Modern Calvinist, Christian Democrat* (Grand Rapids: Eerdmans, 2013), 360–63.

51. H. Richard Niebuhr, *Christ and Culture* (1951; repr., New York: Harper & Row Publishers, 1975), 32. Henry Van Til also takes up this definition (*Calvinistic Concept*, 26–27, 32–33, and 58); cf. Mouw, "Creational Politics," 109.

52. Niebuhr, 194. For Mouw's adoption of this language, see "Weaving a Coherent Pattern," 731; *Politics*, 137–38; and *Adventures*, 157–58.

53. Abraham Kuyper, *Guidance for Christian Engagement in Government: A Translation of Abraham Kuyper's Our Program*, 1879, trans. and ed. Harry Van Dyke (Grand Rapids: Christian's Library Press, 2013), III.1.28.

54. David Naugle, *Worldview: The History of a Concept* (Grand Rapids: Eerdmans, 2002), 265.

55. Albert M. Wolters, *Creation Regained: Biblical Basics for a Reformational Worldview*, 2nd ed. (Grand Rapids: Eerdmans, 2005), 57–59.

56. Wolters, 59. Cf. John Calvin, *The Institutes of Christian Religion*, 1559, ed. John T. McNeill and trans. Ford Lewis Battles, 2 vols. (Philadelphia: The Westminster Press, 1960), I.14.20.

57. Wolters, 57.

58. Wolters, 59.

59. John Calvin, *Commentary on the Epistles of Paul the Apostle to the Corinthians*, trans. and ed. John Pringle (Edinburgh: The Calvin Translation Society, 1848), 1 Cor. 6:16.

60. Mouw and Griffioen, 14–17.

61. Mouw and Griffioen, 16.

62. Mouw, *When the Kings*, 48.

63. Mouw and Griffioen, 16.

64. Mouw and Griffioen, 17–18.

65. Mouw and Griffioen show that Kuyper, Herman Bavinck, and others have "attempted to ground associational pluralism in the very nature of things is by insisting that associational diversity has a creational status" (Mouw and Griffioen, 125).

66. Mouw, *Adventures*, 32.

67. Richard Mouw, *Called to Holy Worldliness* (Philadelphia: Fortress Press, 1980), 21–22. Cf. Mouw, *Adventures*, 140.

68. Mouw, *When the Kings*, 55. Mouw is aware of the potential danger of sliding into racial essentialism, and he clearly does not intend anything of the sort; however,

he neither criticizes essentialism, in general, nor offers much guidance for contesting it at this specific site (i.e., race). See his commentary on *apartheid* in *When the Kings*, 51–53, and *Adventures*, 138–40.

69. Mouw and Griffioen, 88.
70. Mouw and Griffioen, 88–89.
71. Cf. Mouw, *Politics*, 31; "Law, Covenant," 84; and *Adventures*, 111 and 203.
72. Richard Mouw, *Distorted Truth: What Every Christian Needs to Know about the Battle for the Mind* (San Francisco: Harper & Row, 1989), 33; cf. 38–39. See also Mouw, *Adventures*, 158.
73. Mouw, *Adventures*, 155. My mind goes to Calvin's portrayal of Aristotle in his commentary on Psalm 104:43: "A man of genius and learning; but being a heathen, whose heart was perverse and depraved, it was his constant aim to entangle and perplex God's overruling providence by a variety of wild speculations; so much so, that it may with too much truth be said, that he employed his naturally acute powers of mind to extinguish all light" (*Commentary on Psalms*, trans. and ed. James Anderson [Edinburgh: The Calvin Translation Society, 1847.])
74. Mouw, *Distorted Truth*, 43.
75. Mouw and Griffioen, 90. On Augustine's view, compare his entries in *City of God*, trans. Henry Bettenson (1972; repr., New York: Penguin Books, 2003), VIII.1 (worship) and XV.22 (love).
76. Mouw, *Distorted Truth*, 43–45 and 100–103. See Mouw situate this "heart" within contemporary personality theory in *Adventures*, ch. 9. Cf. Richard Mouw, "Modal Diversity in Dooyeweerd's Social Thought," 1995, in *Challenges*, 61–62.
77. "Proper reasoning must always flow out of a trust in God. We cannot reason toward this trust; we can only argue *from* it" (Richard Mouw, *The God Who Commands: A Study in Divine Command Ethics* [Notre Dame: University of Notre Dame Press, 1990], 68). Cf. Kuyper's view of "affinity" with God in chapter 1.
78. Richard Mouw, *Uncommon Decency: Christian Civility in an Uncivil World*, 2nd ed. (Downers Grove, IL: InterVarsity Press, 2010), 85.
79. Mouw and Griffioen, 90.
80. Mouw and Griffioen, 90. Cf. Mouw, *Distorted Truth*, 102; and *Uncommon Decency*, 85.
81. Mouw, *Distorted Truth*, 103.
82. Mouw and Griffioen, 89.
83. Richard Mouw, "Evangelicalism and Philosophy," *Theology Today* 44, no. 3 (October 1987): 344.
84. Mouw names this dividedness in *God Who Commands*, 140–41. He also tells us we should recognize both that common grace can help non-Christians outperform their principles and their fallen nature and that Christians "continue to be plagued by their innate sinfulness. The antithesis reaches into each of us" (*Personal Introduction*, 110). Cf. Mouw, *Distorted Truth*, 18.
85. Mouw, *Distorted Truth*, 9. Cf. Mouw, *Called*, 9–10.
86. Mouw, *Distorted Truth*, 17. Mouw cites hardline Calvinists who have contended that some disastrously wrong theologian or another was yet loving, seeking, and worshipping the triune God in *Adventures*, ch. 15. For example, Charles

Hodge thought this of Friedrich Schleiermacher, and Cornelius Van Til of Karl Barth.

87. Richard Mouw, "An Open-Handed Gospel," *Christianity Today* 52, no. 4 (April 2008): 46. Cf. Mouw, *Sawdust*, 116–17.

88. Mouw, *Sawdust*, 118.

89. Mouw, *Personal Introduction*, 110.

90. Mouw, "Life in the Spirit," 126.

91. Charles Partee, "Calvin's So-Called Epistemology" (paper presented at the 12th Colloquium on Calvin Studies, Due West, SC, January 27–28, 2006), 79, accessed December 16, 2016, http://foundationrt.org/bw/wp-content/uploads/2016/03/Partee_Calvin_Epistemology.pdf.

92. Calvin, *Institutes*, I.5.14–15. Cf. Mouw, "Law, Covenant," 82.

93. Mouw, *Adventures*, 108; cf. 111, 203. Of the immutability of God's lawlike will, Kuyper magnified, "Can we imagine that at one time God willed to rule things in a certain moral order, but that now, in Christ, He wills to rule it otherwise? As though He were not the Eternal, the Unchangeable, Who, from the very hour of creation even unto all eternity had willed, wills, and shall will and maintain one and the same firm moral world-order! Verily Christ has swept away the dust with which man's sinful limitations had covered up this world-order, and has made it glitter again in its original brilliancy" (*Calvinism*, 89). Cf. Mouw, "Life in the Spirit," *passim*; "Some Reflections," 42; and "Law, Covenant," 84.

94. Cf. "The condemnation of the human race is thus imprinted on the heavens, the earth, and all creatures" (John Calvin, *Commentary on Romans*, ed. David W. Torrance and Thomas F. Torrance and trans. Ross Mackenzie [1960; repr., Grand Rapids: Eerdmans, 1995], 8:21).

95. Calvin, *Institutes*, I.6.1. Cf. Mouw, *Adventures*, 98 and 103–5; and "Some Reflections," 55.

96. Mouw, *Distorted Truth*, 112.

97. Mouw, "Life in the Spirit," 118.

98. Mouw, *Politics*, 29.

99. Mouw, "Creational Politics," 117.

100. Mouw, *Politics*, 21–22.

101. Mouw, *Politics*, 32–36.

102. Mouw, *Politics*, 105; and "Creational Politics," 119.

103. Kuyper, *Calvinism*, 101.

104. Mouw, *Personal Introduction*, 32–34. Cf. Kuyper, *Calvinism*, 124–25; and Mouw, "Some Reflections," 34–37.

105. See Mouw, *Politics*, 109; Mouw, *Restless*, ch. 12.

106. Kuyper, *Calvinism*, 100–105. Furthermore, Mouw has also argued that we should not expect the fourth act to bring the return of a prehuman king theocracy in *When the Kings*, 30 and 33–35; cf. *Restless Faith*, 153. We might wonder which other spheres could have similar, postlapsarian traits. And here we might also ask whether our imaginations might tell us about life in the age to come and what to make of our imaginings about that act for sociality in the present. If there is anything "already" about that future reality, would it ever amend or override the creational?

107. A provocative commentary on the epistemological arguments missing from Calvin but (sometimes) supplied by his later devotees can be found in Charles Partee, *The Theology of John Calvin* (Louisville: Westminster John Knox Press, 2008), 299ff.; cf. Partee's punchier argument in "Calvin's So-Called Epistemology."

108. Partee, "Calvin's So-Called Epistemology," 74.

109. Partee, "Calvin's So-Called Epistemology," 77.

110. Partee, "Calvin's So-Called Epistemology," 77.

111. Mouw, "Some Reflections," 43.

112. Mouw, "Creational Politics," 118.

113. Mouw refers these terms to Arthur F. Holmes, *Contours of a World View* (Grand Rapids: Eerdmans, 1983), 128.

114. Richard Mouw, *Called*, 26; cf. 71. See also Mouw, *Adventures*, 33; and Mouw, *Restless Faith*, 154–56.

115. Mouw, *Called*, 23, *et passim*. Cf. Mouw, *Sawdust*, 148–49. Mouw's most detailed work on the anticipated impact of the final consummation can be found in *When the Kings*, but this act plays no substantive role in Mouw's ethics.

116. Mouw, "Some Reflections," 56.

117. Mouw, *Personal Introduction*, 93; and *Restless Faith*, 17–18.

118. Mouw, *Called*, ch. 15.

119. Mouw, "Evangelicals and Political," 1318.

120. Mouw, *Uncommon Decency*, 34.

121. Mouw, *Uncommon Decency*, 35.

122. Mouw, *Political Evangelism*, 26–27. Mouw makes a more formal argument about the task of discerning God's will vis-à-vis bad, even evil, concretions when arguing against Karl Barth's "*Nein!*" to natural theologies; see, for instance, *Adventures*, 98–105.

123. Mouw, *Political Evangelism*, 106. See also Mouw, *God Who Commands*, 103.

124. Richard Mouw, "The Church and Social Specifics," *Reformed Journal* 19, no. 6 (July 1969): 4.

125. Mouw, "Church and Social," 4. Mouw toned down this rhetoric in *Political Evangelism*, offering a general rule for the preacher in a language reminiscent of some early neo-evangelicals: "enunciate the principles and guidelines that will aid [Christians] in their own decision-making" (Mouw, *Political Evangelism*, 82). See also his later, more patient approach in *Restless Faith*, 140–43 and ch. 13.

126. Mouw, *Uncommon Decency*, 93. Mouw's rhetoric is sometimes distasteful, and it seems dishonest to erase this feature from an account of his views. To avoid lifting samples out of their contexts to cheap rhetorical effect, I will provide references to three examples that also represent bad or fallacious argumentation: ad hominem in Richard Mouw, "On Being Permissive about Filth," *Reformed Journal* 26, no. 2 (February 1976): 3; guilt by association in Mouw, *Uncommon Decency*, 141; and slippery slope (his most common move) in Mouw, *Uncommon Decency*, 91.

127. See, for instance, Mouw, *Uncommon Decency*, 23–24; Richard Mouw and Virginia Ramey Mollenkott, "Gay Marriage: Broken or Blessed? Two Evangelical Views," interview by Krista Tippett, *Speaking of Faith*, aired August 3, 2006, on NPR, accessed February 20, 2016, http://www.onbeing.org/program/gay-marri

age-broken-or-blessed-two-evangelical-views/transcript/924; and Mouw, *Distorted Truth*, 63.

128. Mouw and Mollenkott.

129. Mouw and Mollenkott.

130. Richard Mouw, "Continuing the Task," in *Beauty, Order, and Mystery: A Christian Vision of Human Sexuality*, ed. Gerald Hiestand and Todd Wilson (Downers Grove, IL: IVP Academic, 2017), 69–70. Here Mouw also offers several stories around empathy and sexuality.

131. See Mouw, *Uncommon Decency*, 93–94; Richard Mouw, "Hanging in There," *Christian Century* 121, no. 1 (January 13, 2004): 22–25; and Richard Mouw, "'Gay' and 'Straight,'" *Reformed Journal* 31, no. 8 (August 1981): 3–4.

132. Mouw, *Uncommon Decency*, 94–99.

133. Mouw says something like this in "Hanging in There," 24.

134. This irony is not lost on Mouw, who acknowledges as much in "Some Reflections," 48.

135. Mouw, "On Being Permissive," 4.

136. Mouw, "On Being Permissive," 4. Whether the scare-quoted phrase refers to another source is not immediately clear, but the language resembles the Westminster Confession of Faith, ch. XIX. Cf. Mouw, *Politics*, 78.

137. Mouw, "On Being Permissive," 3.

138. Mouw, *Uncommon Decency*, 92.

139. Cf. Richard Mouw, "My Turn: Less Shouting, More Talking," *Newsweek* 153, no. 6 (February 9, 2009): 26.

140. On Calvin's three reasons for marriage, see John Witte Jr. and Robert M. Kingdon, *Sex, Marriage, and Family in Calvin's Geneva*, vol. 1 (Grand Rapids: Eerdmans, 2005), 39 and 94.

141. Mouw and Mollenkott; emphasis added.

142. Speaking of the antithesis, Kuyper wrested the concept of "natural" human capacities from Modernists, whose lack of regeneration left them in a truly "unnatural" or "abnormal" state (e.g., *Calvinism*, 176–77).

143. Mouw and Mollenkott. Cf. Mouw, "Continuing the Task," 67–68.

144. More recently, Mouw has expressed concern about contemporary Christians misusing such passages, for example, assuming the punitive mode of Leviticus 20:13 ("Continuing the Task," 64–65).

145. Richard Mouw et al., "Just Saying 'NO' Is Not Enough," *Christianity Today* 43, no. 11 (October 4, 1999): 51. See also Mouw's argument about the purchase of divine command arguments with unbelievers in *God Who Commands*, 20.

146. Mouw, *Uncommon Decency*, 99–102.

147. Mouw, "On Being Permissive," 4.

148. Mouw, "On Being Permissive," 4.

149. Mouw, *Politics*, 79.

150. Mouw, *Politics*, 80.

151. Mouw, "Weaving a Coherent," 728. Cf. Mouw, *Politics*, 16.

152. Mouw seems to express an evolving perspective about addressing concrete problems in more recent work, noticing the importance of good pastoral theology—or,

referring to Holmes's *Contours*, Mouw names the distinction between academic philosophy and theology and "worldviewish" philosophy and theology that "wrestle[s] with questions that emerge out of the daily living" ("Continuing the Task," 61). Cf. Mouw, *Restless Faith*, 17–20.

153. Mouw and Mollenkott. Mouw exercised similar "thoughtfulness" about definitions for "coercion, violence, and domination" in *Politics*, 71–73.

154. Mouw and Mollenkott.

155. For more context, see Robert P. Jones, *The End of White Christian America* (New York: Simon & Schuster, 2016), 121–22.

156. Mouw referred to his *Newsweek* article like this in *Uncommon Decency*, 89.

157. Mouw, "My Turn," 26. The phrase "my turn" in Mouw's title refers his brief piece to the December 15, 2008, issue of *Newsweek* and Lisa Miller's controversial cover article, "The Religious Case for Gay Marriage."

158. Mouw, "My Turn," 26.

159. Mouw, *Uncommon Decency*, 90.

160. Richard Mouw, "Tolerance without Compromise," *Christianity Today* 40, no. 8 (July 15, 1996): 34. Cf. Richard Mouw, "Looking Through the Eyes of Parents," *Theology Today* 58, no. 1 (April 2001): 53; and Mouw, *Sawdust*, 145–46.

161. On evangelical criticism of the BLM movement, see Mika Edmondson, "Is Black Lives Matter the New Civil Rights Movement?," The Gospel Coalition, June 24, 2016, accessed February 18, 2021, https://www.thegospelcoalition.org/podcasts/tgc-podcast/is-black-lives-matter-the-new-civil-rights-movement/. Edmondson concludes, "Despite the challenges, I think the church is called by God to critically engage and address the ethical issues and concerns related to Black Lives Matter today."

It is also worth recalling from chapter 3 that the notion of "identity politics" first appeared just a few years after the young evangelicals' Chicago Declaration in a statement laying out the moral-political priorities of the "Combahee River Collective," a group of prominent Black feminist leaders—some identifying as queer, not unlike the #BlackLivesMatter leadership.

162. Kristen Kobes Du Mez teases out how traditional family values and the accompanying complementarian gender roles were bound up in this complex of anxieties in "Donald Trump and Militant Masculinity," in *Religion & Politics*, January 17, 2017, accessed December 29, 2020, https://religionandpolitics.org/2017/01/17/donald-trump-and-militant-evangelical-masculinity/.

163. Mouw, "My Turn," 26. Cf. Mouw, *Uncommon Decency*, 90–91; and "Continuing the Task," 66–67.

164. Mouw, "On Being Permissive," 4.

165. Richard Mouw, "Educational Choice and Pillarization: Some Lessons for Americans from the Dutch Experiment in 'Affirmative Impartiality,'" 2003, in *Challenges*, 95–96.

166. Richard Mouw, "Culture, Church, and Civil Society: Abraham Kuyper for a New Century," in *Challenges*, 28. Cf. Mouw, "Educational Choice," 100; and Mouw, "Some Reflections," 27. Mouw's explanation of emergency functions is anticipated in Kuyper's view of the threefold duty of the state—particularly the intra- and intersphere roles, which cannot help but specify the content and dynamics of the spheres.

In this case, the church needs to compensate for the state. Cf. Mouw, *Personal Introduction*, 121–22.
167. Mouw, "Culture, Church," 27–28.
168. Mouw, "On Being Permissive," 4.
169. Mouw, "Educational Choice," 87 and 90.
170. Mouw, "Educational Choice," 92. For Mouw, the state may violate or lend its support to a world-view, but hopefully not on purpose (i.e., the doctrine of double effect).
171. Mouw, "Educational Choice," 91–92. Cf. Mouw, *Politics*, 64; cf. 66–67.
172. Mouw, "Educational Choice," 106. Cf. Mouw, *Distorted Truth*, 16.
173. Richard Mouw, "Dutch Pillars," *Reformed Journal* 32, no. 5 (May 1982): 2.
174. Mouw, "Dutch Pillars," 2.
175. Mouw, "Dutch Pillars," 2.
176. Mouw, "Dutch Pillars," 3.
177. Cf. Mouw, "Evangelicals in Search," 43.
178. One might start with Ed Stetzer, "Names Removed from the Evangelical Manifesto," *The Exchange*, May 15, 2008, accessed February 22, 2021, https://www.christianitytoday.com/edstetzer/2008/may/names-removed-from-evangelical-manifesto-updated-below.html.
179. "Evangelical Manifesto," 13.
180. "Evangelical Manifesto," 13–14.
181. Mouw, *Sawdust*, 146; emphasis added.
182. Richard Mouw, "Is Tolerance the Enemy of Religious Freedom?" *Evangelicals* 1, no. 1 (Fall 2015): 15.
183. Mouw, *Adventures*, 147–48.
184. Ian Buchanan, "Floating Signifier," in *A Dictionary of Critical Theory*, 2nd ed. (New York: Oxford University Press, 2018).
185. "The Chicago Declaration of Evangelical Social Concern (1973)," November 25, 1973, accessed February 17, 2021, https://sojo.net/sites/default/files/chicagoinvitationformatted_final.pdf.
186. Mouw, "Despite Trumpism." Cf. Mouw, *Restless Faith*, 128.
187. Khaled Abou El Fadl, Richard Mouw, and Yossi Klein Halevi, "The Power of Fundamentalism," interview by Krista Tippett, *Speaking of Faith*, aired April 18, 2002, on NPR, accessed June 9, 2020, https://onbeing.org/programs/khaled-abou-el-fadl-richard-j-mouw-and-yossi-klein-halevi-the-power-of-fundamentalism/.
188. Mouw, "Some Reflections," 48. Cf. Mouw, "Culture, Church," 23; *Personal Introduction*, 80–85; and *Uncommon Decency*, 81–82.
189. Mouw, *Uncommon Decency*, 162. Cf. Mouw, *Restless Faith*, 130–31; and *Personal Introduction*, ch. 1.
190. See both sentiments in Mouw, *Restless Faith*, ch. 1.
191. Mouw commonly borrows this phrase from Niebuhr, 194. See, for instance, Mouw, *Adventures*, 98–99. On the broader point, he has argued this against Karl Barth and his unqualified "*Nein!*" to Emil Brunner's call to recover a true natural theology. See Mouw, "Law, Covenant," 70–78; and Mouw, *Adventures*, 98–105.

192. At the time of this writing, one could still get a sense for the moment of protest by searching for the #ToxicFuller and #SeminaryWhileBlack hashtags on Twitter. To see how Fuller Seminary summarized and responded to the advocacy students, staff, and faculty in this season and following, see https://www.fuller.edu/inclusion/.

193. Esperanza Gene, "Seminary While Black: Why Calling out #ToxicFuller Matters," July 20, 2018, accessed June 8, 2020, https://medium.com/@esperanzagene/seminarywhileblack-why-calling-out-toxicfuller-matters-a64a7abd252.

194. For another example, Mouw recognizes a deeply evangelical sentiment expressed by Virginia Ramey-Mollenkott ("Hanging in There," 25) while advocating social policy about same-sex relationships that would disorder her life.

195. Elisabeth Schüssler Fiorenza, *Wisdom Ways: Introducing Feminist Biblical Interpretation* (Maryknoll, NY: Orbis Books, 1970), 118–22. Relative to this language, it is worth noting that a fair amount of current discussion around how to interpret New Testament passages dealing with same-sex sexual intercourse, as in Romans 1, centers on the prevailing understanding of "natural" positions of power and submission in male-female sexuality in the context of first-century Roman rule.

196. Schüssler Fiorenza, 119.

Chapter 6
A Theological Criticism of the Modern Preoccupation with Epistemology

Turning in this final chapter to consider an alternative theological method appropriate to human beings as creatures of God, I aim to shift our thinking about "world-viewing" to make as clear as possible that God alone could endeavor to do such a thing. Human beings can ever only take in so much of the world, from a vantage point within that world—not the fabled Archimedean point. Our working constellation of self-representations may be harboring commitments untouched by the light of the Holy Spirit, and yet the stories we tell about ourselves and our God may well enshrine those commitments and play with the power of divine sanction. Our formative social groups may complicate this reality by extending narrative marriages across generations and locking us into patterns of blindness to faith as understood by those who do not share our other loyalties. From our lowly vantage, we may hear the call of Jesus to come and follow in a living relationship of continuous formation in which we will learn what it means to be faithful daily. This kind of growth is possible only to the extent that we relinquish the false security we find in having and holding more certain knowledge of good and evil and of God than our counterparts in the garden. I have stated my claim provocatively here, but I will unearth the tension between modern epistemology and created relationality in the pages that follow.

While I will focus my energies here on the life and work of Dietrich Bonhoeffer (1906–1945), I am not particularly interested in the static, systematic results of his labor. This chapter will not follow threads or themes throughout his later and most beloved works (*Life Together*, *Discipleship*, and *Ethics*), nor will I draw much from the letters and papers he wrote from his prison cell, which attracted much of the early American attention on him to his advocacy for "religionless Christianity." Instead, I will focus on how his theology developed in and around his conversion to genuine faith in Jesus *after* completing his doctorate in theology. All at once, he discovered the living, Black Jesus of Harlem and the biblical-historical Jesus who lived and preached the Sermon on the Mount in earnest—not as the unattainable ideal that too many have mistaken it to be. We will see his perspective developing in the crucible of an impossible season of life and over-against the active counter-witness and judgment of others who claimed to hold the traditional Christian high ground. Bonhoeffer makes everything from the role of human reason to the meaning and impact of God's mandates or orders for human sociality relative to the person of Jesus Christ. If taken seriously, his approach would check the world-viewing impulse and require twenty-first-century Christians to listen for God speaking a present, preserving word to them from not our lost beginning but our promised end in the evangel.

To cut to the heart of Bonhoeffer's theological project, I will forgo even the simplest treatment of the history of World War I, the global depression beginning in the late 1920s, and the short Weimar period. Rather, I will briefly pose the problem of an idealist, principial "orders of creation" theology gone wrong in one of Bonhoeffer's contemporaries: Paul Althaus (1888–1966). Althaus's political-theological world-view provided much-needed justification for Christians involved in, or more passively party to, the Nazi project. A brief study of Althaus following Robert Ericksen's historically minded account of his theology will help us anticipate many aspects of Bonhoeffer's work. These include Bonhoeffer's criticism of cheap grace and orders-of-creation thinking, as well as his particular views of revelation, the limits of human knowledge, discipleship, and the God who commands and lives. When I turn to Bonhoeffer's work, I will focus largely on his dissertations, the works representing his teaching in Berlin, and his public theology dating from 1927 to 1933. But as we will observe early on, the young Bonhoeffer we encounter through his dissertations has not yet deliberated on the way his nationalism, with its racial and ethnic overtones, has quietly supplied many of the details of his world-view. During the period to be studied, he has experiences that surface his deeper, divided loyalties and help him hear the call of the living, biblical, historical Jesus to follow after him, especially during his 1930–1931 Sloane Fellowship at Union Theological Seminary in New York. The ensuing transformation enables Bonhoeffer to see and criticize Germany's deteriorating situation with greater clarity and from an earlier date than most of his contemporaries. Here we have embodied an alternative to the problem we have encountered throughout this project. Unlike chapters 2 and 4, I will not directly address the contrast with Richard Mouw here. Instead, I will bring this project's themes together in final conclusions and prospects in a coda following this chapter.

My account of Bonhoeffer's work will be framed less as a "response" to folks like Althaus than a constructive whole with wide-ranging implications that include a refutation of such theological programs. In fact, much of what appears in the section on Althaus reflects his work in the mid-1930s as he sought to clarify the meaning of the orders of creation when Bonhoeffer had already been making his public stand against them. The scarce Althaus material to be cited from the 1920s reflects the same kind of blood and soil nationalism evidenced in Bonhoeffer's thought before his transformation. Records show the two were acquaintances; Althaus reviewed and recommended Bonhoeffer's second dissertation, *Act and Being*, for publication, and he sent Bonhoeffer an advance copy of one of his books in 1931.[1] But their collegiality cooled after that point. For instance, as historian Charles Marsh narrates, "Professors Paul Althaus of Erlangen and Emmanuel Hirsch of Göttingen coauthored a scathing response [to an ecumenical conference in Cambridge, England, at which Bonhoeffer spoke] in the daily called the *Hamburger Nachrichten*, decrying the closing of the German Protestant mind. . . . Given the current state of affairs there could 'be no understanding between us Germans and the nations that were victorious in the World War.'"[2] As he sensed the mainstream pressure to realign the values expressed in the Bethel Confession he had labored to produce in 1933, Bonhoeffer abruptly left the project and Germany to pastor congregations in London. Marsh explains what followed, "Exploiting his power over the younger churchmen at Bethel as well as Bonhoeffer's departure for London, Althaus, the forty-five-year-old Göttingen professor, had taken a red pen to Bonhoeffer's forthright and reverential defense of Judaism; all criticisms of the Aryan paragraph were deleted," among other significant changes relative to the state (e.g., keying on its glory and Christians' "'joyful collaboration' in its aims").[3] With these notes in mind, as Althaus makes his somewhat general arguments about how humans should live in the world through the orders of creation based on a particular view of divine revelation, one might slip into thinking he was merely defending *evangelische Orthodoxie* against young interlopers like Bonhoeffer.

PAUL ALTHAUS: A BRIEF CASE IN COUNTERPOINT

While Bonhoeffer is scarcely found criticizing Paul Althaus by name, his theology provides a particular instance of a problem Bonhoeffer increasingly criticized. In his doctoral work and early teaching career, he is particularly concerned with the total loss of transcendence in German Idealism after Kant (as in G. W. F. Hegel's phenomenology of spirit) and the modern fixation on epistemology, which bled from philosophical discourses into theological ones. According to Bonhoeffer, these moves were dislocating theology from its rightful context of sociality within church-community and warping a truly

Christian posture toward God, revelation, and human nature (among other issues). In this vein, Althaus grounded a static, principial framework of so-called *Schöpfungsordnungen* (orders of creation) as God's law for humankind in an idealist epistemology. And he embraced the fruitfulness of an individual mind's (namely his own) logical and imaginative work with the data of creation to fill out a more comprehensive world- and life-view. Revealingly, Althaus and others ascribed the force of God's will to the contemporary concept of *Volkstum* (peoplehood), in general, and to the diversity of that concept's historically concrete forms, as in the particular *Volksdeutsche* (German people). In turn, peoplehood served as the primary organizing factor for the lives of those who were identified as part of that *Volk*, and against others who stood in their way.

Because these thinkers claimed and (ab)used a shared Lutheran tradition, they were particularly vulnerable to the criticism of others who shared that tradition. But reading Lutheran tradition against Althaus was no light burden, even for someone of Bonhoeffer's skill, considering both Althaus's apparently "moderate" theological formulations and his renown as a (possibly *the*) leading authority on Martin Luther in his day.[4] It can be argued, as Ericksen mentions, that it is precisely the moderateness of Althaus's theological formulations (as primarily an abstract system of principles) that make them so vulnerable to servicing corrupt ends.[5] Without always being problematic in a straightforward way, the carefully produced theological system leaves the audience to intuit and "discern" its meaning in their sociohistorical context. (Although, as we will see, Althaus did sometimes use his principial framework for specific identity-political ends; and, in other ways, the political landscape upon which he formulated his principles made clear their "practical applications.") In Bonhoeffer's view, "pseudo-Lutheran"[6] theologians were unknowingly stuck within their own sinful minds, ultimately granting supposedly eternal orders undue reprieve from the scrutiny and judgment of the living Lord, Jesus Christ *here and now*.

Althaus's approach to *Offenbarung* (revelation) enfolded his understanding of the *Schöpfungsordnungen*. While he preserved the rootedness of *Heilsoffenbarung* (revelation of salvation) in the gospel of Jesus Christ as revealed in Scripture, Althaus conceptualized *Uroffenbarung* (general or "primeval" revelation) next to this as God's message in and through creation. He saw the latter as not a "natural theology" (or, if so, only superficially) but "the revelation of God in nature [that] can only be properly understood if one knows the message of God in Christ."[7] Within this concept, he defined *Schöpfungsordnungen* as "forms of social life of people, which are the indispensable conditions for the historical life of humanity."[8] Althaus recognized that any concrete iterations of such orders would be "imperfect, a part of the sinful world," but nevertheless urged their acceptance "as a human representation of God's order in an imperfect world."[9] One could oppose concretized orders on two (albeit totally subjective) grounds: (1) when God calls a person into opposition or (2) when a person's sense of what the order should be compels them into opposition.[10] But *normatively*, Althaus resolved the tension between the eternal orders and their historical forms, between the created and the fallen world, with a leap of faith, namely, accepting forgiveness and redemption in Christ and embracing one's thrownness in history.[11] Coming to terms with grace, a person is free to live in the imperfect world through the orders' concrete iterations, within which God has created them. God is merciful and blesses the faithful intentions of those who live in and through the historical-institutional concretions of the eternal-creational orders, even if they are not always in the right. (Ethics in this fashion would become subject to Bonhoeffer's criticism in *Discipleship* as the stuff of "cheap grace" that brings comfort to people in their unchanged lives and closes them to the call of the living Jesus.)

With regard to *das Volk* as a *Schöpfungsordnung*, Althaus had to address the nonexistence of any biblical or confessional basis for considering such a recent historical development as eternal or "creational." Noted Lutheran theologian Paul Hinlicky describes static Lutheran theories of *Schöpfungsordnungen* as "a reactionary ideological defense against progressive social change in nineteenth-century Germany," and he names Althaus as (further) corrupting the concept into the twentieth century with his presuppositional approach to their progressive revelation.[12] For Althaus, the responsibility of human beings, each to their own *Volk*, was not so much a *new* "revelation" or mandate, at least not in the sense of *creatio continua*. He invoked the continuous change that characterizes the world in which we live and the historical observation that the biblical authors lived and spoke in their own world, which was not aware of God's general will for *Volkstum* as such.[13] So, while the orders were established with the foundations of the earth, *truer human knowledge of them* is generated dynamically over time (note the Hegelian tinge here). As such, *Volk* and race were freshly-revealed-but-eternal orders to be understood through one's own historical context as providential relations of obligation—with the force of revealed divine law.

Within his principial framework of God's providential and lawful ordering of creation, Althaus knew the static order would be concretized particularly (and thus diversely) for each person in history. Here the so-called *Zwei-Reiche-Lehre* (the two kingdoms doctrine identified by Karl Barth among others) comes into focus, for "a Christian man is indeed a double person functioning in a twofold office and living under a twofold law."[14] If God has created the orders out of love for the world, then participating in those orders is a meaningful form of obedience to God's will—God's chosen way of ordering human life.

The belief that God has created me includes also my *Volk*. . . . God has determined my life from its outermost to its innermost elements through my *Volk*, through its blood, through its spiritual style, which above all endows and stamps me in the language, and through its history. My *Volk* is my outer and my inner destiny. This womb of my being is God's means, his *Ordnung*, by which to create and to endow me. . . . The special style of a *Volk* is his creation, and as such it is for us holy.[15]

Althaus's approach to *das Volk* was, in fact, more qualified than the most radical Nazi supporters; for instance, he argued for supporting one's *Volk* not "because it is grander than others" but only "because it is my *Volk*."[16] He seemed to be speaking more generally, working out the principial framework of good Lutheran theology.

But the line from Althaus's abstract or generalized theological principles to a defense of the real-life political status quo as created and willed by God—particularly the strengthening of one's *Volk* under a virulent *Führer* at whatever cost to other *Völker*—proved to be rather straight. Althaus warmly greeted Adolf Hitler's accession to power in 1933 and readily used his seemingly pious, imaginative framework of theological principles to support concrete Nazi forms. "We Christians know ourselves bound by God's will to the promotion of National Socialism, so that all members and ranks of the *Volk* will be ready for service and sacrifice to one another."[17] And he further detailed his principial frame to include a preference for a totalitarian state that serves the needs of a *Volk* and its attendant *Führerprinzip* (leader principle) in full view of Hitler's actual use of it.[18] In the twilight of the history unfolding around him, Althaus's *Uroffenbarung* communicated one clear message for the German people, Christian or otherwise. And public theology like this occasioned Bonhoeffer's argument against principle-based ethics as leaving too much room for the individual agent to choose how the principles apply in the situation without leaving room for the living God to guide, direct, and scrutinize our lives.

For many theologically minded students of this period in German church history, the 1934 Barmen Declaration is articulate, nuanced theological response to a social crisis *par excellence*, but it was not received as such by Althaus. In no uncertain terms, Barth and other drafters rejected the method and message of the *Deutsche Christen* (lit. German Christians)—a key Nazi-supporting advocacy group—and clarified the possible sources of God's revelation. Representing the *Bekennende Kirche* (Confessing Church)—a key Nazi opposition movement within German Protestantism—the Synod of Barmen admonished Christians to recognize only the authority of the one clear word of God in Christ, as attested in Scripture. The faithful should neither search creation and its history for a more comprehensive world-view nor accept detailed guidance from theological

A Theological Criticism of the Modern Preoccupation with Epistemology 251

leaders proposing them on such grounds. But as Ericksen explains, the synod made at least two major errors in Althaus's view: (1) it inadequately dealt with some genuine *völkisch* concerns; and (2) it "emphasize[d] gospel to the exclusion of law, and excluding law it exclude[d] the *revelatio generalis* in which God's law is amplified for man's understanding."[19]

Perhaps too eager for a public opportunity to contest the Barmen Declaration, Althaus signed the 1934 *Ansbacher Ratschlag*, drafted by a colleague and printed within two weeks of the Barmen Declaration. Received with glee by the *Deutsche Christen*, this memorandum promoted itself as "finally the genuine Lutheran voice" (notice the politics of identity here) and boldly pronounced, "As Christians, we honor with thanks towards God every order, therefore also every authority, even if deformed, as a tool of divine preservation."[20] Further, the law of God "binds each in the position to which he has been called by God and commits us to the natural orders under which we are subjugated, such as family, *Volk*, [and] race (i.e., blood relationship).... In that the will of God also meets us continually in our here and now, it binds us also to a specific historical moment of family, *Volk*, and race."[21] At least this much of the Ansbach conceptuality fits Althaus's theological views, but he ultimately published a more measured criticism that identified the potential *Deutsche Christen* abuse of his revelation concept. As Ericksen explains, "Misuse would include the de-Judaizing of Christianity or placing the German experience on the same level as God's message in Christ. But Althaus believe[d] Barmen should affirm that *Ordnungen*, e.g., the German *Volk*, are a part of God's creation and therefore, a part of God's law."[22] Somewhat contrarily, Althaus criticized the theological liberalism of the *Deutsche Christen* that included their wedding of *Heilsgeschichte* (salvation history) to German national history. He denied the messianic role of any *Volk*, arguing that the mission of any *Volk* is internal to itself—even if over-against other *Völker*.[23] (Bonhoeffer noticed the similarly problematic views of revelation and history in both German Idealists and American "social gospel" preachers.[24]) So, while his theology has some strongly idealist themes, Althaus did not partake in a specifically Hegelian-dialectical view of history.[25] Yet in his support of his particular people, as the organizing context in his life, Althaus seemed to have no theological grounds for resisting the way his own *Volk* was driving his overall world-view.

THEOLOGY DEVELOPED UNDER COMPLETELY DIFFERENT CIRCUMSTANCES

Bonhoeffer was already on the outs with the philosophical idealism prevailing in the social and academic currents around him in his dissertations. But, as Christian ethicist Reggie Williams explains in *Bonhoeffer's Black Jesus* (Baylor University Press, 2016), central ideas in that early work remained empty in his real-world experience.[26] For example, where could he find an actual local church making real for him the concept of "Christ existing as church-community"? The gap between second-order reflection and first-order realities can be wide and painful to navigate for young theologians. And following our review of Paul Althaus, we should note that Bonhoeffer carried a strain of *völkisch*-ness that seems to have silently furnished his actual sense of basic community, as displayed in a public lecture before German ex-pats in Barcelona, Spain, in early 1929:

> Every people . . . has within itself a call from God to create its history. . . . Now, should a people experiencing God's call in its own life, in its own youth, and in its own strength, should not such a people also be allowed to follow that call even if it disregards the lives of other peoples? God is the Lord of history; and if a people bends in humility to this holy will guiding history, then with God in its youth and strength it can overcome the weak and disheartened. Then God will be with it.[27]

As Williams points out, Bonhoeffer had argued in a previous lecture, "If there is something in Christ that makes claims upon my entire life, from top to bottom, and does so with the full seriousness of the realization that it is God who is speaking here, and if it is only in Christ that God's word once became a present reality, then Christ possesses for me not only merely relative but also absolutely urgent significance."[28] Juxtaposing these two passages, Williams does not sugarcoat his conclusion: Bonhoeffer's world-view "was missing critical substance. At this point in his theological career, Bonhoeffer did not refer to the Bible for Christian discipleship. As a result of that glaring omission, it was easy to blend the way of Jesus with German nationalism and to consider patriotism an element of Christian discipleship."[29] In his fellowship application, Bonhoeffer named a desire to understand Christian theology "as it has developed under completely different circumstances."[30] And that is precisely what he attempted, as I will relay through key examples from Williams's groundbreaking study of Bonhoeffer's personal and theoethical transformation around his year at Union and time in neighboring Harlem.

While he was relatively unimpressed with the theology he encountered in the seminary community, Bonhoeffer made some friends whose presence occasioned real and significant growth. For example, another Sloane Fellow named Jean Lasserre represents a constellation of important nodes in Bonhoeffer's developing theological network. In one moment, Williams describes how Bonhoeffer and Lasserre went together to see the first film

A Theological Criticism of the Modern Preoccupation with Epistemology 253

adaptation of *All Quiet on the Western Front*, which tells the story of World War I from the German perspective. As Williams narrates,

> German anti-French resentment was clear in the film; for example, when a German soldier shot a French soldier, the American audience cheered. American military fought alongside the French in World War I, but ironically the American audience was persuaded by the film's German viewpoint against the French. Lasserre was deeply grieved and Bonhoeffer was embarrassed. But Bonhoeffer was also pained, being moved by empathy with Lasserre in the theater. Bonhoeffer witnessed his friend experiencing something like the racial acrimony that his friends in the Harlem community knew.[31]

As a French Reformed pastor with Huguenot lineage, Lasserre represents both a national and theological "other." As an individual, he held a strong conviction that (contra young Bonhoeffer) living an authentic Christian life would require a concrete, biblical Christian ethics with a special focus on taking Jesus's teachings (beginning with the Sermon on the Mount) seriously no matter the cost.[32] So, in addition to opening Bonhoeffer's heart to the fruitful possibilities of transnational ecumenism, this friendship with Lasserre sparked significant insights—ranging from the import of biblical teachings for all of life, the costliness of grace, and the self-evidence of Christian pacifism.

For another example, a friendship with Albert Franklin Fisher, an African American student at Union, introduced Bonhoeffer to Black church life in Harlem amid its renaissance. His activities during this critical moment included regular attendance and assistance teaching a Sunday school class at Abyssinian Baptist Church, swimming in the literature being produced and circulated (e.g., works by W. E. B. Du Bois and Alain Locke), and otherwise occupying himself with Harlem life and culture. Bonhoeffer's own summary of the Black literature he was encountering has been lost to time, but he had an abiding interest in this work—even inquiring about the essay (lent to one Jim Dombrowski, a doctoral student who went on to be a civil rights activist) in a letter to Union theologian Reinhold Niebuhr.[33] As a sample of what he was encountering, Williams draws from one of Du Bois's parables called "Jesus Christ in Texas," placed in the center of his 1920 composition *Darkwater*. In the closing sequence, a Black man running toward Jesus in repentance collides with a white woman running away from a Black "stranger" who has asked whether her neighbor-love extends to the Black persons around her. "The farmer's wife finally recognizes the stranger as Jesus when she observes the innocent black man swaying in a noose from a tree. The farmer's wife sees the stranger with him, above and behind him on a cross, superimposing himself on the dying man's image."[34] Interpreting this passage, Williams continues, "Jesus is found among the victims of systemic and structural oppression, repeatedly rejected, and finally killed by its guardians, because of his empathic identification with all victims of injustice. Du Bois' narrative suggests that to die at the hands of white supremacist Christians is tantamount to Christian martyrdom."[35] Bonhoeffer's intent to understand the theologies emerging in other contexts, as Williams narrates, "made him vulnerable to an empathic theological experience that took Bonhoeffer into the context of oppressed people. There he learned of his own disturbing theological commitments from the perspective of others in critical engagement with the lethal white Christ."[36] And as Williams narrates, "At Abyssinian with Fisher, Bonhoeffer found Christ existing as community where historically marginalized and oppressed black people knew Jesus as cosufferer and the gospel spoke authoritatively into all areas of life."[37] Noticing his participation in the disease of whiteness helped facilitate his recovery.

Williams demonstrates how, in the preaching of Abyssinian's pastor Adam Clayton Powell Sr., Bonhoeffer "encountered an African American interpretation of the immanent yet transcendent God, which helped inspire the German teacher in the Sunday school to push back against injustice in simple obedience to Christ."[38] During his time in New York City, he saw Powell launch church-based hunger and clothing relief programs—directly connecting Jesus with the hungry and naked in his preaching of Matthew 25 and setting an example by donating a third of his salary to the new relief efforts.[39] Bonhoeffer returned from his fellowship to the crumbling Weimar Republic. The depression was deepening, and that fall, unemployment numbers soared, and Germany's second-largest bank collapsed.[40] How the church and its people could faithfully respond, attending to and caring for those who suffered under such conditions, was an active part of Bonhoeffer's thought life. In the period after New York, he got involved in international ecumenical work and engaged in ministry with folks suffering under depressed conditions in Berlin's urban center.

As he comes to note what is distinctive about Bonhoeffer's theoethics in comparison with even his confessing church colleagues, Williams describes how his time in Harlem showed him that authentic Christian discipleship could not abide the suffering and oppression of neighbors whom one is called to love—not least those who are assumed to be outside neighbor status because they do not belong to what turns out to be one's primary community (i.e., as determined by race or ethnicity).[41] We do not get to preselect who partakes in community with us, partly because God shows up to us in others to share words we need to hear—words we might not otherwise select for, and even still might struggle to hear and grapple with, ourselves. "For modification to happen," Williams tells us, "Bonhoeffer had to allow himself to be vulnerable to seeing himself and society from the perspective of others, just as discipleship to the empathic and vicarious *Stellvertretung* Christ whom he described in his two dissertations required."[42] He saw the deeper impact of an idealism that can be read to support imperialism and racism, how it facilitates Christians grinding others into dust, and thus mounted a vigorous and multifaceted argument against such thinking as the stuff of Christian faith. Furthermore, as he wrote to his brother in early 1935, Bonhoeffer is aware that his emerging perspective may come off as

> fanatical and mad about a number of things. . . . But I know that the day I become more "reasonable," to be honest, I should have to chuck my entire theology. When I first started in theology, my idea of it was quite different—rather more academic, probably. Now it has turned into something else altogether. But I do believe that at last I am on the right track, for the first time in my life. . . . I think that I am right in saying that I would only achieve true inner clarity and honesty by really starting to take the Sermon on the Mount seriously.[43]

Before closing the letter, he mentions having discovered the tale of "The Emperor's New Clothes," suggesting its relevance to their time and the need for a child to come along and point out to the emperor—or, we might assume, the Christian secure in their abstract, idealist world-view—that they are actually naked.

Having already earned his doctorate in theology, Bonhoeffer starts to move "from the phraseological to the real" during and after his time in NYC.[44] But he also begins sharpening his analysis of biblical themes and theological doctrines with an attentiveness to what may be known in relation to the living, biblical, historical Jesus whom he met in Harlem and who addresses contemporary disciples with the simple call to come follow him. In fact, Bonhoeffer later reflected on how his life and approach to his theological career changed, starting with how he thought prior to his time in New York:

> I threw myself into my work in an extremely un-Christian and not at all humble fashion. A rather crazy element of ambition, which some people noticed in me, made my life difficult and withdrew from me the love and trust of those around me. At that time, I was terribly alone and left to myself. It was quite bad. But then something different came, something that has changed and transformed my life to this very day. For the first time, I came to the Bible. That, too, is an awful thing to say. I had often preached, I had seen a great deal of the church, had spoken and written about it—and yet I was not yet a Christian but rather in an utterly wild and uncontrolled fashion my own master. I do know that at the time I turned the cause of Jesus Christ into an advantage for myself, for my crazy vanity. . . . The Bible, especially the Sermon on the Mount, freed me from all this. Since then everything has changed. . . . It became clear to me that the

life of a servant of Jesus Christ must belong to the church, and step-by-step it became clearer to me how far it must go. Then came the crisis of 1933. This strengthened me in it.

I also met others who shared the same goal. For me everything now depended on a renewal of the church and of the pastoral station. Christian pacifism, which a brief time before—at the disputation where Gerhard was also present!—I had still passionately disputed, suddenly came into focus as something utterly self-evident. And thus it went, step-by-step. I no longer saw or thought about anything else.

My vocation now stands before me. I do not know what God will make of it. There is still a great deal of disobedience and insincerity in my own relation with my profession. I catch myself at it every day. But I must traverse this path its entire length. Perhaps it will not last much longer now. Sometimes we probably do wish it thus for ourselves (Phil. 1:23). But it is, after all, wonderful having this profession.[45]

In what follows, we will encounter the work of a theologian who takes seriously his vested interest in being seen as a theological light, who is attentive to this temptation in an ongoing way, and who theologizes an openness to the biblical-historical Jesus as a living person who can always call the fruits of his own brilliance into question.

DIETRICH BONHOEFFER ON CREATION, FALL, AND HOW WE KNOW

As we take account of Bonhoeffer's constructive theological agenda in the early 1930s, centering on his book *Creation and Fall* may prove most helpful. Based on his lecture manuscripts for a "Creation and Sin"[46] seminar he taught at the University of Berlin in the fateful winter months of 1932–1933, this important work creatively frames his wider argument for a "theology of relationality" within the narrative of Genesis 1–3. As he walks through the drama of the first humans' creation in the *imago dei*, their life *coram deo*, and their grasping after "life" *sicut deus*, Bonhoeffer exposes the original sin as the original epistemological turn—the pious humans' attempt to know God's will and to serve it based on their own inner resources, out of themselves as their own centers. And with the core language and conceptuality here, Bonhoeffer simultaneously develops and extends his earlier, more philosophical arguments (represented in his dissertations) and situates the "orders of preservation" concept that he deploys against the pseudo-Lutheran abuse of idealist "orders of creation" theology (i.e., in support of the prevailing "blood and soil" nationalism). There are many other ways

A Theological Criticism of the Modern Preoccupation with Epistemology   257

to organize even these same themes, but the following account accents how Bonhoeffer's work presents a vital alternative to idealist systematic theological systems. By the end of this chapter, the connections between his early concern with epistemology and his criticism of theologies like Althaus's will become abundantly clear as we see how Bonhoeffer marshaled his philosophical and biblical-theological arguments against the timeless theological principles propping up Nazism. For reasons that will become clear soon enough, I will begin with his Christology lectures from the summer of 1933.

Where to Begin?

Bonhoeffer opens his Christology lectures with a meditation on the silence that precedes teaching about Jesus Christ.[47] Decidedly, this is not a "mystagogical silence"[48] in which one could "chatter away secretly in their soul by themselves" (a vulnerability not only in mystics but also in idealists, as we will see).[49] The quietness Bonhoeffer is after is the silence of the church-community before the Word through which the risen Christ reveals himself.[50] Starting here resituates theology within its first-order, worshipful space as a "function of the church" and, perhaps more importantly, recenters Christology not simply on a haveable *object* for studying but rather on its living *subject*: the person of Jesus.[51] Starting here also throws Althaus's view of revelation into sharp relief: we do not properly set out to explore *this* subject, Bonhoeffer argues, by reaching behind his person searching for first principles (e.g., a broader theory of revelation) that establish his trustworthiness. Bonhoeffer allows for no path to get behind Christ as the Logos of God to some supposedly wider, *more ultimate* reality in which *we know* the Christ participates (i.e., the concept of logos or reason itself).

Starting from the side of human reason, we might ask questions of classification to understand and assimilate what we observe and experience according to the order already present in our minds. Such questions, as Bonhoeffer stylizes them, derive from a more basic question of epistemology: "How is it possible to classify an object?"[52] And *the human logos* provides itself as the answer, offering all the tools one could need. The empiricist is searching out the order baked into the material world and trying to realize itself; the idealist believes the human mind participates in a sense of order that stands above and makes sense of the material world. "But what if," Bonhoeffer asks, such self-assured responses are "subject to doubt? What happens if it is claimed that the human logos is dead, condemned, superseded?"[53] In his view, the living Christ presents just this challenge to the omnicompetent human mind, particularly as one tries to understand what they encounter as a transcendent object.

So, the way this challenge comes to us is significant, Bonhoeffer explains, for the *Gegenlogos* (counter-Logos, i.e., divine Logos as cutting against human logos), has come in "a wholly new form, so that it is no longer an idea or a word that is turned against the autonomy of the [human] logos, but rather the counter Logos appears . . . as a human being, and as a human being sets itself up as judge over the human logos and says, 'I am the truth,' I am the death of the human logos, I am the life of God's Logos."[54] When confronted by this "object," who cannot be assimilated without violence, there are two basic options: kill or be killed. The human logos can either kill the Logos of God or realize that its own death is necessary to participate in reality as defined by this counter Logos.[55] Faced with the *Gegenlogos*, "horrified, dethroned human reason" and faith alike ask, "Who are you?"[56] That is a different kind of question, and Bonhoeffer contrasts the questions of "who" and "how" as an important test for concepts of personhood and approaches to identity.

Merely *asking* the "who" question is not enough to make it out of this experience alive because the human mind continues to interpret any response (real or imagined) through the categorical "how" question. "How?" seeks the information necessary to assimilate another person into the thought-world of the questioner. Prefiguring what we will discover in his wider account of the fall below, Bonhoeffer continues, "When we ask, 'Who are you?,' then we speak the language of the obedient Adam, but we think the language of the fallen Adam, which is, '*How* are you?' In this way, the first language was ruined."[57] In getting to know a person, one often asks a "question of classification. . . . Tell me how you are, tell me how you think, and I will tell you who you are."[58] The real problem of critical thinking in this scenario is that, while we need to be asking the "who" question, our minds are only capable of asking "how." "We are chained to our own authority. It is the *cor curvum in se*."[59] That is, at least, until the genuine, self-revealing other who is God incarnate steps into our situation, resisting any attempts at assimilating their person; the "who" question only applies when one has actually encountered another person who embodies a limit to their knowledge.

In too many theologies, the move to second-order reflection loses God's personhood as a God-concept is vaulted high out of contemporary human lives, and then theologians approach the transcendent as an *object* with imagination and speculation. But humans do not even adequately understand who (or what) they are without this living, personal question of transcendence. In terms introduced in Bonhoeffer's first dissertation, *Sanctorum Communio*, the epistemological subject-object relation is fundamentally different from the social I-You relation, and the varieties of knowing appropriate to each are quite different as well.[60] He draws a distinction between (a) the human desire to possess knowledge of God and (b) the relationship of the human being with God—as a subject, a "You" to my "I," whom I encounter and come to know personally. As a second-order exercise, theology is done (i.e., in his classroom, among his students) in the space of reflection, cognition, and systematization. But only when the living *Gegenlogos* has judged us can "the old logos learn anew to comprehend the relative rights to which it is entitled. Only from the question of transcendence does the human logos receive the rights peculiar to it, its necessity and also its limits."[61]

Consequently, another kind of question cannot be allowed: "how the 'that' of the revelation can be *conceived*. This question leads in the direction of trying again to get behind Christ's claim and to ground it on our own. In doing so, our own logos is presuming on the role of the Father of Jesus Christ himself, when all we actually know is the fact of God's revelation."[62] From his earliest work, Bonhoeffer talks of Christ as *Stellvertreter*, the one who steps in to stand with and for (and sometimes over-against) humankind as God's "loving-action for humanity," Green explains, "In this context, the abstract noun 'revelation' is unsatisfactory. For this reason, Bonhoeffer does not use it very much; when he does he usually puts it in the form of a verb describing personal *self-giving*."[63] As such, sociality rather than epistemology provides the only appropriate "method" for locating God's transcendence. Thinking of the context for faith created within the church-community, Bonhoeffer says, "The question, 'Who?' presupposes an answer which has already been given."[64] The presence of the living person of Jesus Christ in the church-community prompts *this* question. Without someone before us, we would ask not "Who are you?" but *What can we know about God?* and *How?*

The Lost Beginning

Considering possible pathways back to the beginning of our story from this point, Bonhoeffer opens *Creation and Fall* with a reflection on humankind's lost genesis. We have fallen away from our origin, and we are situated between the beginning and the end—neither of which can we see from the middle ground we occupy.[65] We may speculate about "the beginning" to a good many interesting, even inspiring, ends, but our thinking is confined to certain creaturely boundaries, whether we recognize them or not. "Our thinking, that is, the thinking of those who have to turn to Christ to know about God, the thinking of fallen humankind, lacks a beginning because it is a circle. We think in a circle. But we also feel and will in a circle. We exist in a circle."[66] The circularity of human thinking is a feature of the *cor curvum in se*. In stark terms, Bonhoeffer refutes modern epistemologies and the philosophical and theological "systems" built upon them in which "thinking looks to itself as the beginning" and "posits itself as an object, as an entity over against itself, and so again and again withdraws behind this object."[67]

With this first move, the thinking "I" usurps God as the original self-revealing "who" and enthrones their own reason to explore every aspect of "how" with the omnicompetent "I" itself as the ground of knowledge. Green summarizes this problem as presented in Bonhoeffer's second dissertation, *Act and Being*,

> Thought is a "lord," "almighty" in its power. The "thinking" and "knowing I" is described as "overpowering" and "violating" all reality. Under the limitless power of intellect and reason, the creation becomes for the fallen man "his own, violated, 'interpreted' world." Such intellectual aggressiveness allows one to . . . imagine that one can seize God in some intellectual system.[68]

No human being can step out of their position in the middle and come to know the genesis, Bonhoeffer argues. Only the living One who alone was in the beginning can speak of it *truthfully*, and human speech about the beginning is only a cloak for our middle-ness. Yet the beginning can still be bandied about *alternatively* by the one who has lied since that beginning and, in this deceit, introduced humankind to the possibility of discovering, even becoming, their own beginning.[69]

Idealist thinking problematically assumes the individual thinker—particularly the self who is doing the philosophizing or theologizing—exhibits a kind of pure psychological unity (as discussed in part I and insinuated in Mouw's appeal to "sanctified imagination"). In such thinking, the regenerate mind seeks and acquires knowledge in the proper "direction" because of a fundamental change within their soul, their controlling/willing center. But, as Bonhoeffer points out (contra his doctoral mentor, Reinhold Seeberg), "The concept of direction does not guarantee the unity of the concept of person. As a psychologically demonstrable fact, direction is still subject to disintegration into individual acts and arbitrary interpretation."[70] With sin lurking behind the door, every act is a point of decision; moreover, individual Christians are not experts on their own direction. "People do not know their motives; they do not know fully their sin; they are unable to understand themselves on the basis of their own psychic experiences, for they are amenable to any arbitrary interpretation."[71] If we allow a sentimental reading of one's own direction, on which everyone seems to be their own expert witness, then nearly anything the person (even in a mature theologian) does or thinks could pass as basically Christian because *their heart is in the right place*. No, we cannot find the unity we seek within the self or its intentions. The Christian desperately needs the church-community before God's word, where alone they may find their unity and, indeed, their true existence.[72] The theologian, in particular, needs to recognize that the church-community bestows meaning upon their work, keeps them humble, and reminds them that their most beautiful system can "never grasp the living person of Christ into itself."[73]

A Theological Criticism of the Modern Preoccupation with Epistemology 261

Christian thinkers often approach the creation stories with questions and concerns that are foreign to the biblical authors and fundamentally insoluble apart from whatever presuppositions the contemporary interpreter supplies. These questions themselves reflect the concerns of those caught in the middle. Among those quandaries which remain unaddressed in the biblical story but that human beings in the middle wish to see answered, perhaps the most significant for the current project is the metaphysical problem of sin's entry into creation. Bonhoeffer explains that the events of Genesis 3 unfold within *Zwielicht* (twilight) conditions, in which what has been created and what is evil appear together so that the two

> cannot in any way be made an unmixed light without destroying something that is decisive. The ambiguity of the serpent, of Eve, and of the tree of knowledge as creatures of God's grace and yet as the place where the voice of evil is heard must be preserved as such; it must on no account be crudely simplified and its two aspects be torn apart to make it unambiguous. For precisely this twilight, this ambiguity, in which the creation here stands constitutes the only possible way for human beings in the middle to speak about this event.[74]

His use of the term *Zwielicht* is a play on words, referring not only to the half-light between day and night but more significantly to a kind of qualitative two-ness (implied in the prefix *Zwie-*).[75] Bonhoeffer finds the essence of the Genesis 3 episode to be "precisely that the whole course of events takes place in the world God has created and that no *diaboli ex machina* are set in motion to make this incomprehensible event understandable or to dramatize it."[76] Appearing all at once to us in the middle as ambiguous *Zwielicht*, the light's sources cannot be clearly distinguished within the story itself. And this entanglement broadly characterizes all human perception and reasoning after the fall: human beings can only speak or know of *anything* in this twilight. We are, indeed, crepuscular creatures.

Christians need to hear a present word of God in these stories, which may require approaching them perennially as if they have not only fresh answers to our questions but also different questions for us to consider from the start. In pursuing answers to general questions like how evil entered the world, the contemporary interpreter of the biblical text risks missing some crucial aspects of this (hi)story that directly address them. One thing the biblical account describes, in this case, is *how falling happens*—in the first humans, to be sure, but also in our repetition of their story.[77] Communicating the force of this similitude is an abiding concern in Bonhoeffer's study. He thinks imagining this beginning in temporal-historical terms as "in the past" is fundamentally unhelpful and instead casts us all as actors playing out this script in our own lives. Specifically, we should attend to the problematic shift from social to epistemological modes of learning, knowing, and relating and the questions this shift puts between us and our "natural" approach to the beginning. More hopefully, perhaps, as we chatter away in our own souls, we must hear the voice interrupting us to ask, "Where are you?" (Gen. 3:9).

The Christian Concept of Person

Addressing the *imago dei* conceptuality in Genesis 1:26–27, Bonhoeffer reiterates his view that the human attempt to recover a concept of human nature from our lost beginning invariably means "identify[ing] our own ideal of humanity with what God actually created."[78] As we might expect, he then argues that what may truly be known about human nature as such can only be known in Christ. For Bonhoeffer, this means at least two things: (1) only in the person of Christ as revealed through Scripture do we see a human being fully alive and (2) only through Christ existing today as church-community is anything revealed. The attempt to recover the genuine, original concept of human nature, including created relationality, without recognizing this dependency is "as hopeless as it is understandable" and "has again and again delivered up the church to arbitrary speculation."[79] And, at first, Bonhoeffer's own concept of human nature created in the *imago dei* appears rather speculative: "To behold oneself means, so to speak, to recognize one's own face in a mirror, to see oneself in an image of oneself. . . . Only in that which is itself free could the free Creator behold the Creator. But how can what is created be free?"[80] Why start here? Is this "freedom" merely Bonhoeffer's own ideal beginning?[81] In short, no, because God demonstrates the quality of God's own freedom (*pace* Barth)[82] as "being-free-for-the-other" *in the person of Jesus Christ*. Put differently, the uncreated freedom of God in which "God wills not to be free for God's self but for humankind" is the substrate of the evangel itself.[83] Only in the context of this God-established relationship may we see how "God's free grace becomes real with us alone."[84] Grace is real insofar as it is at work preserving the relationship between infinite Creator and finite humankind, and grace is ever the only security for this relationship.

What this means for Bonhoeffer is that the *imago dei* is fundamentally an *analogia relationis* (analogy of relation)—a "given" relation, not merely a calling or a capacity at human disposal (e.g., Abraham Kuyper's microcosmic consciousness).[85] The qualitative difference between God's freedom and the analogous human freedom is in our creatureliness: human beings are created in mutual dependence. As such, our creatureliness (like our freedom) is not an immanent quality of each individual or an individually possessable entity; it is located in the social "existence of human being over-against-one-another, with-one-another, and in-dependence-upon-one-another."[86]

In the language of the Bible, freedom is not something that people have for themselves but something they have for others. No one is free "in herself" or "in himself"—free as it were in a vacuum or free in the same way that a person may be musical, intelligent, or blind in herself or in himself. . . . Anyone who scrutinizes human beings in order to find freedom finds nothing of it. Why? Because . . . freedom is a relation between two persons. Being free means "being-free-for-the-other," because I am bound to the other. Only by being in relation with the other am I free.[87]

The prototypical relation between God and humankind establishes the freedom of human creatures before the person of God, and what may be known about human nature is "true" only in its analogy to that relation. We can understand the human being's freedom-for-others only by way of analogy to God's freedom-for-us.

In the second creation account, two trees rise as reference points for human existence. Life before the fall "is not something problematic or to be sought after or snatched at; instead, it is just there, as a given life, indeed life before God."[88] What may appear to us as a temptation—to reach out and seize life for ourselves—does not appear that way to Adam; he did not need to be told not to eat from "the tree of life," which only becomes an object of interest later in the story. When Adam hears the command not to eat from "the tree of knowledge" in his life *coram deo*, Adam receives this as the word of the living God, through whom he exists and with whom he is in a relationship. Being addressed in the prohibition reminds him of his humanity, that is to say, his freedom before God as well as his limit or *creatureliness*.[89] Anything Adam "knows" at this point arises out of his creaturely freedom, his ignorance. Without knowledge of evil, Adam could not confuse his limit with a boundary that stands beyond himself as something that he could "transgress"; rather, he receives his "knowledge" of the limit as God speaks to him.

To elaborate on the meaning of creatureliness in this sense, Bonhoeffer plays with the typical understanding of a "limit" or boundary (*Grenze* in German)[90] as something at the end of oneself, that is, on the margins. Anticipating his depiction of the fall (and integrating his ongoing critique of German Idealist epistemology), he argues, "Knowledge of the limit or constraint on the margin is always accompanied by the possibility of failing to know any internal limit. Knowledge of the boundary at the center means knowing that the whole of existence, human existence in every possible way that it may comport itself, has its limit."[91] God is the other with whom Adam is in relation and who establishes within Adam a limit that pertains to his entire existence: the living, free, and willing Creator walks with Adam in the garden and speaks a word for him to obey. The word about the tree of knowledge is not itself the limit, nor is the tree standing in the garden's center;

both are gifts to Adam, reminding him of his creaturely existence before and dependence upon the living God, who *is* his limit. This relationship is the very ground of Adam's existence, creating a limit at his "center"—though again not "within" Adam in an immanent, self-sufficient way. A radical intersubjectivity delimits his whole life such that he lives only as he knows and relates to God *as God*. Adam does not "think" God (or God's will) as an object to be known and internalized and then served on those grounds. God's presence is integral to his being, and his ongoing existence as a being as well as whatever may be his calling (i.e., what is sometimes framed as the *analogia entis* and the *analogia operationis*) is contingent upon God's ongoing presence as the One who calls.

At the most basic level, the second human more tangibly personifies the limit that alterity (including God's own) creates in the center of Adam's existence. This other reiterates Adam's creaturely limit as a person he can love and, in so loving, not wish to violate that limit (i.e., by seeking to possess or internalize any other); instead, the two love and know each other in the course of life before God.[92] Bonhoeffer describes the love between persons as preserving each person in the creaturely life lived in freedom for and before God; together they cobear the *imago dei*, living in freedom for God and, by analogy, for each other. "The Creator knows that this free life as a creature can be borne within its limit only if it is loved, and out of unfathomable mercy the Creator creates the helper."[93] So, the limit of the person in the "other" is still not located in transgressable boundaries at the end of the self-sufficient "I," nor is it merely generated as a thought in Adam's mind. Eve (and other persons by extension) incarnates the limit, and Adam would violate her personhood if he took her as an object of his own ends (including "knowledge of") rather than addressing her as an end in herself. "By the creation of the other person, freedom and creatureliness are bound together in love. That is why the other person is once again grace to the first person. . . . In this common bearing of the limit by the first two persons in community, the character of this community as the church is authenticated."[94] As much as the relationship between the first two humans suggests something significant about "marriage," it truly reveals the character of the "church" before God. In sum, we are not created to pursue boundless knowledge, particularly when it extends to assimilate others and their identities and wills; rather, we can ever only pursue this knowledge in our love of the other, with whom we are patient enough to allow for their self-revelation.

The elements of relationality and revelation seem ever at hand as Bonhoeffer explores the predominate philosophical concepts of person since modernity's epistemological turn. Several aspects of René Descartes's thinking make him a pivotal figure despite the overall paucity of propositional claims in his body of works. As Bonhoeffer explains, "Descartes's transformation of the metaphysical question into an epistemological one casts the concept of person into a different light from previous theories. . . . The knowing I becomes the starting point of all philosophy."[95] After Descartes's *cogito*, making the turn into post-Kantian idealism, the epistemological concept of person relocates the unity from the eternal realm to an immanent, rational *Geist*. Against this concept of person, Bonhoeffer develops a Christian one along the lines of the I-You language introduced above, which he hopes will "overcome" and "replace" the idealist conceptuality, thus "preserv[ing] the individual, concrete character of the person as absolute and intended by God," that is, of the person as particular social being rather than a generic unit of conceptual totality.[96] An idealist methodology cannot tell us anything about what we discover in the social sphere where we encounter others as subjects, as something more (mysterious) than mere objects of our knowledge.[97] "All cognitive methods of idealism are included in the realm of personal mind, and the way to the transcendent is the way to the object of knowledge," Bonhoeffer observes.[98] Idealist moral judgments are based neither on *who* the person is nor to *whom*, in particular, they are relating, but *how* they are acting; we could just as well translate the whole scenario into propositional logic, identify the person with a variable, and apply our laws or principles to the same ends. But in this process, we fail to take responsibility for the actual person, not to mention for the impact of our actual judgments on the lives of those people, especially if we have any tangible power over them.

We reach genuine social-ethical experience only when we are forced out of the mode of the self-sufficient, thinking "I" by some other who confronts us from beyond ourselves and puts us in "a state of *responsibility* or, in other words, of decision."[99] An encounter with another person can make known a boundary (*Schranke* in Kant's terminology) to the reasoning self and to the knowledge it seeks on its own terms. In the other, we experience the limit (*Grenze* in Kant's terminology) of not only some noumena—implying existence, but only knowable in our experience of it—but of another willing "I" who is fundamentally ungraspable by the single, solitary intellect.[100] And exactly here, in the moment of being addressed, is any given course of action faced with its value—not in the abstract consideration of whether, based on supposedly timeless principles of ultimate value, one should will that all other people would take up such-and-such an action. "Only in concrete time is the real claim of ethics effectual; and only when I am responsible am I fully conscious of being bound to time. It is not that I make some sort of universally valid decision by being in full possession of a rational mind. Rather, I enter the reality of time by relating my concrete person in time and all its particularities to this imperative."[101]

As Bonhoeffer's concept unfolds, its ramifications for the "social basic-relation" and the concept of God (and thus revelation) become increasingly clear. His turn toward a theological concept begins with an emphatic statement: *"The attempt to derive the social from the epistemological category must be rejected as μετάβασις εἰς ἄλλο γένος [changing to a different category]. It is impossible to reach the real existence of other subjects by way of the purely transcendental category of the universal."*[102] That fact does not keep humans from trying. Descartes identified the source of his own intellectual errors in his will's tendency to extend beyond what is reasonably knowable.[103] And Kant recognized that (a) reason meets an impermeable boundary as it seeks out content for metaphysical concepts (e.g., God and soul) and (b) humans are ceaselessly tempted to fill out those concepts nonetheless. (Thus, encountering a limit on the margins is accompanied by the failure to know any internal limit.) Those who discover these concepts in their minds (as a priori categories) will always feel their thought-world is incomplete until they have found satisfactory content to "synthesize" with categories as metaphysical knowledge.

Becoming *sicut deus* as Falling Away from the Origin (i.e., Death)

Enter the serpent (Gen. 3:1), not to *dispute* God's command—would the first humans entertain such impiety?—but to pose a question that "opens the eyes of the human being to a depth of which the human being has until now been unaware."[104] With the proposition that "on the basis of an idea, a principle, or some prior knowledge about God, humankind should now pass judgment on the concrete word of God," the serpent portrays human beings as above God's word rather than in simple obedience under it.[105] In *reality* there is only God's command and human obedience in the context of an ongoing, grace-filled relationship, but by craftily introducing the category of *possibility*, the serpent offers human beings a handle for seizing hold of themselves and living out of their own centers (even when living by their *knowledge of God the Creator*).[106] What the first humans hear from the serpent is a *pious* question: "the possibility of Adam's *own* 'wanting to be for God,' as Adam's own discovery."[107] Ignorant about deceit and evil, Adam could only receive the serpent's word of life *sicut deus* as "the possibility of being more pious, more obedient, than he is in his *imago-dei*-structure," which, it bears repeating, is a relational structure operating with an apposite way of knowing.[108] But given the creaturely mode of living "out of the life that comes from God," the humans' effort to live a life they *know* to be "good" *coram deo* is just as much "an unthinkable falling away" as living a life in evil.[109] Created in the *imago dei*, human beings are "bound to the word of the Creator and deriving life from the Creator"; but when they become *sicut deus*, each human being is "bound to the depths of [his or her] own knowledge of God, of good and evil."[110] Any difference between *sicut deus* and death is only salient in the serpentine realm of "possibility." Humankind is put in the middle, living neither within its limit nor from the center; with hearts curved in on themselves, human persons are utterly alone in the twilight.[111]

For twenty-first-century Christians living in the middle as we do, it is easy to lose sight of the subtlety of the loss here. Tersely describing the event in the garden as "disobedience" is deceptively simplistic—an explanation from the middle where we languish (or, tellingly, live confidently) in crepuscular knowledge of good and evil, under human traditions built around God's law. One of the more simplistic forms of the pious inquiry today starts with the assumption that God wants us to know his will, so we must be able to discover it—and, as the saying goes, "the plain things are the main things" and vice versa. This is where we might hear new questions being put to us. It is particularly important to understand the Genesis 3 episode well because it is not merely a story of, or from, *the* beginning but *our own history*—as Bonhoeffer told us up front. We are not talking merely about an epistemological problem or the disruption of our created "noetic" capacity. We are talking about epistemology *as* the problem, the abandonment of a social way of being and "knowing" God and one another that fits humans' contingent, relational nature as creatures. "For their knowledge of God, human beings renounce the word of God that approaches them again and again out of the inviolable center and boundary of life."[112] What happens in the fall is

> the creature's stepping outside of the creature's only possible attitude, the creature's becoming creator, the destruction of creatureliness, a defection, a falling away from being safely held as a creature. As such a defection, it is a *continual* fall, a *dropping* into a bottomless abyss, a state of being let go, a process of moving further and further away, falling deeper and deeper.[113]

Creatureliness is not only corrupted but abolished in this falling away; the crepuscular creature really becomes a creator *sicut deus*—generating not material worlds but ideal ones in which to move and have our being (though the distinction may turn out to be no difference).[114] This standing must be borne in mind when we say anything whatsoever about human beings or God from the middle. God alone can express a word to the contrary, which comes to us unimaginably (and surreptitiously) in and through our middle-ness—and yet as more than a mere instantiation of our middle-ness—in the person of Jesus Christ.

Having hidden from each other in shame, the first humans also flee from God. This moment represents another aspect of *our* history, but in a way that would vex those with idealist ethics, including many contemporary Christian moralists. Bonhoeffer provocatively identifies our flight from God as "conscience" itself, explaining, "Here, far away from God, humankind itself plays the role of being judge and in this way seeks to evade God's judgment."[115] That is not to say that human beings seek to avoid judgment altogether, but specifically, judgment that comes from beyond the self (i.e., from God but also from others) and, thus, reinforces our creaturely limit. One could say that the moment of hesitation in which Adam does not return from conscience to stand naked before his Creator is when the free fall begins. "He has not recognized the grace of the Creator that shows itself precisely in that God calls Adam and does not let him flee. Instead, Adam sees this grace only as hate, as wrath, a wrath that inflames his own hate, his rebellion, his desire to get away from God. Adam keeps on falling."[116] The hiding sequence is the original claim that *I already know what you are going to say*. If only the human beings would return to the presence of the living God as the One who speaks to them, who exists at their limit and resists any attempt to be internalized as a mere object or as the mere figure of the Lawgiver, they could hear God's judgment and receive it as the grace that shows them their limit anew. But by remaining in the conscience, centered in the self even when standing before God, we serve as our own judges, feigning within ourselves the presence of the other-who-is-our-limit, thus evading any real "others" (beginning with God).

> Humankind knows, however, what it has lost in being *sicut deus*. . . . In conscience and in remorse one human being constantly seeks to imagine the presence, the reality, of another in his or her life. Humankind accuses itself, torments itself, and glorifies itself only in order to lie its way out of the dreadful loneliness of a solitude in which no voice echoes to its own.[117]

In Bonhoeffer's view, the church-community helps human beings bear their creaturely limit again by opening space for confession. To stand before an other, to confess one's sins rather than suffering in the knowledge of them and of their evil, and to hear the words of forgiveness from the other is not only a sign but God's grace itself.[118]

Though we have not yet come to the point of discussing the so-called orders of creation from Bonhoeffer's perspective, the fall sequence gives us a view of how even the clearest divine orders become corrupted. God speaks a word about the tree of knowledge to the first humans as the Creator speaking to creatures in the context of an ongoing relationship, through which those creatures come to know their Creator as their gracious Sustainer. Then the serpent suggests that the first humans can internalize that word as an object for their consideration and speculation rather than simply the word of their Creator, a person they know and love. In *Act and Being*, Bonhoeffer describes the vulnerability of the category of "revelation" to becoming just another way that the independent "I," *incurvatus in se*, can justify (or is it torture?) itself. *Yes, yes, we have the revelation of God*, crepuscular humans are tempted to say, *let me tell you what it says.* "In philosophical reflection, God is not an objective existent, but is only in the execution of that philosophizing. . . . Idealistic philosophical reflection implies the system in which God's own self resides."[119] In practice, idealist philosophy subordinates the living God to human conscience, to thought, and this word is no less true of its theological kin. And in the contingencies of history, this subordinating became the work of people who imagined themselves as white—indeed, became white in these very processes.

From our position in the middle of history, either the person has met Jesus and found in him their proper limit or they have not. "Existence has or has not been truly touched as a concrete, spiritual-embodied whole at that 'boundary' that is no longer located in or can be established by human beings."[120] Whatever happens to a person when they meet Jesus—when the *Heilsoffenbarung* finds them—we must not mistake it for the sanctification or restoration of a capacity to seek out knowledge of persons (particularly God) without the intimate involvement of those persons in an ethical-social situation of responsibility. As Bonhoeffer explains, "To say that human beings cannot place themselves into the truth is not the kind of self-evident proposition on the basis of which one must or can postulate a revelation capable of supplying truth. On the contrary, the untruth of human self-understanding is made clear only from within revelation and its truth, once it has taken place and has been believed."[121] Kant came up short, as the most hopeful candidate among the idealists, in his weak concept of the transcendent; because he situated revelation within the bounds of human reason, at least regulatively, he knew no real limits. "But all this is comprehensible only for the person who *is* placed into the truth, to whom, through the person of Christ, the other has become a true person. For those people in untruth, revelation remains something that exists, as a person does, a thing, something that 'there is.'"[122] If revelation has a kind of "being," it can only be that which is appropriate to persons—not that of a static, "haveable" object.

There is a contingency to speaking about revelation that always somehow relativizes a priori what I know or pronounce to be true.[123] Green is perhaps more direct than Bonhoeffer, which in this case helps land the point: "Whether a person will in fact remain 'in relation to' transcendence, and not assume that the I can understand itself from itself, is no theoretical question of epistemology but a decision of practical reason, i.e., of the ethical person."[124] Observing idealism's full-orbed intellectual fruits all around him, Bonhoeffer is painfully aware that "theology [can turn] revelation into something that exists," so he attempts to defend against and correct these excesses by limiting its practice to "where the living person of Christ is itself present and can destroy this existing thing or acknowledge it."[125]

The Upholding and Preserving Word of God

We should now consider God's words to humankind beginning with the immediate postfall context but with a weather eye on the eschatological horizon upon which the incarnate Word appears. God does not annihilate Adam, and neither does God deny Adam the word that upholds his existence in the face of nothingness; rather, God gives Adam a *new* word. "That humankind is *allowed* to live in this world and that it will not be deprived of the word of God, even though that word be the word of the God of wrath, the God who expels, who pronounces a curse—that is the *promise*."[126] One iteration of God's preserving activity materializes in Genesis 3:21 (i.e., God made garments for the first humans), where Bonhoeffer sees the starts of how "God's action accompanies humankind on its way."[127] God's new activity here provides a site for Bonhoeffer to directly address static, principial ways of systematizing creational order (like Althaus's) that objectify revelation, subjecting "it" to the omnicompetent "I." But, in this verse, we see the ordering work of God *within the destroyed world* as both an affirmation of that world and a demonstration of its limits: "God's action is now one that orders and restrains. It does not break the new laws that now apply to the earth and humankind after the fall; it participates in them. At the same time, however, by participating in them, it imposes on them restraint and order [*Ordnung*]; that is, it points to the wickedness, the fallen state, of those laws."[128] Such orders, though of God, belong fully within the fallen world (i.e., after Gen. 3:14–20) as *Erhaltungsordnungen* (orders of preservation)—and decidedly not in the original creation (e.g., in an imaginative construal of the command to "fill the earth" [Gen. 1:28]).

Any attempt to discern something like these orders as "eternal-creational" can only occur under twilight conditions, under which the commanded structures and their concrete forms must appear together, "confused" in the original sense of the word. (This is certainly the case in the systematizing theological work of folks like Althaus, and Bonhoeffer will say as much below.) From this point in the narrative arc, Bonhoeffer disallows thinking of these orders of our fallen world as having "any eternal character, for all are there only to uphold or preserve life . . . only until it finds its end—in Christ."[129] Prior to Jesus's incarnation, the orders (e.g., family, work, government, and church) stood together as divine mandates in the destroyed world with the joint purpose of commandeering patterns of human relating so that each might become a merciful reminder of our limit and so that in each we might be open to the gift of real others who simultaneously make us responsible and help us bear our limit. This is what "preservation" means in the fallen world, and any command or mandate endures only inasmuch as God speaks them to us today, graciously acting to pattern our lives so that we may be preserved in relationship with God on toward Christ and his kingdom.

In no way does the postlapsarian context diminish the God-givenness of these preserving words, but human beings living *sicut deus* and yet still before God—whose activity accompanies humankind on its way—often fail to see these penultimate orders in light of their ultimate goal. We labor to uncover the lawful patterns within the natural world, but even the most rigorous intellectual activity does not generate for us the word of God that upholds the world.

> Law and life that creates life are, as God's work, created out of nothing and exist only in the midst of nothingness, only in the freedom of God's word. If God withdraws the word from the work, it sinks back into nothingness. Thus neither the subjection of the course of the world to law nor the living nature of what has been created is to be identified with God's upholding activity; on the contrary, law and life are upheld only by the free word of God.[130]

Here Bonhoeffer counters those who either understand the Spirit to be working itself out in history or otherwise speculate about God's eternal-creational will based on their static object of "revelation." If nature itself did "hold" such revelation without being subject to the *Zwielicht* conditions of the fall, perhaps human beings could strive to discern how God has ordered things and receive their discoveries as truth—with the primary *Heilsoffenbarung* of Christ enabling the believer to do this searching from a sanctified vantage. But even in the full light of day, would the lawlike regularities or the perceptible nature of things themselves preserve anything in this world? Even the most pious humans, when laboring to unearth indubitable *knowledge of good and evil and of God*, are not upheld within their ethical-social limit by what they find; rather, in evading the living God who asks for simple obedience (and offers unconditional grace), in their quest for possession, for defying creatureliness, they slip deeper and deeper into the fall. "The community of faith knows that making general pronouncements makes sense only where Christ confirms it in each instance. . . . For only when Christ himself speaks these words *hic et nunc* are they really about God and about sin—that is about my sin, in a truly existential way."[131] Our new (daresay epistemological) nature is to deny our contingency and instead to continue from our own center, seeking to possess, assimilate, and imaginatively elaborate such divine commands within our own knowledge, rather than learning again through them (or being humbled again by them into) the limit of our creatureliness before the God who preserves and sustains us.

As he sharpens his arguments against idealism through his reading of the Genesis 2–3 account of *Creation and Fall*, Bonhoeffer offers a stark contrast to the "pseudo-Lutherans" who have indulged the "natural" *impulse after an unitous organic knowledge*. I have intentionally cribbed the emphasized wording here from Abraham Kuyper, who spoke optimistically when he said it. My point is to demonstrate, exactly here, how the world-viewing impulse drives us to improperly seize personal-ethical subjects as objects of our knowledge such that we try to know them in the "how" form without the accountability of any living "who." Althaus and company have been all-too-eager to spell out a comprehensive world-view by way of imaginatively filling out God's eternal-creational intentions for humankind (on a very thin biblical-theological basis, I might add). Cognition aims to close the system of knowledge, but, Bonhoeffer argues, "If this happens, the I has become lord of the world. For that reason, revelation stands against the system, for God is lord of the world, and the true system is but an eschatological possibility."[132] In terms more familiar to my project, the crepuscular world-viewing impulse pushes us to pursue closure in our system of knowledge.

PUTTING THE CRITICISM TO WORK

Bonhoeffer's involvement in the joint youth commissions of two ecumenical bodies during the early 1930s reveals something about how he operationalized these convictions for public-facing theology. And reviewing this material will further situate our understanding of his approach within its *Sitz im Leben*: conversations in and around the changing landscape of German social and political life. Bonhoeffer called Christians to hear the voice of the living God, to turn away from all particular historical forms idolized as "orders of creation," and to support German churches in their struggle. Against other public theologians, he argued that because "original creation" has no revealed content of its own, a theologian or leader can present something as "creational" only on the basis of their own authority, for example, as the product of a sanctified imagination working with some objectified "revelation." At a conference a few months prior to his "Creation and Sin" seminar, Bonhoeffer argued,

> A special danger lies in this argument [from orders of creation], . . . basically that everything can be justified on its basis. One need only portray something that exists as willed and created by God and then everything that exists is justified for eternity: the strife among the peoples of humanity, national struggle, war, class distinctions. . . . Nothing is easier than portraying and sanctioning that all this is intended by God simply because it exists.[133]

Importantly, the word of the church does not cut against or categorically deny that God issues commands; rather, that word can only be understood as God's commandment when it is also understood as gospel (i.e., as the word of the living Christ *hic et nunc*).[134] The underlying truth shining through here holds for any abstract theory of orders within God's original creation: only the crepuscular judgment of actual human beings stands between a "good" and a "bad" theory of such orders or between "good" and "bad" concrete forms of those orders.[135] Claims to indubitable (but contentious) grounds of knowledge can only mask the messiness of this reality, and to what end? In his historical context, Bonhoeffer could not rely on the goodwill of those human beings making the practical application in the way that contemporary evangelicals seem to be willing.

There is an explicit standard by which to discern whether a particular iteration of an "order of preservation" should be opposed in Bonhoeffer's view: openness to the living, biblical, historical Jesus. "*Every order*—be it the oldest and holiest—*can be broken*—and must be, when it is locked within itself, hardened, and when it no longer permits the proclamation of the revelation."[136] Here Christ revealed in the church-community before Scripture is made the standard of judgment for any theological system as well as its situation within the world. To be clear, we hear the word of God only when the living God speaks here and now, which happens not in every pulpit every Sunday as a function of the static pastoral office but here and there. Thus, among the first few lines of his 1937 classic *Discipleship*, Bonhoeffer says, "It is not ultimately important to us what this or that church leader wants. Rather, we want to know what Jesus wants."[137] And insofar as this standard continues to be addressed as a person, he will actively resist all attempts to assimilate him to one's own ideals, and he will resist in a way that broad "creational" or "divine" categories—as enabling of idealist-epistemological speculation—simply cannot. By the time he is working on his *Ethics* manuscript (in the early 1940s), Bonhoeffer shifts from "orders of preservation" language to "divine mandates," which he seems to think better resists the misconception of these relationships as concrete instances of supposedly eternal forms. His basic conceptuality remains: the living God speaks a word in history to humans, who are created in freedom-for-one-another and preserved not in general but toward Christ. Yet the call of the resurrected Christ and the life of discipleship displace these "penultimate" goods with the "ultimate" concern, namely, the restoration of the relation of basic trust (i.e., faith in communion) between humans and God.[138] As such, God's word arrives not as an echo from a lost beginning but as a theophany from out of the unconsummated future. This revelation is fit for an age that receives its significance not according to the moment of creation but in light of what is to come. So, rather than merely preserving human life in this world toward

Christ, divine *mandates* are those sites where the word of God emerges to orient human beings toward the kingdom come, toward the future, toward participation in the resurrected life, the body of Christ, by the power of the Spirit. The mandates' ultimacy is denied in view of this end.

In Bonhoeffer's view, Althaus and others were not wrong to receive *Ordnungen* as a feature of thick, Lutheran theology or to understand the Christian's engagement in their concrete, historical offices as an important aspect of creaturely life. Part of the rub between Bonhoeffer and world-viewing idealists like Althaus is how a sense of divine ordering could possibly relate to Christian engagement in concrete historical forms. For Bonhoeffer, the answer is eventually spelled out, at least partly, in terms of the mandates being not only for- and with-one-another, but also *over-against*-one-another; for example, the independence of the church from the state (in principle and concrete forms) gives it some critical distance. (His discussion of the mandates in *Ethics* does fill out the conceptual picture with some elements reminiscent of the sphere sovereignty framework we explored in chapter 5.[139]) When these limits go unrecognized, these social entities can collude together or (more likely) try to sublimate one another, trapping persons into relations of power that are closed to the scrutiny and intervention of Christ. So, in terms of his broader argument, Bonhoeffer is calling others to recognize the dubious nature of spending too much time speaking of Christian ethics in terms of timeless principles left up to us to apply to our cultural contexts, that is, too much time building a system we can live within without really expecting to hear Jesus's voice calling for us to follow him. More than principles, Christians must engage the actual human beings and the actual communities around them as real persons or "collective persons" that create in and for them a kind of responsibility—a duty to act. And in this situation, what is most important is to recognize how the mandates can function as God's words to us *hic et nunc* only to the extent that they order our lives toward the living Christ and his inaugurated-but-not-consummated kingdom. When a mandate fails to do this, in concreteness or principle, it must be cast into the fires—not as a destructive act, but as a matter of making the mandates pliable once again such that they can serve the one who speaks them as words of preservation.

The question of a failing mandate was imminent as the discriminatory Aryan paragraph began making its encroachments in the spring of 1933.[140] That summer, Bonhoeffer published his well-known essay, "The Church and the Jewish Question," which opens with the idea that racial discrimination is a matter of church concern, not least because it represents the state breaking into the church-community and ripping members out of Christ's existence today.[141] One lesson from this essay is his approach to the question of the church and the state as orders of preservation in light of the race question pressing into German life. The problems of the state were spilling into the church's space, where religious authorities should make the call on internal grounds as to who counts as members—and, particularly, who should be excluded from membership once baptized into the congregation. Bonhoeffer insists that the state is no order of creation but an order of preservation and that its relative value can only be known and maintained by a church that knows its own role in being with, for, and over-against the state.[142] The state does not have a standing, creational telos that is independent of the basic role it plays in preserving the world so that people may flourish and the church may go about its work.

Correlatively, Bonhoeffer does not see the church as having any standing vocation in terms of direct action against any state; rather, the church must continually serve as a check on the state's performance of its duties and care for the state's victims all the while. In doing the latter, the church discovers concrete sites at which it must hold the state responsible for its judgments and actions. All of this traces back to the question of what humans can possibly know about God's will from our place in the middle. What God wills for human governance in any detailed sense is not at all obvious, and even if we were to merely distill some basic civil needs for authoritative oversight, we would still not know what God would have us do relative to them for all of time. The relationship of the Christian to the state is always ambiguous because, while the state is bent on its own flourishing and expansion, the church seeks first the kingdom of God and, as such, fosters lives bent on following Jesus in all sectors. This reality pushes the disciple to pursue a more concrete ethics, centered in the person and teaching of the living, biblical, historical Jesus. It is clear that Bonhoeffer found this path and found it to be life-changing. Over-against the abstract ethics built upon an orders-of-creation basis, Bonhoeffer argues for a very different faith posture, offering his rebuke right at the source, namely, in a reading of Genesis 1–3 as supported by his understanding that "Christ as *Stellvertretung* is the revelation of God and the demonstration of God's freedom for humanity."[143]

Thus, we should not read Bonhoeffer's criticism as "against" whatever concrete pronouncements and frameworks Christians work out for life in this world. Rather, his approach requires that we be as honest as we can about them and how we know them and what they are for and that we hold them as humbly as we ought, knowing that we cannot appeal cheaply to God's will as the support for our particular positions—certainly not without fully embracing the sense that we are responsible for these formulations before God and will bear the grace of God's judgment for them. Given the kind of theology being pumped out by scholars like Althaus, maintaining distinctions between Christian piety and a creational ethics facilitated by a faulty reading of Luther's *theologia crucis* (in which Christian life remains hidden), it should be no surprise that many Christians would have had neither the skill nor the will to see issues of race and peoplehood as doctrinal problems or matters of faith. "Seeing society from the hidden perspective of Harlem helped Bonhoeffer to recognize white supremacy in Germany and to see it as a Christian problem that might demand Christian political action."[144] When Jesus is the source of your ethics, it is harder to grasp a firm basis to coerce others into compliance, harder to send the claims for responsibility upstream to a haveable basis for making such judgments. As Bonhoeffer continues to develop this concept as he moves out of his teaching in Berlin and into his underground work at Finkenwalde, where *Discipleship* becomes the curriculum, "Christ *pro nobis* takes on ethical implications as *Stellvertretung* becomes an imperative for Christian moral living in solidarity with suffering Jews. Concretely this means that Christians act on their Jewish neighbors' needs for justice and value them as they value their own."[145] But Bonhoeffer is not excited about the possibility of deriving a new, abstract, lofty-ideal ethic from Jesus's teachings and then trying to live it out on our own steam. Many distinctives he becomes known for in his later works begin with his rejection of the natural-theological basis for moral knowledge, and they flow from a mode of knowing that is appropriate to creatures in relationship with the living, biblical, historical Jesus—who exists today as church-community and, in another sense, appears to those who have eyes to see in the hungry, naked, imprisoned of Matthew 25.

Thinking of the role of the church, which Bonhoeffer had hoped could stand together in resistance to the creeping ethnonationalism of his time, he argued that as the church makes pronouncements in the name of God, "it is possible therewith to take the name of God in vain, and that the church is in error and is sinful"; nevertheless, as persons and groups of persons make the church a responsible agent in time and space, it can (and indeed must) own its judgments and its actions, living "in faith in the word of the forgiveness of sins that holds true for the church as well."[146] This way of approaching cultural engagement both restores epistemological humility—for there is really no absolute ground for knowledge except that God lives and speaks—and frees us to pronounce and act concretely in our contingent positions. Sure, we strive together to discern God's will, and doubtless we intend to be-for-God with our very lives, but the implication that by the work of Christ we are absolved of any responsibility for what we do in this name—and that this is grace—sets us up to evade Christ and to try shrugging off criticism as part of "the cost of discipleship" (ever reading Matthew 5:10 in our favor). For Bonhoeffer, we make concrete judgments in our historical moments based on our communal reading of Scripture and in openness before the living Word, but in full responsibility for those claims and how their concrete impacts in the lives of our actual neighbors without beckoning God's will *ex machina* to substantiate our claims. We are bold, we stand before the living God, and we alone bear the blame for the moral overreach to which humans *sicut deus* are prone.

ON MARRIAGE AS A MANDATE

Over his all-too-brief career, Bonhoeffer shifts his conceptuality from "orders of creation" to "orders of preservation" to "divine mandates," all while trying to nurture a generation of Christians ready to take free, responsible action within a reality framed by the living, biblical, historical Jesus. Judging from student notes on his lecture about the creation of the second human being in the "Creation and Sin" seminar, he ruled out identifying even "marriage" as an order within creation. More significant about the first humans' relationship is its status as a prototype for human sociality on analogy with God's relationship to us.[147] Whatever can be said of the fundamental human sociality on display in the relationship between the first humans, that relationship is a context of love in which each free human being is held within the world, preserved in their life within the limit set for them as creatures. As the archetype of all relationships with human others, the structure of the first relationship can be distilled only in this way. And the fulfillment of this "type" of human relation is the social relation between Christ and the church, such that marriage in the male-plus-female sense cannot be regarded as an ideal to be realized but rather as a generative social dynamic across difference to be fulfilled in a distinct form (i.e., in the bonds of Christ and church body).

When Bonhoeffer speaks of the new thing that happens in the first two human beings hiding from each other, he talks about human sexuality as "a *passionate hatred* of any limit."[148] In a life without limits, human beings fail to recognize the other as another "I" to whom I relate as a "You," and instead tend to treat others as objects orbiting around the only "I" that I recognize (i.e., myself, the subject) as the center. Self-seeking sexual desire is that fallen trait that savages the limit and lusts after others as objects of the self's ends rather than loving others as creatures of God. "The protest that appeals to the natural character of sexuality is unaware of the highly ambivalent character of every so-called 'natural' aspect of the world. The way in which sexuality is sanctified is by being restrained by shame, that is, by being veiled, and by the calling of the community of marriage, which is under this restraint, to be in church."[149] I will return to this last notion below, but first I want to note there is something deeply Augustinian about this argument (which makes sense given Bonhoeffer's indebtedness to Martin Luther, an erstwhile Augustinian monk). Sexuality, not least when circumscribed by the "natural" binary of sexes, is a site at which humans seek their own completion or sense of inner unity by way of disordered love—something Augustine himself found true in his earlier life. And as such, appeals to natural sexuality in daily life and in public theology both provide and exact a wage from the soul much like W. E. B. Du Bois identified with whiteness in chapter 1. The romance and presumed virtue of innocent sexuality (i.e., the moral line along which "straight" refers simply to heterosexuals) benefit those who cognitively assent to the norms even when their concrete (or imagined) relationships with other persons are less than ideal.[150] If God were merely interested in our *preservation* in view of lonesome and death-dealing human life *sicut deus*, then marriage might take on a certain cast.

But Bonhoeffer works evangelistically to free us *and the mandates under which we live* to serve the living God, partly by declaring those mandates penultimate to something new—not referring to the antecedent that is pristine creation (i.e., the lost beginning) or post hoc to the fall. He contests the cultural mandate as such, opposing the notion that God wills us to bring "culture" into alignment with biblical code rather than guiding us in Christ to see one another more truthfully, reinterpreting that code again and again according to the Spirit by which it is fulfilled in a life of loving God and one another. What is required after the fall, and particularly in following Jesus, is not what was required in the garden in any detailed sense; and it is not merely living in the destroyed world but still before God as in the generations between Eden and Christmas. What we call by the name "marriage" is no order of creation, but a divine mandate that receives its limited blessing in light of the ultimate kingdom purposes to which it is merely penultimate. More than the direction incumbent on all biological life—to be fruitful and multiply—surely this penultimate status in light of the inaugurated fourth act of human history (i.e., the eschaton) determines marriage's most important functions. We must not deal with the penultimate forms too gravely in their own right, for these forms of life are freed for Christian "use" by Jesus, and only in the sense that the weak come to embody the Christ of God.

To be sure, Bonhoeffer's more detailed expositions of marriage assume not only a gender binary but also complementarian gender roles; in fact, before he stopped participating in the process of drafting the Bethel Confession, he did not reject naming the sexes among the orders.[151] But inasmuch as marriage preserves the lives of two people in a way that looks forward to life in the consummated kingdom of God, it fulfills the divine order only when it structures human lives to "be-for-each-other," with their mutual love as that which helps them bear their creaturely limit.

> The community of husband and wife is a community of love that is accepted as given by God and that glorifies and worships God as the Creator. It is therefore the church in its original form. And because it is the church, it is a community

A Theological Criticism of the Modern Preoccupation with Epistemology 279

bound with an eternal bond. Such statements for us do not mean the glorification of marriage as we know it; instead they point out that at any rate for us the bond between husband and wife does not partake of this unambiguous reality, and that the most questionable of all the church's official functions may be precisely its role in officiating at marriage.[152]

Not all relationships defined as "marriage" here below serve its preserving function, and this prognosis makes the real-life blessing churches give to any marriages a precarious one. The church's blessing of a particular marriage is predicated on the ongoing participation of the two persons wedded together in the sociality called "church," which is itself the utmost order of preservation. The eschatological fulfillment of marriage in the New Testament involves prioritizing singleness, precisely because of the sociality it nurtures.

The sense that we can wrap our minds around all that is required—and even translate it into a language that would benefit other people apart from a relationship with the living God—is one problem with assuming that all humans have incumbent upon them an unchanging "mandate" (or four or seven). With any given concrete instantiation of a supposedly general or universal mandate, we must ask whether "Christ himself speaks these words *hic et nunc.*" In this sense, one might also wonder if it would be possible to imagine an interpretation of marriage that thinks it better for same-sex couples to marry than for their participation, baptism, and membership in the church (Christ existing as church-community today) to be conditioned upon their celibacy (cf. 1 Cor. 7). Though she does not reference Bonhoeffer's view of the mandates, Karen Keen has argued that an ongoing deliberative process is required to faithfully apply them (including perceived creational ordinances).[153] She is especially interested in biblical models for expanding mandates to *enhance* the precedent's objective "by expressing *greater* care for the people involved."[154] And even the reader who ultimately disagrees with her conclusions here or there must wrestle honestly with her biblical reasoning and interpretation around this point. In any case, life with God in Christ is not about humans grasping and fulfilling God's lawlike will as uncovered and organized into a comprehensive (abstract) life-system, but about humans living as creatures before the person of God, within their creaturely limit.

I should also address Marsh's suggestion that Bonhoeffer may have harbored and suppressed sexual desire for Eberhard Bethge, his former student and best friend ever after.[155] Bonhoeffer's numerous letters to Bethge reveal a very high degree of nonsexual intimacy that many in the modern West would think romantic, even if platonic. In fact, within some of these letters and poems, as Marsh highlights, Bonhoeffer extols the virtues and fecundity of friendship in contrast to the duties of marriage under the constraint of the curse and the law.[156] And, in his last will and testament, Bonhoeffer left nearly all his worldly possessions to Bethge—with the allowance that Bonhoeffer's young fiancée, Maria Wedemeyer, could select a token to have "as a remembrance."[157] For my part, I think it more likely that we see reflected in Bonhoeffer's correspondence the complexities of his actual relationships in terms that reflect the self-transcending limit of specific persons. "Perhaps you are surprised at such a personal letter," Bonhoeffer wrote to Bethge in the summer of 1944. "But when I feel like saying such things sometimes, who else should I say them to? Perhaps the time will come when I can speak to Maria this way, too; I do very much hope so. But I cannot put that burden on her yet."[158] There is no reason to think of sexual desire as an element in his friendship with Bethge, even if their intimacy ranks them among the deepest of friends. In fact, the way this correspondence brings to light his complicated feelings about marriage and friendship, Wedemeyer and Bethge, might also help us understand why officiating at marriage is "the most questionable of all the church's official functions." The mandate and its structure (however one may conceive of it) matter less than the actual lives being joined together, the fruit of the relationship, the way life together preserves the couple toward Christ. There simply is no guarantee biblical or otherwise that it is good for any given man and woman—however free they may be in their choice of one another—to get married.

BRIDGE

Within the framework of life *sicut deus*, divine words are prone to human assimilation into sacred and unassailable mental constructs, which in turn function to internalize faceless other human beings and order their lives without appropriately encountering each and every concrete other as one who embodies the limit to my pretensions of power. Losing sight of the orders' ultimate goal—to preserve us toward Christ and within the limit of our creatureliness—we develop affection for the ordering word itself, particularly conceived as governing laws and principles. The orders take on rather uncharacteristic destructive power when we take our knowledge of God's preserving word to be stable enough itself in time and space to hold us and others within this world. Inspired by a seemingly complete view of the world reconstructed in this knowledge, the Christian sets out to fully embrace within (or, we might add, to comprehensively impress upon) the world those forms deemed eternal structures of God's design. Put differently, when understood as ultimate in form and eternal in force, these life-structures as conceived by crepuscular theorists can also become to us objects of desire and defense in their own right, and as such receive our worship and service as *idols*. Even the word of

God delivered to Israel in the Law functions within the frame established by this conversation.

Since Adam's fall God sent the divine *word* to sinful humanity, in order to seek and *accept* us. This is why we have received God's word, to reconcile our lost humanity with God. God's word came as promise and as law. For our sake God's word became weak and lowly. But human beings rejected this word, refusing to be accepted by God. They offered sacrifices; they performed good works which God was supposed to accept in their stead, thereby letting them go free.[159]

The chief problem plaguing God's people is not unrighteousness owing to their inability to fulfill the Law (as revealed by its so-called elenctic purpose in Calvinist theology), but the intermittence of their openness to the law's Lord while enslaved to its letters. We are drawn ever and again to theology's system instead of the living God whose self-revelation amid the destroyed world it remembers and organizes—we turn out to love our thoughts more than God.

Such is the situation within the world that Jesus enters as the Word of God who lives and breathes and thus resists, as *Gegenlogos*, fallen human attempts to assimilate him into their sure knowledge of good and evil. Christian discipleship is not pure reason grasping timeless metaphysical essences and applying them, to the best of one's practical-reasoning ability, to their concrete lives—sometimes hitting, sometimes missing, ever forgiven. Epistemology is the wrong category altogether for searching out the commands of the living God, who took on flesh in Christ to exhibit the sociality entailed by God's freedom, God's sovereignty. Bonhoeffer resists the objectification of God in any sense, including the frequent appeal of some evangelicals to Scripture's verbal inspiration. Scripture as an epistemological resource in the way that modern philosophy has taught us to hold it must be sacrificed to God in faith that it will be given to us, as a way of knowing, as the (sub)text of a conversation between God and humankind. "We cannot speak of God as of something there for the finding. On the contrary, God alone can speak of God."[160] Thus, social sensibilities better prepare humans-as-creatures to meet God *as* our Creator who issues words over our lives meant to order them so that our relationship can continue, with repentance (on our part) and grace (on God's) as a continuous, relationship-preserving dynamic.

NOTES

1. See correspondence in Dietrich Bonhoeffer, *Ecumenical, Academic, and Pastoral Work, 1931–1932*, English ed., Dietrich Bonhoeffer Works (Minneapolis:

Fortress Press, 2012), series hereafter cited as DBWE, 11:44–45; and *Berlin: 1932–1933*, DBWE (Minneapolis: Fortress Press, 2009), 12:73.

2. Charles Marsh, *A Strange Glory: A Life of Dietrich Bonhoeffer* (2014; repr., New York: Vintage Books, 2015), 142.

3. Marsh, 191.

4. Robert P. Ericksen, *Theologians under Hitler: Gerhard Kittel, Paul Althaus, and Emanuel Hirsch* (New Haven, CT: Yale University Press, 1985), 79–81 and 116.

5. Ericksen, 116.

6. For a short treatment of "pseudo-Lutheranism," as Bonhoeffer termed it, see the Dietrich Bonhoeffer Works (German ed.) editor's afterword translated in Dietrich Bonhoeffer, *Ethics*, DBWE (Minneapolis: Fortress Press, 2005), 6:415–19. For a glimpse of Althaus's use of Lutheran tradition to make a case for natural orders as explained below, see his *Der Geist der lutherischen Ethik im Augsburgischen Bekenntnis*, 1930.

7. Ericksen, 99. Cf. Matthew D. Kirkpatrick, *Attacks on Christendom in a World Come of Age: Kierkegaard, Bonhoeffer, and the Question of "Religionless Christianity"* (Eugene, OR: Pickwick Publications, 2011), 51.

8. Paul Althaus, *Theologie der Ordnungen*, 1934, quoted in Ericksen, 100. All translations of Althaus's work are by Ericksen, unless otherwise noted.

9. Ericksen, 100.

10. Ericksen, 101.

11. Ericksen, 101.

12. Paul R. Hinlicky, *Beloved Community: Beloved Community after Christendom* (Grand Rapids: Eerdmans, 2015), 792–93.

13. Ericksen, 102.

14. Paul Althaus quoted in Kirkpatrick, 49.

15. Paul Althaus, *Völker vor und nach Christus*, 1937, quoted in Ericksen, 103.

16. Paul Althaus, *Kirche und Volkstum*, 1928, quoted in Ericksen, 85.

17. Paul Althaus, *Kirche und Staat nach lutherische Lehre*, 1935, quoted in Ericksen, 86.

18. Ericksen, 106–7.

19. Ericksen, 88.

20. *Ansbacher Ratschlag* quoted in Ericksen, 87.

21. *Ansbacher Ratschlag* quoted in Ericksen, 87.

22. Ericksen, 100; cf. 89f.

23. Ericksen, 90–92. Interestingly, the *Deutsche Christen* argument against him was grounded in experiential-presuppositionalist terms—that is, you have to experience it to believe it—which extended to the sense that German national history itself "becomes *Heilsgeschichte* for those who are able to see it as such" (93).

24. Kirkpatrick, 62.

25. As Kirkpatrick writes, "Althaus never affirmed a nationalism that considered one *Volk* as necessarily better than another. In this way, Althaus was Lutheran but not Hegelian" (59).

26. Reggie L. Williams, *Bonhoeffer's Black Jesus: Harlem Renaissance Theology and an Ethic of Resistance* (Waco, TX: Baylor University Press, 2014), 9.

27. Dietrich Bonhoeffer, *Barcelona, Berlin, New York: 1928–1931*, DBWE (Minneapolis, MN: Fortress Press, 2008), 10:373.
28. DBWE 10:343.
29. Williams, 11.
30. Dietrich Bonhoeffer quoted in Marsh, 103.
31. Williams, 28.
32. Cf. Williams, 26–33.
33. DBWE 11:95
34. Williams, 61.
35. Williams, 62.
36. Williams, 41. Williams also helpfully details and distinguishes between the shape white imperialism took in the United States versus Germany, especially in a post-World War I world (ch. 2).
37. Williams 26.
38. Williams, 78.
39. Williams, 99–101.
40. Williams 108–9.
41. Cf. Williams, 122–24.
42. Williams, 79.
43. Dietrich Bonhoeffer, *London: 1933–1935*, DBWE (Minneapolis: Fortress Press, 2007), 13:284–85.
44. This popular way of referring to Bonhoeffer's transformation comes from a letter he wrote in the spring of 1944, as he reflected (in part) on the consistency and change in his thinking over time (*Letters and Papers from Prison*, DBWE [Minneapolis: Fortress Press, 2009], 8:358).
45. Dietrich Bonhoeffer, *Theological Education at Finkenwalde: 1935–1937*, DBWE (Minneapolis: Fortress Press, 2013), 14:134–35; cf. 112–13.
46. Note the slight change in title from the course to the book, which seemed necessary because Emmanuel Hirsch had recently (1931) published a book by the title *Creation and Sin*; see the editor's forward in Dietrich Bonhoeffer, *Creation and Fall*, DBWE (Minneapolis: Fortress Press, 1997), 3:1–2. Hirsch wrote his dissertation on the idealist philosopher Johann Gottlieb Fichte, and his reading of history and of human knowledge/consciousness bears idealist marks. He supported the Nazi project from the start, increasingly becoming something of a public theologian for the party (Ericksen, 129ff.).
47. For these lectures, I have drawn from two different reconstructions published as follows: Dietrich Bonhoeffer, *Christ the Center*, trans. Edwin H. Robertson (New York: HarperCollins Publishers, 1978), hereafter *CC*; and DBWE 12:299–360.
48. DBWE 12:300.
49. Bonhoeffer, *CC*, 27.
50. Bonhoeffer, *CC*, 27.
51. Dietrich Bonhoeffer, *Act and Being Transcendental Philosophy and Ontology in Systematic Theology*, DBWE (Minneapolis: Fortress Press, 1996), 2:130.
52. DBWE 12:302.
53. DBWE 12:302.

54. DBWE 12:302.

55. DBWE 12:307. "What the [human] logos does under attack from the other Logos represents . . . a great insight into its power of self-negation, for self-negation signified the self-affirmation of the logos" (302). G. W. F. Hegel killed the *Gegenlogos* and assimilated what he took to be its function into a depersonalized philosophical system as the principle by which reason advances in human history. In other words, the threat of self-negation manifest in Christ is drawn into the very logic of human philosophizing.

56. DBWE 12:302.

57. Bonhoeffer, *CC*, 31.

58. Bonhoeffer, *CC*, 31.

59. DBWE 12:303. Bonhoeffer regularly uses this phrase, which leans on Martin Luther's concept of *homo incurvatus in se* (a deeply Augustinian insight into Romans). Cf. Bonhoeffer, *CC*, 31; and DBWE 3:165n[76].

60. Dietrich Bonhoeffer, *Sanctorum Communio: A Theology Study of the Sociology of the Church*, DBWE (Minneapolis: Fortress Press, 1998), 1:41ff.

61. DBWE 12:304–305.

62. DBWE 12:304.

63. Clifford J. Green, *Bonhoeffer: A Theology of Sociality*, Rev. ed. (Grand Rapids: Eerdmans, 1999), 56. At Larry Rasmussen's suggestion, I have shifted my own conceptualization of Bonhoeffer's theology from Green's "a theology of sociality" to "a theology of *relationality*" to expand the sustaining basis of human identity to include nonhuman creation.

64. Bonhoeffer, *CC*, 31–32; cf. 36.

65. DBWE 3:28.

66. DBWE 3:26.

67. DBWE 3:27. Cf. DBWE 2:33; cf. 142–44.

68. Green, 79–80. For the quotation about "his own, violated, 'interpreted' world," see DBWE 10:406.

69. DBWE 3:28–29.

70. DBWE 2:102.

71. DBWE 2:102.

72. Nowhere is this clearer than in the opening chapter of Bonhoeffer's *Life Together*, DBWE 5 (Minneapolis: Fortress Press, 1996).

73. DBWE 2:132.

74. DBWE 3:104.

75. DBWE 3:104n[5].

76. DBWE 3:104.

77. DBWE 3:83.

78. DBWE 3:62.

79. DBWE 3:62.

80. DBWE 3:60–61.

81. Mouw characterizes Karl Barth's view of the *imago dei* as "reading more recent philosophical notions into the text with his use of the Buberian 'I-Thou' construction" (Richard J. Mouw, "The *Imago Dei* and Philosophical Anthropology,"

Christian Scholar's Review 41, no. 3 [Spring 2012]: 256). Watch Bonhoeffer avoid this same accusation by appealing to the person of Jesus as revealed in Scripture.
82. DBWE 2:81–91. Cf. Kirkpatrick, 99.
83. DBWE 3:63.
84. DBWE 3:63.
85. DBWE 3:64–65. Notice how the shift to relational terms also repudiates Kuyper's speculation about the original priority of individual, "concreate theology" in the *imago dei* (cf. chapter 1).
86. DBWE 3:64.
87. DBWE 3:62–63. Cf. Bonhoeffer's conversation about "nothingness" as establishing the complete freedom of God in creating (32–34).
88. DBWE 3:83.
89. DBWE 3:85–87.
90. In the background is Hegel's criticism of Immanuel Kant's metaphysics, which plays heavily on the concept of *Grenzen* (typically translated as "boundaries," referring to noumena) vis-à-vis *Schranken* (typically translated as "limits," as in the limits of reason). See Kant's discussion in *Prolegomena to Any Future Metaphysics*, 2nd ed., trans. James W. Ellington (Indianapolis: Hackett Publishing Company, 2001), 88ff. Compare with Hegel, who speaks of the knowledge of God as, "more precisely, . . . an *elevation to God*" in his *Lectures on the Philosophy of Religion: The Lectures of 1827*, one vol. ed., ed. Peter C. Hodgson (Berkeley: University of California Press, 1988), 162ff. Against this backdrop, Bonhoeffer's insistence on a personal-relational knowledge of God—the possibility of a living God actively interacting with humankind, as presenting a *Grenze*—is a shock to the philosophical system. What Bonhoeffer is doing is strictly theological in defiance of the expectation that one should operate primarily within epistemological categories.
91. DBWE 3:86; see editor's note 17 on this page about Bonhoeffer's criticism of Hegel on this point.
92. DBWE 3:99.
93. DBWE 3:98.
94. DBWE 3:99.
95. DBWE 1:40.
96. DBWE 1:45.
97. See Bonhoeffer's conversation about the mystery of beloved persons close to us in his 1934 Trinity Sunday sermon in DBWE 13:361–62. Cf. Green, 32; DBWE 1:41ff.
98. DBWE 1:45.
99. DBWE 1:48.
100. I acknowledge that, at times, I may be deploying this distinction a bit differently than Bonhoeffer, particularly by referring to the German words *Grenze* and *Schranke*. My intention is to demonstrate something of the influence of Kant's thinking.
101. DBWE 1:48.
102. DBWE 1:45.
103. René Descartes, *Meditations on First Philosophy*, 1641, trans. by Donald A. Cress, 3rd ed. (Indianapolis: Hackett Publishing Company, 1993), AT 7:58.

104. DBWE 3:106.
105. DBWE 3:108.
106. DBWE 3:108–9. This concern for "reality" is a recurrent theme in his later works, as in DBWE 6:53–57.
107. DBWE 3:109; cf. 106–7. Bonhoeffer routinely uses the name "Adam" as representative of the first human pair and as prototypical of humankind, after Paul's usage (e.g., Rom. 5:12ff.).
108. DBWE 3:113.
109. DBWE 3:87–88.
110. DBWE 3:113.
111. DBWE 3:115.
112. DBWE 3:116–17.
113. DBWE 3:120.
114. DBWE 3:116.
115. DBWE 3:128. Cf. DBWE 2:136ff.
116. DBWE 3:130.
117. DBWE 3:142.
118. DBWE 5:108ff.
119. DBWE 2:50.
120. DBWE 2:82.
121. DBWE 2:81; cf. 80.
122. DBWE 2:115–16.
123. DBWE 2:124.
124. Green, 82.
125. DBWE 2:131.
126. DBWE 3:132.
127. DBWE 3:139.
128. DBWE 3:139.
129. DBWE 3:139–40.
130. DBWE 3:58–59; cf. 45–47.
131. DBWE 2:131.
132. DBWE 2:94.
133. DBWE 11:363.
134. DBWE 11:359.
135. Cf. Kirkpatrick, 69.
136. DBWE 11:364.
137. Dietrich Bonhoeffer, *Discipleship*, DBWE (Minneapolis: Fortress Press, 2001), 4:393.
138. See how Bonhoeffer develops the concepts of "ultimate" and "penultimate" things in *Ethics*, 146ff. As Rachel Muers argues, "To recognize the world as penultimate is to be prepared, not merely to seek to preserve the order of the world as it is given, but to look for a 'better future' of *this* world" (*Keeping God's Silence: Towards a Theological Ethics of Communication* [Malden, MA: Blackwell Publishing, 2004)], 88).

139. For example, Bonhoeffer claims that concrete instances of the divine mandates only communicate God's commandment in Jesus in "their being with-one-another (*Miteinander*), for-one-another (*Füreinander*), and over-against-one-another (*Gegeneinander*)" (DBWE 6:393). Not one of them is self-sufficient in any person's life in the destroyed world, nor is any one capable of subsuming all the others; in fact, each one (as a kind of "collective person") exists as a decisive limit for the other, staking out social territory for its own concern and defending itself against the encroaching strictures of the others.

140. Cf. Williams, 120–24.
141. DBWE 12:362.
142. DBWE 12:363–65.
143. Williams, 125.
144. Williams, 111.
145. Williams, 126.
146. DBWE 11:361.
147. DBWE 3:95n[5].
148. DBWE 3:123; cf. 99.
149. DBWE 3:125–26.

150. The leading line of this sentence is taken from the title of Geoffrey Rees's fascinating reading of Augustine in light of twenty-first-century conversations around sexuality in *The Romance of Innocent Sexuality* (Eugene, OR: Cascade Books, 2011).

151. See, for instance, his sermon (written from prison) for the wedding of his niece Renate and his beloved student Eberhard Bethge in DBWE 8:82–87. On the Bethel Confession, see DBWE 12:388.

152. DBWE 3:100–101.

153. Karen R. Keen, *Scripture, Ethics, and the Possibility of Same Sex Relationships* (Grand Rapids: Eerdmans, 2018), chs. 5–6.

154. Keen, 61.
155. Marsh, 384–85.
156. Marsh, 362–64.
157. DBWE 8:193.
158. DBWE 8:486.
159. DBWE 4:214.
160. DBWE 2:92.

Coda

The theological moves I have offered as prospects along the way, anticipating Dietrich Bonhoeffer's contribution to this moment in the project, together push us not only to think, but to hold and practice Christian identity in a fundamentally different way. Such an identity is no graspable, possessable thing, nor is it a quality within the individual person so much as a reality that arises again and again in the course of our restored life *coram deo*. I have heard some scholars constrain to "the early Bonhoeffer" this idea of the self or personal "identity" that rises in moments of social-ethical encounter and falls away again; for my part, I see value in maintaining that whoever we are, as persons in our very existence, is inextricably bound up in our relationships with others—God foremost among them. Our hope is not built upon a static, haveable system that helps us feel secure in our grasp of the world or our place in it, that gives us a sensible basis for political action and social engagement. Rather, assurance comes to us amid a living, growing relationship with God in Christ, in the grace that preserves that relationship when we own our judgments and actions, when we seek repentance and forgiveness. Looking not at grand-vision politics, this discovery drives us more proximately into local ways of relating, holding each other accountable, advocating for one another's needs, and using whatever power our status at the higher degrees of collectivity affords us for the sake of those who make us responsible. In what space remains, I will engage Bonhoeffer's ideas with a view to how his thick way of being evangelical, if we should call him that, challenges the world-viewing swagger on display in my major case studies with a dramatically different methodology.

Key to Bonhoeffer's clarity about what was going on in Germany—from a much earlier time than many of his contemporaries—were the Jesus he met in the Harlem and the emerging ecumenical and transnational relationships he developed. Put more directly, his actual relationships in history not only made him responsible but *made him who he was*. Bonhoeffer started his reflecting about the meaning of Christian faithfulness in a fallen and falling world well before Ockenga got about the work of organizing the evangelicals at the national level, but he encountered Black voices amid the Harlem Renaissance as well as committed Christians of other stripes and made a very different series of turns. So, Bonhoeffer is interesting not only because he inhabited a different approach to faith, not only because he criticized the general "orders" framework, but also because as he made his case public and argued specifically about identifying with the oppressed as identification with and like Christ. And he does so after listening deeply to Black American Christians. This empathy pushed him in different directions, and his letters reveal that he knew he sounded a bit fanatical. But he was concerned less with the overt rationality of his approach than fidelity to the living, Black Jesus he met. Precisely because he escaped the world-viewing impulse, Bonhoeffer was able to resist Nazism. His case encourages us, however we may be identified relative to religion and church, to renounce our false world-view security and to hear the word of God in Christ calling us to discover others and ourselves in encounters powered by God's gift of faith.

CONCLUSIONS ABOUT WORLD-VIEW SECURITY IN LIGHT OF BONHOEFFER

First, the world-viewing impulse fuels our confidence in what we can grasp, the thin concept of "the biblical world-view," as the stuff of a haveable identity. It is supposedly who we are and how we live and move within this biblical world, and while we may acknowledge that we have some growing to do in our fidelity to that view, we can be identified as those who are trying to live what we believe. But the basis of this identity is a static object—supposed revelation that we read to be on our side and in our corner—such that God can be understood as stirring us to proceed with our best intentions because there is grace for those who try to do God's will. To engage in "biblical worldviewing" has meant applying God's will "as I know it" to life in the world we have, each thinker expecting that whatever they come up with is logical and coherent vis-à-vis the Bible. At a conference in Geneva, Bonhoeffer named the problem like this, "We prefer our own thoughts to those of the Bible. We no longer read the Bible seriously. We read it no longer against ourselves but only for ourselves."[1] For Kuyper, Ockenga, and Mouw, the world-viewing impulse is a fixture in human nature, and born-again Christians possess a renewed inner capacity to grasp the basic outline of how God wants human life to be structured and to exercise a more expansive, sanctified imagination.

I submit that world-viewing does not flow from the reversal of our cognitive rebellion; rather, it is the cognitive structure of that very rebellion once we have abandoned our limit as creatures within the created world. Here, epistemology is the foundational question, which each of my case studies resolves with his take on the doctrine of revelation. One piece of this is, of course, the false closure of a person or group's identity in terms of something noetic as if a supposedly infused epistemological power told us anything meaningful or reliable about who people are. Bonhoeffer would remind us that epistemology cannot actually do what we need it to do and moving from there to a theology of relationality requires μετάβασις εἰς ἄλλο γένος (changing to a different category). The basis of a Christian identity can only be ongoing communion in that social body in which Christ exists today, such that the solid ground we seek is not haveable, possessable by us. Christian identity as understood in terms of "who"—that is, identity that observes our creaturely limit—errs on the side of nonpossession and is integrated only in its identification with others, often at significant cost to self, whatever the guilt that follows, always at risk of coming apart if judged by visible standards (but never undone in view of Christ's hidden holding of all things together). Only in the context of such relationships is anything really "known" in the sense that they become familiar not possessed over against others, and a great deal must be, in fact, subjected to "unknowing." When Bonhoeffer speaks of an Archimedean point in letters from prison, he points to the resurrection of Jesus—rather weak ground by modern standards, but really only weak in the same way that Jesus's identity and authority as Messiah were incognito in his incarnation (cf. Phil. 2).[2]

In its best and most honest use, the world-view concept is a heuristic device without a singular cognitive-intuitive structure as its referent, let alone a claim to comprehensively reflect God's own (mode of) self-revelation. Articulating our most cherished principles and the stories we live by, we may seize the world-view concept for confidence that we can logically and comprehensively organize all our thoughts and the rest of life, and even communicate them to others. We may imagine that we view the whole world. Fathoming the perspectives of others, especially very different others, we might organize their views into a grid like our own. But the philosophical theory that we and others live and move and have our being primarily within these world-views is manifestly false and, I have argued, ultimately unhelpful. Hypothetical structures like "world-view" only help us insofar as they lend insight into the phenomena they attempt to describe, but they mislead when reified into ideals or demands with divine gravitas and when used self-descriptively for exclusive and self-serving ends. None of this is to deny that thoughts shape our interpretations of and actions in the world; in fact, that much is all the clearer after our case studies. What I am saying is: our thoughts do not shape us in the way world-view theory trains us to think they do. I am not hopeful about improving world-view theory or getting the underlying theology just right; in fact, I believe those who follow Jesus must abandon it and begin to repent from our false world-view security.

Second, the world-view concept pushes us to organize and externalize the details of our inner life, such that a number of convictions generated from non-Christian grounds fly under the radar of Christological scrutiny—not ideally but descriptively. When the basis of Christian identity is seen as a haveable, creational world-view, the omnicompetent theorist locates whatever they take to be the fundaments of biblical world-viewing within the creational order that all should use as the lens for understanding the Jesus we encounter in the gospels. This Jesus, like the theorist, is merely working to restore creational order. But regarding the *Schöpfungsordnungen*, Bonhoeffer takes a concept that had become not only static but also ossified in the worldly realm, apart from the active scrutiny and rule of Christ, and he transfigures it so as to exceed the orders as "under" Christ and, thus, dynamic and actively submissive to the ultimate reality emanating from the future rather than eternal, formulable, and possessable fixtures of a lost beginning. By concretizing the focus on the contemporaneity of Jesus in the church-community and not a vaguely biblical God-concept, it is harder to project whatever law we have onto Christ. Bonhoeffer is not so naive as to think that one could not instrumentalize the work of Christ to continue imagining the Christian's place in a world replete with God-ordained spheres. This is where posture starts to matter because what we need is not merely a principle of Christ's sovereignty but a dynamic sense of Christ's living reign and presence in the community as revelation.

The human problem vis-à-vis God's will is not merely about noetic access to, and the desire to obey, God's will; it also emerges from human beings who imaginatively (even if intended in piety) fill out *God's* will and live within their most certain knowledge of that static will rather than receiving the living God's word as a creaturely limit. It is not about the orders, per se, but about the ultimacy that we ascribe to particular historical forms, and this in a way that stands removed from God's salvifically oriented realm. We are to have relationships of mutual service and obligation under headings like marriage and economy, but any forms are penultimate; if they are to be useful in view of the ultimate, they must share in the aim of fostering and abetting God's inbreaking reign in contradistinction to any Christian attempt to be-for-God primarily by obedience to a possessable set of laws called "divine." In view of God's self-revelation in Christ, the world-viewing impulse can be checked by the awareness that God has broken into that world-view not to give us proper grounds for confidence in our knowledge of good and evil but to restore to us the personal knowledge of God, of the world as God's, and ourselves as graciously limited creatures within it. We cannot view the whole, and more importantly, even what we can "know" of those with whom we are socially engaged is only by way of their self-revelation, such that we cannot possess the other or seek to assimilate them to the self.

Even what seems to be a properly functioning political authority can lull Christians into a false sense of security, keep their focus off of the very real injustice and oppression around (and within) them. This is a lesson Bonhoeffer learned in Harlem. In recent writing, Mouw has defended government as an order of creation with reference to Bonhoeffer, acknowledging the predicament he was in and praising his "active resistance to the horrors of Nazism."[3] Mouw insists that a "more cohesive interpretation [of Romans 13] can be found by seeing Paul as setting forth a 'normative' view of government" and "the relationship of a Christian citizen to a *properly functioning* political authority."[4] In keeping with the distinction we saw in chapter 5 between evil as perversion versus badness of being, Mouw argues, "The problem with the Nazi regime, then, was that it was not conforming to the standards that inform God's purposes in instituting political authority. In that case, it was not Bonhoeffer who was violating the norms set forth in Romans 13—it was the Nazi regime!"[5] He published these words less than a year after then-attorney general Jeff Sessions cited Romans 13 to defend the Trump-era policy of prosecuting everyone who crosses the US border illegally; we might have done better if Mouw had addressed the tension around the principles and applications of the text at that exact moment. That complaint aside, he does not account for the way Bonhoeffer denies any order "creational" status, arguing that when we try to establish such knowledge of good and evil on our own, even with Scripture in front of us, we risk setting up philosophical systems that help us evade Jesus when he calls. Similarly, each of our evangelical world-viewers failed to see how their world-viewing was grounded in a theologically problematic self-understanding and social imagination that hid their own ambiguous agency in what they saw and in their way of seeing it. Even if world-viewers may piously admit to unknown bias and invite criticism so that they can reevaluate, their goal would still be to see the whole world better. They will not stop world-viewing or using the Bible as a basis for supporting essential, categorical distinctions in "identity." In the end, we are given no real criteria for protecting against the sinful concretions of the world-view's ideals.

Third, the world-viewing impulse as it has funded evangelical identity politics warps the way evangelicals relate to and think about other persons—starting, perhaps, with other evangelicals. Evangelicalism, as represented by our case studies, is at risk for defining persons by their principles. When the world-viewing impulse is funding the politics of evangelical identity, membership is ascribed not on the basis of relationships among real-live persons within concrete institutions and social groups that share in an evangelical spirit but based on certain abstract details that seem salient to visible leaders with supposedly representative power. Without considering the concrete ethical claim the individuals may have on the institutions, the investment they may have in the mission, leaders say, in effect, "Tell me how you are, tell me how you think, and I will tell you who you are." Thin concepts like "the biblical world-view" or "piety" are used to settle the anxiety about evangelical identity as a matter of rhetoric, but in practice, they are put to use in "how" questions by the human *logos* to sort people into categories. Thus, world-viewing not only resists the scrutiny of the living Christ, since Christ is also expected to conform to the evangelical world-view, but it also represents the way reason is reseated within the person, such that the level of questioning remains in the "how" rather than "who." And to continue in world-viewing in this fashion is to close our minds to God and one another, to evade responsibility for our judgments (pointing a finger, like the first humans, at an other), and to give our pious machinations the support of a well-articulated God-concept that we (fail to) serve on our own steam.

Although I have centered this study on the reality of world-view as the particular language game played by evangelicals even as their form of life became an identity-political project, it is worth noting that other terms and concepts seem to occupy a similar space in other historical Christian traditions or social groups. For example, it is worth asking whether the use of "gospel" as an adjective among Southern Baptists and company serves to signify a similar (or the same) complex of ideas and historical problems. But such possibilities must be studied more granularly than I could possibly accomplish here. This "space" is what Claude Lévi-Strauss termed a "floating signifier," which is a concept that is both specific enough to engender loyal activism and empty enough for individuals to bring their own complex sense of meaning to it. American evangelicalism is a fruitful test case for how the concept of a manifestly *biblical* or *Christian* or *evangelical* or *gospel* worldview or, to shift language games, *story* or *narrative* in postliberal circles serves visible leaders as they claim support from those who hold the thin line while simultaneously limiting membership in the orthodox party with a thicker, more defined set of expectations. The "story" concept in popular usage does not seem to have changed the basic way people *hold* what they take to be true. In a sense, my project is partly framed by what we might call "the politics of identity," which encompasses the political jockeying within an identity group, questions of representation when diversity goes unrepresented, and how this identity spills (or is it charges?) into public even amid the internal diversity.

As we have seen, the world-viewing impulse drives us to box God and one another into static limits and distinctions that compromise our presence to those who do not fit well into our idealist mental categories, as if our insular world-view were a unified, Spirit-driven view of all creation. When we relate to God, to others, to the creation through a world-view—as a kind of cognitive mediator—the granular and dynamic sociality revealed in Christ as our own telos is diminished. The urgency with which much world-viewing impulse pushes us to engage the world is proven to be little more than the nervous energy of human beings working out of their own centers, concerned about the fit between themselves and their world and whatever they imagine to be God's will for God's creation. Thus, we need to hear the gospel again: "God has done what the law, weakened by the flesh, could not do: by sending his own Son in the likeness of sinful flesh, and to deal with sin, he condemned sin in the flesh, so that the just requirement of the law might be fulfilled in us, who walk not according to the flesh but according to the Spirit" (Romans 8:3–4). The concern with an internal "limit" and seizing "knowledge of" as the beginning of the fall amounts to this: faithfulness means tending to the actual relationships of our lives within the limit of radical intersubjectivity. The heart turned in upon itself, the omnicompetent "I" living out of its own center, suffers from a self-inflicted wound that joins us to the original humans in their falling. This "hidden wound" (as Wendell Berry has poetically named it in his soul-searching about racism) is mirrored in others whose personhood shows us our limit, helps us learn who we are, and makes us responsible but who instead become objectified in our systems of knowing, possessing, and ordering.

PROSPECTS FOR A VIABLE THEOLOGY OF IDENTITY

Such a wound can only be healed over time in painful acts (and often unpredictable consequences) of opening oneself to concrete others in vulnerability. In Christ, we see how God created humans in freedom for others such that we can relate properly only as we allow others to address us on their own terms. We decidedly do not exist under a general vocation to exercise a dominion that means grasping at comprehensive knowledge of how God orders the world and imposing that envisioned order over all concrete beings with little regard for the actual others whose lives we are thus ordering. This we could do while preserving, in theory, the formal distinction between what one advocates for as a matter of principles versus how one pastors actual persons in their churches, where it becomes more painfully clear that one must own their judgments. Such world-viewing seems like a pious way to be for God, but too often it turns out to be a (to me) reasonable and (sometimes) conceptually articulated way of living out of one's own center (i.e., viewing the world, sicut deus). By contrast, what we need is a view from within the world as exactly one creature before God, who loves us and invites us into life together. This God appears to us in freedom in Jesus to look us in the eye and tug at our hearts-curved-in-on-themselves.

The human mode of knowing is short-circuited by the Christ who comes incognito, who lives in relationship with God but without pretensions of power or claims to knowledge or identity on any basis other than that relationship. In Christ, we see not only the living God, but also the image of God as a human person who lives within his limit, knowing God as well as his fellow creatures *as persons*. Looking exactly here for his guidance, Bonhoeffer emphasizes the freedom we have to be *for one another*, to know one another in self-revealing communication without attempting to assimilate or possess others on the basis of our clear and reasonable principles—whether in individual knowledge or exertions of power. Bonhoeffer describes a subversiveness in the mode of God's self-revelation in Christ; for inasmuch as the Christ comes incognito, he does not correct the intellectual errors of the past in any form that is now "haveable" separate from his person, in relationship. And, at the same time, he demonstrates the priority of social ways of knowing partly by attending to the spirit of the law rather than its humanly articulated letters, as one who is in an active relationship with God through the Holy Spirit. The experts of the law were not particularly competent judges of Jesus's actions given their own commitment to the knowledge of God as possession; to those who trusted their knowledge of good and evil, particularly under the aegis of God's law, Jesus appeared indisputably as a transgressor of the law.

It should come as no surprise to followers of Jesus today—those who know his person in the church-community—that whenever we legislate discipleship and thereby judge ourselves and litigate others, Christ should appear to us as one who transgresses the law in order to expose our pretense and open us to his presence in one another. Precisely because we wrongly wield our convictions about the good life under the right world-view, the living, biblical, historical Jesus upsets our expectations by demanding that we simply obey his living word in concrete encounters. When we ask this Jesus, "Who are you?" we must resist the temptation to judge him based on what we know of the law and instead trust his response. In issuing the call to follow him, Jesus makes his move, stepping into the center of each disciple's life and confronting them with their limit. For those whose confidence rests in the grace of God manifest in the person of Jesus Christ, his relationship to God, his way of fulfilling the law (the spirit of which was meant to preserve humans toward God), the relationship of faith takes priority, such that convictions about eternal law and order can and must be evaluated in terms of their ongoing openness to judgment and fulfillment in Christ.

Along the way, I have sometimes asked whether any practice might enable or enact a methodological openness to Jesus's scrutiny. I suspect that Bonhoeffer's preference for making concrete, rather than general, pronouncements goes a long way in this direction. Considered in light of the free responsibility before God and for others borne by those who make any pronouncements, a word in history is always open to scrutiny—from Jesus Christ, those who share in the church-community, and all who stand to be affected by such pronouncing. To make a general claim on others' lives without having to look them in the eye and, thus, take responsibility for that claim, is an evasion of responsibility and a violation of the creaturely limit. This much, Bonhoeffer tells us, is true also of humans' relationship with nonhuman creation:

> This freedom to rule includes being bound to the creatures who are ruled. The ground and the animals over which I am lord constitute the world in which I live, without which I cease to be. . . . I am not free from it in any sense of my essential being, my spirit, having no need of nature, as though nature were something alien to the spirit. On the contrary, in my whole being, in my creatureliness, I belong wholly to this world; it bears me, nurtures me, holds me.[6]

If this is true of the ground upon which we walk, how much more the ground of ideas for how humans should live together. The humility of the concrete pronouncement in the end also includes the demand that we explain clearly how any order as we preach it, as we practice it, actually serves the kingdom of God rather than preserving some arbitrary, neurotic institution(s). Bonhoeffer tells the theologian, the church, and the individual follower of Jesus that they must test their moral convictions against the standard of whether/how *this* principle, *this* rule participates in the ultimate. What, exactly, is its relative, penultimate value? To the theologian, he also issues the reminder that their solitary projects are given their value by the church that puts it into practice (or not). And to the individual follower, theologian or not, he issues the clarion call to encounter every other as a limit who creates for them a moral responsibility and, more than that, who makes *them* a responsible actor in the moments of life. Real persons can ask questions about how you figure—how you justify your convictions—that will not be satisfied by mere appeal to sanctified imaginations or prestigious theological tradition or to thin, publicly inscrutable definitions of "the common good" or "piety" or "biblical tradition."

In Christ we may live in free responsibility with God and others, owning our actions and judgments as our own, and continuously practicing repentance and forgiveness in the context of the church such that we bear our limit. This is why the church, and no other social structure, is first among and paradigmatic for human relations. Among other things, *this* community reminds us that our sins entail violating the limit manifest in real persons (including the living God), that in confessing our sins we can be forgiven, and that God's grace is deep enough and true enough to maintain the relationships between and among God and God's creatures. Attention to our creaturely limit requires that we engage with other persons as persons, as independent, willing I's. To all such creatures, the message of the gospel is first and foremost Jesus's personal restoration of life with God. Faith is predicated on meeting the risen Jesus who shows us, as a living person to whom we relate, who God is and what God wants with us. We could not hope to know anything about God outside of that context—not least because this risen Christ comes to us from the most unexpected of places and at the most unexpected of times. Yet to this day, as in the beginning, we need others to help us bear our creaturely limit. And at the same time, all real-life others are limits to us. We cannot adequately deal with them as decisively internalized, categorized into this or that class of persons. Thus, followers of Jesus live before God in free responsibility, hearing and simply obeying the word of God in Jesus existing as the church-community, and bearing again the judgment of God—not as wrath, but as the grace that maintains the relationship when we fail and take responsibility, confess and repent, and hear the words of forgiveness from others who help us bear our limit. We are each but one creature within a world that only the living God can truly, personally "view."

NOTES

1. Dietrich Bonhoeffer, *Ecumenical, Academic, and Pastoral Work, 1931–1932*, English ed., Dietrich Bonhoeffer Works (Minneapolis: Fortress Press, 2012), series hereafter cited as DBWE, 11:377.
2. Dietrich Bonhoeffer, *Letters and Papers from Prison*, DBWE (Minneapolis: Fortress Press, 2009), 8:333 and 500. Rachel Muers has provided a sustained and inspired treatment of the resurrection as the Archimedean point—deepening the incognito in terms of personal-relational mystery and unknowability—in *Keeping God's Silence: Towards a Theological Ethics of Communication* (Malden, MA: Blackwell Publishing, 2004), ch. 3.
3. Richard J. Mouw, *Restless Faith: Holding Evangelical Beliefs in a World of Contested Labels* (Grand Rapids: Brazos Press, 2019), 134.
4. Mouw, *Restless Faith*, 135.
5. Mouw, *Restless Faith*, 136.
6. Dietrich Bonhoeffer, *Creation and Fall*, DBWE (Minneapolis: Fortress Press, 1997), 3:66.

Bibliography

Abou El Fadl, Khaled, Richard Mouw, and Yossi Klein Halevi. "The Power of Fundamentalism." Interview by Krista Tippett, *Speaking of Faith*, aired April 18, 2002, on NPR. Accessed June 9, 2020. https://onbeing.org/programs/khaled-abou-el-fadl-richard-j-mouw-and-yossi-klein-halevi-the-power-of-fundamentalism/.

American Psychiatric Association. *Diagnostic and Statistical Manual of Mental Disorders: DSM-5*. Arlington, VA: American Psychiatric Association, 2013.

Appiah, Kwame Anthony. "The Politics of Identity." *Daedalus* 135, no. 4 (Fall 2006): 15–22.

Augustine. *City of God*. Translated by Henry Bettenson. 1972. Reprint, New York: Penguin Books, 2003.

———. *On Christian Doctrine*. Translated by J. F. Shaw. Mineola, NY: Dover Publications, Inc., 2009.

Bacote, Vincent E. *The Political Disciple: A Theology of Public Life*. Grand Rapids: Zondervan, 2015.

Bailey, Sarah Pulliam. "A New Group of Evangelical Leaders Forms in Support of Biden." *The Washington Post*, October 12, 2020. Accessed January 25, 2021. https://www.washingtonpost.com/religion/2020/10/02/new-evangelical-leaders-support-biden/.

Barna Group. "Black Lives Matter and Racial Tension in America." May 5, 2016. Accessed January 5, 2021. https://www.barna.com/research/black-lives-matter-and-racial-tension-in-america/.

———. "Black Practicing Christians Are Twice as Likely as Their White Peers to See a Race Problem." June 17, 2020. Accessed January 5, 2021. https://www.barna.com/research/problems-solutions-racism/.

———. "What Is the Church's Role in Racial Reconciliation?" July 30, 2019. Accessed January 5, 2021. https://www.barna.com/research/racial-reconciliation/.

Barron, Jessica M. "Managed Diversity: Race, Place, and an Urban Church." *Sociology of Religion* 77, no. 1 (Spring 2016): 18–36.

Barth, Karl. *Church Dogmatics III.1: The Doctrine of Creation.* Edinburgh: T. & T. Clark, 1958.
Barthes, Roland. *Mythologies.* Translated by Richard Howard and Annette Lavers. New York: Hill and Wang, 2012.
Bebbington, David W. *Evangelicalism in Modern Britain: A History from the 1730s to the 1980s.* 1989. Reprint, New York: Routledge, 1993.
Berry, Wendell. *The Hidden Wound.* New York: North Point Press, 1989.
Blum, Edward J. *W. E. B. Du Bois: American Prophet.* Philadelphia: University of Pennsylvania Press, 2007.
Boesak, Allan. *The Tenderness of Conscience: African Renaissance and the Spirituality of Politics.* Stellenbosch, South Africa: Sun Press, 2005.
Bonhoeffer, Dietrich. *Act and Being Transcendental Philosophy and Ontology in Systematic Theology.* English ed. Dietrich Bonhoeffer Works 2. Minneapolis: Fortress Press, 1996.
———. *Barcelona, Berlin, New York: 1928–1931.* English ed. Dietrich Bonhoeffer Works 10. Minneapolis, MN: Fortress Press, 2008.
———. *Berlin: 1932–1933.* English ed. Dietrich Bonhoeffer Works 12. Minneapolis: Fortress Press, 2009.
———. *Christ the Center.* Translated by Edwin H. Robertson. New York: HarperCollins Publishers, 1978.
———. *Creation and Fall.* English ed. Dietrich Bonhoeffer Works 3. Minneapolis: Fortress Press, 1997.
———. *Discipleship.* English ed. Dietrich Bonhoeffer Works 4. Minneapolis: Fortress Press, 2001.
———. *Ecumenical, Academic, and Pastoral Work, 1931–1932.* English ed. Dietrich Bonhoeffer Works 11. Minneapolis: Fortress Press, 2012.
———. *Ethics.* English ed. Dietrich Bonhoeffer Works 6. Minneapolis: Fortress Press, 2005.
———. *Letters and Papers from Prison.* English ed. Dietrich Bonhoeffer Works 8. Minneapolis: Fortress Press, 2009.
———. *Life Together* and *Prayerbook of the Bible.* English ed. Dietrich Bonhoeffer Works 5. Minneapolis: Fortress Press, 1996.
———. *London: 1933–1935.* English ed. Dietrich Bonhoeffer Works 13. Minneapolis: Fortress Press, 2007.
———. *Sanctorum Communio: A Theology Study of the Sociology of the Church.* English ed. Dietrich Bonhoeffer Works 1. Minneapolis: Fortress Press, 1998.
———. *Theological Education at Finkenwalde: 1935–1937.* English ed. Dietrich Bonhoeffer Works 14. Minneapolis: Fortress Press, 2013.
Bounds, Elizabeth M. *Coming Together/Coming Apart: Religion, Community, and Modernity.* New York: Routledge, 1997.
Bracey, Glenn E., II, and Wendy Leo Moore. "'Race Tests': Racial Boundary Maintenance in White Evangelical Churches." *Sociological Inquiry* 87, no. 2 (May 2017): 282–302.
Brannon, Tiffany N., Hazel Rose Markus, and Valerie Jones Taylor. "'Two Souls, Two Thoughts,' Two Self-Schemas: Double Consciousness Can Have Positive

Academic Consequences for African Americans." *Journal of Personality and Social Psychology* 108, no. 4 (2015): 586–609.

Bratt, James D., ed. *Abraham Kuyper: A Centennial Reader*. Grand Rapids: Eerdmans, 1998.

———. *Abraham Kuyper: Modern Calvinist, Christian Democrat*. Grand Rapids: Eerdmans, 2013.

Brown, Warren S., Nancey Murphy, and H. Newton Maloney, eds. *Whatever Happened to the Soul? Scientific and Theological Portraits of Human Nature*. Minneapolis: Fortress Press, 1998.

Bruce, Dickson D., Jr. "W. E. B. Du Bois and the Idea of Double Consciousness." *American Literature* 64, no. 2 (June 1992): 299–309.

Buchanan, Ian. "Floating signifier." In *A Dictionary of Critical Theory*, 2nd ed. New York: Oxford University Press, 2018.

Butler, Anthea. *White Evangelical Racism: The Politics of Morality in America*. Chapel Hill, NC: The University of North Carolina Press, 2021.

Calvin, John. *Commentary on Psalms*. Translated and edited by James Anderson. Edinburgh: The Calvin Translation Society, 1847.

———. *Commentary on the Epistles of Paul the Apostle to the Corinthians*. Translated and edited by John Pringle. Edinburgh: The Calvin Translation Society, 1848.

———. *Commentary on Romans*. Edited by David W. Torrance and Thomas F. Torrance. Translated by Ross Mackenzie. 1960. Reprint, Grand Rapids: Eerdmans, 1995.

———. *The Institutes of Christian Religion*. 1559. Edited by John T. McNeill. Translated by Ford Lewis Battles. 2 volumes. Philadelphia: The Westminster Press, 1960.

Carter, J. Kameron. *Race: A Theological Account*. New York: Oxford University Press, 2008.

Carter, Joe. "No, the Majority of American Evangelicals Did Not Vote for Trump." The Gospel Coalition, November 15, 2016. Accessed March 2, 2021. https://www.thegospelcoalition.org/article/no-the-majority-of-american-evangelicals-did-not-vote-for-trump/.

Casey, Shaun. *The Making of a Catholic President: Kennedy vs. Nixon 1960*. New York: Oxford University Press, 2009.

"Chicago Declaration of Evangelical Social Concern (1973)." November 25, 1973. Accessed February 17, 2021. https://sojo.net/sites/default/files/chicagoinvitationformatted_final.pdf.

Cladis, Mark S. "Du Bois: The Poet-Sociologist." Paper presented at the Annual Meeting of the American Academy of Religion (San Diego, CA, November 2019).

Cobb, Ryon J., Samuel L. Perry, and Kevin D. Dougherty. "United by Faith? Race/Ethnicity, Congregational Diversity, and Explanations of Racial Inequality." *Sociology of Religion* 76, no. 2 (Summer 2015): 177–98.

Combahee River Collective. "A Black Feminist Statement." April 1977. In *Capitalist Patriarchy and the Case for Social Feminism*, edited by Zillah R. Eisenstein, 362–72. New York: NYU Press, 1979.

Cook, Jacob Alan. "Toward an Incarnational Theology of Identity." In *Justice and the Way of Jesus: Christian Ethics and the Incarnational Discipleship of Glen Stassen*, edited by David P. Gushee and Reggie L. Williams, 25–38. Maryknoll: Orbis Books, 2020.

Cooper, Betsy et al. "Anxiety, Nostalgia, and Mistrust: Findings from the 2015 American Values Survey." Public Religion Research Institute, November 17, 2015. Accessed December 17, 2015. http://publicreligion.org/research/2015/11/survey-anxiety-nostalgia-and-mistrust-findings-from-the-2015-american-values-survey/.

Cooper-White, Pamela. *Braided Selves: Collected Essays on Multiplicity, God, and Persons*. Eugene, OR: Cascade Books, 2011.

Descartes, René. *Meditations on First Philosophy*. 1641 Translated by Donald A. Cress. 3rd ed. Indianapolis: Hackett Publishing Company, 1993.

Dougherty, Kevin D., Mark Chaves, and Michael O. Emerson. "Racial Diversity in U.S. Congregations, 1998–2019." October 12, 2020. Accessed January 5, 2021. https://sites.duke.edu/ncsweb/files/2020/10/Racial-Diversity-in-U.S.-Congregations-1998-2019.pdf.

Du Bois, W. E. B. "The Conservation of Races." 1897. In Sundquist, *Du Bois Reader*, 38–47.

———. *Darkwater*. 1920. In Sundquist, *Du Bois Reader*, 481–623.

———. *The Souls of Black Folk*. 1903. In Sundquist, *Du Bois Reader*, 97–240.

———. "The Souls of White Folk." *The Independent* 69 (August 18, 1910).

Du Mez, Kristen Kobes. "Donald Trump and Militant Masculinity." *Religion & Politics*, January 17, 2017. Accessed December 29, 2020. https://religionandpolitics.org/2017/01/17/donald-trump-and-militant-evangelical-masculinity/.

———. *Jesus and John Wayne: How White Evangelicals Corrupted a Faith and Fractured a Nation*. New York: Liveright, 2020.

du Toit, André. "Puritans in Africa? Afrikaner 'Calvinism' and Kuyperian neo-Calvinism in late nineteenth-century South Africa." *Comparative Studies in Society and History* 27 (1985): 227–34.

Duffett, Robert G. "The Gospel according to George McGovern." Sojourners, March 2014. Accessed March 17, 2015. http://sojo.net/magazine/2014/gospel-according-george-mcgovern.

Dunn, Amina, et al., "Voters Say Those on the Other Side 'Don't Get' Them. Here's What They Want Them to Know." Pew Research Center, December 17, 2020. Accessed March 2, 2021. https://www.pewresearch.org/politics/2020/12/17/voters-say-those-on-the-other-side-dont-get-them-heres-what-they-want-them-to-know/.

Edmondson, Mika. "Is Black Lives Matter the New Civil Rights Movement?" The Gospel Coalition, June 24, 2016. Accessed February 18, 2021. https://www.thegospelcoalition.org/podcasts/tgc-podcast/is-black-lives-matter-the-new-civil-rights-movement/.

Edwards, Korie L. *The Elusive Dream: The Power of Race in Interracial Churches*. New York: Oxford University Press, 2008.

Emerson, Michael O. and Christian Smith. *Divided by Faith: Evangelical Religion and the Problem of Race in America*. New York: Oxford University Press, 2000.

Englizian, H. Crosby. *Brimstone Corner: Park Street Church, Boston.* Chicago: Moody, 1968.
Ericksen, Robert P. *Theologians under Hitler: Gerhard Kittel, Paul Althaus, and Emanuel Hirsch.* New Haven, CT: Yale University Press, 1985.
Erikson, Erik H. *Identity and the Life Cycle.* New York: W. W. Norton and Company, 1959.
———. *Young Man Luther: A Study in Psychoanalysis and History.* 1958. Reprint, New York: W. W. Norton and Company, 1993.
"An Evangelical Manifesto: A Declaration of Evangelical Identity and Public Commitment." May 7, 2008. Accessed February 23, 2021. http://www.ntslibrary.com/PDF%20Books/Evangelical_Manifesto.pdf.
Evans, Curtis J. "White Evangelical Protestant Responses to the Civil Rights Movement." *Harvard Theological Review* 102, no. 2 (2009): 245–73.
Fanon, Frantz. *Black Skin, White Masks.* 1952. Translated by Richard Philcox. New York: Grove Press, 2008.
Farrer, Lauralee. "This Is Then, That Was Now." *FULLER*, no. 1 (2014): 16–22.
Ferguson, Niall. *Civilization: The West and the Rest.* New York: Penguin Books, 2011.
Fitzgerald, Frances. *The Evangelicals: The Struggle to Shape America.* New York: Simon & Schuster, 2017.
Garvey, Hannah. "The Form of the Color Line: Du Boisian Charts, Antiabsorption, and the Strange Meaning of Being Black." Paper presented at the Annual Meeting of the American Academy of Religion (San Diego, CA, November 2019).
Gene, Esperanza. "Seminary While Black: Why Calling out #ToxicFuller Matters." July 20, 2018. Accessed June 8, 2020. https://medium.com/@esperanzagene/seminarywhileblack-why-calling-out-toxicfuller-matters-a64a7abd252.
Gergen, Kenneth J. *The Saturated Self: Dilemmas of Identity in Contemporary Life.* 1991. Reprint, New York: Basic Books, 2000.
Green, Clifford J. *Bonhoeffer: A Theology of Sociality.* Rev. ed. Grand Rapids: Eerdmans, 1999.
Grem, Darren E. *The Blessings of Business: How Corporations Shaped Conservative Christianity.* New York: Oxford University Press, 2016.
Haidt, Jonathan. "The Emotional Dog and Its Rational Tail: A Social Intuitionist Approach to Moral Judgment." *Psychological Review* 108, no. 4 (October 2001): 814–34.
Haidt, Jonathan, Jesse Graham, and Craig Joseph. "Above and Below Left-Right: Ideological Narratives and Moral Foundations." *Psychological Inquiry* 20, no. 2/3 (April 2009): 110–19.
Hamedani, MarYam G., Hazel Rose Markus, and Alyssa S. Fu. "My Nation, My Self: Divergent Framings of America Influence American Selves." *Personality and Social Psychology Bulletin* 37, no. 3 (March 2011): 350–64.
Hamilton, Michael S. "A Strange Love? Or: How White Evangelicals Learned to Stop Worrying and Love the Donald." In Noll, Bebbington, and Marsden, 217–27.
Harvey, Jennifer. *Dear White Christians: For Those Still Longing for Racial Reconciliation.* Grand Rapids: Eerdmans, 2014.

———. "What Would Zacchaeus Do?: The Case for *Disidentifying with Jesus.*" In *Christology and Whiteness: What Would Jesus Do?*, edited by George Yancey, 84–100. New York: Routledge, 2012.
Hegel, G. W. F. *Lectures on the Philosophy of Religion: The Lectures of 1827.* One Vol. ed. Edited by Peter C. Hodgson. Berkeley: University of California Press, 1988.
———. *Phenomenology of Spirit.* 1807. Translated by A. V. Miller. New York: Oxford University Press, 1977.
———. *The Philosophy of History.* 1892. Translated by John Sibree. New York: Dover Publications, 1956.
Heidegger, Martin. *The Basic Problems of Phenomenology.* Translated by Albert Hofstadter. Bloomington: Indiana University Press, 1982.
Helm, Paul. *John Calvin's Ideas.* New York: Oxford University Press, 2004.
Henderson, Roger D. "How Abraham Kuyper Became a Kuyperian." Appendix to Kuyper, *Problem of Poverty.*
Henry, Carl F. H. *The Drift of Western Thought.* Grand Rapids: Eerdmans, 1951.
———. *Evangelicals at the Brink of Crisis.* Waco, TX: Word Books, 1967.
———. *A Plea for Evangelical Demonstration.* Grand Rapids: Baker Book House, 1971.
———. *The Uneasy Conscience of Modern Fundamentalism.* 1947. Reprint, Grand Rapids: Eerdmans, 2003.
———. "What Social Structures?" In *The Best of the Reformed Journal*, edited by James D. Bratt and Ronald A. Wells, 75–76. Grand Rapids: Eerdmans, 2011.
Heslam, Peter S. *Creating a Christian Worldview: Abraham Kuyper's Lectures on Calvinism.* Grand Rapids: Eerdmans, 1998.
Hinlicky, Paul R. *Beloved Community: Beloved Community after Christendom.* Grand Rapids: Eerdmans, 2015.
Holmes, Arthur F. *Contours of a World View.* Grand Rapids: Eerdmans, 1983.
Hume, David. *A Treatise of Human Nature.* 1739–40. Reprint, New York: Penguin Books, 1986.
Huntington, Samuel P. *The Clash of Civilizations and the Remaking of World Order.* New York: Simon & Schuster, 1996.
James, William. *The Principles of Psychology.* Volume 1. New York: Henry Holt and Company, 1890.
Jenkins, Willis. *The Future of Faith and Ethics: Sustainability, Social Justice, and Religious Creativity.* Washington, DC: Georgetown University Press, 2013.
Jennings, Willie James. *After Whiteness: An Education in Belonging.* Grand Rapids: Eerdmans, 2020.
———. *The Christian Imagination: Theology and the Origins of Race.* New Haven, CT: Yale University Press, 2010.
Jones, Jeffrey M. "U.S. Church Membership Falls Below Majority for First Time." Gallup, Inc., March 29, 2021. Accessed April 6, 2021. https://news.gallup.com/poll/341963/church-membership-falls-below-majority-first-time.aspx.
Jones, Robert P. *The End of White Christian America.* New York: Simon & Schuster, 2016.

Kant, Immanuel. *Critique of Judgment*. Translated by Werner S. Pluhar. Indianapolis: Hackett Publishing Company, 1987.

———. *Prolegomena to Any Future Metaphysics*. 2nd ed. Translated by James W. Ellington. Indianapolis: Hackett Publishing Company, 2001.

Keen, Karen R. *Scripture, Ethics, and the Possibility of Same Sex Relationships*. Grand Rapids: Eerdmans, 2018.

Keller, Catherine. *From a Broken Web: Separation, Sexism, and Self*. Boston: Beacon Press, 1986.

Kirkpatrick, Matthew D. *Attacks on Christendom in a World Come of Age: Kierkegaard, Bonhoeffer, and the Question of 'Religionless Christianity.'* Eugene, OR: Pickwick Publications, 2011.

Kuykendall, Ronald. "Hegel and Africa: An Evaluation of the Treatment of Africa in The Philosophy of History." *Journal of Black Studies* 23, no. 4 (June 1993): 571–81.

Kuyper, Abraham. *Calvinism: Six Stone Lectures*. Amsterdam: Höveker & Wormser Ltd., 1899.

———. "Calvinism: Source and Stronghold of Our Constitutional Liberties." In Bratt, *Centennial Reader*, 279–322.

———. "Common Grace." In Bratt, *Centennial Reader*, 165–201.

———. "Confidentially." In Bratt, *Centennial Reader*, 45–61.

———. *Encyclopedia of Sacred Theology: Its Principles*. Translated and edited by J. Hendrik de Vries. New York: Charles Scribner's Sons, 1898.

———. *Guidance for Christian Engagement in Government: A Translation of Abraham Kuyper's Our Program*. Translated and edited by Harry Van Dyke. Grand Rapids: Christian's Library Press, 2013.

———. "It Shall Not Be So Among You." In Bratt, *Centennial Reader*, 125–40.

———. "Modernism: A Fata Morgana in the Christian Domain." In Bratt, *Centennial Reader*, 87–124.

———. "Our Instinctive Life." In Bratt, *Centennial Reader*, 255–77.

———. "Perfectionism." In Bratt, *Centennial Reader*, 141–63.

———. *The Problem of Poverty*. 1891. Edited and translated by W. Skillen. 1991. Reprint, Sioux Center, IA: Dordt College Press, 2011.

———. "The South African Crisis." In Bratt, *Centennial Reader*, 323–60.

———. "Uniformity: The Curse of Modern Life." In Bratt, *Centennial Reader*, 19–44.

———. *The Work of the Holy Spirit*. Translated and edited by J. Hendrik de Vries. New York: Funk & Wagnalls Co., 1900.

Labberton, Mark, ed. *Still Evangelical?: Insiders Reconsider Political, Social, and Theological Meaning*. Downers Grove: InterVarsity Press, 2018.

Lettow, Susanne. "Modes of Naturalization: Race, Sex and Biology in Kant, Schelling and Hegel." *Philosophy and Social Criticism* 39, no. 2 (2013): 117–31.

LifeWay Research. "Most Evangelicals Choose Trump Over Biden, But Clear Divides Exist." September 29, 2020. Accessed March 2, 2021. https://lifewayresearch.com/2020/09/29/most-evangelicals-choose-trump-over-biden-but-clear-divides-exist/.

Lindsell, Harold. *Battle for the Bible*. Grand Rapids: Zondervan, 1976.

Linville, Patricia W. "Self-Complexity and Affective Extremity: Don't Put All of Your Eggs in One Cognitive Basket." *Social Cognition* 3, no. 1 (1985): 94–120.
Lorde, Audre. "Age, Race, Class, and Sex: Women Redefining Difference." 1980. In *Sister Outsider: Essays and Speeches*, 114–23. 1984. Reprint, Berkeley: Crossing Press, 2007.
Lyotard, Jean-François. *The Postmodern Condition: A Report on Knowledge*. Translated by Geoff Bennington and Brian Massumi. Minneapolis: University of Minnesota Press, 1984.
Machen, J. Gresham. *Christianity and Liberalism*. Grand Rapids: Eerdmans, 1923.
MacIntyre, Alasdair. *Whose Justice? Which Rationality?* Notre Dame, IN: University of Notre Dame Press, 1988.
Markus, Hazel Rose. "Self-Schemata and Processing Information about the Self." *Journal of Personality and Social Psychology* 35, no. 2 (February 1977): 63–78.
———. "Who Am I? Race, Ethnicity, and Identity." In *Doing Race: 21 Essays for the 21st Century*, edited by Hazel Rose Markus and Paula M. L. Moya, 359–89. New York: W. W. Norton & Company, 2010.
Markus, Hazel Rose, and Alana Conner. *Clash: How to Thrive in a Multicultural World*. New York: Plume, 2013.
Markus, Hazel Rose, and Paula Nurius. "Possible Selves." *American Psychologist* 41, no. 9 (September 1986): 954–69.
Markus, Hazel Rose, and Shinobu Kitayama. "Culture and the Self: Implications for Cognition, Emotion, and Motivation." *Psychological Review* 98, no. 2 (April 1991): 224–53.
———. "Cultures and Selves: A Cycle of Mutual Constitution." *Perspectives on Psychological Science* 5, no. 4 (July 2010): 420–30.
Markus, Hazel Rose, and Elissa Wurf. "The Dynamic Self-Concept: A Social Psychological Perspective." *Annual Review of Psychology* 38, no. 1 (February 1987): 299–337.
Marsden, George. *Reforming Fundamentalism: Fuller Seminary and the New Evangelicalism*. Grand Rapids: Eerdmans, 1987.
Marsh, Charles. *The Beloved Community: How Faith Shapes Social Justice, From the Civil Rights Movement to Today*. New York: Basic Books, 2005.
———. *A Strange Glory: A Life of Dietrich Bonhoeffer*. 2014. Reprint, New York: Vintage Books, 2015.
Marshall, Paul A., Sander Griffioen, and Richard J. Mouw, eds. *Stained Glass: Worldviews and Social Science*. New York: University Press of America, 1989.
McAdams, Dan P. "The Psychological Self as Actor, Agent, and Author." *Perspectives on Psychological Science* 8, no. 3 (May 2013): 272–95.
———. *The Redemptive Self: Stories Americans Live By*. Rev. ed. New York: Oxford University Press, 2013.
———. *The Stories We Live By: Personal Myths and the Making of the Self*. 1993. Reprint, New York: The Guilford Press, 1997.
McClendon, James Wm., Jr. *Ethics: Systematic Theology, Volume 1*. Rev. edition. Nashville: Abingdon Press, 2002.

Milkman, Katherine L., Modupe Akinola, and Dolly Chugh. "Temporal Distance and Discrimination: An Audit Study in Academia." *Psychological Science* 23, no. 7 (July 2012): 710–17.

Miller, Lisa. "The Religious Case for Gay Marriage." *Newsweek* 152, no. 24 (December 15, 2008).

Moore, Wendy Leo. *Reproducing Racism: White Space, Elite Law Schools, and Racial Inequality*. Lanham, MD: Rowman & Littlefield, 2008.

Mouw, Richard J. *Abraham Kuyper: A Short and Personal Introduction*. Grand Rapids: Eerdmans, 2011.

———. *Adventures in Evangelical Civility: A Lifelong Quest for Common Ground*. Grand Rapids: Brazos Press, 2016.

———. *Called to Holy Worldliness*. Philadelphia: Fortress Press, 1980.

———. *The Challenges of Cultural Discipleship: Essays in the Line of Abraham Kuyper*. Grand Rapids: Eerdmans, 2012.

———. "The Church and Social Specifics." *Reformed Journal* 19, no. 6 (July 1969): 2–4.

———. "Continuing the Task." In *Beauty, Order, and Mystery: A Christian Vision of Human Sexuality*, edited by Gerald Hiestand and Todd Wilson. Downers Grove, IL: IVP Academic, 2017.

———. "Creational Politics: Some Calvinist Amendments." In *Challenges of Cultural Discipleship*, 108–23.

———. "Culture, Church, and Civil Society: Abraham Kuyper for a New Century." In *Challenges of Cultural Discipleship*, 16–32.

———. "Despite Trumpism, I'm Not Quitting Evangelicalism." *Religious News Service*, December 13, 2016. Accessed June 4, 2020. https://religionnews.com/2016/12/13/richard-mouw-despite-trumpism-im-not-quitting-evangelicalism/.

———. *Distorted Truth: What Every Christian Needs to Know about the Battle for the Mind*. San Francisco: Harper & Row, 1989.

———. "Dutch Pillars." *Reformed Journal* 32, no. 5 (May 1982): 2–3.

———. "Educational Choice and Pillarization: Some Lessons for Americans from the Dutch Experiment in 'Affirmative Impartiality.'" In *Challenges of Cultural Discipleship*, 87–107.

———. "Evangelicalism and Philosophy." *Theology Today* 44, no. 3 (October 1987): 329–37.

———. "Evangelicals and Political Activism." *The Christian Century* 89, no. 47 (December 27, 1972): 1316–19.

———. "Evangelicals in Search of Maturity." *Theology Today* 35, no. 1 (April 1978): 42–51.

———. "'Gay' and 'Straight.'" *Reformed Journal* 31, no. 8 (August 1981): 3–4.

———. *The God Who Commands: A Study in Divine Command Ethics*. Notre Dame: University of Notre Dame Press, 1990.

———. "Hanging in There." *The Christian Century* 121, no. 1 (January 13, 2004): 22–25.

———. "How to Change Hearts on Race." *Religious News Service*, January 23, 2018. Accessed June 4, 2020. https://religionnews.com/2018/01/23/how-to-change-hearts-on-race/.

———. "The *Imago Dei* and Philosophical Anthropology." *Christian Scholars Review* 43, no. 3 (2012): 253–66.
———. "Is Tolerance the Enemy of Religious Freedom?" *Evangelicals* 1, no. 1 (Fall 2015): 14–17.
———. "Just Saying 'NO' Is Not Enough." *Christianity Today* 43, no. 11 (October 4, 1999): 50–55.
———. "Law, Covenant, and Moral Commonalities: Some Neo-Calvinist Explorations." In *Challenges of Cultural Discipleship*, 69–86.
———. "Life in the Spirit in an Unjust World." *Pneuma* 9, no. 2 (September 1987): 109–28.
———. "Looking Through the Eyes of Parents." *Theology Today* 58, no. 1 (April 2001): 51–57.
———. "Modal Diversity in Dooyeweerd's Social Thought." In *Challenges of Cultural Discipleship*, 58–68.
———. "My Turn: Less Shouting, More Talking." *Newsweek* 153, no. 6 (February 9, 2009): 26.
———. "On Being Permissive about Filth." *Reformed Journal* 26, no. 2 (February 1976): 3–5.
———. "An Open-Handed Gospel." *Christianity Today* 52, no. 4 (April 2008): 44–47.
———. *Political Evangelism*. Grand Rapids: Eerdmans, 1973.
———. *Politics and the Biblical Drama*. Grand Rapids: Baker Book House, 1976.
———. *Restless Faith: Holding Evangelical Beliefs in a World of Contested Labels*. Grand Rapids: Brazos Press, 2019.
———. *Smell of Sawdust: What Evangelicals Can Learn from Their Fundamentalist Heritage*. Grand Rapids: Zondervan, 2000.
———. "Some Reflections on Sphere Sovereignty." In *Challenges of Cultural Discipleship*, 33–57.
———. "Tolerance without Compromise." *Christianity Today* 40, no. 8 (July 15, 1996): 33–35.
———. *Uncommon Decency: Christian Civility in an Uncivil World*. 2nd ed. Downers Grove, IL: InterVarsity Press, 2010.
———. "Weaving a Coherent Pattern of Discipleship." *The Christian Century* 92, no. 27 (August 20, 1975): 728–31.
———. *When the Kings Come Marching In: Isaiah and the New Jerusalem*. Grand Rapids: Eerdmans, 1983.
Mouw, Richard J., and Sander Griffioen. *Pluralisms and Horizons: An Essay in Christian Public Philosophy*. Grand Rapids: Eerdmans, 1993.
Mouw, Richard J., and Virginia Ramey Mollenkott. "Gay Marriage: Broken or Blessed? Two Evangelical Views." Interview by Krista Tippett, *Speaking of Faith*, aired August 3, 2006, on NPR. Accessed February 20, 2016. http://www.onbeing.org/program/gay-marriage-broken-or-blessed-two-evangelical-views/transcript/924.
Mouw, Richard J., and John Howard Yoder. "Evangelical Ethics and the Anabaptist-Reformed Dialogue." *The Journal of Religious Ethics* 17, no. 2 (Fall 1989): 121–37.

Muers, Rachel. *Keeping God's Silence: Towards a Theological Ethics of Communication*. Malden, MA: Blackwell Publishing, 2004.
Naugle, David K. *Worldview: The History of a Concept*. Grand Rapids: Eerdmans, 2002.
Newport, Frank. "Religious Group Voting and the 2020 Election." Gallup, Inc., November 13, 2020. Accessed March 2, 2021. https://news.gallup.com/opinion/pol ling-matters/324410/religious-group-voting-2020-election.aspx.
Niebuhr, H. Richard. *Christ and Culture*. 1951. Reprint, New York: Harper & Row Publishers, 1975.
Noll, Mark A. *American Evangelical Christianity: An Introduction*. Malden, MA: Blackwell Publishers, 2001.
———. "One Word but Three Crises." In Noll, Bebbington, and Marsden, 1–13.
———. *The Scandal of the Evangelical Mind*. Grand Rapids: Eerdmans, 1994.
Noll, Mark A., David W. Bebbington, and George M. Marsden, eds. *Evangelicals: Who They Have Been, Are Now, and Could Be*. Grand Rapids: Eerdmans, 2019.
Ockenga, Harold John. "The Challenge to the Christian Culture of the West." Presidential address, opening convocation of Fuller Theological Seminary, Pasadena, CA, October 1, 1947. Accessed March 9, 2020. https://fullerstudio.full er.edu/the-challenge-to-the-christian-culture-of-the-west-opening-convocation-oc tober-1-1947/.
———. "Christ for America." Presidential address, meeting of the National Association of Evangelicals, Chicago, May 4, 1943. In National Association of Evangelicals, *United . . . We Stand: A Report of the Constitutional Convention of the National Association of Evangelicals, May 3-6, 1943*, 9–16. Boston: NAE, 1943.
———. *Faith in a Troubled World*. Wenham, MA: Gordon College Press, 1972.
———. *Faithful in Christ Jesus*. New York: Fleming H. Revell Company, 1948.
———. "Fulfilled and Unfulfilled Prophecy." In *Prophecy in the Making*. Messages Prepared for Jerusalem Conference on Biblical Prophecy, edited by Carl F. H. Henry. Carol Stream, IL: Creation House, 1971.
———. *Our Evangelical Faith*. Grand Rapids: Zondervan, 1946.
———. *Our Protestant Heritage*. Grand Rapids: Zondervan, 1938.
———. "The New Evangelicalism." Societal Questions and Problems, Part 5. Sermon, Park Street Congregational Church, Boston, MA, January 5, 1958. Accessed August 10, 2015. http://www.parkstreet.org/library/sermons/speaker/ Harold-Ockenga.
———. "The New Reformation." *Bibliotheca Sacra* 105, no. 417 (Jan.– Mar. 1948): 89–101.
———. "The Unity Christ Seeks." *The Christian Century* 73, no. 9 (Feb. 29, 1956): 266–67.
———. "The Unvoiced Multitudes." In *Evangelical Action!*, 18–39. Boston, MA: United Action Press, 1942.
Orr, James. *The Christian View of God and the World as Centering in the Incarnation*. New York: Anson D. F. Randolph and Co., 1893.
Pangritz, Andreas. *The Polyphony of Life: Bonhoeffer's Theology of Music*. Edited by John W. de Gruchy and John Morris. Translated by Robert Steiner. Eugene, OR: Cascade Books, 2019.

Pannell, William E. "The Evangelical Christian and Black History." *Fides et Historia* 2, no. 2 (1970): 4–14.

———. "Evangelism and the Struggle for Power." *International Review of Mission* 63, no. 250 (April 1974): 201–10.

———. *My Friend, the Enemy*. Waco, TX: Word Books, 1968.

Partee, Charles. "Calvin's So-Called Epistemology." Paper presented at the 12th Colloquium on Calvin Studies, Due West, SC, January 27–28, 2006. Accessed December 16, 2016. http://foundationrt.org/bw/wp-content/uploads/2016/03/Partee_Calvin_Epistemology.pdf.

———. *The Theology of John Calvin*. Louisville: Westminster John Knox Press, 2008.

Pew Research Center. "In a Politically Polarized Era, Sharp Divides in Both Partisan Coalitions." December 17, 2019. Accessed March 2, 2021. https://www.pewresearch.org/politics/2019/12/17/in-a-politically-polarized-era-sharp-divides-in-both-partisan-coalitions/.

———. "On Views of Race and Inequality, Blacks and Whites Are Worlds Apart." June 27, 2016. Accessed January 8, 2021. https://www.pewsocialtrends.org/2016/06/27/on-views-of-race-and-inequality-blacks-and-whites-are-worlds-apart/.

———. "Racial and Ethnic Composition." Religious Landscape Study. Accessed May 20, 2020. https://www.pewforum.org/religious-landscape-study/racial-and-ethnic-composition/.

———. "Why America's 'Nones' Don't Identify with a Religion." August 8, 2018. Accessed February 27, 2020. https://pewresearch.org/fact-tank/2018/08/08/why-americas-nones-dont-identify-with-a-religion/.

Public Religion Research Institute. "Summer Unrest over Racial Injustice Moves the Country, But Not Republicans or White Evangelicals." August 21, 2020. Accessed January 5, 2021. https://www.prri.org/research/racial-justice-2020-george-floyd/.

Qvortrup, Matt. "G.W.F. Hegel: An Introduction." *Philosophy Now* 140 (2020). Accessed January 29, 2021. https://philosophynow.org/issues/140/GWF_Hegel_An_Introduction.

Rader, William. *The Church and Racial Hostility: A History of the Interpretation of Ephesians 2:11–22*. Tübingen: J. C. B. Mohr (Paul Siebeck), 1978.

Rasmussen, Larry L. *Moral Fragments and Moral Community: A Proposal for Church in Society*. Minneapolis: Fortress Press, 1993.

Rees, Geoffrey. *The Romance of Innocent Sexuality*. Eugene, OR: Cascade Books, 2011.

Reynolds, Jason. "Fortifying Imagination." Interview by Krista Tippett, *On Being*. Aired June 25, 2020, on NPR. Accessed January 7, 2021. https://onbeing.org/programs/jason-reynolds-fortifying-imagination/.

Rosell, Garth M. *The Surprising Work of God: Harold John Ockenga, Billy Graham, and the Rebirth of Evangelicalism*. Grand Rapids: Baker Academic, 2008.

Schneider, Laurel C. *Beyond Monotheism: A Theology of Multiplicity*. New York: Routledge, 2008.

Schulz, Kathryn. "On Being Wrong." Filmed March 2011 in Long Beach, CA. TED video, 17:36. https://www.ted.com/talks/kathryn_schulz_on_being_wrong.
Schüssler Fiorenza, Elisabeth. *Wisdom Ways: Introducing Feminist Biblical Interpretation.* Maryknoll, NY: Orbis Books, 1970.
Sire, James W. *Naming the Elephant: Worldview as a Concept.* 2nd ed. Downers Grove, IL: InterVarsity Press, 2015.
Smietana, Bob. "Sunday Morning in America Still Segregated – and That's OK with Worshipers." LifeWay Research, January 15, 2015. Accessed January 21, 2016. http://www.lifewayresearch.com/2015/01/15/sunday-morning-in-america-still-segregated-and-thats-ok-with-worshipers/.
Smith, James K. A. *Letters to a Young Calvinist: An Invitation to the Reformed Tradition.* Grand Rapids: Brazos Press, 2010.
Stein, Karen Farchaus, and Hazel Rose Markus. "The Role of the Self in Behavioral Change." *Journal of Psychotherapy Integration* 6, no. 4 (December 1996): 349–84.
Strachan, Owen. *Awakening the Evangelical Mind: An Intellectual History of the Neo-Evangelical Movement.* Grand Rapids: Zondervan, 2015.
Stetzer, Ed. "Defining Evangelicals in Research." *Evangelicals* 3, no. 3 (Winter 2017/18): 12–13.
———. "Names Removed from the Evangelical Manifesto." The Exchange, May 15, 2008. Accessed February 22, 2021. https://www.christianitytoday.com/edstetzer/2008/may/names-removed-from-evangelical-manifesto-updated-below.html.
Sundquist, Eric J., ed. *The Oxford W. E. B. Du Bois Reader.* New York: Oxford University Press, 1996.
Sutton, Matthew Avery. *American Apocalypse: A History of Modern Evangelicalism.* Cambridge, MA: The Belknap Press, 2014.
Swartz, David R. *Moral Minority: The Evangelical Left in an Age of Conservatism.* Philadelphia: University of Pennsylvania Press, 2012.
Sweeney, Douglas A. "The Essential Evangelicalism Dialectic: The Historiography of the Early Neo-Evangelical Movement and the Observer-Participant Dilemma." In Noll, Bebbington, and Marsden, 56–73.
Tanner, Kathryn. *Theories of Culture: A New Agenda for Theology.* Minneapolis: Fortress Press, 1997.
Thielicke, Helmut. *Theological Ethics.* 3 vols. Philadelphia: Fortress Press, 1966–69.
Turman, Eboni Marshall. *Toward a Womanist Ethic of Incarnation: Black Bodies, the Black Church, and the Council of Chalcedon.* New York: Palgrave Macmillan, 2013.
Turner, Léon. *Theology, Psychology, and the Plural Self.* Burlington, VT: Ashgate Publishing Company, 2008.
US Census Bureau. "Income and Poverty in the United States: 2019." Accessed January 6, 2021. https://www.census.gov/content/dam/Census/library/publications/2020/demo/p60-270.pdf.
———. "Educational Attainment in the United States: 2019." Accessed January 6, 2021. https://www.census.gov/content/census/en/data/tables/2019/demo/educational-attainment/cps-detailed-tables.html.
Van Til, Henry R. *The Calvinistic Concept of Culture.* 1959. Reprint, Grand Rapids: Baker Book House, 2001.

Van Til, Kent A. "Abraham Kuyper and Michael Walzer: The Justice of the Spheres." *Calvin Theological Journal* 40 (2005): 267–89.
Vandermaas-Peeler, Alex, et al. "Partisan Polarization Dominates Trump Era: Findings from the 2018 American Values Survey." Public Religion Research Institute. October 29, 2018. Accessed June 8, 2020. https://www.prri.org/rese arch/partisan-polarization-dominates-trump-era-findings-from-the-2018-american -values-survey/.
Walzer, Michael. *Spheres of Justice*. New York: Basic Books, 1983.
———. *Thick and Thin: Moral Argument at Home and Abroad*. Notre Dame, IN: University of Notre Dame Press, 1994.
Warren, Dan R. *If It Takes All Summer: Martin Luther King, the KKK, and States' Rights in St. Augustine, 1964*. Tuscaloosa, AL: University of Alabama Press, 2008.
Westen, Drew. "The Cognitive Self and the Psychological Self: Can We Put Our Selves Together?" *Psychological Inquiry* 3, no. 1 (1992): 1–13.
———. "Personality, Culture, and Science: Contexts for Understanding the Self." *Psychological Inquiry* 3, no. 1 (January 1992): 74–81.
———. *The Political Brain: The Role of Emotion in Deciding the Fate of the Nation*. 2007. Reprint, New York: PublicAffairs, 2008.
———. *Self and Society: Narcissism, Collectivism, and the Development of Morals*. New York: Cambridge University Press, 1985.
Williams, Reggie L. *Bonhoeffer's Black Jesus: Harlem Renaissance Theology and an Ethic of Resistance*. Waco, TX: Baylor University Press, 2014.
Witte, John, Jr., and Robert M. Kingdon. *Sex, Marriage, and Family in Calvin's Geneva*. Vol. 1. Grand Rapids: Eerdmans, 2005.
Wittgenstein, Ludwig. *Philosophical Investigations*. 4th ed. Edited by P. M. S. Hacker and Joachim Schulte. Translated by G. E. M. Anscombe, P. M. S. Hacker, and Joachim Schulte. Malden, MA: Blackwell Publishing, 2009.
Wolters, Albert M. *Creation Regained: Biblical Basics for a Reformational Worldview*. 2nd ed. Grand Rapids: Eerdmans, 2005.
Worthen, Molly *Apostles of Reason: The Crisis of Authority in American Evangelicalism*. New York: Oxford University Press, 2014.
Young, Iris Marion. *Inclusion and Democracy*. New York: Oxford University Press, 2000.
———. *Justice and the Politics of Difference*. 1990. Reprint, Princeton, NJ: Princeton University Press, 2011.
Zinn, Howard. *A People's History of the United States*. New ed. New York: Harper Perennial, 2010.

Index

abstraction, 13, 15, 58, 59, 61, 70, 87, 94, 100, 109n129, 139, 175, 182, 185, 187, 203, 206, 220, 223, 248, 250, 255, 259, 265, 273, 275, 276, 279, 294. *See also* depersonalization; ecclesiology, abstract wish-dream; generalization
Abyssinian Baptist Church, 18, 188, 253–54
accidental qualities, 55–56, 58, 74, 185, 214
accountability, 56, 117, 139, 234, 289; unaccountability, 139, 142, 189, 233–34, 272
Act and Being, 247, 260, 268
Adam, 36, 207, 208, 258, 263–64, 266, 268, 270, 281
aggregate associations, 3, 16, 55, 79–80, 115, 140, 167, 211. *See also* class; gender; race; sexuality; voluntary associations
All Quiet on the Western Front, 253
Althaus, Paul, 18, 246–52, 257, 270, 272, 274, 275
Anabaptists, 33, 136, 204
ancient Greek philosophy, 41, 55–57, 67n156. *See also* Aristotle; Plato
Ansbacher Ratschlag, 251
antithesis (theological concept). *See* radical antithesis

apartheid (South Africa), 51
Archimedean point, 13, 41–42, 56, 245, 291, 298n2
Aristotle, 55, 209, 238n73
Aryan, 53; paragraph, 247, 274
assimilation, 79, 179, 181, 257–58, 264, 271, 273, 280, 281, 284n55, 293, 296. *See also* epistemology, colonial; human logos; objectification
The Atlantic, 71, 75
Augustine, 44, 81, 212, 277–78, 287n150

Bacote, Vincent, 54
Baptists, 226
Barcelona, 252
Barmen Declaration, 250–51
Barna Group, 4, 162, 166, 167
Barth, Karl, 208, 230, 238n86, 249–51, 262, 284n81
Barthes, Roland, 181
basic trust, 42, 212–13, 219, 227, 273. *See also* direction
Bebbington, David, 136; quadrilateral definition of evangelicalism, 4, 20n9, 152n163
Bell, L. Nelson, 132
Berlin, 71, 246, 254, 256, 276
Berry, Wendell, 74, 295

313

Bethel Confession, 247, 278
Bethge, Eberhard, 279–80, 287n151
Bible (Christian Scripture), 35, 39–47, 49, 56–57, 72, 73, 76, 97, 117, 119–22, 125, 130, 131, 134, 165, 189, 201, 215–19, 220–21, 232, 233, 252, 255, 263, 273, 276, 290, 293; as divine revelation, 40–43, 45, 119–21, 205, 212, 215, 217, 248, 250, 262; doctrine of, 4, 7, 44, 116, 120–21, 145n6, 204–5, 281; principles of, 15, 40–41, 57–59, 120, 132, 137, 220, 233; uninterpreted (rhetoric), 45–47, 70, 120–24, 173, 183, 217. *See also* biblical Christianity; Biblical Theism; biblical world-view; revelation, special
biblical Christianity (rhetoric), 5, 16, 116–18, 121, 124, 156, 226–27. *See also* Biblical Theism
Biblical Theism, 120, 122, 125, 139
biblical world-view, the (rhetoric of), 6–8, 12, 13, 16, 17, 23n45, 47, 50, 59–60, 70, 89, 95–97, 113–14, 116, 121, 126, 132, 137–38, 143, 157, 171, 202, 205–7, 213, 214, 220, 221, 224–27, 230, 232, 290, 292, 294. *See also* floating signifier
Biden, Joe, 4, 202
Black Lives Matter movement, 134, 140, 201, 223, 242n161
Blum, Edward, 73, 76
Blumhardt, Christoph, 27
Boesak, Allan, 54
Bonhoeffer, Dietrich, 18, 67n157, 101, 187–88, 245–81, 289–93, 296–97
Brannon, Tiffany, 80
Bratt, James, 28, 29, 48, 49, 53–55, 67n155
Brown v. Board of Education of Topeka (1954), 133. *See also* desegregation; integration
Bruce, Dickson, 75
Brunner, Jerome, 90
Bush, George W., 2, 4, 137

California Proposition 8, 222–23, 226, 230
Calvin, John, 30, 40, 41, 44, 210, 214–17, 220–21, 238n73
Calvinism (tradition, adherents), 10, 27, 30–34, 39, 43–44, 49, 51–57, 59, 73, 101, 136, 202, 204–7, 209, 212, 214, 221, 225, 232, 234, 281. *See also* neo-Calvinism
Calvinist world-view (rhetoric of), 30–31, 33–34, 52, 53, 59–60
capitalism, 27, 32, 48, 73, 115, 123, 129, 132. *See also* economic inequality; free enterprise
Carmichael, Stokely, 3
Carnell, E. J., 114, 149n89
Carter, Jimmy, 143, 201
Chicago Declaration (1973), 204, 228, 242n161
Christian nationalism, 2, 6, 16, 28, 29, 31, 52, 115, 117, 122, 137, 152n166, 156, 161, 179, 205
Christological scrutiny. *See* divine scrutiny
church (congregations, traditions), 1, 2, 4, 14, 17–19, 30–32, 42, 44–46, 48, 59, 95–96, 116, 120, 122, 126, 128, 130, 132, 135, 141, 142, 157, 159, 161, 201, 217, 221, 224, 226, 242n161, 252, 254–56, 272, 280, 295; multiracial, 17, 156, 164, 167–71, 173–74; and race, 155–57, 161, 163–64, 166–74, 274–75. *See also* ecclesiology
civility, 10, 202, 219, 220, 222, 224, 232
civilization, 10, 12, 14, 21n26, 33, 49–52, 54, 56, 72–73, 76, 113, 145n6, 160, 175–78, 181. *See also* cultural chauvinism
civil rights, 16, 115, 118, 129, 133–35, 142, 165, 202, 203, 228, 230, 253; legislation, 129, 132–35; movement (midcentury), 3, 114, 129, 132, 133, 141, 150n115, 158–59, 181, 207, 223, 229

class (economic division), 1, 5, 6, 16,
  48, 49, 52, 72–73, 76, 80, 96, 97,
  116, 129, 130, 136, 140, 141, 156,
  159, 162, 181, 184, 185, 191n23,
  211, 225, 232, 272. *See also*
  economic inequality; preferential
  option for the poor
Clinton, Hillary, 4
coercion, 1, 14, 18, 171, 186, 203, 216,
  221–23, 228, 231, 234, 242n153,
  276, 295. *See also* control
cognition, 29, 36, 71, 81, 83, 84, 95, 97,
  139, 259, 272; structural complexity
  of, 9, 14–16, 71, 75, 79–82, 84, 97,
  213, 234. *See also* consciousness
cognitive-evaluative mismatch, 82, 85–86
colonialism, 9–11, 13–15, 17, 49–58,
  71–74, 76, 174–79, 181–82. *See also*
  epistemology, colonial; Abraham,
  Kuyper, advocacy for colonialism
colorblind (argument relative to race).
  See race, and colorblindness
Columbus, Christopher, 176
Combahee River Collective, 140, 242n161
common grace, 28, 34, 38, 49, 52, 72,
  126, 210, 216, 221, 238n84
common sense, 16, 90, 117, 179–80, 183
communion (with God, others), 2,
  14, 16, 18–19, 29, 46, 48, 53, 74,
  90–91, 93, 95, 100–101, 174–75,
  179, 184–87, 189, 273, 291. *See also*
  relationality
Communism, 5, 12, 49, 113–14, 118–
  19, 122, 123, 127, 128, 133, 134,
  145n8, 150n115, 159, 160, 229
compromise formations, 83, 91, 93–94,
  98, 136
conceptually articulated thought, 7, 8,
  16, 19, 28, 29, 44–45, 59, 93, 141–
  42, 291, 294–96. *See also* revelation,
  human participation in; speculation
concreteness in ethics, 60, 61, 84, 91,
  101–2, 127, 160, 189, 210, 213,
  219, 225–26, 230, 233–34, 241n152,
  248–50, 253, 265, 266, 270, 273–77,
  280–81, 287n139, 293–97. *See also*
  fallacy of misplaced concreteness;
  world-view, general *vs.* specifics in
Confessing Church, the, 250, 254
confession (as a practice), 268
conscience, 32, 36, 54, 126, 128, 132,
  142, 187, 189, 268–69
consciousness, 34–37, 39, 40, 45–47,
  72, 75, 100, 265, 283n46; collective,
  9–10, 42–44, 46, 56, 59, 95;
  structural unity of (theory), 15,
  39–41, 43–44, 46, 56–58, 61, 70, 71,
  77, 84–87, 94–96, 98–99, 101, 212,
  260. *See also* double consciousness;
  microcosmic consciousness
consensus, 8, 90, 129, 136, 142, 202,
  206–7, 218–19, 221, 227–28
conservatism, 16, 28, 115, 116, 122, 130,
  131, 136, 137, 152n166, 155, 156,
  158–61, 165, 166, 168, 181, 219, 226
contingency (of human life), 56,
  100–102, 104n36, 141, 185, 262–64,
  266–67, 269, 271, 276, 296–98. *See
  also* creatureliness
control, 16, 101, 102, 179, 205. *See also*
  coercion
coram deo, 256, 263, 266, 289
cor curvum in se, 258, 259, 267–69,
  284n59, 295–96. *See also*
  epistemology, as the problem; fall;
  omnicompetence; sin
cosmonomic, 209–10
counter-schematic feedback, 79, 85–86,
  92, 94, 97, 100, 102, 184
creation, 39–40, 101, 160, 176–77,
  189, 216, 248–50, 256; as fallen,
  12, 18–19, 37, 57–59, 63n35, 160,
  209–12, 215–16, 248–49, 260–61,
  270–71, 277–78; original-creational
  (as ideal, by design), 18, 27, 32,
  34–36, 42, 44, 48, 56–58, 95, 131,
  158, 189, 207, 209–10, 215–17, 220,
  232–33, 237n65, 239n106, 249–51,
  270–73, 275, 279, 292–93. *See
  also* creatureliness; lost beginning;

natural theology; orders of creation; revelation, general; sphere sovereignty framework; twilight
Creation and Fall, 256, 259, 272
creatureliness (creatures), 1, 14, 15, 18, 29, 30, 35, 53, 87, 100, 102–3, 158, 187, 190, 210, 212–13, 218, 228, 245–48, 259, 261–64, 266–68, 271, 274, 276–79, 281, 291–92, 295–98. *See also* contingency
crepuscular, 261, 267, 269, 272, 273, 280. *See also* twilight
Criswell, W. A., 132
cultural chauvinism, 11, 29, 47, 54, 56–57, 73, 109n129, 175–76, 182; examples of, 9–10, 49–53, 66n138, 178. *See also* worldview, development and competition in history
cultural discipleship. *See* discipleship, cultural
cultural mandate, 11, 50, 55, 176–77, 182, 207–9, 211, 220, 236n40, 278
cultural toolkit, 164–71, 173–74, 184, 193n63
curse of Ham, 50, 55, 131, 151n124

democracy, 3, 32, 54, 113, 115, 118, 160
Democratic Party, 4, 128
demonization, 148n79, 213–14
depersonalization, 44, 55, 59, 88, 92, 94, 214, 233, 284. *See also* abstraction; generalization; objectification; theological anthropology, abstract theories of
Descartes, René (Cartesian), 40, 264–66
desegregation, 16, 115, 130. *See also* racial integration
Deutsche Christen, 250–51, 282n23
direction (as a theological judgment), 38–40, 44, 84, 87, 91, 113, 115, 185, 210–14, 229, 260. *See also* basic trust
Discipleship (book), 101, 245, 249, 273, 276
discipleship (following-after Jesus, spiritual formation), 3, 5, 14, 17–19, 33, 43, 47, 85, 93, 95, 99–102, 141, 143–44, 185–86, 207, 215, 245–46, 252, 254–55, 273–76, 278, 281, 292, 296–97; cultural, 202, 204, 208, 215, 224, 231
dissent, 7–8, 18, 121, 138–39, 142, 147n41, 147n60, 218, 222–24, 228–30; dissenting insider, 8, 18, 202, 229–30, 233–34
dissociative identity disorder, 75–77, 84–85, 98, 104n21
diversity, 52, 91, 101, 119, 129, 157, 167, 187, 207, 211–14, 221–22, 225–26, 294; managed (i.e., diverse faces *vs.* voices), 6, 17–18, 55, 169, 171, 174, 178, 194n98, 231. *See also* dissent; evangelicalism, diversity within
divine command, 124, 131, 208, 209, 221, 246, 263, 266, 268, 270, 271, 273, 281; as commandment, 273, 287n139; as law, 13, 102, 113, 124, 125, 165, 188, 208–10, 212, 214–15, 218, 220–21, 230, 233, 239n93, 248, 249, 251, 267, 268, 270–71, 279–81, 292, 295, 296; as mandate, 11, 50, 55, 56, 58, 146n25, 176–77, 182, 207–9, 211, 220, 234, 236n40, 246, 249, 270, 271, 273–74, 277–80, 287n139; as ordinance, 208, 209, 212, 279. *See also* orders of creation; orders of preservation; sphere sovereignty framework
divine scrutiny, 59, 230, 248, 250, 274, 292, 294, 296–97
Dombrowski, Jim, 253
Dooyeweerd, Herman, 209–10
double consciousness, 13, 15, 71–72, 74–77, 80, 84, 85, 93, 97, 98, 102, 109n134, 142, 181
double effect (doctrine), 234, 243n170
Du Bois, W. E. B., 13, 15, 56, 71–77, 80, 81, 84, 93, 95, 96, 98, 161, 176, 183, 253–54, 278; parable of *Jesus Christ in Texas*, 253–54

ecclesiology (theology of church-community), 14, 16, 19, 30, 32, 33, 42, 46, 59, 95, 101, 121–22, 124–25, 130, 135, 141, 149n82, 177–78, 180, 186–88, 206, 208–9, 211, 219, 222, 224–25, 228, 247–48, 254, 257, 259, 260, 264, 268, 270, 272–79, 292, 296–98; abstract wish-dream, 122, 138–39, 187–88, 234, 252; the body of Christ existing today, 186, 188, 252, 254, 262, 276, 279, 298. *See also* church; religious freedom
economic inequality, 7, 14, 48–49, 72–73, 126, 129–30, 160, 162–63, 166–67, 203, 229
ecumenical work, 115, 205, 247, 253, 254, 272, 289
Edwards, Korie, 6, 168–72, 179, 181
Eisenhower, Dwight, 133
election (theological concept), 33, 52, 55–57, 59, 66n130, 73, 176, 178. *See also* predestination
elections (political), 127, 128, 134, 160, 191n37; 2016 US presidential, 4, 142–43, 201, 230; 2020 US presidential, 1, 202
Ellison, Ralph Waldo, 13, 80
emergency: functions in cases of, 224–25, 242n166; state of, 219, 225
Emerson, Michael O., 163–68, 173
Emerson, Ralph Waldo, 74
The Emperor's New Clothes, 255
empty signifier. *See* floating signifier
England, 11, 31, 52, 53, 247
enlightenment (theological concept), 40–42, 46, 52, 58, 60–61, 70, 76, 96–97, 99, 100, 121, 212–14, 217, 230, 245. *See also* sanctification; sanctified imagination
epistemic certainty (hope), 15, 17–19, 39, 43–45, 53, 87, 99, 121–22, 177, 187, 203, 207, 216–19, 233–34, 291–92. *See also* sanctified imagination
epistemic humility, 58, 100, 217–18, 276. *See also* sin, noetic effects of

epistemological confidence. *See* epistemic certainty
epistemological turn, the. *See* epistemology, turn to
epistemology, 2, 3, 7, 9, 11–15, 17–19, 36, 69–70, 93, 190, 203, 205–6, 214, 216–18, 232–34, 245, 247–48, 257–59, 266, 272, 276; colonial (imperial), 13–15, 17, 18, 29, 53–58, 69, 71, 74, 96, 176–78, 181–83, 188–89, 203, 233–34, 255, 258; idealist (ideals as a philosophical abstraction), 2, 9, 10, 15, 29–30, 32, 34–36, 53, 57–58, 68n159, 87, 97, 114, 230–34, 246–48, 251, 255–57, 260, 263, 265, 267, 269–70, 272–74, 283n46, 294–95; presuppositionalist, 14, 212, 249, 282n23; as the problem, 14, 18, 234, 264–67, 271, 273, 281, 291; rationalist, 5, 9–10, 31–32, 72, 113, 121, 212; turn to, 18, 247, 256, 261–62, 264–67, 271. *See also* knowledge of good and evil; regeneration, noetic effects of; relationality, as opposed to epistemology; sin, noetic effects of; world-view
Ericksen, Robert, 246, 248, 251
Erikson, Erik, 90–91
essentialism (essence, structure), 18, 37, 55–56, 58, 67n155, 78, 87, 176–77, 179, 196n146, 203, 209–10, 214, 220, 222, 232–34, 237n68, 262, 293, 297. *See also* gender, hierarchy of; race, hierarchy of; universal
evangelical Christians: Black, 4, 6–7, 16–17, 130, 132, 135, 138, 143, 150n115, 157–58, 166, 180, 193n68, 229; as a voting bloc (conception), 2, 4, 7, 128, 143, 150n106, 155; white, 3–8, 14, 17, 28, 50, 70, 126, 136, 141, 143, 152n166, 155, 157–60, 162–70, 173–74, 177, 181–84, 188–89, 202, 223, 234. *See also* evangelicalism
evangelicalism (as a historical movement/project), 3–8, 10–13, 17–18, 28, 33,

48, 63n31, 69–70, 99, 101, 114–15, 120, 126, 155–70, 172–74, 176, 179–84, 201–8, 226–31; claims to represent, 4, 8, 18, 114, 117, 119, 126–27, 136–38, 141–43, 155–56, 179–81, 201–2, 204–5, 207, 219, 223–24, 226–29, 234, 294; defining/identifying, 4, 8, 116, 135–39, 142–43, 155, 157, 161, 180, 201–2, 205–7, 213–14, 226–30, 289; diversity within, 6–8, 119, 128–29, 132, 135–38, 143, 150n110, 155–56, 180–81, 202, 204, 206, 226, 228–30; entrepreneurial nature of, 122–23, 143, 148n61, 180, 227; generic (thin), 204–7, 227, 229; self-identification of, 7, 136, 143, 157, 189, 201–2, 205, 228, 229. *See also* evangelical Christians; evangelical world-view; neo-evangelicalism; young evangelicals

An Evangelical Manifesto, 154n183, 201, 226–27, 243n178

evangelical world-view, the (rhetoric of), 6, 8, 12, 95, 114–15, 119, 123, 137–38, 141, 143, 156, 176–77, 182–83, 207, 224, 294. *See also* biblical world-view; floating signifier

Evans, Curtis, 123, 135

exnomination, 115, 137–38, 142, 156, 160, 171, 179–81, 183, 233, 245. *See also* hegemony; whiteness, transparency of

faith, 3–5, 8, 18, 31, 32, 43, 46, 51, 76, 93, 114, 128, 135, 166, 183, 229, 231, 249, 276; as a faculty (function) of the soul, 36–38, 40–43, 60, 83, 95, 258; instinctive life of, 43, 46, 60, 71; statements of, 6, 122, 138, 142–43, 156, 180, 217; as a theological concept, 5, 14, 19, 30, 33, 40, 43, 46, 63n50, 101–3, 175, 181, 203, 245, 255, 258–59, 271, 273, 275, 281; as a tradition/set of beliefs, 14, 76, 99, 114, 118, 125, 132, 136, 137, 165, 166, 173, 175–76, 201, 204, 217, 219, 220, 223, 224, 271, 276

fall, the (theological concept), 18, 39, 53, 186, 211–12, 258, 259, 261, 263, 266–71, 278, 295; *vs.* falling (away), 186, 261–62, 266–68, 271, 290, 295. *See also* sin

fallacy of misplaced concreteness, 87, 99, 123–24, 188

Fanon, Frantz, 13, 74, 80, 85

fascism, 5, 12, 113

Federal Council of Churches, 115–16, 120, 130, 138, 161

feminism, 3, 140, 153n170, 159–60, 226, 232. *See also* gender; womanism

Finkenwalde (underground seminary), 276

first principles, 12, 30–32, 37–41, 49, 53, 59, 65n97, 69, 72–73, 113, 118–19, 144, 209, 212, 257. *See also* world-view, principial nature of

Fisher, Albert Franklin, 253–54

floating signifier, 119, 142, 206, 227, 273, 294; biblical/evangelical world-view as, 115, 119, 137–38, 141–42, 227, 233, 292, 294; other examples, 294

forgiveness, 159, 188, 249, 268, 276, 281, 289, 297–98. *See also* grace

formation (moral, spiritual). *See* discipleship

Fosdick, Harry Emerson, 128

free enterprise, 6, 48, 72–73, 114, 122–23, 127, 129, 132, 139, 160, 161, 170, 189, 205

free responsibility (freedom for others), 17, 18, 101, 113, 122, 135, 158, 164, 185, 187, 189, 234, 249, 262–65, 269, 271, 273–78, 289–90, 295–98; evasion of responsibility (for actions, to others), 18, 59, 143, 230, 233–34, 265, 268, 271, 276, 293, 294, 297. *See also* Jesus, as free for others

freewill individualism, 17, 95, 122, 126, 164–65, 180, 184

Index 319

French Revolution, 31, 67n142, 132
Freud, Sigmund, 70, 103n1
Führer (prinzip), 250
Fuller Theological Seminary, 16, 114, 118, 122, 123, 135, 136, 157, 174, 175, 202, 231
fundamentalism (Christian), 5, 10–11, 16, 69, 113, 116–18, 120, 129, 132, 136, 138, 145n6, 155, 158, 160, 180, 205, 229

Gallup, Inc., 2, 143
gender, 2, 5–7, 58, 79, 80, 96, 98, 140, 141, 163, 185, 204, 211, 229, 230, 232, 277–78; hierarchy of (complementarianism, patriarchy), 3, 9, 15, 56, 58, 64n55, 67n155, 153n170, 209, 214, 216, 220, 229, 232, 233, 278
generalization, 55, 57, 61, 91, 174, 213, 216, 222, 250; in psychology, 78, 81. *See also* abstraction; generalization
Germany, 12, 18, 27, 54, 71, 145n6, 246, 247, 249–51, 254, 276, 283n36, 289
God: kingdom of, 14, 16–19, 87, 100–102, 127, 185, 188, 219, 232, 271, 274, 275, 278, 297; knowledge of, 34–35, 39, 41–43, 46, 117, 187, 190, 214–17, 232–34, 245, 258–59, 266–67, 271, 285n90, 292, 295, 296; as a living person, 2, 14, 18, 19, 38, 39, 47, 56, 67n157, 99, 101, 187, 213, 221, 234, 246, 250, 260, 263–64, 268–69, 271–73, 277–79, 281, 285n90, 292, 296–98; as only true world-viewer, 14, 95, 245, 298; preserving word of, 270–74, 280; simple obedience to, 254, 258, 263, 266, 271, 296, 298; the will of, 5, 15, 16, 18, 28, 33, 35, 55, 60, 101, 117, 121, 135, 159, 182, 185, 203, 208–10, 214, 217–19, 221, 232–34, 248–51, 256, 264, 275–77, 290, 292, 295. *See also* divine command; revelation; self-revelation, of God

good and evil, knowledge of. *See* knowledge of good and evil
government (civil order), 1, 64n59, 113, 117, 123, 124, 134–35, 153n166, 165, 216, 225, 270, 293. *See also* orders of creation, state as; state
grace, 125, 126, 178, 188, 218, 219, 253, 261, 271; cheap, 246, 249, 276, 290; in God's judgment, 268, 270, 296, 298; as a relational concept, 100–101, 187, 262, 264, 266, 268, 275, 281, 289, 292, 296–98. *See also* common grace
Graham, Billy, 132, 203
Great Depression (1920s), the, 113, 114, 127, 137, 246, 254
Griffioen, Sander, 211–13

Harlem, 18, 188, 246, 252–53, 255, 276, 289–90, 293; Renaissance, 253, 290
Hegel, G. W. F., 9–11, 29–30, 32, 34, 36, 37, 42, 46, 49, 53, 56, 57, 62n6, 71, 75, 95, 160, 247, 249, 251, 284n55, 285n90
hegemony, 11, 14, 55, 138, 159, 170–74, 176, 179, 181–82
Henry, Carl F. H., 10–11, 114, 116, 120–21, 125–27, 135, 161, 193n76, 203, 204
Henry the Navigator, Prince, 175–76
highly generative individuals, 91–93
Hinlicky, Paul, 249
Hirsch, Emmanuel, 247, 283n46
Hitler, Adolf, 250
Holmes, Arthur, 217, 241n152
Holy Spirit, 14–16, 30, 31, 34, 39–42, 44–47, 52, 57, 59–61, 81, 101, 120, 123, 214, 232, 245, 271, 274, 278, 295, 296
homophily, 167–68, 174
Hoover, Herbert, 127, 132
human logos (rational mind, reason), 31–32, 35, 36, 57, 120–21, 182, 212, 246, 257–59, 264, 265, 269–70, 284n55, 294. *See also* Jesus Christ,

as Logos of God and *Gegenlogos*; revelation, human participation in; sanctified imagination; sin, noetic effects of; speculation
human nature. *See* theological anthropology
Hume, David, 93, 106n76
Huntington, Samuel, 66n139, 160

idealism. *See* creation, original-creational; epistemology, idealist
identity, 3, 14, 17, 29, 72, 76–79, 84, 87–90, 98, 101–2, 177; denied to others, 18, 138, 180, 204–5, 227–30; and encounter, 100–102, 185, 289–91, 297; theology of, 15, 71, 86, 99–103, 138, 157, 178, 184–90, 289–98. *See also* multiplicity; plural selves
identity politics, 3–5, 8, 16, 20n7, 27, 114, 137–42, 155, 179, 201, 203, 220, 226, 242n161, 258, 293, 294; and intersectionality, 140, 153n170, 223
ideological setting, 90–94. *See also* social location; world-view
idolatry, 87, 99, 125, 158, 212–13, 272, 280–81
imago dei, 34–35, 39, 42, 45, 48, 53, 55, 57, 59, 100, 208, 211, 256, 262, 264, 266, 284n81, 296; analogies, 208, 262–64. *See also* Jesus Christ, as free for others
Industrial Revolution, 27, 32, 47
internalized oppression, 72, 74–75, 98, 158–59
intuition, 9, 37, 57, 81, 182

James, William, 70, 74, 77, 89
Jennings, Willie, 10, 67n157, 141, 157, 174–79, 181–83, 189
Jesus Christ, 3, 5, 17–19, 30, 39, 46, 48, 58, 74, 76, 85, 93, 95, 100–102, 117, 120, 122, 125, 130, 132, 141, 157–59, 161, 184–89, 190n5, 203, 205, 215, 228, 231, 239n93, 245–46, 248–57, 259, 260, 262, 267, 269–71, 273–81, 289–98; as Black, 18, 76, 158–59, 246, 253–54, 290; as free for others, 262–63, 276, 278, 296; incarnate, 42, 102, 187–89, 232, 258, 270, 291; incognito, 291, 296; as a living person, 18, 187, 205, 246, 248, 249, 255–60, 269–70, 273–77, 290, 292, 294, 296–98; as Logos of God and *Gegenlogos*, 257–59, 272, 281, 284n55, 296; silence before teaching about, 257; speaking a word here and now, 18, 102, 248, 271, 273–74, 279; as *Stellvertretung*, 255, 275–76. *See also* discipleship
Johnson, Lyndon B. (LBJ), 128, 133
Judaism, 247, 251

Kant, Immanuel, 9, 11, 182, 247, 265–66, 269, 285n90
Keen, Karen, 279
Kennedy, John F. (JFK), 128, 133
King, Martin Luther, Jr., 3, 133, 164, 229
kingdom of God. *See* God, kingdom of
knowledge of God. *See* God, knowledge of
knowledge of good and evil, 18, 19, 90, 99, 187, 230, 232–34, 245, 266–67, 271, 281, 292, 293, 295, 296
Kuyper, Abraham, 10–11, 13, 15, 18, 27–61, 69–73, 78, 83, 85, 86, 88, 92–101, 114, 123, 175, 178, 182, 184, 202, 208–9, 212–17, 220, 221, 225, 229–31, 233, 262, 272, 290; advocacy for colonialism, 29, 47, 54–56, 92; tainted legacy of, 29, 54–57, 92–93, 229–30
Kuyperianism. *See* neo-Calvinism
kyriarchy, 153n170, 231–32. *See also* gender, hierarchy of; mythical norm; race, hierarchy of

Lasserre, Jean, 253–54
law and order, 25, 129, 133, 134, 160, 296
Lévi-Strauss, Claude, 294
liberal individualism, 17, 32, 33, 48, 62n24, 72–73, 95, 108n127, 122,

132, 136–37, 139, 147n60, 160, 164, 165. *See also* freewill individualism
liberation, 3, 76, 85, 98, 122, 131, 140, 179, 187, 219, 220
liberty (individual), 6, 9, 95, 131–32, 160. *See also* free responsibility
LifeWay Research, 4, 167
limit (concept of). *See* persons, as limits
Lindsell, Harold, 204
Locke, Alain, 253
logos (human reason). *See* human logos
London, 247
Lorde, Audre, 140–41
lost beginning, the, 18–19, 246, 259–62, 272–73, 278, 292
Luther, Martin, 30, 90, 248, 277, 284n50; and the two kingdoms doctrine, 249
Lutheranism (theology, adherents), 32, 204, 248–51, 256, 274; claim to represent, 250, 251; pseudo-Lutheran (criticism as), 248, 272, 282n6

Mammonism. *See* materialism
Markus, Hazel Rose, 78–82, 85, 89, 108n127
marriage, 127, 149n100, 158, 209, 210, 219–27, 232, 264, 277–80, 292; definition of, 220, 222–23, 226, 229, 230, 232, 233, 278–79; interracial, 127, 149n100, 158, 233; officiating as the church's most questionable function, 279, 280; same-sex, 18, 203, 219–28, 230, 232, 233, 279. *See also* orders of creation, marriage as
Marsden, George, 115, 122, 136, 138
Marsh, Charles, 129, 247, 279
materialism, 5, 27, 28, 32, 48–49, 72–76, 98, 113, 160–61
McAdams, Dan P., 88–92, 96, 97
McGovern, George, 129, 202
McIntyre, Carl, 219
Methodism, 33, 51, 129, 147n60, 217
microcosmic consciousness, 35–36, 57, 59, 196n148, 262

middle, the (theological location), 58, 259–61, 267, 269, 275
miracle motif, the, 48, 165, 166, 193n76. *See also* regeneration, and social change
Modernism, 5, 11, 12, 27–34, 38, 69, 113, 116, 120–21, 124, 125, 144, 145n6, 147n49, 148n60, 182–83; as a *Fata Morgana*, 32
Moore, Wendy Leo, 172–73, 179, 181
Moral Majority, 7, 114, 137, 201
moral realism, 210, 232. *See also* sphere sovereignty framework
Mouw, Richard J., 7, 12–13, 17–18, 67n155, 128, 155, 186, 201–34, 246, 260, 290, 293
multiplicity, 58, 71, 77–79, 84–86, 89, 93, 99–100, 104n21, 156. *See also* plural selves
multiracial churches. *See* church, multiracial
mystification, 15, 45–46, 58, 60–61, 65n108, 96–97, 213–14, 231. *See also* piety
myth, 13, 161; communal, 88–89, 91–92, 96–97, 101–2, 141, 143–44, 183; personal, 88, 89, 91, 97, 183. *See also* mythical norm
mythical norm, the, 5, 13, 85, 137, 140–41, 153n174, 181. *See also* hegemony; power

NAE. *See* National Association of Evangelicals
narrative marriages (consolidation), 5, 90, 93, 137, 140, 177, 180, 183, 245. *See also* exnomination
narrative theology, 70, 88–89, 294
National Association of Evangelicals (NAE), 6, 16, 113–14, 117–18, 122, 127, 132, 142, 143, 156, 161, 180
National Black Evangelical Association (NBEA), 7, 143
National Congregations Survey (NCS), 163–64, 168

nationalism, 12, 32, 161, 182n25, 246–47, 252, 256, 276. *See also* Christian nationalism
natural theology, 14, 35–36, 38, 41, 93, 95, 142, 203, 214–16, 220–21, 230, 232, 237n48, 243n191, 248, 250–51, 262, 271–72, 277–78. *See also* creation; orders of creation; revelation, general; sin, noetic effects of
Naugle, David, 9–10, 12, 13, 22n34, 103n1, 209
Nazism (National Socialism), 11–12, 18, 54, 113, 118, 130, 145n6, 246, 250, 257, 283n46, 290, 293
neo-Calvinism (Kuyperianism), 10, 17, 28, 33, 34, 49, 51, 54, 55, 57, 72, 202, 207–9, 214, 215, 217–18, 220, 230, 232
neo-evangelicalism (the new evangelicals), 5–7, 11–12, 16–17, 47–48, 69, 113–29, 136–38, 140–41, 143–44, 171, 179–84, 202–5, 207, 227–28. *See also* fundamentalism
Netherlands, 11, 31, 52, 53, 67n155, 225
New Deal, the, 127
Newsweek, 201, 222–24, 227, 242nn156–57
New York City (NYC), 203, 246, 254, 255. *See also* Abyssinian Baptist Church; Harlem; Union Theological Seminary
Niebuhr, H. Richard, 209, 230
Niebuhr, Reinhold, 120–21, 147n47, 253
Nixon, Richard, 128–29, 133, 134, 160, 202
Noll, Mark, 4, 28, 116, 136, 145n7
nonviolence (pacifism), 128, 185, 228, 253, 256

objectification, 61, 74, 258, 264, 265, 268–70, 272, 277, 280, 281, 294–95. *See also* subject-object relation; theological anthropology, abstract theories of

Ockenga, Harold John, 5–7, 10, 12–13, 16–18, 47, 113–44, 155, 156, 159–61, 164, 165, 171, 172, 175, 179–84, 186, 202–5, 213, 219, 223, 226, 228–30, 233, 290
omnicompetence, 16, 61, 94, 95, 141, 142, 203, 232, 257, 260, 264, 270, 292, 295. *See also cor curvum in se*; human logos; world-viewing, as a posture
orders of creation (*Schöpfungsordnungen*), 12, 18, 120, 210, 216, 246–49, 251, 256, 268, 272–73, 275, 292; *das Volk* as, 12, 18, 249–51; marriage as, 220, 232, 277–80; state as, 208, 209, 216, 220, 270, 275, 293. *See also* sphere sovereignty framework
orders of preservation (*Erhaltungsordnungen*), 246, 256, 270–71, 273–75, 277–80
original creation. *See* creation
Orr, James, 10–11, 22n29, 146n35
orthodoxy, 54, 116–18, 121, 137, 140, 147n44, 155, 156, 158, 179, 183, 204–6, 229, 230, 247, 294

palingenesis. *See* regeneration
Pannell, Bill, 7, 16–17, 135, 142, 152, 156–62, 171, 172, 177, 180, 181, 183, 190nn2–5, 204, 205, 231; on thinking whitely, 17, 157–58, 171, 181, 231
Partee, Charles, 214, 216–17, 240n107
party politics (partisanship), 1–2, 6, 16, 28, 70, 114, 123, 127–29, 137, 141, 142, 155, 156, 161, 162, 184. *See also* Democratic Party; Republican Party
patriarchy. *See* gender, hierarchy of
Paul (apostle), 40, 73, 117, 186, 293
penultimate, the, 19, 271, 273–74, 278, 286n138, 292, 297. *See also* ultimate
Perkins, John, 129
personal transformation. *See* regeneration

persons (personhood as a concept): collective, 274, 287n139; as limits, 2, 246, 258–60, 263–72, 277–80, 285n90, 291, 292, 294–98; as with, for, and over-against others, 2, 18, 259, 262, 274, 278. *See also imago dei*; God, as a living person; Jesus Christ, as a living person; self-revelation; theological anthropology; transcendence; who *vs.* how questions
Pew, J. Howard, 123
Pew Research Center, 1–2, 154n184, 190n4
phenomenology, 9, 34, 42–43, 247, 265, 285n90
physicalism, 78, 104n36
piety (pious, wanting to be for God), 5, 101, 202, 207, 217, 234; dubious, 15, 48, 99, 101, 106n71, 161, 206, 228, 232, 233, 250, 275, 293; and knowledge of God, 46, 57, 95, 123, 271; pious question (the serpent's), 266–67; self-centered, 58–60, 96, 256, 292, 294, 295. *See also* mystification
Plato, 3, 123
Plessy v. Ferguson (1896), 131
pluralism, 28, 70, 86, 120, 211–13, 225
plural selves, 15, 71, 77–81, 84–86, 97–101
polarization, 1–2, 8, 14, 18, 19
polyphony, 103
possible selves, 80–82, 85–86, 89, 99, 100
postmodernism, 12, 69, 78, 87, 119
Powell, Adam Clayton, Sr., 254
power (e.g., economic, social, theopolitical), 3, 5, 6, 8, 10, 18, 48–49, 56, 69, 75, 86, 90, 96, 100, 120, 130, 131, 138–42, 153n170, 158, 162, 167–69, 171–73, 176, 181–85, 203, 228, 229, 231–32, 234, 245, 247, 250, 255, 274, 280, 294, 296; analysis of, 12, 17, 69, 120–21, 158–59, 232; ascription of, 5, 136, 185, 293–94; levers of, 2, 17, 28; powerful subjects, 3, 13–15, 29, 30, 48, 55–57, 71, 73, 74, 97, 98, 102, 176, 182, 228, 234, 260; principalities and powers (spirits), 14, 17, 59, 68n161, 97, 118, 125, 141, 143–44, 148n77, 159, 181, 185–87, 189, 196n152, 274; subversive use of, 185–86, 289; theopolitical, 5, 185; will to, 32, 228. *See also* hegemony
preferential option for the poor, 48, 76
preserving word of God. *See* God, preserving word of
presuppositionalism. *See* epistemology, presuppositionalist
Princeton Theological Seminary, 10–11, 27, 34, 52, 148n61
principalities and powers (spirits). *See* power, principalities and powers
Protestantism (tradition, adherents), 4, 7, 10, 12, 30–33, 48, 53, 72, 73, 113, 115–16, 120, 122, 124–25, 128, 129, 137, 140, 146n25, 147n44, 161, 162, 168, 180, 204, 205, 220, 225, 226, 247, 250
prototypical self-concept, 81, 84, 87, 89, 95, 101
PRRI. *See* Public Religion Research Institute
psychology (psychological), 42, 53, 57–58, 61, 64n68, 70, 74, 77–97; cognitive, 15, 78–82; developmental, 15, 89–91; experiential, 78, 85, 87–92; health (wellbeing) in, 15–16, 84–85, 87, 93; motivation in, 47, 71, 79–86, 90, 93–94, 97, 101; narrative, 15–16, 71, 87–94; representational, 78–84, 88. *See also* cognition; conscience; consciousness; compromise formations; counter-schematic feedback; dissociative identity disorder; identity; ideological setting; plural selves; prototypical self-concept; self-schemas

public education policy, 132, 160, 223–25
Public Religion Research Institute (PRRI), 162, 166, 167

race: and colorblindness, 6, 55, 174, 181; hierarchy of (white supremacy), 6, 9–11, 13–14, 29, 50–53, 55–56, 72–73, 92, 129–31, 158–59, 161, 176–78, 207, 230, 254, 276; pseudoscientific theories of, 9–10, 49–52, 71; racialization (as a structural reality), 17, 72, 75, 155, 156, 159, 164, 165, 167–68, 173, 181–82, 184, 186, 189, 192n60. *See also* church, multiracial; church, and race; curse of Ham; racial justice
racial justice, 2, 7, 161–62, 165, 167, 190n5, 203, 229
racial scale. *See* race, hierarchy of; whiteness, as a scale
racism, 15, 17, 47, 54, 55, 57, 58, 69, 97, 126, 129–35, 165, 167, 168, 170–71, 182, 203, 205, 255, 295; examples of, 6, 49–52, 130–31, 159, 163, 166; structural (systemic), 3, 7, 14, 129, 134–35, 159–60, 162–66, 169, 172, 173, 183–84, 202, 228, 254
Rader, William, 130–31
radical antithesis, the, 38–40, 42–43, 49, 57–59, 68n158, 94–95, 117, 120, 182, 212–14, 221, 224, 228, 238n84, 241n142
Rauschenbusch, Walter, 27, 219
reconciliation, 2, 51, 157, 281
Reformation, the, 30–32, 90, 120
regeneration (conversion), 15, 20n9, 30, 33, 39–46, 57–60, 80, 87, 94, 99, 107n79, 160, 205, 208, 260; noetic effects of, 13, 29, 40–42, 95, 97–98, 120–21, 184, 207, 212, 214–19, 232, 241n142, 260, 291; and social change, 125–27, 129, 132, 134–35, 142, 159–60, 165–66, 184, 193n76. *See also* miracle motif

relationality (theology of), 2, 16, 40, 42, 56, 95–96, 100–102, 120, 187, 189, 208, 234, 245, 255, 256, 258–59, 262–69, 273, 276–79, 281, 284n63, 289–98; as opposed to epistemology, 2, 17–19, 53, 58, 245–48, 255–71, 279, 281, 285n90, 291. *See also* communion; free responsibility
relativism, 69, 113, 120–22, 186, 269
religious freedom, 222, 224–26, 230, 274–75
repentance, 14, 17, 19, 60, 73, 85, 91, 97, 101, 119, 129, 143, 160, 184–85, 228, 233, 253, 281, 289, 292, 297, 298
Republican Party, 16, 115, 127–29, 137, 141, 155, 161, 162, 180
revelation (divine), 13, 41–42, 44, 45, 55, 56, 59, 63n50, 120, 130, 177, 215–18, 230, 233, 246–51, 257–59, 262, 264, 268–73, 281, 290–91; general, 41, 121, 248–49, 251; human participation in (e.g., logical action), 34–36, 42–47, 217; special, 39–41, 44, 45, 116, 119–21, 144n3, 189, 212, 215, 248, 250, 262, 275, 285n81, 292. *See also* microcosmic consciousness; self-revelation
revolution, 6, 44, 49, 119, 122, 124, 130, 133–35, 137, 161. *See also* French Revolution; Industrial Revolution; sexual revolution
Riverside Church, 116, 128
Roman Catholicism, 30, 113, 120, 124, 128, 143, 145n8, 204, 219, 225
Romanticism, 9, 32, 58, 68n160, 74
Roosevelt, Franklin Delano (FDR), 127–28
Rosell, Garth, 151n121
Ruether, Rosemary Radford, 159–60

same-sex relationships, 219, 221–24, 230, 244nn194–95, 279–80; and disordered friendship, 219. *See also* marriage, same-sex

sanctification, 40, 46, 58, 60, 61, 92, 96, 99, 149n89, 213–14, 217, 269, 277, 297. *See also* enlightenment; sanctified imagination
sanctified imagination (or reason; appeals to), 51, 60, 187, 213, 214, 217–18, 231–34, 260, 271–72, 290
scale, 171; of human life, 99, 175, 187, 233. *See also* racial scale; whiteness, as a scale; world-viewing, scale of
Schelling, Friedrich Wilhelm Joseph, 9
Schulz, Kathryn, 94
Schüssler Fiorenza, Elisabeth, 153n170, 232
science, 5, 19, 32, 35, 37–39, 44, 69–70, 74, 78, 113, 145n6, 193n66; philosophy of, 83–84; pseudo-, 66n129, 71, 78; spiritual (Kuyper), 37, 39, 41, 57, 83; theology as, 35, 39–40, 43–45
Scripture (Christian). *See* Bible
security (being held), 2, 14, 17, 100–101, 185, 187, 262, 267, 268, 271, 277, 289, 291–93; *vs.* closure, 96–97, 272, 291; false sense of, 2, 14, 18, 19, 39, 94, 96, 157, 177, 184–85, 187, 188, 245, 255, 271, 280, 289–93
Seeberg, Reinhold, 260
segregation, 55, 114–15, 165, 167, 168, 173, 226; voluntary, 132. *See also* desegregation; racial integration
self-communication. *See* self-revelation
self-deception, 15, 38, 47, 58–61, 71, 82–83, 85–88, 91, 93, 97, 99, 101, 147n47, 189, 221, 233, 260
self-normativity, 15, 16, 56–57, 61, 71, 73, 85, 96–98, 141, 174, 175, 178, 182, 203, 269. *See also* double consciousness; whiteness, transparency of
self-revelation, 102, 257, 264, 268–70; of God, 32, 34–36, 39, 42, 44–45, 47, 53, 59, 93, 189, 216, 257–59, 265–67, 272–73, 276, 281, 291, 292, 296; of humans, 37, 57, 71, 83, 84, 88, 100, 293, 296. *See also* persons; revelation; subject-object relation; who *vs.* how questions
self-schemas, 78–89, 91–95, 97, 100, 101, 105n48, 108n127, 174
self-theory, 72, 77–81, 86–87; diachronic unity in, 15–16, 78, 80, 87, 89, 99; synchronic unity in, 77, 78. *See also* plural selves
Sermon on the Mount, 246, 253, 255, 276
sexuality (sexual orientation), 5, 6, 80, 85, 86, 96, 97, 118, 119, 125, 127, 140, 141, 160, 180, 185, 210, 219–27, 230, 233, 244n195, 277–80, 287n150; homosexuality (term), 127, 220–21, 223, 226; interracial, 50–51; LGBT+, 2, 203, 220, 222, 223, 230; and virtue, 278, 279. *See also* marriage; same-sex relationships; sexual revolution
sexual revolution, 202, 223–25
sicut deus, 234, 256, 266–71, 277, 278, 280
Sider, Ron, 128, 202, 204
silent majority (rhetoric). *See* unvoiced multitudes
sin: noetic effects of, 12, 14, 32, 36–40, 42, 45, 92, 93, 95, 120–21, 207, 212, 214–19, 230, 232–34, 248, 258–62, 267, 292; original, 215, 234, 256; privative quality of, 36, 38, 56; as rebellion, 14, 132, 212, 215, 221, 234, 268, 291; social-structural (corporate), 17, 48–49, 125, 129, 147n44, 151n121, 159–60, 164, 183–84, 203–4. *See also cor curvum in se*; creation, as fallen; radical antithesis
Sloane Fellowship, 246, 252, 254
Smedes, Lewis, 135, 149n94
Smith, Christian, 163–68, 173
Smith, James K. A., 54
social change (transformation), 30, 74, 118, 124–27, 129, 132, 138, 164–66,

193n68, 193n76, 209, 211, 231–32, 249. *See also* regeneration, and social change
social crisis (early-19th century), 27, 48–49, 72–74, 130. *See also* economic inequality
social gospel, 124, 126, 129, 219, 251
socialism, 32, 48–49, 113, 114, 119, 124–25, 127, 132, 159, 160, 223. *See also* Communism; Nazis
social justice, 124, 134, 162, 207, 228, 231
social location, 8, 18, 54–57, 59, 69–70, 91, 115, 141, 179–80, 183, 189, 212, 261. *See also* middle; whiteness, transparency of; world-viewing, objectivity in
social networks, 6, 8, 141, 142; homogeneity in, 6, 8, 16, 17, 115, 137–38, 167, 169, 179–80, 183
social question, the. *See* social crisis
sociology, 71, 74, 77, 155–56, 158, 162–74
soul (spirit), 69, 71–74, 76, 98, 126, 130, 132, 208, 257, 262, 278; of a group (metaphor), 116, 123, 124; as a metaphysical concept, 10, 35–37, 40–41, 43, 57, 59, 64nn68–69, 78, 83, 104n36, 260, 266. *See also* microcosmic consciousness; physicalism
South Africa, 50–51, 66n133; Dutch colonies in, 11, 31, 47, 50, 52
Southern Baptists, 132, 190n5, 294
speculation (philosophy/theology), 15, 29, 31, 35, 53, 70, 71, 92, 132, 215–18, 230, 238n73, 258, 259, 262, 268, 271, 273
sphere sovereignty framework, 28, 34, 208–14, 216–18, 220–22, 224–25, 232, 233, 239n106, 242n166, 274, 292. *See also* cosmonomic; essentialism; orders of creation
state (political community), 124, 125, 128, 225, 242n166, 247, 274–75. *See also* government; orders of creation, state as
Stetzer, Ed, 143
Stone (Levi P.) Lectures, 11, 27, 28, 33, 34, 39, 48–51, 54, 57, 71
structural sin. *See* sin, structural
student demonstrations, 133–34, 229, 231
subject-object relation (non-haveable object), 37–39, 42–43, 47, 100, 187, 257–58, 265, 269, 276, 289, 291, 296. *See also* objectification; who vs. how questions
Sutton, Matthew Avery, 20n20, 122, 136, 149n100
Swartz, David, 21n17, 132, 150n110, 190n5

Taft, Robert A., 115, 128
Taylor, Herbert J., 123
teleology (telos), 9, 14, 35, 39, 41, 56, 175, 179, 209, 215, 275, 295. *See also* essentialism; universal
theologia crucis, 275–76
theological anthropology, 58, 70, 86, 97, 177, 289; abstract theories of, 13, 15, 17, 53, 57–61, 86–87, 91, 94–95, 99–101, 177, 179, 182, 203, 213–14, 233–34, 262–65, 272, 290–93; being-nature distinction, 36, 41, 55–58, 84; social nature of human beings, 17, 48, 157, 208, 262–66, 281. *See also* creatureliness; enlightenment; fall; *imago dei*; persons; radical antithesis; regeneration; sanctification; *sicut deus*; sin
theological education, 121–22, 171, 175, 177–79, 203, 259
Thomism (Thomas Aquinas), 28, 209, 214, 237n48
thrownness, 91, 180, 196n146, 249
transcendence, 247, 254, 257–59, 265, 266, 269, 280. *See also* persons, as limits
Truman, Harry, 127–28, 151n132
Trump, Donald, 4, 143, 155, 201–2, 293

truthfulness (honesty), 19, 37, 61, 86, 96, 101, 143–44, 157, 185, 187, 260, 269, 275, 278. *See also* self-deception
Turman, Eboni Marshall, 98, 109n134
Turner, Léon, 78, 86–89
twilight (*Zwielicht*), 39, 53, 190, 261, 267, 270, 271. *See also* crepuscular; creation, as fallen

ultimate, the, 16, 19, 34, 39, 41, 90, 186, 211, 257, 265, 271, 273–74, 278, 280, 292, 297. *See also* penultimate
Union Theological Seminary, 116, 149n94, 246, 252, 253
universal (form/structure), 9, 13, 15, 17, 29, 55–58, 61, 67n156, 100, 102, 175–76, 182, 186, 188, 196nn148–49, 212, 234, 266, 279. *See also* essentialism; teleology
unvoiced multitudes (rhetoric), 6, 34, 117, 122, 137, 139, 141, 152n165, 155, 228

Vietnam War, 7, 128, 134, 160, 202, 203, 218, 228, 229
violence, 76, 133, 134, 139, 159, 224, 228, 231, 242n153, 258. *See also* coercion; war
Volk, das, 248–52. *See also* orders of creation, *das Volk* as
voluntary associations, 6, 17, 132, 137–38, 167, 170, 171, 173, 174, 180–81, 211. *See also* aggregate associations

Wallis, Jim, 7, 128, 204
Walzer, Michael, 206–7, 236n47
war, 2, 7, 116, 117, 124, 126, 128–29, 134, 142, 148n77, 160, 218, 228–29, 272. *See also* nonviolence; Vietnam War; World War I; World War II
Warfield, B. B., 11, 34
watchwords, 205, 228
Wedemeyer, Maria, 280
Westen, Drew, 81–83, 85, 89, 106n62, 196n151

Westminster Confession of Faith, 217
Westminster Theological Seminary, 10–11
Wheatley, Phillis, 74
white institutional space, 6–7, 17–18, 137–38, 163, 168–74, 178–80, 231–32
whiteness, 3, 6, 8–10, 13–14, 16–17, 47, 53, 57, 59, 70, 72–73, 76, 85, 86, 98, 141–42, 144, 155–58, 171–79, 181–83, 186, 231, 254, 269, 278; as a scale, 10, 53, 56–57, 175–77, 203, 231–32; transparency of, 6–7, 13, 16–17, 71, 73, 85, 138, 142, 156, 158, 164, 167–75, 179, 181–84, 203, 231, 293; and virtue, 15, 72–74, 96–97, 101, 175–76; wage of, 72–74, 76, 278. *See also* diversity, managed; hegemony; power; race, hierarchy of; self-normativity; white institutional space; white racial frame embraced by non-white persons
white racial frame embraced by nonwhite persons, 168–70, 172, 179, 181, 231–32. *See also* epistemology, colonial; internalized inferiority; Bill Pannell, on thinking whitely
white supremacy. *See* race, hierarchy of
who *vs.* how questions, 258–60, 265, 272, 291, 294
Wilberforce, William, 11
Williams, Reggie, 188, 252–54
witness, 2, 3, 6, 8, 16, 44, 102, 143, 144, 176, 180, 183, 219, 223, 246
Wittgenstein, Ludwig, 23n44
Wolters, Albert, 210
womanism, 3, 98, 109n134, 140, 242n161. *See also* identity politics, and intersectionality
working self-concept, 80–82, 84–85, 87, 89, 95, 97, 100, 101
world-view (conceptuality/theory of, *Weltanschauung*), 2, 3, 5, 8–15, 19, 21n19, 29, 33–36, 40–47, 53, 55–60, 70, 71, 83, 90–93, 99, 113–15,

119, 121–22, 142, 182, 186, 207, 212–14, 218, 291–92; development and competition in history, 1–2, 11–14, 27–28, 30–33, 49, 51–53, 66nn138–39, 97, 115, 118, 119, 122, 160, 211–13, 224–26, 233; general *vs.* specifics in, 55, 69–70, 109n129, 119, 123–24, 132, 135, 138, 142, 206–7, 214, 229–31, 233, 247–50, 265, 274, 293; principial nature of, 29, 30, 36–39, 41–42, 44–45, 49, 55–59, 87, 113, 118–20, 126, 142, 144, 203, 212–14, 220, 227, 233, 248, 250, 265; psycho-political, 17, 156, 160–61, 177, 182. *See also* biblical world-view; evangelical world-view; floating signifier; ideological setting; world-viewing

world-viewing: as an impulse, 3, 5, 10, 11, 14–16, 29, 34–35, 38, 43, 44, 50, 52, 57, 59, 71, 93, 98–99, 135, 157, 175, 182, 184, 189–90, 220, 229–30, 234, 246, 272, 290, 292–95; as a posture, 13, 19, 28, 29, 53, 55, 57–61, 70, 97–99, 176, 178, 181–84, 218, 230, 232–33, 245, 272, 280, 289–95; scale of, 10, 12, 13, 15, 50, 56–57, 175–77, 182, 186, 203, 231–32, 245, 291

World War I, 145n6, 246, 247, 253, 283n36

World War II, 28, 47, 114, 117, 118, 127, 128, 157, 180

Worthen, Molly, 11–12, 20n6, 136

Yoder, John Howard, 204

Young, Iris Marion, 153n169, 167, 173, 181

young evangelicals, the, 7, 21n17, 135, 202, 204–5, 218, 227–29

Zinn, Howard, 133

About the Author

Jacob Alan Cook (PhD, Fuller Theological Seminary) is a postdoctoral fellow at the Wake Forest University School of Divinity, where his research and teaching center on forming agents of justice, compassion, and reconciliation. He has published chapters on Christian identity, peacemaking, and ecological theology.

www.ingramcontent.com/pod-product-compliance
Lightning Source LLC
Chambersburg PA
CBHW021342300426
44114CB00012B/1051